# Crime, Reason and History
## A Critical Introduction to Criminal Law

**Alan Norrie**
Edmund-Davies Professor of Criminal Law and Criminal Justice
King's College London

Butterworths
A Member of the LexisNexis Group

**Members of the LexisNexis Group worldwide**

| | |
|---|---|
| United Kingdom | Butterworths Tolley, a Division of Reed Elsevier (UK) Ltd, Halsbury House, 35 Chancery Lane, LONDON, WC2A 1EL, and 4 Hill Street, EDINBURGH EH2 3JZ |
| Argentina | Abeledo Perrot, Jurisprudencia Argentina and Depalma, BUENOS AIRES |
| Australia | Butterworths, a Division of Reed International Books Australia Pty Ltd, CHATSWOOD, New South Wales |
| Austria | ARD Betriebsdienst and Verlag Orac, VIENNA |
| Canada | Butterworths Canada Ltd, MARKHAM, Ontario |
| Chile | Publitecsa and Conosur Ltda, SANTIAGO DE CHILE |
| Czech Republic | Orac sro, PRAGUE |
| France | Editions du Juris-Classeur SA, PARIS |
| Hong Kong | Butterworths Asia (Hong Kong), HONG KONG |
| Hungary | Hvg Orac, BUDAPEST |
| India | Butterworths India, NEW DELHI |
| Ireland | Butterworths (Ireland) Ltd, DUBLIN |
| Italy | Giuffré, MILAN |
| Malaysia | Malayan Law Journal Sdn Bhd, KUALA LUMPUR |
| New Zealand | Butterworths of New Zealand, WELLINGTON |
| Poland | Wydawnictwa Prawnicze PWN, WARSAW |
| Singapore | Butterworths Asia, SINGAPORE |
| South Africa | Butterworths Publishers (Pty) Ltd, DURBAN |
| Switzerland | Stämpfli Verlag AG, BERNE |
| USA | LexisNexis, DAYTON, Ohio |

A CIP Catalogue record for this book is available from the British Library.

ISBN 0 406 93246 8

Typeset by B & J Whitcombe, Nr Diss, Norfolk, IP22 2LP
Printed and bound in Great Britain by William Clowes Limited, Beccles and London

**Visit Butterworths LEXIS direct at: http://www.butterworths.com**

If you call me brother
Forgive me if I inquire
Just according to whose plan?

*Leonard Cohen*


Our external symbols must always express the
life within us with absolute precision; how
could they do otherwise, since that life has
generated them? Therefore we must not blame
our poor symbols if they take forms that seem
trivial to us, or absurd for . . . the nature of
our life alone has determined their forms.

A critique of these symbols is a critique of
our lives.

*Angela Carter*

*To Gwen,*
*with love and respect*

# Preface to the second edition

It is eight years since the first edition of this book was published. Where relevant, I have sought to update the argument with new case and statute law. I have also developed the analysis, especially in Chapter 3, where a closer link between the two main sections, on motive and intention and indirect intention, is established. There, I have sought to bring out the conflict between 'factual and cognitivist' approaches to intention on the one hand and 'morally substantive' approaches on the other. This seems to me to involve a conflict central to criminal law, as is evidenced by its repetition in many areas. It is paralleled in the law of recklessness (Chapter 4), in the law of strict liability (Chapter 5) and in the law of acts (Chapter 6). Its existence spills over into defences like necessity and duress (Chapter 8) and the principles of sentencing (Chapter 10). Elsewhere, I have argued that it also underlies acute problems in the law of provocation (Norrie, 2001). Recognising the problem helps explain tensions in the law between formalism and informalism (below, pp 44–6), and many logical inconsistencies and contradictions with which criminal lawyers grapple.

The idea that the general principles of criminal law might be founded on conflicts or contradictions seems hard to grasp. It runs up against the assumption that arguments of underlying principle should resolve problems by finding a better, or even a right, solution. Analyses of the moral significance of motive, or generally of a morally substantive approach, to formulating intention are assumed to lead directly to proposals for legal reform (see eg Clarkson and Keating, 1998, 144; Horder, 2000; Smith, 2001, 402). My argument is that such analyses are indeed relevant to the law, but are at the same time repelled by its structural tendency to deny moral substance through its general principles. The law has a complex dilemmatic structure involving inclusion and exclusion of the morally substantive within an overall framework based on the psychologically factual and cognitive.

The name given to the dominant psychologistic approach is 'orthodox subjectivism'. It informs the great post-war textbooks on criminal law, as it does the work of the early law reformers, the Victorian Criminal Law Commissioners. My argument is that its dominance stems from how it reflects the historical, legal and political value structure of modern Western societies. It is this that explains its enduring importance even if it is seen by many as problematic for its evasion of issues of moral substance. My own position is that both orthodox subjectivism and moral substantivism have value, though both are also morally inadequate. It is this complex relationship of the positive and the negative, of the legal, the historical and the moral, that makes legal change inherently problematic.

*Crime, Reason and History* has turned out to be the second of three books on modern Western ideas of criminal law, responsibility and punishment. The relationship between it and its predecessor, *Law, Ideology and Punishment* (1991) is described in the Preface to the First Edition below. Its successor, *Punishment, Responsibility and Justice* (2000) is a more ambitious philosophical and theoretical work. It advances what I call a relational theory of justice against both the orthodox subjectivists and the moral substantivists referred to above. It seeks in brief to identify and explain the ambivalence and ambiguity which accompany judgments of individual responsibility in modern law and morality. It does so by revealing the intrinsic yet occluded links (relations) between individual and social responsibility, between doing individual and doing social justice. The broad connection between these two books is that *Punishment, Responsibility and Justice* develops, underpins and defends the analysis presented here. I briefly refer to it at various places in this edition, but I have in general not sought to rewrite the earlier book in the light of the later one. The exception to this is Chapter 3, where the argument of the first edition needed development. I stress, however, that no knowledge of the later book is presupposed below.

Once more, I would like to thank the many academic friends and colleagues who through their agreements and, as important (and more frequent!), disagreements support the intellectual dialogue of which this book is a part. I also thank once more Gwen, Stephen and Richard for being there.

Alan Norrie
*September 2001*

# Preface to the first edition

The impetus to write this book came from an earlier work (Norrie, 1991) which considered the broadly 'Kantian' historical development of the modern philosophy of punishment, and explained the concept of justice and the contradictions within it in terms of the ideological premises upon which it was based. Those premises, I argued, stemmed from the ideological form of the abstract juridical individual at the heart of modern legal theory. Towards the end of that work, I began to develop the central argument of the present book. If the philosophy of punishment is essentially contradictory in its forms, and if these forms are based upon legal ideology, then it ought to be possible to understand not only the philosophy of punishment but also the theory and practice of the criminal law as contradictory.

Sustenance for this view was derived from the North American Critical Legal Studies approach, but such work remained peculiarly 'legal' in an inverted way: it retained an insider's commitment to law at the same time as it challenged law's central premises. Critical Legal Studies has had surprisingly little to say about criminal law, but the leading work in the field (Kelman, 1981) does not move significantly beyond the activity of 'trashing', simple negation, of the rationalist premises of orthodox criminal law theory. This work is important, but in presenting a systematic critical introduction to the law's general principles, I try to move beyond it. I have sought to synthesise a critical 'internal' account of criminal law which 'takes doctrine seriously' with an 'external' commitment to presenting law as a social and historical practice emerging in the first half of the nineteenth century.

I regard the practical work of the penal reform movements of this period as crucial in establishing a criminal law project that was deeply influenced by the philosophy of the Enlightenment. That influence remains at the heart of orthodox legal practice and scholarship through the commitment to liberal subjectivist and legal positivist analysis. It is the marriage of social practice and philosophical ideology that links my earlier concerns in the philosophy of punishment with the present work, and which provides the bridge for an analysis that seeks to break down any inside/outside distinction in legal scholarship.

The main title of this book reflects these concerns, but perhaps a word is required about the subtitle. The idea of 'critique' as in 'Critical Introduction' is that of starting from the forms of law in orthodox usage and showing the contradictions within that usage. From there, one moves to examine the fault lines that underlie the operative forms and to explain their existence in a particular social and historical context. In this way, one shows how the legal forms 'hang together' within criminal law discourse, and that there is an historical logic which underlies, suffuses and explains its intrinsic illogic.

This is, however, a 'Critical Introduction' and not an 'introductory critique'. I have sought to make the argument as accessible as I can, in particular by developing it slowly in the first few chapters. My aim, however, has been to develop it to meet some of the very sophisticated orthodox analyses head on, and this requires an approach that cannot be too simplistic. Where the work is introductory is in the scope of its coverage of the law's general principles. I examine the most important areas of criminal responsibility, and treat them to critical analysis. These are also the central areas that need to be covered, alongside the substantive crimes, in an under-graduate criminal law course.

This book is in many ways a companion volume to the other criminal law text in the *Law in Context* series (Lacey, Wells and Meure, 1990). Although the two works share many sympathies, they are also remarkably different. Lacey, Wells and Meure deal primarily with the substantive crimes and the contexts which generate the particular shape of the laws that protect and control (some forms of) social life. I start with the central categories of the orthodox approach to criminal law, and seek to locate them in a social and ideological context. The former approach locates criminal laws in the diversities of social life and the differentials of social power, while I begin with the ideal of unity within orthodox scholarship, and show both its intellectual limits and the social conditions of its possibility. At the risk of consid-erable oversimplification, it might be said that Lacey, Wells and Meure's primary focus is the *content* of the criminal law, whereas mine is its *form*. It may be that neither approach tells the whole story, and that therefore the two books genuinely complement each other. Perhaps subsequent work will be in a position to seek a further, deeper synthesis of form and content, in part on the basis of these two books.

In writing this book, I have incurred a large number of debts to friends and col-leagues. At Warwick, I would like to thank Roger Burridge and John McEldowney who welcomed me onto the criminal law course some years ago, and encouraged me in the development of the arguments presented here. I would also like to thank Davina Cooper, Robert Fine and Linda Luckhaus for reading and commenting on specific chapters, and a number of colleagues for their comments at staff seminars I gave at the beginning and end of the project. These include Hugh Beale, Julio Faundez, Laurence Lustgarten, Sol Picciotto and Geoffrey Wilson. More generally, I would like to acknowledge the value of being in a Law School like Warwick which has a self-conscious tradition of encouraging innovative approaches to legal study. Beyond Warwick, I would like to thank a number of people for their help, including Andrew Ashworth, Antony Duff, John Gardner, Peter Glazebrook, Jeremy Horder, Nicola Lacey, Roger Leng, Peter Rush, Stephen Shute, Clive Unsworth, Tony Ward and Celia Wells. Roger Leng in particular read and commented on every chapter except the last to my great benefit. From Andrew Ashworth (1991), I have borrowed the realist usage of the male-gendered pronoun to denote the criminal subject. William Twining and Chris McCrudden were supportive Series Editors, while Benjamin Buchan at Weidenfelds was both patient and cracked the whip at appro-priate times. Versions of Chapters 3, 4 and 7 have appeared in the *Criminal Law Review* [1989] 793, the *Oxford Journal Of Legal Studies* (1992) 12, 45 (and appears here by permission of Oxford University Press), and the *Modern Law Review* (1991) 54, 685.

Finally, I would like to thank my wife Gwen for her love, support and encouragement, particularly in the trying final stages of writing. Stephen and Richard were understanding and unselfish in letting me disappear for hour upon hour when I could have been doing other things with them. I hope their view of academic life has not been too coloured by observing the process of book-writing at close proximity. I am grateful to Stephen for his increasingly mordant wit, and to Richard I owe the Prologue from bedtime reading of *The Phantom Tollbooth*. It is an indication of how long I have been working on the book that he was recently created a High Court judge. Without them all, I doubt if this book would have been written; for them, it is the best I could do.

Alan Norrie
*December 1992*

# Contents

# Table of statutes

# List of cases

# A brief history of the ancient juridical city of Fictionopolis

## (with apologies to Norton Juster)

Fact is often stranger than fiction, and fiction can sometimes help us understand fact. Let me tell of an old world with a wise ruler and some enlightened advisers.

One day, the old King was picking through a thick pile of papers. These were tedious to him, though important to their writers, and the chore of reading them caused the king to yearn for some change, if only he could think of one. Fictionopolis had a good name as a city in which all were happy and each knew his or her place, but it must be said that there was a dark side to it. This took the shape of horrific laws under which a person could be put to death, often most unpleasantly, for a wide variety of not very good reasons (and in some cases for no reason at all). The laws were neither fair nor just, and it was because of this that the king had to perform the daily chore of picking through the papers. For these were requests for pardon from execution, and the King really had to make an effort, stifling a yawn, to preserve some semblance of caring for his people. Day in, day out, he would divide the pile into two – this side for the gallows, that side for transportation to some bizarre-sounding island many thousands of miles away where the lucky pardonees could do what they liked, out of sight, out of mind.

The King was bored and there was some word (he refused to believe it) that the people were not wildly happy either. Some got extraordinarily angry at the sight of 'justice' being done to their family and friends. To make matters worse, there was a growing gang of malcontents, claiming to speak for the people, who kept on muttering to anyone who would listen that the system was not only unfair but also downright inefficient. Eventually, the old King decided, for want of anything better, that perhaps the mutterers' hearts were in the right place and he should listen to them. They might not be 'his sort' but one had sometimes to do that which was distasteful. Besides, if it meant getting out from under the daily ordeal of the two piles – well, almost anything was better than that.

The malcontents were a new sort of people, lacking in breeding and culture, but with an impressive measure of brash self-confidence which was not unrelated to a vulgar ability to make rather large sums of money. Their ideas were pretty new-fangled and the King was inclined to send them packing with a flea in the ear. As we said, however, the old monarch of Fictionopolis was a wise man. Although what he heard grated terribly, and although, were he to agree, he would lose some of his own power, he began to see how things might not be so bad under a new régime. These rather offensive upstarts might not even be bad partners in the business of rule. Thus it was that the malcontents became transformed rather rapidly into enlightened advisers.

They said that the old system was unjust and did not work. If evil, wicked people (of whom there were many) got caught, they could really get it in the neck – but not many were caught and the penalties were so severe that juries kept on acquitting them. Even His Majesty connived at this situation (they tactfully pointed out that he too was a victim of the system) by giving out so many pardons. The King pricked up his ears. The system of pardons, said the advisers, had to go. 'But', said the King suspiciously, 'how will my people be protected from harsh laws otherwise?' 'Simple,' said the advisers, 'we will amend the laws and make them less harsh.'

Then they got down to brass tacks. The present system was old-fashioned. It relied too much on the undoubtedly present but personal ties between His Majesty and the people. They loved the King, but there was rather a lot of temptation about on account of the recent activities of the advisers themselves (here they puffed out their chests) as Creators of Wealth. 'We are the new men,' they said (their women were at home attending to domestic matters), 'and we see the world differently. His Majesty sees loving subjects who know their place and obey the rules out of respect for the past and the King. We are the new men of the future, a world in which a man does what a man must (their women were still at home). A man must be free and all men must be equal for we are all the same – all out to get for ourselves what we can. We know what is best for ourselves, and the law must respect our rights as individuals.'

By this point, the King's eyes were beginning to glaze over. 'Yes, yes,' he said, 'enough of the harangue. What has this got to do with law and order in the city?' 'Everything', said the advisers. If every man was an individual, and all were the same, and each was able to look out for himself, then, properly set, the laws could act as a genuine deterrent to crime. Everyone had to realise that any crime would be followed by a penalty matched to it. There would be a scale of crimes and punishments and (provided that there was a more efficient police force and an effective prison system) everyone would work out for themselves that no crime was worth committing. 'Trust the people,' said the advisers, 'they are like us. Grade the punishments and make them less harsh, make the laws rational, certain and fair and the people will obey them.'

The King could see what they were getting at, but he had some doubts. These advisers might be a common lot, but they weren't half as common as the rabble whose petitions he had to read. Would *they* obey these laws? Terror seemed a better prospect. Then he thought of his brother-in-law, who just happened to be Lord High Chief Justice of Fictionopolis. He could just imagine his reaction! Do you expect the judges to go along with this, he asked? The advisers took a deep breath, for they had anticipated this difficult question. The judges would have to be controlled. They enjoyed too much discretion and power, which they used viciously (despite much cant to the contrary). Their job would be only to apply the law, and not to make it up as they did at present. People had no security when the judges kept reinventing the rules. They must be bound by the rules themselves. New rules should be made by a new body (they crossed their fingers) called Parliament. This would be made up of men like themselves plus some of His Majesty's old hunting friends. The judges might get a bit of a say, but the law was to be applied as it stood and without jiggery-pokery. If it were any consolation, they concluded, the judges would enjoy new respect among the people because they applied just laws fairly to all.

The King had felt a certain urge to call the guard at the mention of Parliament, but, being wise, he could see the value of what was said. True, he and his brother-in-law would be shackled by this new system (which he disparagingly referred to as 'the rule of law') but they would gain a certain amount of kudos from that very fact. If the system were to be effective in preventing crime (he still had his doubts), well it couldn't be all bad. Besides, these adviser chaps did have a lot of money to play about with . . . He agreed.

How fared the new régime in Fictionopolis? It 'worked' – after a fashion. There were three problems. First, the idea that the world was full of free and equal individuals calculating their self-interest was (as the King had sensed) both a blessing and a curse. It transpired that the advisers had been rather optimistic in their view of things (to what extent deliberately was hard to say). The law was tailored to respect individual freedom and choice but what the advisers had not seen, or not accounted for, or deliberately ignored (here lies the uncertainty) was the extent to which individuals would be divided into distinct social orders by factors of wealth and power. To give the advisers the benefit of the doubt, they had not realised that for all their talk about everyone being free and equal, the reality would be that in matters of property distribution, some (including the advisers) were decidedly more free and equal than others. It was not that their talk (and their laws) were lies or mere rhetoric. Everyone was (more or less) free and equal in the eyes of the law. It was that legal freedom and equality was rather badly matched to the economic distri-bution of resources and the political distribution of power. It thus transpired that while the law was expressed in universal terms as applying to all classes of people, individuals from the lower classes were much more likely to contravene it. Occasionally, the odd well-to-do person (even one of the advisers in a particularly scandalous episode) would come before the courts, and when the poor came before them, they were treated reasonably fairly (according to the law). It was just that despite this universality of application, the bulk of the criminals did tend to be drawn from the lower echelons.

The cynics said that this was hardly surprising. The advisers had proclaimed themselves Creators of Wealth and it was their own wealth that they wanted to protect. The new laws were very fine and fancy in their respect for individuals, but they were there to protect property in the main. Inevitably they ended up protecting those who had the most property and prosecuting those who had little and who either committed crimes in order to get wealth or in reaction to the conditions in which they lived. This disparity between form and substance did not appear in the law itself. Whether knowingly or not, the advisers had concocted a clever scheme which under the guise of protecting all (and this was not a sham) protected mainly the few against the many. Of course the law had to manage this gap between the legal categories which respected individuals as free and equal beings and the realities of social life, but lawyers are intelligent and resourceful people and this was more or less possible.

The second problem concerned the judges. The old King's brother-in-law had not liked the new set-up one little bit and fought a determined rearguard action against it. Indeed he succeeded in ensuring that not all the law would be made by Parliament and that the judges would still have considerable say in what the laws should be. He had to accept the general notion of the 'rule of law', however, and as time passed, he and his colleagues began to get the hang of it. For one thing, as the King had foreseen, resentment at being tied down by the law was offset by a new respect shown to the judges (who continued to be drawn from the city's upper ranks) by the common people. In any case, being bound by the law proved not quite so constraining as had at first seemed to be the case. They still had substantial control over the law and it was possible to manipulate it this way and that where necessary.

In this respect, they saw themselves as being in a bit of a cleft stick. They were charged with applying a set of rules designed to be fair, just and respectful to all individuals, but after a while working in the law, it became clear that each individual was simply another manifestation of serious social problems which the law had to control. At the end of the day, the law was about achieving good order in the city. All the talk about individual rights and responsibilities, frankly, got in the way. So sometimes, they did what they were not supposed to and bent or broke the rules (in effect remade them) to suit the situation as they saw it. Respect for the law was one thing, respect for good order quite another. Occasionally the odd tiresome teacher of the law would complain but, due to the general respect that the judges enjoyed, this could be patched over.

Finally, it has to be said that the advisers were sorely disappointed in the results of their system. There was much debate on the matter but it was plain that over the years the amount of crime did not diminish and disappear as the advisers had predicted. Individuals just did not see the reason to obey the law, and were not deterred. Some people said that criminals just weren't rational. Others said that it all depended upon what 'rational' meant. It might be quite rational for those in poor social conditions to steal or hit someone, and not consider the penalty. Still others said this was claptrap and all that was needed was greater penalties and detection (this view generally prevailed). Those who favoured it (the King's brother-in-law was a keen advocate) often claimed that the law itself was a problem, and that what was needed was a better balance between the rights of the criminal and society (the criminal not being a part of society for this purpose).

Sadly for this latter view, it never did seem to do much good. A recent traveller to Fictionopolis reports that the criminal courts are as busy as ever applying (and occasionally bending) the law to 'individuals' who come before them in an unaccountably incessant stream. The Parliament has meantime prudently sanctioned the building of a brand new prison, to be run as a business by certain offspring of the old King's original advisers.

# Part 1

# Context

# Chapter 1

# Contradiction, critique and criminal law

By and large, the dominant tradition in Anglo-American legal scholarship today is unhistorical. It attempts to find universal rationalising principles . . . The underlying structure of the law class remains that of forcing the student to reconcile contradictions that cannot be reconciled. If you do it very well, you then become a professor and you demand it of your students and you continue to do it in your legal scholarship. The ideological 'tilt' of current legal scholarship derives from this attempt to suppress the real contradictions in the world, to make the existing world seem to be necessary . . . to be part of the nature of things. It is history that comes to challenge this approach by showing that the rationalising principles of the mainstream scholars are historically contingent. Consequently, analytic scholarship is anti-historical: it regards history as subversive because it exposes the rationalising enterprise. (Horwitz, 1981, 1057)

## I   INTRODUCTION

The quotation from Morton Horwitz with which I begin this introductory chapter contains two main arguments which are central to the analysis of criminal law attempted here. First, there is the identification of traditional, legal scholarship as entailing a 'rationalising enterprise'. The standard textbooks affirm the possibility of a rational (logical) approach to criminal law based upon the identification, elucidation and application of certain general principles to the existing law. Williams, for example, prefaces the first edition of his *Textbook on Criminal Law* with the statement that he has sought to show 'that the law is mainly rational', joining in criticism so that it may be improved through 'the effort to expose its shortcomings' (Williams, 1978, v). Smith and Hogan heap praise on one case as 'a major step towards a rational and principled criminal law' while criticising other cases for 'the mischief wrought by those extraordinary decisions' (Smith and Hogan, 1983, v). What makes those decisions 'extraordinary' is that they are irrational and unprincipled. The orthodox approach to criminal law scholarship is committed to what MacCormick (1993) has termed 'rational reconstruction', the 'production of clear and systematic statements of legal doctrine, accounting for statute law and case law in terms of organising principles'.

The argument of this book, to the contrary, is that criminal law is neither rational nor principled, so that the 'extraordinary' is as much the norm as the ordinary. It is not that there is no rationality or principle in the law at all, but rather that the elements of reason and principle are constantly in conflict with other elements in the law itself. This means that the 'rationalising enterprise' is frequently rationalisation only in the pejorative sense of an apparent rationality papering over the cracks of deeper contradictions.

The second point drawn from Horwitz concerns the relevance of history. If legal rationalism is for much of the time only rationalisation in the pejorative sense, why should this be so? Traditional legal scholarship, if it saw the question, would have no answer to it. For it, the principles upon which the criminal law is founded are natural and ahistoric, in the sense that they are never seen as the product of a particular kind of society generating particular historical forms of social control peculiar to itself. This is what Horwitz means when he says that current legal scholarship attempts to make the world seem 'necessary . . . part of the nature of things'. To the extent that lawyers think historically about the law, they tend to think in terms of the slow evolution of legal forms from the crude to the sophisticated, and not in terms of the particular connections between different legal forms and different kinds of society. When lawyers look back, they tend to discover no more than the present writ small in the past (Gordon, 1981). They propagate a closed version of legal history that can be described as 'mythical' (Fitzpatrick, 1992).

By contrast, the argument of this book is that the modern criminal law was formed in a particular historical epoch and derived its characteristic 'shape' from fundamental features of the social relations of that epoch. Its principles, therefore, are historic and relative rather than natural and general. Furthermore, these principles were established in the crucible of social and political conflict, and bear the stamp of history in the always-contradictory ways in which they are formulated. Historical analysis shows that, far from being free-standing foundations for a rational criminal law, the central principles of the law are the site of struggle and contradiction. This can only work its way through the legal rules themselves. Thus it is that the fate of law as a rationalising enterprise is tied up with the nature of law as a social, historical force. In the Prologue, I have tried to sketch in an imaginary way the social and historical contradictions from which the law emerges and whose marks it bears. In the next chapter, we will go into things in a less imaginary way. In this introduction, I want to consider what the fundamental principles of the criminal law are, and to show why it is fair to suggest that they are contradictory.

## 2  RATIONALITY AND LEGALITY

These two values are intertwined. Legality (the 'rule of law') depends upon making and applying legal rules in a non-arbitrary way. It depends upon a system of norms that do not contradict each other, that are consistent and coherent. It requires that judges recognise and obey already existing rules through a system of precedent. All these things can only happen if the 'glue' that holds a system of laws together is logic or reason. Rationality is fundamental to legality. The link is well brought out within legal theory by MacCormick, for whom legal reasoning must be rational:

> . . . the essential notion is that of giving (what are understood and presented as) good justifying reasons for claims, defences or decisions. The process which is worth studying is the process of argumentation as a process of justification. (MacCormick, 1978, 15)[1]

It is the rationality of legal decision-making which constrains judges to 'do justice according to law, not to legislate for what seems to them an ideally just form of society' (MacCormick, 1978, 107). It is only respect for reason and logic that maintains the basic tenet of law-making under the rule of law:

> 'Thou shalt not controvert established and binding rules of law' is a commandment which applies to both [statute and case law], and which imposes genuine and important limits to judicial freedom of action even after we have made all appropriate qualifications to allow for the possibility of restrictive interpretation and explaining and distinguishing. (MacCormick, 1978, 227)

Nor is this view the preserve of legal theory alone. The Chairman of the Law Commission writes that –

> ... if there is one quality which a judge seeks to impart in his judgment, it is that of a logical approach. Not of course in the sense of the formal logic of the syllogism but in the search for principle, the ascertainment of fact and the application of the principle to the facts of the particular case. (Beldam, 1987, 9)

Logical reasoning, he says, is a key element in legal reasoning. Similarly, take two cases of the recent past. In *Morgan*, Lord Hailsham stated:

> I cannot myself reconcile it with my conscience to sanction as part of the English law what I regard as logical impossibility, and if there were any authority which, if accepted, would compel me to do so, I would feel constrained to declare that it was not to be followed. (*DPP v Morgan* (1976) at 213)

In the case of *Abbott*, Lord Edmund-Davies, in a strongly worded dissenting judgment, drew together the issues of logic and legality with this comment:

> It has to be said with all respect that the majority opinion of their Lordships amounts, in effect, to side-stepping the decision in *Lynch* and, *even were that constitutionally appropriate*, to do it *without advancing cogent grounds* ... (*Abbott v R* (1977) at 772; see below, Chapter 8)

One would think that there is a clearly recognised principle of rationality and thence legality recognised within the law, and one that therefore coheres with the method of the textbook writers. But if one looks a little further, one finds only contradiction. Thus Williams, whose work seeks to show that the law is 'mainly rational' reveals elsewhere (in discussing legality) that the opposite is the case:

> It would be pleasant to be able to assert that the root principle underlying the administration of the criminal law is that of legality. Unfortunately ... there is no unanimity about anything in criminal law: scarcely a single important principle but has been denied by some judicial decision or by some legislation. The principle of legality is a notable sufferer from this lack of agreement. (Williams, 1961, 575)

Or take Lord Hailsham, who could not reconcile it with his conscience to allow illogic into the law in *Morgan*, in the later case of *Howe*:

> Consistency and logic, though inherently desirable, are not always prime characteristics of a penal code based like the common law on custom and precedent. (*R v Howe* (1987) at 780)

Or Lord Edmund-Davies, so critical of his fellow judges for their lack of logic in *Abbott*, in the slightly earlier case of *Majewski*:

> I have respectfully to say that were such an attitude rigorously adopted and applied [ie the attitude of Lord Hailsham in *Morgan*], it would involve the drastic revision of much of our criminal law. Many would say that this would not be a bad thing, but it is well to realise clearly that such would be the consequence, for the criminal law is unfortunately riddled with illogicalities. (*DPP v Majewski* (1976) at 166)

In these passages, a commitment to rationality is proclaimed and denied. Rationality is both a central legal virtue and an impossibility. Lawyers, both practising and academic, make their arguments on the assumption that logical reasoning is a central requirement, but in their moments of doubt, or when pushed to a position they do not accept, they jettison logic or insist on its limits. Yet those limits are never understood as I suggest they should be understood: as historical and social limits on a reasoning process that is necessarily contradictory. Nor does a recognition of such limits lead to a restructuring of legal discourse or a reconsideration of the legal enterprise as a whole. Even where writers recognise the myriad problems of the law, or concede that there might be underlying tensions (as does Glanville Williams in some of the passages quoted in this chapter), they still proceed on the basis that a rational principled criminal law could be achieved. The possibility of 'rational reconstruction' remains the central organising theme of their work. I wish to stress, in contrast, the historical, political and ideological limits upon rationality within the law and the way in which these limits inform its fundamental principles and undermine the rationalistic enterprise. This is not a question of bad lawyering, archaic rules, or general dim-wittedness getting in the way of an otherwise rational process: it is the way that the law fundamentally is.

## 3   INDIVIDUAL JUSTICE

It can be said that the ultimate principle at the root of criminal law, and one which includes the principles of logic and legality, is the requirement of doing justice to individuals (cf Williams, 1961, 575–6; Lacey, 1988, 149). At the core of the philosophy behind the criminal law is a moral individualism which proclaims that for the state to intervene against the individual, it must have a good and clear licence to do so (Dennis, 1997). Hence the relevance of fault liability to criminal law, and the principle of giving the individual the benefit of the doubt in a number of important situations. Criminal law is, at heart, a practical application of liberal political philosophy. Thus the legal theorist Hart writes that criminal liability can be founded upon –

> . . . the simple idea that unless a man has the capacity and a fair opportunity or chance to adjust his behaviour to the law its penalties ought not to be applied to him. (Hart, 1968, 181)

There is an *intrinsic* connection between criminal punishment and individual justice:

... the principle that punishment should be restricted to those who have voluntarily broken the law ... incorporates the idea that each individual person is to be protected against the claim of the rest for the highest possible measure of security, happiness or welfare which could be got at his expense by condemning him for a breach of rules and punishing him. For this a moral licence is required in the form of proof that the person punished broke the law by an action which was the outcome of his free choice ... *it is a requirement of Justice*. (Hart, 1968, 22) (my emphasis)

The idea of a fault element at the heart of the criminal law is embraced by both Williams and Smith and Hogan. They insist that the root of responsibility lies in the subjective mental attitude of the accused (the 'orthodox subjectivist' approach which dominates the modern textbook tradition: Dennis, 1997). Without this, fair opportunity and voluntariness cannot exist. The fault element is 'a mark of advancing civilisation' required by 'the criminal law in respect of offences traditionally regarded as serious' because they involve 'so drastic an interference with the liberty of the subject' (Williams, 1983, 70). The legal term mens rea 'denotes the mental state (subjective element)' (Williams, 1983, 71) which supplies the element of fault.

Also consistent with the requirement of individual justice is the 'rule of strict construction' which gives the accused the benefit of the doubt in cases of genuine doubt as to the interpretation of a law. As Lord Reid put it in the case of *Sweet v Parsley*:

... it is a universal principle that if a penal provision is reasonably capable of two interpretations, that interpretation which is most favourable to the accused must be adopted. ((1969) at 350; see below, Chapter 5)[2]

The precise nature of the rule of strict construction needs to be specified,[3] but this does not concern us here. Williams in fact amends it, consistently with the principle of individual justice, by arguing that a rule of *liberal* construction applies in relation to defences, where giving the benefit of the doubt to the individual involves broadening, not narrowing the rules (Williams, 1961, 591–2; 1983, 452).

Thus, we might think that the principle of individual justice is present within the criminal law through the fault requirement and the rule of strict construction. Again, however, we face quite contradictory statements. Whereas Williams commences his discussion of mens rea with the claim that subjective fault is central to criminal liability, he ends it, four chapters later, as follows:

To wind up this discussion of mens rea, it was the judges who invented the doctrine, but ... some have fought a long rearguard action against it. The mental element has been virtually eliminated from many offences, while it has been watered down in others. (1983, 143)

Similarly, in a discussion of the rule of strict construction, he writes that –

Courts still pay lip-service to the ancient principle that in case of doubt a criminal statute is to be 'strictly construed' in favour of the defendant; but the principle is rarely applied in practice, if there are social reasons for convicting. (1983, 12)

In similar vein, Spencer slams the rule in terms of Williams' proposed amendment with regard to defences:

English judges seem to have a longstanding love of broadly defined offences and a deep suspicion of broad defences. This leads to a very strict rule of criminal law, tempered only by the judges' liking for the administrative discretion to give a light sentence. These are the real limits of criminal liability. The attitude is ancient, durable and widespread, and most judges past and present seem to share it . . . (Spencer, 1984, 1270)

Finally, we began this discussion of individual justice within criminal law with the view of the legal philosopher Hart. We have so far considered contradictory statements about one particular *application* of his fundamental principle concerning the respect for individuals embodied within the law. I want to end with a full-frontal challenge to the principle itself from another legal philosopher. Vining argues that the individualism within the law –

... has nothing to do with concern for the dignity, happiness or importance of the individual. It defines rather a particular way of populating our thought with living units of reference, no more universal or basic than the various personifications of wind and water which have lost their vivid meanings for most of us . . . (Vining, 1978, 2)

This is abstractly expressed and perhaps not easy to grasp, but it is important. Vining sharply contrasts the law's view of what individuals are like ('legal individualism') and the realities associated with actual individual lives ('human individuality'). Legal individualism affixes a badge to our clothing or a mask to our face which has nothing to do with what we really are or resemble. Law dresses us with a veneer of rights, duties and responsibilities (legally conceived) that have nothing to do with the real needs and attributes of human beings. Real justice to individuals has nothing necessarily in common with legal justice. The latter obscures the former:

... respect for each man as such and for what he truly is in all the fullness of his life and hopes – is only now coming into its own as it is perceived that individuals are not in fact known to the law. We achieve our ends, which we cherish as individuals, and we realise ourselves, precisely because individuals are not legal persons. (Vining, 1978, 2; cf Hudson, 1987)

We will return to this in due course. It is a complex argument, and I will suggest that Vining overstates his case. For now, as with the other points we have considered, we need only note the impressive disparity, contradiction and dispute in abundance concerning the basic principles of the law. The concept of individual justice is problematic both in terms of its instantiation within the criminal law and in terms of its own fundamental character. Yet this is the concept that is expected by liberal criminal law theory to play the part of a central organising principle within a rational, principled criminal law. In this light, how successful can it be in playing this part?

## 4   UNDERSTANDING THE CONTRADICTIONS

The aim of this book is to try to understand how it can be that criminal law attracts such contradictory assessments. More precisely, what is the *real* nature of the law, and how can it generate such conflicting views from within its own practice? The answer lies in a two-handed approach which both rejects the view that the law is (in principle) rational and just, but equally rejects the view that it is wholly irrational. There are principles of rationality and justice in operation within the law but they must be seen as elements in tension with other contradictory elements. In examining criminal law, we must recognise the *limits* of rationality and justice: limits which are a central and necessary part of the enterprise and not the result of chance or contingency (cf Norrie, 1996). Criminal law is relatively unpredictable in its development and this stems from the fundamental ambiguity of its central organising principles.

To apply this to our previous discussion, we saw how the principles of rationality and legality (offshoots in fact of the basic principles of liberal individualism) are *both* central to the self-understanding of the legal role *and* denied by it. The approach of this book is not to take up either the former or the latter view in isolation. To take only the former view would lead to an important misunderstanding of the necessary elements of irrationality in the law, while the latter view alone would lead to a too-rampant irrationalism in which 'anything goes' (Kelman (1981) comes close to this position). The truth is that when Lord Edmund-Davies attacked the majority in *Abbott* for their lack of logic, he was acting in an identifiably legal way. But the same is *also* true when he conceded and defended illogic in *Majewski*.[4] There is in short a deep-seated tension within the law between elements of rationality and irrationality.

What is true of rationality is also true of individual justice. One can find examples of restrictive (*Anderton v Ryan* (1985) on attempts) and broad (*Caldwell* (1981) on recklessness) constructions of offences, of liberal (*DPP v Camplin* (1978) on provocation) and narrow (*Abbott v R* (1977) on duress) constructions of defences. Similarly, one can find examples of decisions based upon subjective fault (*DPP v Morgan* (1976)) just as readily as decisions which deny the requirement (*Caldwell* (1981)). A T H Smith, commenting on the 'classical view' that courts give individuals the benefit of the doubt and contrasting it with the developing academic consensus that they do the reverse, writes:

> Even if it is true that neither view applies with any consistency, justice is reduced to a matter of chance, or the temperament of individual judges. ((1984) at 48)

It is this inconsistency of approach that has to be accounted for. It will be argued that while justice may become a 'matter of chance', the explanation for this must be sought more deeply than in the temperament of individual judges, although it would be foolish to deny that that plays a part.[5] One must seek understanding of the inconsistency first and foremost in the intellectual structure of the law, a structure that has developed in the crucible of particular, historically developed social relations. It is helpful here to recall the opinion of Williams in the summary of his discussion of mens rea. It will be remembered that his conclusion was that the principled element of subjective fault had in fact been grossly undermined by the judges' decisions. He then went on to say this:

> In short, the law on mens rea illustrates the eternal tension in the position of the judge. He is supposed to be an impartial adjudicator, applying the existing law and protecting the rights and liberties of the subject; but he is also a State instrumentality – in the wider sense, an organ of government. In general it is the second concept of the judge's role that shapes judicial attitudes on the issue of fault in the criminal law. (Williams, 1983, 143–4)

It is not this view which *structures* Williams' analysis of the law which, as we have seen, involves the effort of 'rational reconstruction', but it does reveal the way into a more firmly based explanation of legal development. It is the 'second concept of the judge's role' which so frequently undermines the principles of subjective fault that Williams sees in the law. Recall also Williams' earlier comment (1983, 143) that 'it was the judges who invented the doctrine [of mens rea]' so that they both promote and oppose the principle of subjective fault: a contradictory role indeed. A more adequate understanding of the law will be built around this kind of insight (cf Lacey, 1985). But we cannot stop there. We need also to know why the contradiction in the judicial role exists. *Why is it* that the law both embodies principles of individual liberty and justice and undermines them? It will be argued, in the next chapter, that an answer to that question, and the key to understanding legal development, must be sought in the historical moment of birth of legal and liberal individualism: the period of the 'Enlightenment'.

Finally, I return to the contrasting views of Hart and Vining as to the fundamental questions of what it means to do justice to individuals, and whether the law has any claims in this area. Again, the answer will be two-handed. The legal definition of justice propounded by Hart is not, as Vining's comment implies, wholly misconceived but nor is it wholly valid. Legal justice is limited and partial because it deals with individuals in a particular abstract fashion. It picks out certain aspects of individuality, but excludes others.[6] There is a legal conception of the individual which ignores, conceals and *discounts* fundamental features of the lives of people. Legal justice cuts across and denies a broader social conception of justice, with which it can be contrasted and in relation to which it can be found wanting.[7] Nonetheless, limited though it is, the liberal legal conception of justice is not a total sham or without value: it can provide an important defence for individuals against the state, and the importance of this should not be overlooked.

It is important to note that the standpoint adopted here of a two-handed approach to law and its claims should not be regarded as a compromise giving 'a bit of this and a bit of that'. The argument is a strong one about law and legal ideology which insists that the key to understanding the law's development is an approach which takes as its starting point historically located contradictions within the law. History explains the 'method behind the madness' and it is to that that we now turn.

# Chapter 2

# The historical context of criminal doctrine

The high and paramount importance of the Criminal Law consists in this consideration, that upon its due operation the enforcement of every other branch of the law . . . depends. [And] there is [no branch] which is so capable of being made intelligible to all classes of persons, or which, in its relations and bearings, is calculated to excite greater attention and interest – none, the knowledge of which can tend more effectually to convince all ranks of Your Majesty's subjects that the laws are founded on just principles, having regard to the protection of all, and equally binding on all, and consequently to impress the duty and induce the habit of prompt obedience. (Criminal Law Commissioners, 1843, 4)

It was easy to claim equal justice for murderers of all classes, where a universal moral sanction was more likely to be found, or in political cases, the necessary price of a constitution ruled by law. The trick was to extend that communal sanction to a criminal law that was nine-tenths concerned with upholding a radical division of property. (Hay, 1977, 35)

## I INTRODUCTION

In the preceding pages, I have considered the orthodox claim that the fundamental bases of the criminal law are principles of rational legalism and individual justice. Although this claim is made in the writings of academic and practising lawyers, we have also seen it negated by these same people. This raises the obvious question, 'Why?' An explanation of this phenomenon must go deeper than the principles of law themselves, to a level at which we can understand the co-existence of principle and its negation within the law. As Horwitz has claimed, to go deeper involves going into history. The Prologue is a starting point. It tells of an imaginary world which, I suggest, corresponds roughly to the historical world of which we are a part. English society (along with most of continental Europe) had its own reactionary, bloody penal system, which gave way to an 'enlightened' project of legal reform in the second quarter of the nineteenth century. But this project of legal reform was not without its contradictions, and a more thorough analysis of the most important developments shows this to be so. That is the task of this chapter, which attempts to substantiate the sketch of the Prologue and provisionally to indicate its significance for modern criminal law doctrine. The two should be read together, but the reader should not need reminding (as lawyers sometimes do) that fact is not the same as fiction.

This chapter is divided into two main sections. The first considers the nature of the legal individualism that came to dominate juridical discourse in the first instance through the work of the penal reform movement of the late eighteenth and early nineteenth centuries. The second looks at the relationship between that individualism and the nature and necessities of state power, as that relationship developed in the period of reform. Both sections reveal the contradictions within this proto-legal discourse which result from the development of legal individualist ideology in a world of social conflict. In a brief concluding section, I move from history to the present by suggesting that it is this setting which forms the intellectual crucible in which modern criminal law doctrine is compounded. I argue that the conflicts, contradictions and tensions of the criminal law result from a theory of individual responsibility that can be described, first, as *psychologically* and, second, as *politically individualistic*.

## 2   LEGAL INDIVIDUALISM AND SOCIAL INDIVIDUALITY

### (i)   Justice and deterrence in the penal theory of the Enlightenment

*(a)   The reformers' task*

Foucault (1979, 3–6, 32–73) has shown how the vicious and bloody penal system of eighteenth century France was institutionally and logically interconnected with the maintenance of absolute monarchy. Through the course of the political struggles of the seventeenth century, England had in contrast abolished absolutism, but in its place had developed a political and social régime disparagingly known as 'Old Corruption' (Corrigan and Sayer, 1985, 87–104; Hill, 1967). The Whig oligarchy of eighteenth-century England ran its criminal law system as if absolutism still existed, so that the bloodiness of the law substantially increased in this period. The number of capital statutes quintupled (from 50 to 250: Radzinowicz, 1948) although comparatively few of the large number of those given the death penalty actually met their end on the gallows. Hay has shown how this system of maximum potential punishment coupled with the use of pardons was employed by the ruling class to affirm the old feudally originated ties between the landed gentry, the king and 'their' people (Hay, 1977). The threat of terror was combined with the application of 'mercy' through the use of the royal prerogative to pardon at the behest of the judge or high standing members of the 'community'. The common people were both cowed by and made grateful to their 'betters' by this manipulative ideological cocktail of terror and mercy. Blackstone, in some but not all (Ashworth, 1978) ways an apologist for the system, was quite clear as to the legitimative effects of the system of pardons:

> . . . these repeated acts of goodness coming immediately from his own head, endear the sovereign to his subjects, and contribute more than anything to root in their hearts that filial affection, and personal loyalty, which are the sure establishment of a prince. (Quoted in Hay, 1977, 48)

Nonetheless, by the end of the eighteenth century, these feudal ideas were becoming ideas whose time had passed. A new social class was coming to the fore, ready to replace the old élite and its particular logic of rule with a new one. In France, things were done dramatically, in England, through the relatively quiet revolution of Benthamism.

The key conception was that the social world was founded upon individual self-interest and right. In the different countries, the emphasis within this liberal individualism was placed differently. In Germany, at one extreme, the language was one of right and reason, expressed in the dramatically metaphysical philosophies of Kant and Hegel (Marcuse, 1941; Norrie, 1991, chs 3, 4). In England, at the other extreme, the language was one of individual self-interest under the prosaic influence of political economists like Smith and materialist philosophers like Hobbes and Hume (MacPherson, 1962; Norrie, 1991, chs 2, 6). Whatever the emphasis, the core idea was that at the heart of moral, political, social, economic – *and legal* – discourse there should be placed the idea of the free individual. This persona was variously free, in the British account, to pursue his (the ideas were predominantly male oriented) economic self interest or, in the German account, to constitute the core of a rational and metaphysical philosophy. The liberal Enlightenment involved the embrace of free individualism in every discourse, and this provided a firm basis for the criticism and rejection of the old absolutist method of social control through a punitive reign of terror. The latter could hardly be held to respect the liberties of the individual subject and was therefore to be abolished.

## (b)   Retributive justice

With regard to punishment and criminal law, the change could be seen in a growing assertion of the need both for individual justice *and* effective deterrence. Both were present in the reform movement that began in the second half of the eighteenth century, particularly in the work of Cesare Beccaria. He justified punishment as a response to a breach of the social contract by a free individual, and argued that only a system of punishments respecting the individual could effectively deter crime (Beccaria, 1966). The time had come to abandon the brutal system which could deliver maximum punishment for the smallest crime in favour of one based upon *proportionality* between crime and its punishment. Right and respect for the individual and public utility all demanded as much.

The emphasis on these questions varied from one country to another. In France, Foucault stresses the moral dimension of the new punishment which 'ceased to be centred on torture as a technique of pain [and] assumed as its central object loss of wealth or rights' (Foucault, 1979, 15). He quotes Mably, a contemporary reformer, who wrote 'Punishment, if I may so put it, should strike the soul rather than the body' (1979, 16). He also gives the vivid example of the guillotine. With its substitution of instantaneous, painless death for torture, it was 'intended to apply the law not so much to a real body capable of feeling pain as to a *juridical subject, the possessor, among other rights, of the right to exist*' (1979, 13) (emphasis added).

It was this view of punishment as the negation of an abstract legal moral right rather than simple pain or psychological terror that was most famously expressed in the retributive philosophy of punishment in Germany. Kant and Hegel insisted that punishment was a matter, first and foremost, of the right of the individual. Because of this, the individual's guilt had to be established in advance of punishment, and, most importantly, punishment had to be equal to the crime. Punishment without guilt or responsibility, or in excess of the wrong done by the individual was unjust. The demand for individual justice was a central demand of liberal thought in this period, and it is crucial to note its theoretical basis in the birth of a particular model of the legal subject as a free and responsible agent. What one might call the 'retributive moment' with its strengths and weaknesses is central to the penal philosophy and doctrinal practice of the criminal law today.[1]

## (c) Utilitarian deterrence

The reformers were not, however, motivated purely by enlightened moral sentiment. They were convinced that the old system of terror did not work. Drawn from the rising middle classes, who owned property as merchants and manufacturers in the cities (where the old feudal ties did not exist), they experienced tremendous levels of loss from theft and other forms of taking. The contemporary reformer Colquhoun collected the estimates of entrepreneurs and insurers in London. Theft of goods from warehouses in the Port stood at £500,000 per annum and from the City itself at £700,000 (Foucault, 1979, 85–7). The middle classes had a 'crime problem' on their hands, and they imagined a more effective way of dealing with it than the increasingly ineffective system of terror and patronage. Under the old system, many criminals went free. Juries refused to convict and pardons were always a possibility. The common people were not, it seemed, intimidated by capital punishment and public executions were themselves occasions for illegality through violent protest and as an easy opportunity for pickpockets.

The reformers conceived of a regular and systematic form of law that would not rely on uncertain terror but on certain calculation. The free rational individual that inhabited their moral and political discourse also underlay and explained their economic activity of calculating costs and benefits. Translating this economic theory of behaviour into the realm of social control, they argued that free individuals could work out for themselves that the costs of punishment might outweigh the benefits of crime and would, therefore, rationally desist from its commission. In looking to self-interest within a more certain system of crime control, it was thought that individuals' conduct could be regulated by a systematic code of rules in which a proportioned weight of punishment would deter the commission of different kinds of crime. In addition to retributive justice based upon moral sentiments concerning individual right, the reformers' liberal individualism thus also gave rise to a utilitarian theory of deterrent punishment based upon the individual's calculation of his self interest.

In England, the utilitarian reformer Bentham wrote that mankind was placed under two sovereign masters, pain and pleasure, and possessed an innate tendency to avoid the one and seek the other. The ability to calculate rationally the consequences of action combined with the pain/pleasure principle to enable the individual to maximise his self-interest (Bentham, 1962; 1975). All punishments were pains and therefore evils in themselves, but they were justified because of their potential to deter the pain and evil (in society and for other individuals) of crime. The pain of punishment must, however, only just exceed the prospective pleasure to the criminal of his crime, for two reasons. First, the aim of the legislator is to diminish the evil of pain in the world, and this includes pain to the criminal as well as to others. To a calculating subject, punishment need only just exceed crime in its severity for it to be an effective deterrent. Any more would be simply needless evil brought into the world (1975, 199–200). Second, a rational system of punishments would match crime to punishment so that more serious crimes can have more serious punishments. Otherwise, the individual has no incentive to commit lesser rather than greater crimes (1975, 202, 287).[2]

Equally and in addition, the utilitarian standpoint pointed the way to the recognition of the need for rules of individual responsibility. The evil of punishment could only be justified where it could be an effective deterrent. Where the individual's mental state was such that he could not help committing the crime because of some excusing condition, he should not be punished. Inefficacious punishment was useless evil. Bentham accordingly supplied a list of candidates for exemption from punishment, which is similar in broad outline to that recognised by the law today: 'individuals who could not know the law, who have acted without intention, who have done the evil innocently, under an erroneous supposition, or by irresistible constraint.' In addition, 'children, imbeciles and idiots', though they may be influenced by punishment, 'have not a sufficient idea of futurity to be restrained by punishments' (1975, 199).

*(d)   The need for legality*

Though utilitarian theory emphasised self-interest and individual calculation rather than justice and individual dignity, it reached a similar conclusion to retributivism in terms of the need for principles of individual responsibility and proportionate punishment.[3] Furthermore, both insisted on the requirement of legality, since both the security of individual liberty *and* the effectiveness of deterrent punishment required a system of law that would be certain and known in advance. This could only occur within a rational system of laws. In England, the old penal laws were hopelessly irrational. The law was technical and formalistic, hidden in innumerable statutes and subject to gross judicial manipulation. Rather than applying the law, the judges had the habit of making it up as they went along. This was neither just nor effective: Bentham called it 'dog law', for it condemned individuals after the event, in the way that a person punishes his dog. The dog only learns after the punishment that what it has done is wrong. Applied to a human being, there can be neither (utilitarian) deterrence nor (retributive) respect in such a process. The law must be known in advance, and be clearly stated. The judges must themselves be bound by it so that their job is to apply existing rules. Change of the law is for the legislators. The proper and logical solution to the problem of law is a comprehensive legal *code*, which in one coherent, logical, concise document establishes the law, its penalties, and the duties of the free citizen. The code both guards individual liberty against the State and safeguards individual property and security through deterrence. It provides the ideal text for the individual to read and calculate by, as well as the maximum protection and respect for his liberty.[4]

## (ii)   Interests and ideology in reform penal theory

The reformers' ideology was one of free individualism, of certitude of rights and deterrence, of liberty and prevention. Men like Beccaria and Bentham, Kant and

Hegel emphasised different elements in their particular national contexts but these were the common foundations of their thought. It is tempting simply to see these ideas ahistorically, as part of the triumph of reason and progress in human affairs associated with a general process of enlightenment. In general, indeed, this is what many lawyers and legal theorists do. They are, however, wrong to do so, for these arguments also served important social interests and embodied particular ideological stances and strategies. It was these ideological positions, I will argue, that embodied particular conflicts and contradictions, and these as a result *became embedded in the law itself.*

### (a)　Middle-class interests

The emphasis on individual rights served as a safeguard for the middle classes against the aristocracy. For this reason, the discussion of retributive right was more crucial to the reformers of continental Europe where absolutism remained in force: in England, Sir Edward Coke and the common law had fought the same battle a century earlier (Little, 1969, 172–89; Hill, 1965). The stress on utilitarian deterrence and legal certainty was equally important to this class because of the need for a firm definition of, and protection for, the new forms of property and wealth that were produced in the periods of mercantile and then industrial capitalism.

The lower classes on the land and in the cities, the peasants and the emerging working class, had to be made to understand that property rights were exclusive and that the 'acquired and tolerated illegalities' (Foucault, 1979, 87) of the past were to be abolished. On the land, the lenient system of accepted use of forests and pastures, and of exploitation of wild animals (known to the common people as 'customary rights') had to give way before land enclosures and intensive capitalist farming methods. Any subsequent invasion of landed property rights was to be clearly labelled as crime.[5] More importantly, in the cities, the urban and industrial middle classes required similar clear definitions of law and effective routine enforcement procedures to protect the wealth in their yards and manufactories. Having connived at illegality in the eighteenth century, for example in the crime of smuggling (Winslow, 1977), they now wished it to be clearly known that the many accepted customs and practice of pilferage of the past constituted theft. An objective, clearcut criminal law in which no doubts as to what was and was not lawful was required (Foucault, 1979, 85–7).[6]

### (b)　Middle-class interests and moral-legal individualism

The ideological corollary of these objective, certain laws was a knowing individual subject, responsible for his actions. The reformers represented middle class interests and expressed these in the individualist ideology of their intellectual spokesmen, the political economists. The individual was conceived of as a rational economic actor, able to calculate what was in his own best interests. Just as the market regulates individual economic actors, so the criminal law regulates social conduct as an adjunct to the market. The task of the law, for Bentham, was to secure the harmony of individual interests – to supplement the 'invisible hand' of the market – by keeping egoism within acceptable bounds (cf Halevy, 1972, 17). Crime and punishment were to be exchanged as costs and benefits like any other commodity, and punishment was an economic disincentive to crime. The Enlightenment gave birth to 'economic man' in the work of the political economists and to the free moral individual of the philosophers, but it also gave birth to 'juridical man' in the work of the penal reformers. The rational calculating individual is the common stem of all three modes of thought, so that, as Halevy expresses it of the utilitarian philosophers, their morality is 'their economic psychology put into the imperative' (Halevy, 1972, 478, 489).

Within the overall context of enlightenment and of a social class not short of self-confidence, this ideology of the penal reformers was an optimistic one. Buttressed by the promise of political economy of a world of social harmony,[7] Bentham thought that a code of law geared to rational conduct would reduce crime virtually to naught. His vision was of a crime-free world where benevolence and self-constraint prevailed.[8] To state it so brings one up short: what went wrong? Such confidence in the potential triumph of legal and economic institutions over the wicked ways of the world! But if Bentham did get it wrong, and with hindsight we know he did, it was not because he was illogical. He merely followed through the logic of his theory. A world of rational individuals, whose self-interests harmonise in the market place and around the law, has as its natural consequence peace and friendship. The problem with these ideas lies not in their lack of coherence, but in the incompleteness of their ideological premises.

*(c)   Abstractions and realities*

In place of real individuals belonging to particular social classes, possessing the infinite differences that constitute genuine individuality, the reformers proposed an ideal individual living in an ideal world. 'Economic man' or 'juridical man' were abstractions from real people emphasising one side of human life – the ability to reason and calculate – at the expense of every social circumstance that actually brings individuals to reason and calculate in particular ways. Crime was a social problem. It arose out of particular social conditions and was brought into being in the midst of struggles between social classes over definitions of right and wrong. For the reformers, the world was constituted by separate individuals operating in the consensual context of the market and the law. They did not recognise in their theories that these individuals came from particular social classes, and that therefore the market and the law were sites of conflict. Individualistic ideological abstractions triumphed over bitter social realities, but the realities did not thereby obligingly disappear. Instead, they crept into the margins of the reformers' arguments as unreconciled or untheorised 'problems' for the project of reform. Their force was so great that the reformers had somehow, unsuccessfully, to accommodate them in their arguments.

Thus Beccaria opposed the death penalty because it prompted dangerous thoughts in the minds of those 'rational' criminal individuals who also just happen to be poor. Legal justice is the product of a universal social contract according to the theory, but the poor come to see the enforcement of the law as the social injustice of one class against another when they are threatened with capital punishment. The poor draw their own conclusions:

> Let us break these bonds, fatal to the majority and only useful to a few indolent tyrants; let us attack the injustice at its source. (Beccaria, 1966, 49)

Similarly, with theft, Beccaria argued in classical individualist style that the most appropriate punishment is deprivation in return of the thief's own property. But he observes that theft is often committed by those without property, and therefore concludes that penal servitude and compulsory labour are more appropriate punishments (Beccaria, 1966, 75). His critics were quick to point out, however, that there could be little deterrent in such a punishment given the living standards of the poor outside the prison.[9] The penal code for a world of ideal individuals ill fitted the real, miserable world of the poor who predominantly came before it.

In Bentham, the contrast between the ideal and the real is even more tantalising. His *Principles of the Penal Code* consists of four parts. In the first three of these, on crime and punishment, he maintains the image of a world of calculating individuals. In discussing the fine, he proposes a flexible punishment to match the pocket of the criminal but does not raise the question of the poor's outright inability to pay at all (1975, 179, 207, 217). His penal theory appears mainly devoid of considerations of social class. Yet in the fourth part, entitled 'Indirect Means of Preventing Offences', by which he means non-legal forms of social control, it becomes clear that the penal code will never successfully combat crime by itself, for social conduct is not, after all, a matter of pure individual choice. The sad truth for his own deterrent theory, Bentham acknowledges, is that people can know what they ought to do, but nonetheless do what they ought not to.[10] Why this should be so in a world of calculating rational agents is not made explicit. The implied answer is seen in the use of 'indirect', social means to reduce crime which work by altering the conditions within which people live and which determine their conduct.

Thus Bentham's discussion focuses upon what he euphemistically calls 'the most numerous class'. In order to avoid the numbers of crimes caused not by rational self-interested choice but by drink and the uncivilised character of the 'labourers and artisans', it is necessary to cultivate as much 'innocent amusement [as] human art can invent'. Music, theatre, literature, the arts, tea-drinking and gardening(!) must all be cultivated (1975, 231) to do what the law cannot.[11] It turns out that far from a legal code being an effective adjunct of natural individual choice in the maintenance of social order, Bentham must reinvent the social world, transform it out of all recognition, for the working class. What of that class of paupers for whom poverty makes crime a necessity? Bentham concedes that 'there are few punishments which can be greater than starvation' (1975, 237) and that no punitive solution will work (1975, 237–8). Prostitution and sexual vice, 'which also springs from inequality of fortune' (1975, 239), are also products of social conditions. As for children, education must play the important role for the poor, lest they become 'the pupils of crime' (1975, 276). Religion can play its part here as 'moral instruction best adapted to the most numerous class of society' (1975, 269). Clearly, this class does not emerge already equipped with the rational self-interest that makes the penal code an effective form of social control.

It transpires that individuals commit crimes under the direct influence of social circumstances and not as the product of rational choices made in abstraction from such circumstances. Social reform, not individual punishment, is required for the full protection of property. The abstract individualism of the reformers' ideology ('juridical, economic man') makes it inadequate either to comprehend or control the reality of crime. The 'criminal classes' are in truth composed of the 'uncivilised' labourers and artisans, paupers, and women and children living in poverty. It is said that Beccaria had a vision 'of a society in which equality no longer existed only in juridical abstractions but was an economic reality' (Venturi, 1971, 101). However, it was an economic reality of overt social *injustice* for which he and Bentham produced the idea of a legal code. There was a fundamental disparity between the economic and social substance of the emerging relations of production and their juridical and economic expression. In legal theory, the contradictions were kept at bay so long as the logic of abstract individualism and the myths of political economy were adhered to. In theory, each individual was the same as every other. All were potential possessors of property rights, all potential offenders against them. That in reality the possessors and offenders came from different social classes constituted hardly a ripple on the millpond of theory.[12] But the logical coherence was bought at the price of practical failure, for the penal code never could diminish crime as its proponents imagined. The penal code's ideology of abstract individualism and consensual sociality doomed it to inefficacy. Yet it was this ideology that came to inform the Anglo-American criminal law.

### (d)    The character of modern law: its repressive individualism

The logic of law is a logic of individual right and self-interest, in a social world presented as resting upon a consensus of individuals. It is a logic which masks and mediates underlying realities of class and conflict. It is this contradictory location that gives rise to the problem of grasping law's peculiar character. As a logic of individual right, law sets up requirements of universality and equality in its application. If all individuals are the same, then they should all be treated the same. At the least, it provides a rhetoric of individual liberty which transcends particular social interests. Yet law is at the same time directed to the defence of the interests of wealth and power in society. This is Thompson's point when he writes that the law entails 'a logic of equity', a tendency to seek 'to transcend the inequalities of class power which, instrumentally, it is harnessed to serve' (Thompson, 1975, 268). Criminal law protects particular social interests but does it through a language that is universal and general, and cast in terms of respect for the individual before it.

But if the logic of individual right provides a measure of legal liberty and fairness to all members of society, it is also a logic which obscures the social realities beneath the legal appearances. If all individuals are responsible citizens, punished as a matter of justice and right, then there is no need to recognise that *this* citizen was poor, unemployed, brought up in deprivation, or the product of a broken family. Fault resides in the individual not in the system. Thus law offers in principle both a defence of the individual's rights and liberties (even the poor individual) at the same time as it is a form of oppression, in the sense that it is a means of controlling those conflicts that have their roots in social inequities and which manifest in certain forms of threat to persons and property. The 'cunning' of the law lies in its ability to mask the onesidedness of its instrumental content through its formal character as a logic of universal individualism.

How can law be about oppression, when every individual is the same before it? The question embodies the 'trick' identified by Hay in the quote which prefaces this chapter, and its message is clearly conveyed in the other quote from the Criminal Law Commissioners. They were Victorian law reformers who, influenced by the Benthamite ideal, first began to articulate the importance of a modern legal code. The criminal law could be 'made intelligible to all classes of persons' and could 'convince all ranks ... that the laws are founded on just principles' (Criminal Law Commissioners, 1843, 4). The law would protect, bind, and secure prompt obedience from all, yet some would have more to be protected while others would feel its bind the more pressing.

How do theorists deal with these observations? If the theory of punishment deals with individuals and their responsibilities, how does it meet the claim, that might be raised by those who gain least from the prevailing social order, that they were not responsible for what they did because of circumstances which excuse, permit or justify their actions? With difficulty, as we have seen. These issues occupy marginal and disruptive places in their thought. How then would law, which is also concerned with matters of individual responsibility, deal with the same issue? My argument is that the same response of attempting to marginalise and exclude it prevails. In other words, the law's logic of individual responsibility, like the Benthamite penal reform project, requires separating off from other logics that would situate individuals in social contexts and locate responsibility in a different way. I will argue in the following chapters that the general principles of the criminal law are crucially shaped *by the law's need to maintain its categories of individual responsibility in a world where actions are socially structured and conditioned.* Legal doctrine at its heart is premised upon the need to 'mind the gap' between the law's form (free individualism) and its content (the control of socially structured individuality). Legal form is created and maintained against the persistent 'threat' of social and political 'leakage' into the process of state judgment and punishment. It is this core characteristic of the law of individual responsibility that shapes modern legal doctrine and underlies its problems. Because neither lawyers nor legal academics generally see this 'downside' of liberal Enlightenment thinking, they cannot understand what lies at the heart of modern law. Failing to understand its historical roots, they are condemned always to repeat its problems. I return to this point in the final section of this chapter, where I refer to this basic aspect of modern law as its *psychological individualist form.*

## 3    LEGAL INDIVIDUALISM AND SOCIAL CONTROL

Law has a logic that is in tension with the deeper social realities to which it is applied. Of course law does not apply itself; it must be applied (and created) by social actors and here the judiciary become an important focus for consideration. In Chapter One, we quoted Williams (1983, 143–4) who wrote that the judges had both created the doctrine of mens rea (the basis of individual responsibility) and had sought to undermine it. He concluded that passage by stating that there was an 'eternal tension in the position of the judge'. He is supposed to be an impartial adjudicator protecting the rights and liberties of the subject, but he is also a 'State instrumentality', an organ of government, and Williams observes that it is the latter role that has shaped judicial attitudes to criminal fault.

Although this conflict in the judicial role is not central to Williams' own rational reconstructive project, the tension is central to the criminal law. It is based upon the conflict between a conception of law based upon a logic of universal individualism, and the need to protect a particular social order. In this section, we trace through this tension in the period of the development of the modern criminal law, showing how the judges both could father doctrines of individual responsibility and reject their offspring as often as they own them. We must also note that to the extent that judges pick up and discard the doctrines of individual responsibility, they pick up and discard the logic of the law itself. Judicial ambivalence tends to judicial incoherence, so that illogic and contradiction as well as injustice are the product of their conduct.

## (i)  The common law and the criminal law in history

The heritage of the modern common law stems from the seventeenth-century writings and case collections of Coke. As we have already said, the revolution against absolutism came early in England, and the common law was instrumental in enshrining the rights and liberties of the subject against the sovereign, and of establishing the role of the judges as impartial interpreters of the law. One hundred and fifty years before the penal reform movement, English lawyers were developing a discourse of individual rights, logic and legality. But why did it take so long to feed the common law tradition into the criminal law?

Little writes (1969, 174) that Coke's 'activity on behalf of the Petition of Right of 1628 has rightly won him the reputation of defender of the "liberty of the subject"', but he adds that '"liberty of the subject" meant for Coke the rights of the propertied'. Liberty, according to Hill, was liberty to do what one liked with one's property [13] – if one had any. From the start, the common law employed a universal language in a world of social inequality and division, a world of private property. The poor on the other hand found themselves on the wrong end of decisions designed to enhance the exclusive rights of property (Thompson, 1975, 24). Access to the law was barred to them by lack of money and social connection (Hill, 1965, 113–14), while their lives were governed by Poor Laws and Vagrancy Acts, harsh and draconian statutes gaining little in the way of libertarian assistance from the common law.

It is in this context that one understands the eighteenth century's bloody penal code. This was often drafted as well as applied by the lawyers. While a show of justice was made by a sometimes pernickety regard for formalities, the substance of the law paid scant regard to the rights of individuals. For example, the infamous Black Acts, which were designed to protect the lands of the rich from poachers and peasant defenders of communal rights (Thompson, 1975; Radzinowicz, 1948, ch 1), were drafted by Philip Yorke in his role as Solicitor General and later Attorney General. Yorke then became Lord Hardwicke, the Lord Chief Justice, and as a judge he pressed for the severest penalties under the Acts. He considered this most infamous of penal measures 'a very useful Act' made necessary by the 'degeneracy of the present times' which had produced 'many (good) new laws necessary for the present state and conditions of things' (Thompson, 1975, 210–11; on Hardwicke, see 1975, 208). When he later came to hear appeals under this law, he 'defended individual liberty' by crucially enlarging the scope of the Act through improbable interpretations of the words (Thompson, 1975, 210, 250).

Against this, it must be noted that some lawyers did seek to systematise the law and promote its logic of individual right and responsibility. Hale and Foster in particular sought to establish system and principle and 'to rid the law of inconsistency and excess' (Ashworth, 1978, 394). But in so doing their application of legal logic ran up against the very clear opposition of class interest within the judiciary itself. Thompson's account of Foster's involvement in the case of *Sims and Midwinter* is revealing (Thompson, 1975, 251–4). Sims had aided and abetted Midwinter in the killing of the mare of the local squire. The offence was capital but made no mention of the position of the aider and abettor. Foster argued, according to the logic of individual liberty, that the offence should therefore be strictly construed 'in favour of life' so as to exclude Sims from conviction. Consultation with the other judges revealed that he was alone in his liberalism, and Sims was sentenced to death, though later pardoned.

Foster still considered he was right and in his *Crown Law* gave his reasons for disagreeing with his colleagues. Before publication, he showed his work to the then Lord Chief Justice, Lord Mansfield. Mansfield conceded that Foster had an argument but thought it 'founded in subtle nicety, and very literal interpretation' while the majority's view was in his opinion 'agreeable to justice'. He insisted that Foster suppress his argument, which he did. Subsequently, Mansfield used the case of *Sims and Midwinter* as a precedent in two other cases in which he failed to develop Foster's argument or to note the list of precedents the latter had marshalled for it. Thus the law developed in opposition to arguments of individual liberty and legal logic, and not through their promotion.

Moving forward to the period of reform of the common law, the first half of the nineteenth century, the Criminal Law Commissioners (1843, 8) acknowledged the issues of social class that underlay the appalling state of the criminal law. The disparity between it and the civil law (where the logic of individual right was well developed) was due to 'the magnitude and extent of pecuniary interests involved in civil proceedings'. These 'have tended to promote argument and discussion, and to cause inquiry, and suggestion of improvement in that branch, to which the means of ordinary delinquents are seldom equal'. Nor had the law produced adequate procedures for these matters of life and death. The 'ordinary course of administering criminal justice' was such as 'in a great measure to exclude such effectual and mature discussion of the rules of law as would tend to its gradual enrichment, and afford the best measure for improvement'.

Thus the character of the law, its means of interpretation and its practical application all reflected the social conflict between rich and poor that the law was designed to control. The tension between the 'rights and liberties of the subject' and the 'State' was not, pace Williams, an 'eternal' one. It was in its initial manifestation a specifically historical reflection of the implicit conflict between the form and content of the criminal law in the English society of the eighteenth and nineteenth centuries.

## (ii)    Logic, 'policy' and social class

Taking this argument to the present day, the judicial attitude to criminal law reform has generally been negative (Gardner and Curtis-Raleigh, 1949; Glazebrook, 1983, 490). In the nineteenth century, the judiciary resisted legal codification on the ground that it would remove their power to develop the law as they saw fit (Glazebrook, 1983, 495–6; Cross, 1978). Nonetheless, the period of the second half of the nineteenth and the twentieth centuries has seen important developments in the practical quality of the criminal law. This is in major part the result of improving access to the law in a society where liberal democratic ideas and forms of government have been important and influential counterweights to underlying social conflicts and inequities (Lacey, 1998). At the actual level of doctrine, it has also been in part due to the influence of liberal legal academics such as Williams and Smith and Hogan who have pushed the subjectivist standpoint of the responsible individual against less liberal 'objectivist' standards, and criticised illogic within the law. When judgments have rejected these positions, they have been subjected to such cogent criticism from the liberal standpoint that they have been difficult to sustain (for example, for the reaction to the objectivist intention case, *DPP v Smith* (1960), see Williams, 1960; this reaction has coloured the whole subsequent development of the law: see Chapter 3, below).

The legal process is undeniably the 'process of argumentation [and] . . . justification' that MacCormick described in Chapter 1. Yet that does not stop it being at the same time a process of rationalisation in the pejorative sense we have also discussed of papering over the logical cracks in order to reach a result not justified on the rules. In the following comment, Williams makes this clear (and also raises the contrast between criminal and civil cases mentioned in the historical discussion above):

> A judgment will marshal the authorities in a manner suggesting, to the uninitiated, that the court is ineluctibly bound to reach the conclusion it does reach, when to the discerning eye it is often no more than what is popularly called 'special pleading' – that is, rationalisation accompanied by misdirection and legerdemain. The legal pros and cons are not fairly stated . . . The court selects the arguments and authorities leading to the conclusion it desires, and minimises or ignores the weight of authority or force of argument going the other way. Ordinary lawyerly reasoning, as generally employed in civil cases, may be rejected in favour of fallacious and shallow arguments. The unavowed premise is that those who break fresh ground in the annals of crime cannot rely upon any previously established rule of law being maintained in their favour. (Williams, 1983, 16)

This brings us to a comparison of the role of the judiciary in modern society with their role in the eighteenth and early nineteenth centuries. The late twentieth century is so different from the earlier period that it would be foolish to suggest a direct comparison. Nonetheless, the commission of crime, as it is defined and processed, remains the province in the main of the lower social classes (Braithwaite, 1979; Quinney, 1980; Box, 1983, 1987), and is primarily crime against property.[14] The judges still remain an élite group drawn from the middle and upper social classes and responding to a conception of the needs of society shared by those groups (Griffith, 1985, 25–31, 229). Griffith writes that –

> Law and order, the established distribution of power both public and private, the conventional and agreed view amongst those who exercise political and economic power, the fears and prejudices of the middle and upper social classes, these are the forces which the judges are expected to uphold and do uphold. (Griffith, 1985, 234)[15]

Although it is rarely expressed as such. When judges are called upon, or volunteer, to make law or traduce authority, they do so not in the name of a social class but in the universal terms of what they call the 'public interest' or 'public policy'. But what does that mean in a world of *conflicting* claims as to what is for the good and bad, what is right and wrong? Griffith again:

> The judges define the public interest, inevitably, from the viewpoint of their own class. And the public interest, so defined, is by a natural, not an artificial, coincidence, the interest of others in authority whether in government, in the City or in the church. It includes the maintenance of order, the protection of private property, the promotion of certain general economic aims, the containment of the trade union movement . . . (Griffith, 1985, 234)

The criminal law is an area where the judges remain keenly aware of the 'public interest' and the functions of the law. Lord Devlin, for example, has written about the tension within the judicial role:

> In theory the judiciary is the neutral force between government and the governed. The judge interprets and applies the law without favour to either . . . British judges have never practised such detachment . . . In the criminal law the judges regard themselves as at least as much concerned as the executive with law and order. (Quoted in Griffith, 1985, 196)

Thus the historical roots of the conflict between a logic of individual fairness, a universal dispensation of rights and liberties, and a functional concern for social order carry through to our day. The law is administered from the perspective of a body of, mainly, men drawn predominantly from one social class and applied to another body, again mainly of men, drawn predominantly from another social class. The law embodies a logic of individual right to be applied universally, but is also applied to one group by another. The tension identified by Williams (1983, 143–4) is a historic one, and its effects, I will argue, necessarily pervade the substantive law. Legal doctrine must 'mind the gap' between the law's form (a logic of free individualism, premised on subjective right) and its content (the protection of a particular social order by the judiciary).

## 4   THE FOUNDATIONAL TENSIONS OF CRIMINAL DOCTRINE

I now consolidate the observations above about abstract individualism and social context, about legal right and state power, into an account of the law's psychological and political individualism, which I see as underlying the problems of principle, legality and rationality in the criminal law. In Chapter 1, we saw that the principles of legality and justice were both regarded as central to the criminal law and yet were 'hostages to its fortune'. It was suggested that in order to understand this, we required the historical perspective developed in this chapter in order to examine the legal issues developing out of and shaped by a particular social and ideological context. Let me now summarise the two main arguments.

### (i)   Law's psychological individualism

First, individual justice and legality were the key principles established by the penal reformers of the Enlightenment (and earlier, though not in the criminal law, by the common lawyers in England). The image of the individual established in this period was an ideal one. It was the image of 'man' as either a metaphysical or a calculating, self-interested being, conceived of in an asocial way in a world whose sociality was no more than the coming together of individuals in a social contract. It was this 'man' who was the key figure in the penal reformers' imagination of a crime-free world: an abstract juridical individual. It is this image that Vining was attacking when he said that the law knew no *real* individuals, only their mystical abstractions. What we have done here is to locate the conflict identified by Vining in an actual historical context: the intellectual birth of liberal Western modernity and legality.

Here is one key to understanding the nature of modern criminal law. At its heart there exists a 'responsible individual', or rather a universe of equally responsible individuals, regarded in isolation from the real world, the social and moral contexts in which crime occurs, of which they are a part. The legal categories rarely take the realities of crime and conflict on board. They operate (and justify both themselves and the system as a whole) by obscuring the world's realities. But just as the realities kept impinging upon Bentham and Beccaria, so they keep impinging on law. One important tension within legal doctrine is accordingly between an abstract individualism and the concrete, social individuality of human beings operating within a conflictual society. This tension will be seen, I will argue, in the ways in which legal concepts, focusing on abstract human faculties like intention (Chapter 3) or recklessness (Chapter 4) are designed to avoid open and contentious moral and political issues. For example, the concept of intention is artificially separated from that of motive because the latter introduces questions of substantive moral evaluation into the question whether an individual is responsible for his acts. The separation, however, cannot be complete, and this leads to difficult conflicts and tensions in the law. There is a basic tension, stemming from the social, political and historical context of the modern law. It involves creating and maintaining 'technical' legal concepts concerning the individual's psychological powers in isolation from the social context in which they operate. This is the conflict around the law's psychological individualism.

### (ii)  Law's political individualism

A second tension stems from the first. The law's individualism may be abstract in its ideology but it is nonetheless real in terms of its possessing practical, legal effects. Legal individualism obscures social realities but, in its universality, also potentially protects social actors. This is the 'logic of equity' of which Thompson (1975, 268) spoke, and which is lacking from Vining's comments in the previous chapter (1978, 2). A logic of individual right has an expressive function in terms of its 'standing up for' the individual before the forces of the state. This is seen in the criminal law's defence of the individual from state punishment when the categories of intention, recklessness and so on lead to an acquittal. This aspect of law's working concerns its political individualism, in contrast to the psychological individualism described above. This second aspect of legal individualism generates a second basic tension in the law between its liberal individualism and the social control needs of the state as envisioned in terms like 'law and order' by a social élite, the judges.[16]

Unlike the first tension, this second one is more recognised within legal discourse.

It is, indeed, Williams's tension between the judge as principled legal logician and 'State instrumentality'. While Williams does not permit his insight to structure his understanding of the law, which he sees as in essence rational and principled, Ashworth's more recent textbook is much more alive to the various manifestations of this conflict in the law (see especially Ashworth, 1999, 66–87). Where the approach offered here primarily differs, therefore, is in my identification of the first, more basic, tension between legal abstraction and social context in the concept of the psychological individual (see further, Norrie, 2000, 47–50).

These two tensions within the law stem from the contradictory foundational elements engendered by its basic liberal individualist structure. Figure 2.1 seeks to represent this standpoint.

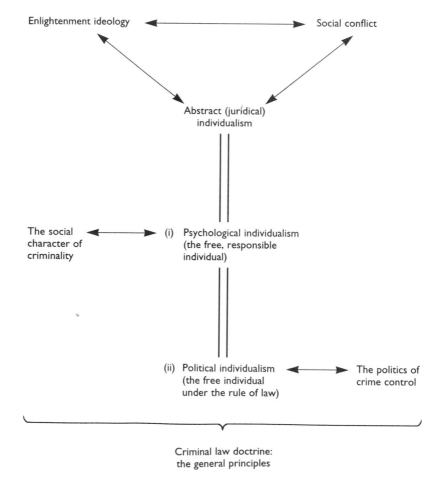

**Figure 2.1**   The structural foundations of the criminal law's contradictions

If we want to understand the nature and logic of developments in the criminal law, I suggest that we should put aside the continuing legal-liberal dream that it is potentially rational, and instead seek to understand the *limits* of legal reasoning. We must understand legal development as founded upon these two historic tensions within English society and English law. It is only in this way that we can understand why the principles of the law are so hard to operationalise logically and without contradiction. There is a deeper, historical logic to the law than that provided by the flawed self-understanding of most lawyers and the more orthodox legal theories. Its effect is to undermine the law's own claims to logic and principle while explaining why those claims might be false or partial. It is because criminal law is a social, historical phenomenon, developed and applied in a particular and contradictory social world, that the getting of wisdom entails recognising that the law's rationality is necessarily limited. The legal compound embodies the contradictory structure and shape provided by its socio-political and ideological context. If we understand this, many longstanding doctrinal mysteries and puzzles in criminal law can be explained.

# Part II

# Mens rea

# Chapter 3

# Motive and intention

It is lamentable that, after more than a thousand years of continuous legal development, English law should still lack clear and consistent definitions of words expressing its basic concepts. (Williams, 1983, 73)

A consideration of motives requires and indicates a much more advanced level of ethical criticism than is involved in appraisals based only on the fact that a harm was inflicted intentionally, not by accident. (Hall, 1960, 83)

## I  INTRODUCTION

Criminal liability for those crimes that are conventionally recognised as the most serious requires not only that a criminal act occur but that the individual be responsible for it through possessing a 'guilty mind'. Mens rea signifies this:

In Latin it means a guilty mind, but in legal use it denotes the mental state (subjective element) required for the particular crime in question. Or it can refer to the mental state commonly required for serious crimes (and a number of lesser offences). (Williams, 1983, 73)

Mens rea is a shorthand term denoting the existence of either *intention* to commit a crime, or *recklessness* (running a risk) as to whether a crime will occur as a result of one's actions. In this chapter we deal with intention, saving recklessness until Chapter Four. Discussion of mens rea, as Williams's definition suggests, may be crime-specific, ie focused upon the particular mental element for a given crime,[1] or more general, considering the common features of the mental element across a range of crimes.[2] It is the latter aspect that is of more interest to us, given our concern with the law's general principles.

We saw in Chapter 1 that an important claim on behalf of law is that it delivers justice to individuals. It does so by way of 'the principle that punishment should be restricted to those who have voluntarily broken the law' or of a capacity conception of criminal responsibility (Hart, 1968, 181; Lacey, 1988, 62–5). The mens rea requirement is often regarded as central to this claim, for it embodies a *fault* element: individuals should only be punished when they have at least recognised the harmful aspect of their conduct or its consequences. Williams accordingly supports mens rea as 'a mark of advancing civilisation' (Williams, 1983, 70). His linking of this moral element with human psychology is interesting: mens rea involves –

> . . . a development that can still be seen among our own young. Small children think of wrongness as any disobedience to rules, irrespective of intention. Later they learn the relevance of wrongful intent, and defend themselves by saying 'I didn't mean to do it'. (Williams, 1983, 70)

The commonsensical logic of this argument seems hard to oppose, but are the responsibility concepts of a small child sufficient to reflect the fault of adult members of a complex society? Jerome Hall suggests another important dimension to individual action which concentration on intention alone misses. Greater maturity than that of the child considers the *motives* that underlie actions too, as the second quote at the head of the chapter indicates.

Here we must note an interesting fact about the law of criminal responsibility. While it claims to be based upon individual justice through the operation of a fault requirement, it completely ignores a normal mental element in human conduct in its attribution of fault. It is as firmly established in legal doctrine as any rule can be that motive is irrelevant to responsibility: 'A crime may be committed from the best of motives and yet remain a crime' (Williams, 1961, 31).[3] Why has legal justice never got beyond the standpoint of the small child?

The importance of logic to legal reasoning and the core value of legality has also been elaborated in the last two chapters. Yet one of the law's core concepts, perhaps *the* core concept, remains obscure and mystifying. Williams's comment at the head of this chapter refers to the law of intention. It is striking that a word used day in and day out in legal practice has evaded precise definition. The law requires 'to have reasonably precise definitions, not too far removed from the ordinary meanings of words, so that the legislature can use them in defining offences and so that a trial judge can explain them confidently to a jury' (1983, 73). The ideology of the rule of law demands this as much as do the practical requirements of law-makers and givers. So why does the law of intention fail this most fundamental test? Why is a central requirement of legal principle unmet by a central element of criminal law?[4]

## 2   MOTIVE AND INTENTION: DESOCIALISING INDIVIDUAL LIFE

### (i)   Conflicting motives and common intentions

Human agency is essentially composed of motives and intentions. Human beings conceive desired ends by a complex psychological and sociological process (the creation of motives for actions), and formulate intentions and perform actions designed to achieve those ends. It is as impossible in practice to imagine people forming intentions without having motives as it is to imagine them developing motives without creating intentions to put them into effect. We are concerned, as Hall puts it, 'with a unified process, a course of action which always, at every step and at each moment involves both motive and intentionality' (1960, 77). We must, however, clarify an ambiguity in the way the terms are used, for motive can be seen both as a *cause* of intention and as a *form* of intention (known as ulterior intention):

> Sometimes, when we speak of motive we mean an emotion such as jealousy or greed, and sometimes we mean a species of intention. For example, D intends (i) to put poison in his uncle's tea, (ii) to cause his uncle's death and (iii) to inherit his money. We would normally say that (iii) is his motive [although it] is certainly also intended . . . it is a consequence ulterior to the mens rea and the actus reus; it is no part of the crime. (Smith and Hogan, 1999, 78; cf Wasik, 1979)

In this discussion, we are concerned with motive in the first sense, of a force inducing intention and action. Ulterior intention entails a rephrasing of this meaning of motive so that instead of talking of the jealousy or greed that impelled D's action, we talk of his ulterior intention to inherit, which amounts to no more than an intention to satisfy his greed (the precipitating motive).

The passage from Smith and Hogan quoted above is instructive in another way. In discussing motive they describe it in the standard terms of utilitarian psychology, within which each individual is seen as a separate monad operating according to discrete personal motivating characteristics or emotions. Individual psychic forces like 'jealousy' or 'greed' (or, we could add, 'anger' or 'love') are seen as the 'springs of action' (Hall, 1960, 84).[5] No thought is given to the social context within which 'jealousy' or 'greed' are stimulated or to the particular content they embody.[6] We would expect as much from utilitarian analysis because, as we saw in Chapter 2, it treats each individual as an isolated psychological figure. Yet it is clear that individual actions, intentions and motives are formed within particular social contexts. For example, in his enquiry into what lay behind the English inner city rebellions of 1981, Lord Scarman explained the anger and other passions that led to the criminal violence as the product of a set of social causes and conditions which were essential to their manifestation. Social conditions like unemployment, racism, bad housing, and unequal opportunity were the context within which motivating passions would emerge:

> Where deprivation and frustration exist on the scale to be found among the young black people of Brixton, the probability of disorder must . . . be strong. (Scarman, 1981, 16)

Police discrimination against black people was both a general cause and a spark which could ignite a fire of anger:

> Deeper causes undoubtedly existed and must be probed: but the immediate cause of Saturday's events was a spontaneous combustion set off by the spark of one single incident. (Scarman, 1981, 37)

I shall argue that it is this link between social causes and individual motives that lies behind the exclusion of motive from the consideration of legal fault and responsibility. The attitude that motive is irrelevant has deep roots within the common law tradition, and is linked to the social conflicts of the period in which the law was developed. First, there was the question of law-breaking on account of acute personal need. Writing in the second half of the seventeenth century, Hale noted the significance of motive only once in his criminal law treatise and that was in order to reject it. Larceny born out of hunger or lack of clothing remained 'a felony and a crime by the laws of England punishable with death' where there existed the *intention* to steal (Hale, 1736, 1, 54).[7] At the beginning of the modern period of development of a systematic criminal law, the early Victorian Criminal Law Commissioners quoted with approval the smug epigram, 'We must not steal leather to make poor men's shoes', and the 'compassionate' words of the Scots criminal lawyer Hume:

> Whatsoever be the cause which impels a person to the doing of those things, which are destructive of the interest or bonds of society, his will is not on that account the less vicious or his nature the less depraved. (1843, 29)

Hume constructs the issue in terms of the breach of a universal social interest (the 'bonds of society'), but universality was proclaimed in opposition to the interests of the poor, for whom poverty was 'the common excuse' in the eighteenth century. Yet it was an excuse which, as Hale's peremptory view makes clear, cut little ice.[8]

The second cause of the rule concerns not the denial of motive out of compassion, where compassion threatened to undermine private property, but the squashing of alternative definitions of right and wrong. The poor might not just claim an absence of malice, but the positive existence of rightful or good motive on their side. A pamphleteer in 1816 gives a clear idea of the social issue at stake:

> The property which [the game laws] protect is viewed with peculiar jealousy, both by those who are precluded from taking it, and those to whom its enjoyment is secured. The former consider it as a common right of which they are unjustly deprived; the latter as more sacred than any other class of property, on account, not only of its intrinsic value, but of the amusement which it affords them. These opposite feelings are continually called into exercise, not only by their immediate object, but by all the local disputes and antipathies with which they mingle. (Quoted in Hay, 1977, 191)

The ruling classes sought a universal definition of right and wrong that could legitimate extremely dubious processes of property expropriation of the poor by the rich. It was the political success of these classes in forcing their will upon the lower classes that ensured that the legal reformers could express the rules of a legal system which were the product of sharp social conflicts in terms of consensus and good common sense. The rule of private property became the 'rule of law', so that attacks on the former could be condemned as attacks on a universal social good. Thus the Criminal Law Commissioners again:

> The motive by which an offender was influenced, as distinguished from his intention, is never material to an offence. If the prohibited act be done, and be done with the intention by law essential to the offence, it is complete, without reference either to any ulterior intention or to the motive which gave birth to the intention.
> To allow any man to substitute for law his own notions of right, would be in effect to subvert the law . . . [A] man's private opinion could not possibly be allowed to weigh against the authority of the law . . . though he (the offender) thought that the act was innocent, or even meritorious . . . (1843, 29)[9]

Desperate social need and indignant claim of right were the motives of the poor in the seventeenth, eighteenth and early nineteenth centuries. These were hardly motives calculated to win favour or compassion from a social class determined to impose a property order on all regardless of the consequences. Small wonder then that motive's relevance to guilt was very firmly squashed, and doing justice to individuals become a matter of 'childish' moral judgment. The law's subjective recognition of individual fault has this fundamental limitation imposed from the very beginning. The law's *content*, the protection of private property and particular social interests, structured its *form*, a narrow conception of individual fault, from which evaluative, morally substantive questions were erased. Separating motive from intention, and focusing on the latter, the law was able to focus on the question of 'how' acts came to be committed, and to exclude the question 'why' they were done. Yet motive could not so easily be expunged from the law or the legal process. Suppressed, it persistently irrupts within legal discourse.

## (ii)  Hidden motives

To proclaim the irrelevance of motive to law is not at a stroke to remove the relevance of motive to human conduct and its judgment. People continue to operate on the basis not only of knowledge of legal right and wrong but also on the basis of moral codes which they regard as transcending the law's code, and in social contexts which create motives which are contrary to the law. Because motive is legally irrelevant, no legal distinction can be drawn between circumstances exhibiting great moral differences: the contract killing of a third party is in law as culpable as the mercy killing of a mortally ill elderly relative (cf Smith and Hogan, 1999, 77). It is true that the law does have a way of reflecting such distinctions, through punishment, but it is a fundamentally *non-legal* way. We will discuss this in subsection (iii). First, we should note what a blunt instrument for the allocation of fault the law is, why it should be convenient for it to be so, and how this can still give rise to problems within its discourse.

### (a)  Individual morality

Occasionally the issue of good motive crops up where an individual acts from a personal moral belief in the rightness of his or her actions. In the main, such claims of good motive will be rejected. In the late nineteenth century, the problem emerged with the so-called 'Peculiar People' cases, in which parents belonging to a religious sect refused to seek medical assistance for their children. In *Hines* (1874) a judge held that a man could not be convicted of manslaughter where he had failed to get medical help if he honestly believed that prayers would save his child's life. Some years later in the case of *Senior* ((1899) at 289), after statutory intervention, a man was convicted of manslaughter in similar circumstances 'no matter what his motive' might be. This latter attitude was also apparent in *Sharpe* (1857) where the accused removed his mother's corpse from a graveyard of Protestant Dissenters to bury it in a churchyard with his recently deceased father. Sharpe was as guilty of the offence of unlawfully removing a corpse as any grave defiler or body snatcher.

More recent cases also illustrate the issue. In *Smith* (1960), the accused promised money to the mayor of a town as an inducement in a property deal. His real motive was to expose corruption in his local council, but he was convicted of an offence of corruption like any genuine corrupter. In the case of *Steane* (1947) by contrast, a man broadcast on behalf of the Germans during the Second World War in order to protect his family from being sent to a concentration camp. His motive – fear and concern for his family – was morally good, yet given the general stance of the law on motive, there was little that the court could do to avoid Steane's conviction. The defence of duress, which we shall see (below, Chapter 8) fits uncomfortably with the general law, in effect does allow motives of extreme fear to avoid conviction, but that defence was not relied on by the court in *Steane*. In this situation, the Court of Appeal admitted motive by the 'back door' method of treating Steane's 'ulterior intention' (to save his family) as his *only* intention. They ignored the obvious fact that in order to save his family, he had to perform intentional acts likely to assist the enemy. Steane's motive required recognition on compassionate grounds, but the court, apparently reluctant to admit the defence of duress in his case, chose to do so by using a very narrow definition of intention. The tension in their position was resolved by constricting the law of intention.

A similar approach to *Steane* is seen in cases involving medical treatment. In *Gillick v West Norfolk and Wisbech AHA* (1986), the question was whether a doctor giving contraceptive advice or treatment to a girl under 16 aids and abets unlawful sexual intercourse. Lord Scarman argued that the 'bona fide exercise by a doctor of his clinical judgment must be a complete negation of the guilty mind' ((1986) at 190) essential to the commission of the offence. The intention to do her professional job excludes any question of the mental state required for the crime. In *Airedale NHS Trust v Bland* (1993), Lord Goff described the 'established rule' that 'a doctor may, when caring for a patient who is . . . dying of cancer, lawfully administer painkilling drugs despite the fact that he knows that [this] will abbreviate the patient's life' ((1993) at 867).

This position is not, however, reconciled with the law of indirect intention, as was seen in the recent trial of Dr Moor, a general practitioner accused of the murder of an elderly patient whom he believed terminally ill. The question was whether a doctor who gives treatment to ease suffering in the knowledge it will hasten death can be said to intend the death. As we will see (below, pp 50–8), the rule is that an intention to do an act with knowledge that it will have a *virtually certain* consequence makes the person responsible for the consequence as having indirectly intended it. It does not have to have been his purpose or desire that the consequence ensue. In Dr Moor's case, however, the presiding judge directed the jury to consider whether the defendant directly intended to kill his patient or thought it was 'only highly probable that death would follow the injection' (Arlidge, 2000, 39). If the former the accused was guilty of murder, if the latter, he was not. The formulation was extremely favourable to the accused because it left out of account the rule that foresight of a virtually certain consequence will also constitute the necessary intention for murder. This seems a good illustration of the law being manoeuvred to produce what Ashworth (1999, 182) calls 'moral elbow-room' in a case of good motive where otherwise the standard formulation of the law of intention would lead to a guilty verdict (see further Ashworth, 1996; Norrie, 2000, 49–50, 174–6).

## (b) Political morality

One of the original grounds for excluding motive from responsibility comes up in those situations where an accused finds a way to argue the moral or political rights and wrongs of his action in the courtroom. Occasionally, a law will not phrase the mental element required for an offence in terms of standard mens rea, and this can lead to the possibility of an argument about the meaning of the mens rea term, which in turn allows discussion of motive. In *Chandler v DPP* (1964), the defendants had broken into a nuclear base in order to protest against nuclear weapons. They were charged with conduct revealing 'a purpose prejudicial to the safety or interest of the state' under s 1 of the Official Secrets Act 1911, but claimed that their *purpose* (the mens rea term under the Act) was not prejudicial. They wished to show the dangers to the state and the people of nuclear armament. The case hinged on competing political claims of rightful conduct and the question of who defined the interest of the state. Lord Radcliffe dismissed the appeal on the basis that the appellants' purpose, as they described it, was really their motive and therefore irrelevant. He stated that he did –

> . . . not think that the ultimate aim of the appellants in bringing this demonstration of obstruction constituted a purpose at all within the meaning of the Act. I think that those aims constituted their motive, the reason why they wanted the demonstration. (1964, 795)

Thus 'purpose' was given a narrow meaning, similar to that given to intention, and excluding motive. Lord Devlin supported this view by arguing that the question of what constituted a purpose prejudicial to the interests of the state was to be judged objectively, that is according to the actual policy of the state. Similarly, Lord Reid, though warning of the dangers of identifying the state with the government of the day, nonetheless held that the armed forces were within 'the exclusive discretion of the Crown' and that the declaration of the Secretary of the State was not open to dispute ((1964) at 791). Thus the 'bottom line' in *Chandler* is not the issue of individual fault but a political defence of the state. To put it another way, the form of individual responsibility with regard to the novel mens rea term arises from the political conflict between the state and the protesters. In this regard it follows the standard reasoning of the law from the eighteenth and nineteenth centuries. Lord Reid makes this clear in his further comment that the argument advanced by the appellants would lead to a plurality and conflict of views which the criminal law 'is not designed to deal with'. It is necessary therefore to consider whether the Act 'can reasonably be read in such a way as to avoid the raising of such issues' ((1964) at 791). The assertion of the irrelevance of motive within criminal law doctrine precisely *allows* the courts to treat essentially political issues (apparently) apolitically, while claiming to respect the individuals who come before it.[10]

## (c)  Social mores

As with political morality, the slightly different question of the nature of social morality can raise questions of right and wrong where the legal terminology is not carefully drawn. Another mens rea term that causes problems is 'dishonesty' under the Theft Act 1968. Theft is defined as a dishonest appropriation of another's property with an intention permanently to deprive (Theft Act 1968, s 1; see Wasik, 1979; Tur, 1985). What does it mean to be 'dishonest'? Whose standards are to be applied – the state's, the accused's, or the jury's? Is there a common standard which all in our society embrace? If a latter-day Robin Hood came before the courts charged with taking from the rich and giving to the poor, would his behaviour be universally condemned as dishonest? Section 2 of the Theft Act 1968 provides a partial definition of the term, giving three instances in which appropriation is not dishonest and one where it may be. It does not, however, give an overall definition, so it has been left to the courts to decide the matter.

The Criminal Law Revision Committee (1966, 20) was responsible for the adoption of the term, and it foresaw no problem with it: ' "Dishonesty" is something which laymen can easily recognise when they see it.' The word could stand without definition and be applied according to the common sense of juries. The courts initially followed this view. In *Gilks* (1972) (see also *Boggeln v Williams* (1978)), the Court of Appeal accepted that where a man kept an overpayment from a bookmaker on the ground that 'bookies' were fair game ('a race apart'), it was proper for the question of his honesty to be left to the jury. However, an alternative view was enunciated in *Feely* where it was stated that the jury should not consider simply the defendant's view but should have regard to the 'current standards of ordinary, decent people' (1973) at 573 (see also *R v Greenstein* (1976)) and judge the defendant against those standards.

The dilemma relates to one's view of society. In the classical penal reformers' view, society was constituted by a consensus of like-minded, rational individuals. In such a society, general agreement about the dishonesty of property appropriations would be relatively easy to achieve, and the common sense of the ordinary member of society could be relied upon. This appears to be the view behind the Criminal Law Revision Committee's suggestion. But what if society is based not on consensus about private property, but, as it was in the beginning, on dissensus and conflict? Williams puts the point well, though he idealises the past:

> The practice of leaving the whole matter to the jury might be workable if our society were culturally homogeneous, with known and shared values, as it once very largely was. But the law of theft is to protect property rights; and disrespect for these rights is now widespread. Since the jury are chosen at random, we have no reason to suppose that they will be any more honest and 'decent' in their standards than the average person . . . (1983, 726)[11]

If the definition of 'dishonesty' is left open to the jury, the standard of right and wrong is not in the hands of the judges and the law, but is 'at large'. It is therefore able to reflect the social standards of a society in which the black and white rights and wrongs of the law have no necessary relevance. Theft, pilferage, fiddling, petty (and gross: Levi, 1987) fraud are commonplace.[12] While it may be that the Criminal Law Revision Committee 'certainly did not contemplate that the jury would be left in complete freedom to uphold a defence that the defendant was carrying out a "Robin Hood" policy of robbing the rich to provide for the poor' (Williams, 1983, 725), the subjective standard of dishonesty equally certainly opens the door to it.

In *Ghosh* (1982), the Court of Appeal sought to consolidate the conflicting cases, to rescue an element of subjective fault, *and* to avoid the 'Robin Hood' problem that goes with too broad a subjective element. Their aim was both to recognise that 'dishonesty' involves a state of mind, and therefore a subjective question, and to exclude the possibility of subjectivism extending to moral debates about the rights and wrongs of private property. It was necessary, for example, to say that it was not dishonest for a foreigner from a country where public transport was free to use an English bus without paying, even though he acted intentionally (ie his motive was honest). But it was also necessary to say that 'Robin Hood or those ardent anti-vivisectionists who remove animals from vivisection laboratories are acting dishonestly' ((1982) at 696), even though *they* believe their motives are honest.

The court adopted a two-part test. A jury must first 'decide whether according to the ordinary standards of reasonable and honest people what was done was dishonest'. If it was not dishonest by this quasi-objective standard, the defendant is acquitted. If it was dishonest by this standard, then 'the jury must consider whether the defendant himself must have realised that what he was doing was by those standards dishonest' ((1982) at 696). Thus the question becomes not whether the accused believed that what he did was honest, but whether he believed that reasonable people would regard it as honest. In this way, it is intended to retain a subjective element, but not pure subjectivism – to acquit the non fare-paying foreigner but convict Robin Hood or the animal rights activist.

There are two problems with this. First, the first rule enunciates only a *quasi*-objective standard because while it takes the definition away from the subjective view of the accused, it leaves it in the hands of the jury. But where, in Williams's words, 'known and shared values' are in decline and a 'poor level of self-discipline' (1983, 726) prevails, the standard of the reasonable and honest person is up for grabs.[13] Second, the subjective element in the rule remains importantly subjective. It would be open for the defendant still to claim not only that he believed his activities to be honest but also that he believed that everyone else felt the same about, for example, pilfering from work or stealing from a supermarket.[14] This *Ghosh* test does not avoid the problems, inherent in the word 'dishonesty', of competing views of good and bad motives for taking property. The individual's private opinion, contrary to the words of the Criminal Law Commissioners, *is* 'allowed to weigh against the authority of the law' (1843, 29), which is tied here to the principle of the sanctity of private property. Ordinary people do not share this tie in many circumstances.

Interestingly, Williams suggests a solution that would exclude motive from consideration entirely. It parallels the approach of the court in *Chandler* by defining honesty objectively, by definition as involving 'respect for property rights'. The judge would rule out as irrelevant any attempt to lead evidence as to the honesty of the motives of the defendant if those revealed a lack of respect for such rights. The meaning of 'dishonesty' would cease to be a question for defendants or juries at all. Williams's objectivism here contrasts markedly with his subjectivism when the mental element is simply a matter of intent or recklessness. The message is clear: subjectivism only goes so far. Where it impinges upon the sanctity of private property, it is rejected. 'Dishonesty' must be defined by the state, 'independent[ly] of prevailing mores' (1983, 726–7). But one can see Williams's point. The mens rea term 'dishonesty' is too clearly a substantive term requiring a moral content, and therefore enabling contestation. Better, within the logic of the law, to shut off that possibility entirely, even if, in so doing, the political commitment of the law's individualist form is revealed as tied to a particular kind of social order, and a particular content of social norms.

### (iii)   Informal remedies to the formal politics of denial

The penal reformers had a vision of a consensual society, but the reality was in the beginning one of intense social conflict. It was only possible to express the law in universal terms after a long political and social process of defeating counterclaims and imposing one definition of lawful and unlawful conduct on a resisting populace. That imposition could only be achieved and managed by recognising individual justice in an abstract fashion. People act from motives and intentions, and it is indeed 'childish' to imagine that culpability can be properly evaluated with reference to intention alone. Motive is crucial, in terms of our evaluation of the goodness or badness of a person, but motive must be irrelevant to the law's evaluation, for once motive rears its head, substantive issues of right and wrong enter the courtroom.

It will be said that law and morality are separate spheres (though the judges do not always recognise this themselves),[15] and that the criteria for the one are not necessarily the criteria for the other. This is true, but not for the reason that is normally given. It is said that in a secular society, the law reflects democratic institutions and liberal political values rather than any particular moral code. Whatever the relevance of that argument elsewhere (Devlin, 1965; Hart, 1963), it is not relevant to the discussion here. The basic issue is the exclusion of *competing* moral and political views, and the imposition of one particular moral view which embraces both the defence of the nuclear state and the sanctity of private property. It is because law *does* reflect one particular, but contestable, moral view of the just social order and excludes others that legal definitions of individual justice have to eschew morally more serious definitions of culpability if they are to operate on the basis of an ideology of individual responsibility. The particular moral and political content of the law is then masked by its individualistic form.

But the suppression of motive still leaves a deep and persistent mark upon the law. We have seen this in different substantive areas. Beyond them, there are the defences of duress and necessity which will be discussed in Chapter 8. There are also a variety of informal remedies to these problems of law, through which non-legal decisions temper legal rules. In *Buckoke v GLC* (1971), Lord Denning had to consider whether a fireman driving through a red light to a fire broke the law. Since there was held to be no defence of necessity, he decided that he had, but that 'the police need not prosecute. Nor need the justices punish'. Rather, the accused 'should be congratulated' ((1971) at 258). The law had been broken but, through various exercises of discretion, the rule of law should be evaded. Three general sites of discretion can be identified.

### (a)   Discretion to prosecute

Prosecutory discretion operates in order to select what is regarded as the morally appropriate solution in light of the defendant's motive. This can be either in terms of not prosecuting at all or of selecting a lesser offence where two offence categories are available. In the first category falls the latitude often shown to medical practitioners in relation to the treatment of the damaged newborn and the terminally ill (Lacey and Wells, 1998, 526–37). In the second come decisions to prosecute factory owners under Health and Safety at Work legislation rather than the law of homicide for deaths at work (below, Chapter 5; Sanders and Young, 2000, 368–71).

Another example is the prosecution of car drivers who kill under the Road Traffic Act 1988, s 1 (causing death by dangerous driving) or s 3A (causing death by careless driving under the influence of drink or drugs) rather than the law of manslaughter. The law in this area has changed since the House of Lords decision in *Seymour* (1983) (see below, p 66), but the view in that case that prosecutors should only prosecute rarely for the offence of 'motor manslaughter', depending on the degree of 'moral turpitude' in the killing, remains relevant.

### (b)   Discretion to convict

Judges display conflicting attitudes to the role of the jury. On the one hand, it is said that the shift to objective standards of fault, for example in the law of recklessness, follows from a suspicion that juries are unreliable and too prone to accept the accused's story. On the other hand, juries are relied upon to exercise good common sense where the law is vague or caught between conflicting standpoints. Examples of this are to be found in the law of indirect intention (see Lord Scarman in *Hancock and Shankland* (1986) at 365), and provocation (see Lord Hoffmann in *Smith* (2000) at 312–13; for discussion, see Norrie, 2001). In gross negligence manslaughter (see below, pp 66–9), the jury also finds justice where the law cannot guide it.

Sometimes, even, a judge may extol the virtue of the jury where it refuses to convict even though the law has been clearly broken. Lord Devlin described the jury as 'the lamp that shows freedom lives' (1956, 164), as playing 'a direct part in the application of the law' (1979, 127). Its role in this view is to intervene on behalf of the ordinary person when the powers that be get above themselves. This is the realm of the so-called 'perverse verdict', and it emerges where law and morality conflict. Thus Clive Ponting was acquitted by a jury for breaching the Official Secrets Act by leaking papers concerning the sinking of the General Belgrano with the loss of many lives during the war with Argentina. Similarly, Pat Pottle and Michael Randle were acquitted on a charge of helping the Soviet spy George Blake to escape prison in 1963. They had in fact confessed to their role in print long before the prosecution, but their moral appeal to the jury was successful (see Berlins and Dyer, 2001). Such 'perversity' is, it is argued, not perverse at all. It is a necessary (if irreconcilable) supplement to a formal legal system which ignores the underlying moral aspects of particular offences.

### (c)   Discretion in sentencing

There is also the final crowning issue of mitigation of punishment after conviction of the accused. As we have seen, actors of very different moral colour can be convicted of the same offence, since their motives are irrelevant to criminal responsibility. The textbooks point out, however, that the rigours of the law are compensated for by compassion at the sentencing stage and beyond, when motive finally does come into the picture:

> Motive is important again when the question of punishment is in issue. When the law allows the judge a discretion in sentencing, he will obviously be more leniently disposed towards the convicted person who acted with a good motive. When the judge has no discretion (as in murder) a good motive may similarly be a factor in inducing the Home Secretary to grant an early release on licence. (Smith and Hogan, 1999, 79)

The possibility of mitigation of sentence is a marvellous mechanism for allowing the criminal process to 'have its cake and eat it'. Having convicted the accused by a strict, unbending set of rules, the rule books are cleared away and judicial or governmental discretion comes in to do 'real' justice to the individual, or to temper legal justice with 'mercy'. None of the orthodox doctrinal scholars appear to appreciate the irony of this. Having insisted upon a strict legal code so as to protect the liberty of the individual, it transpires that the individual's liberty is ultimately dependent not upon the rule of law at all but on a group of men operating with a wide discretion at the sentencing stage.

The penal theory of the Enlightenment had two catchphrases: 'nullum crimen sine lege' and 'nulla poena sine lege' (Hall, 1960, ch 2) – no crime *or* punishment without law. In admitting a wide flexibility with regard to mitigation while insisting upon a strictly defined criminal law, English lawyers in effect slam the stable door while overlooking the gaping hole in the back wall through which the horse of discretion bolts at will. Yet arguably the issue of disposal is much more important to the individual than that of conviction so that an unregulated discretion at this stage is very dangerous in terms of the ideology of the rule of law. The sentencing style represents the 'scandal' of the liberal criminal justice system,[16] yet it is a scandal that is necessitated *by the very certainty* of the rest of the law.

The question of motive and the ensuing moral judgments of right and wrong re-emerge at the sentencing stage from the purdah which the law imposes upon them. They have to, if the law's crude judgments of individual fault are to be tempered by a genuine regard for individual wrongdoing. But when they do so, they undermine the law's claims to justice *and* legality. To the extent that judges mitigate punishment, they punish according to an individualised view of the defendant and a discretionary view of their role that has little to do with the necessary generality of the rule of law, or a legal conception of justice.

The conflict is built into the system, and it might be thought just as well that discretion exists, even if it undermines the ideology of the law. But we should note the *political* limits of the 'mercy' function. The judgments of right and wrong employed in the use of discretion at the sentencing stage are placed firmly in the hands of that 'State instrumentality' (Williams, 1983, 143), the judges. What counts for good or bad motive is not left at large in the community: it is kept politically safe with the judges, far away from the noise and conflict of the world outside. The social mores of the 'common people' are mediated, for good or ill, by the judges' perception of them.

## 3   INDIRECT INTENTION: LEGAL AND MORAL JUDGMENT

Having followed through the historic logic of the motive/intention division and the tensions thrown up by it, it might be thought that we could now enter the calmer judicial waters of the law of intention itself. One might expect, on the lawyer's own chosen ground, a smooth, logical, solidly based example of the legal art. In fact, the law in this area has been deeply problematic for a number of years. Matters have, however, changed with the recent House of Lords decision in *R v Woollin* and in this section I seek to analyse the development of the law up to and including this case. *Woollin* seems to have laid to rest many of the problems of the previous case law, though I will suggest that those problems may rather be seen as lying dormant than as resolved.

One of the fundamental aims of the nineteenth-century penal reform movement was the replacement of legal artifice, fictional constructions of the law, with clear and simple terms rooted in what was seen as natural understandings of the citizen (see eg the Criminal Law Commissioners, 1834, 3–9). In a rational world, individuals could be knowledgeable of the law and educated by it only where the law did not indulge in arcane meanings knowable only to lawyers. The legal code was designed for lay people, not for an élite. This is the context of liberal principle in which we can situate Williams's comment on the need for 'reasonably precise definitions, not too far removed from the ordinary meanings of words' (Williams, 1983, 73). Logic, legality and individual justice all require clarity and lack of confusion in the law, but it may be the nature of law that its judgments embody conflicts that stem from its characteristic forms. I shall argue that just as the distinction between motive and intention becomes inevitably blurred, so too does the meaning of intention.

## (i)    Two approaches to direct and indirect (oblique) intention

It will be helpful if we begin by exploring the meaning of the concept of intention. This is not straightforward for we can identify not one but two conceptions, both of which are relevant to the law. The first is the one that is favoured by the 'orthodox subjectivists' such as Williams and Smith and Hogan, and which has a prominent position in the law itself. It is a formal, 'factual', psychological definition. The second is a more morally substantive, less factual and psychological, account which is reflected in the work, for example, of Antony Duff (1990), John Gardner (1998) and Jeremy Horder (2000). Here, the emphasis is not on whether the individual as a matter of fact conceived an intention, revealing psychological control of the ensuing action, but rather whether that person's intention was *in its intrinsic quality* morally good or bad. I argue that this latter understanding is also to be found in or behind the law, often in conflict with the first approach, and that we need to understand this interlacing of conflicting views.

### (a)    The formal psychological ('orthodox subjectivist') approach

In this approach, the paradigm case is the easiest. To talk of intending to do something is to talk of 'meaning' or 'aiming' to do it. It concerns applying one's mind to a particular task and directing one's action to a particular 'aim', 'end' or (the standard lawyer's synonym) 'purpose' (Smith and Hogan, 1999, 54). Our 'purpose' is what we intend to bring about through our actions.

In perhaps most situations it will be relatively clear that an outcome was the direct product of an individual's purpose. A punch on the nose will normally (though not always) be brought about by an intention to punch someone on the nose, so that outcome and intention are directly linked. But there are other situations in which an outcome will not be directly linked to an intention or purpose (end) but will be either a means to a particular end or a by-product or side-effect of such an end. The outcome is not the product of a direct intention, but emerges *obliquely*, as the consequence of the achievement of a desired end (Williams, 1987). Where the outcome is indirectly achieved as a means to an end or as a side-effect (which may not be desired in itself), can one be said to intend it?

Where the means are *necessary* to the desired end, and knowingly undertaken in that light, it is argued that the individual intends the means as well as the end, even if he does not desire (or like) the means themselves. Where the side-effect is known to be a *certain* by-product of achieving one's purpose, it is also argued that one intends the side-effect in addition to the purpose. This analysis conforms with that of Lord Hailsham in *Hyam* ((1974) at 52) where he stated that 'intention' must 'include the means as well as the end and the inseparable consequences of the end as well as the means . . .' [17] For the 'orthodox subjectivist', this linking of what was intended to matters that were strictly not intended involves no element of artificiality: it is quite acceptable to talk of intentions as being either direct or indirect (oblique) (cf Williams, 1987; Goff, 1988, 45–7; Smith and Hogan, 1999, 55). Where artificiality would enter the analysis would be if the means or side-effect were not a *necessary* consequence but a consequence about which there was a degree of chance or probability of its occurrence. Where a side-effect was known to be likely, possible, or probable, one could say that the person *took the risk* that the consequence would occur, but not that he intended it to occur. In other words, he was *reckless* as to its occurrence (see further, Chapter 4 below), rather than intending it.

Finally, an important point of qualification. In the last paragraph, we spoke of *necessary* means and *certain* side-effects of one's actions. But the world is such that we can never act with one hundred per cent certainty that a particular means will be necessary or that a by-product is bound to be created. The world is full of unanticipatable and unanticipated effects which alter or wreck the best-made calculation. I intend to injure my enemy standing behind a closed window by throwing a stone. In 999 cases out of 1000, I must break the window in order to achieve my purpose. On the occasion in question, by a fluke, the window is thrown open as the stone leaves my hand. Or, I intend to collect the insurance on a parcel on a plane by timing a bomb to explode in mid-air. I know it to be a plane without parachutes or ejector seats. It is as certain as can be that the pilot will be killed but, by a freak, he falls from a great height and lives. Could the stone thrower or the bomb planter claim that the possibility of a fluke or freak stopping the means or side-effect occurring meant that he did not intend it, since it was not *absolutely bound* to happen? Could he rely on the chance in a thousand to say that the means or side-effect was not intended since it was not *genuinely* certain to occur? Could he claim that he very much hoped that the window would be thrown open or the pilot would be saved, and that given the possibility of the outside chance, he therefore did not intend the side-effect?

The answer on this analysis is that our actions and plans are always subject to the intervention of the unexpected and this is as true of our direct purposes as of the means to our ends or side-effects of our purposes. The unexpected may defeat the achievement of our purpose or render our calculation of means and side-effects wrong, but it does not cancel our intentions or purposes whether those are either direct or indirect. We need therefore to qualify the argument about the certainty of means or side-effects by talking of certainty 'for all practical purposes'. Judges have used the phrases 'moral' or 'virtual' certainty to denote a situation where an event will occur 'barring some unforeseen intervention' (*Nedrick* (1986)). The important point to note is that 'virtual certainty' *is* a kind of certainty (the only kind in fact that ever exists) and not a kind of high probability or chance.

## (b)   The morally substantive approach

Duff's critique of the foregoing approach is that it fails to reflect the way in which we understand wrongdoing. Orthodox subjectivism splits one moral judgment, whether a person directed his moral energies into doing something wrong, into two (subjective and objective) components. The 'objective' component is the harm that constitutes the wrong or the crime, which is measured in terms of the bad consequences it produces. The 'subjective' element is the fault of the wrongdoer, which is judged by whether the objective consequences were *as a matter of fact* known, foreseen or intended. For Duff, this approach is inadequate for it fails to reflect the nature of our moral judgments, in which 'objective' wrongdoing and 'subjective' fault are always combined. Thus to judge harm, we need to know about the *moral* quality of what was intended:

> Both the murder victim and the victim of natural causes suffer death: but the character of the harm that they suffer surely also depends on the way in which they die. One who tries to kill me . . . *attacks* my life and my most basic rights; and the harm which I suffer in being murdered . . . essentially involves this wrongful attack on me . . . The 'harm' at which the law of murder is aimed is thus not just the *consequential* harm of death, but the harm which is *intrinsic* to an attack on another's life. (Duff, 1990, 113)

And to judge intention, we need to know its moral quality:

> Human actions are purposive: they are done for reasons, in order to bring something about; their direction and their basic structure is formed by the intentions with which their agents act. It is through the intentions with which I act that I engage in the world as an agent, and relate myself most closely to the actual and potential effects of my actions; and the central or fundamental kind of wrong-doing is to *direct* my actions towards evil – to *intend* and to *try* to do what is evil. (Duff, 1990, 112–13)

The intention to do wrong is not a crime because a person has a psychological intention to do a criminal act, but because that intention manifests moral wrong-doing. The idea that intentions reveal bad moral attitudes leads to less emphasis on the precise forms of intention and more on what they reveal about the wrongdoer's motives. For the orthodox subjectivist, a person is guilty of murder where he intends to kill or cause serious ('grievous bodily') harm, or foresees death or serious injury as a virtual certainty, but not where he foresees death or serious injury as a probability. (These are the law's requirements too.) For the orthodox subjectivist, there is doubt as to whether intending to cause serious harm ('implied malice') is a sufficient alternative mental state to a direct intention to kill. Even foreseeing death as a virtual certainty (indirect intention) smacks to some of a false constructivism because there is no direct link between what was intended and the outcome of death. Only an intention actually to kill truly links with the result. Certainly foreseeing death or serious injury as a probable consequence (reckless killing) does not link what was intended sufficiently to the outcome of death to count as murder.

For Duff, the killer in all these situations may legitimately be convicted of murder. Where there is foresight of virtual certainty of death or serious injury, the killer displays 'an utter indifference to [the victim's] rights or interests' (Duff, 1990, 114). Further, where a person foresees the probability of death by exposing his victim to its serious risk (which English law does not see as murder), Duff argues that it is legitimately charged as murder. Such a person is 'wickedly reckless' and guilty of murder, for death 'is an integral aspect of his intended attack' (Duff, 1990, 177). On the orthodox subjectivist approach, as with the law of murder, such a person is guilty only of reckless manslaughter. With the morally substantive approach, this is not so. The moral quality in the act is more important than a precise distinguishing of different psychological states.

### (c)   Summary of the two approaches

To summarise the foregoing discussion, the 'orthodox subjectivist' approach deploys a formal, psychological, 'factual' view of responsibility based on the accused's mental control over actions. It is opposed by a 'morally substantive' approach concerned with the moral values identified in a particular action and the mental state accompanying it. The former approach appears to offer a neat, logical framework for understanding intention by removing itself from the 'messy' moral issues the latter insists on identifying. It seems much easier to talk about what the defendant intended or foresaw, than about how one evaluates the wrongdoing in his actions. Orthodox subjectivists certainly believe that this is so, and it is their approach which has by and large driven the modern law on direct and indirect intention. There is, however, a very big question mark against this approach. It is whether the law also needs to be supplemented in a manner akin to Duff's moral substantivism. Does the law also need moral concepts like 'wicked recklessness' in order to make appropriate judgments of guilt in murder cases? In the most recent House of Lords case, *Woollin*, Lord Hope referred to cases of what he called 'indiscriminate malice'. Such cases cannot really be included within the framework of an orthodox subjectivist approach, yet they may be relevant to establishing guilt. Similarly, what if a person kills with the required mental state but with a morally good motive, as in the case of the mercy killer? Again, the orthodox subjectivist approach, with its emphasis on mental states like intention, would not recognise this issue. We have seen the problems cases of good motive pose for the division between motive and intention. Turning to the subjectivist case law on indirect intention, how does it deal with issues of moral substance?

### (ii)   The law of oblique intention: *Moloney*

In the last forty years, the House of Lords has considered the law of oblique intention five times (four times since the mid-seventies). The current story begins with *Hyam* (1974) where the accused poured petrol through a letter box and lit it in order, she claimed, to frighten the woman in the house. In the ensuing fire, two of the women's daughters died. Hyam claimed she had not intended to kill them. In *Moloney* (1985) the accused killed his step-father with a shotgun at close range but, he claimed, without any intention to kill or hurt his victim when he unthinkingly pulled the trigger. In *Hancock and Shankland* (1986), two miners on strike dropped concrete blocks off a motorway bridge on a car, killing the driver. They claimed that their intention was to frighten, not to kill, and that they thought the blocks would land on a different lane to the one on which the car was travelling. The case law development is completed by the Court of Appeal case of *Nedrick*, with facts similar to those in *Hyam*, and the most recent House of Lords case of *Woollin*, where a father killed his infant child by throwing it across the room in a fit of frustration. All these cases raised the issue of death resulting where there was no direct intention to kill or cause grievous bodily harm, and therefore, depending upon whether their mental states were defined as indirectly intentional, whether the accused was guilty of murder or, in the alternative, manslaughter.

In *Hyam*, the House held[18] that Mrs Hyam may not, as she had claimed at her trial, have intended the death of the two girls; but that if she had foreseen that their deaths were a probable consequence of her actions, she was guilty of murder. 'Intention' was accordingly defined in a broad way to include both direct and indirect intention *and* foresight of a probable consequence. Note that this definition effectively brings 'intention' within the sphere of recklessness as briefly defined in the previous subsection. Mrs Hyam claimed that the death of the two girls was not her purpose, nor was it foreseen as a virtually certain side-effect of her actual purpose. If she was believed, there was a foreseen risk of death, but no more than that.

In *Moloney*, by contrast, the House discarded this element of recklessness, narrowing their definition to include indirect side-effects *only* when the latter were foreseen as 'morally' certain to occur. Lord Bridge, giving the judgment of the House, stated that 'the probability of the consequence taken to have been foreseen must be little short of overwhelming before it will suffice to establish the necessary intent' ((1985) at 1036). He gave the example of a person who boards a plane for Manchester without any desire to go there but in order to escape pursuit. In boarding the plane, the person demonstrates his intention to go there. The plane *may* develop engine trouble and be diverted elsewhere, but in the normal course of events it is a 'moral certainty' that the person will arrive in Manchester ((1985) at 1037). A person can be said to intend a side-effect of his actions when the effect will occur 'unless something unexpected supervenes to prevent it' ((1985) at 1039). Thus, Lord Bridge's statement of the law in *Moloney* brought it into line with the orthodox subjectivist definition of intention and oblique intention that we outlined in the previous section. It discarded what was seen as the artificial, constructive definition employed in *Hyam* which extended the term to cover foresight of probable consequences, that is, recklessness.

All the cases since *Moloney* have agreed with its formulation of *the law* and rejected the broader *Hyam* approach. What has changed is that in the later Court of Appeal case of *Nedrick* (1986), the test was reformulated as one of 'foresight of virtual certainty', to clarify the otherwise difficult concept of 'moral' certainty. Yet there were problems with the decision in *Moloney* which ensured that it would lead to further litigation. These concerned the *guidelines* to a jury offered in *Moloney* as to how the foresight of virtual/moral certainty test should be applied. They also relate, however, to the practical and broader moral question of which killers should be labelled murderers. This issue lurks behind the legal discussion, which is cast in orthodox subjectivist terms. It reveals, I will suggest, the relevance of the morally substantive approach discussed above for the legal meaning of intention.

*(a)    Guidelines to a jury in Moloney*

Lord Bridge in *Moloney* laid down the following guidelines that a trial judge might use to explain to the jury how the law might be applied to the facts before them:

> First, was death or really serious injury . . . a natural consequence of the defendant's voluntary act? Second, did the defendant foresee that consequence as being a natural consequence of his act? The jury should then be told that if they answer Yes to both questions it is a proper inference for them to draw that he intended the consequence. ((1985) at 1039)

The crucial word here is 'natural'. In using it, Lord Bridge intended to convey the notion of moral certainty, that is a consequence that is virtually bound to follow:

> In the old presumption that a man intends the natural and probable consequences of his acts the important word is 'natural'. The word conveys the idea that in the ordinary course of events a certain act will lead to a certain consequence unless something unexpected supervenes to prevent it. One might almost say that, if a consequence is natural, it is really otiose to speak of it as also being probable. ((1985) at 1039)

Given that 'natural' means virtually certain (as in 'the horse is a "natural" – a certainty – to win the race'), 'probable' in the old phrase 'natural and probable consequences' does indeed become redundant, for virtual certainty necessarily includes and subsumes any degree of probability within it.

However, there is an ambiguity for 'natural' *can* mean, in addition to virtual certainty, following 'in an unbroken causal chain from [an] initial event' (*Hancock and Shankland* (1986) at 644). When the word is used in this sense, it may not involve a particularly high degree of probability at all, let alone certainty. A causal connection between two events may be both 'natural' in this latter sense and highly unlikely. For example, there was a natural (causal) connection between the actions of Hancock and Shankland and the death of the taxi driver, but that did not mean that death was virtually certain to occur.[19] We will return to this point below.

*(b)    Moloney's intended practical impact*

Lord Bridge discussed the liability of a person who plants a bomb giving timely warning to evacuate the public. The person knows that it is virtually certain that a bomb disposal squad will be called and in the event a disposal expert is killed. Although he does not say so directly, it appears from the context of the example ((1985) at 1037–8; cf Smith and Hogan, 1988, 59) that Lord Bridge considers that such a bomber would be guilty of murder on the *Moloney* rules. But this is not so. The virtual certainty that a squad would be called is not the same as the virtual certainty that the expert would be killed. Death in such an occupation is a possibility, not a virtual certainty. The liability of a bomber in this example is for the crime of manslaughter, not murder, for intention in the *Moloney* sense is lacking.

Yet, as I have said, Lord Bridge appears to think the opposite. The point is an important one, for the example of the bomber is a persistent one in judicial ruminations. Lord Bridge describes his example as 'an all too tragically realistic illustration' ((1985) at 1037). The assumption appears to be that such a person *should* be guilty of murder (cf Goff, 1988, Lord Hailsham in *Moloney* (1985) at

1027, and now Lord Hope in *Woollin* (1998) at 393). Yet the rules do not run that far. We return to this point below.

### (iii) Having one's subjectivist cake and eating it: interpreting *Moloney*

When we move on to *Hancock and Shankland* and the Court of Appeal case of *Nedrick* (1986), we see the ways in which the ambiguities in *Moloney* between the law and the guidelines were exploited. They were used to achieve a strict rule of intention on the one hand and a broad practical application of it on the other.

#### (a) Guidelines to a jury: Hancock and Shankland

While honouring in words the restrictive and principled meaning of intention established in *Moloney*, these cases produced the possibility of by-passing it in practice. The appeal in *Hancock and Shankland* stemmed from the ambiguity in the word 'natural' discussed above, and the concern that a jury might take it only to entail a foreseen causal connection of any level of probability, not one of moral certainty. At the Court of Appeal, Lord Lane conceded the ambiguity, but instead of explaining 'natural' in Lord Bridge's terms, as involving a certainty 'unless something unexpected supervenes to prevent it' ((1985) at 1039), he stated that it –

> . . . means that it must have been *highly likely* that the defendant's act would cause death or serious injury before the inference can be drawn that he had the necessary intent. ((1986) at 644) (emphasis added)

'Likely' is a synonym for 'probable' so that Lord Lane is in effect couching the definition of 'natural' in terms that hark back to the old *Hyam* recklessness standard of foresight of probability, not moral certainty. The questions for the jury become:

> Are you sure that the defendant's act was of a kind which was likely to cause death or really serious bodily injury? . . . are you sure that the defendant appreciated that what he did was highly likely to cause death or really serious bodily injury? ((1986) at 645)

There is no difference in substance between 'appreciation of a likelihood' and foresight of a risk. In other words, the Court of Appeal rightly recognised the problem in the word 'natural' in the *Moloney* guidelines, but in dealing with it, they transformed the substance of Lord Bridge's formulation away from certainty and towards *Hyam*-style recklessness. In the House of Lords, Lord Scarman followed Lord Lane's logic by re-inserting the word 'probable' that Lord Bridge had taken out of the phrase 'natural and probable'. Lord Bridge had taken it out as unnecessary because 'natural' meant morally certain and therefore included any degree of what was 'probable' anyway. Lord Scarman put it back in order to avoid the ambiguity Lord Bridge had failed to notice in 'natural'. However, in so doing, he only managed to dilute the meaning of 'natural' and return the guidelines to a probability test. Lord Bridge, he said:

> . . . omitted any reference in his guidelines to probability. He did so because he included probability in the meaning which he attributed to 'natural' . . . I agree with the Court of

Appeal that the probability of a consequence is a factor of sufficient importance to be drawn specifically to the attention of the jury and to be explained . . . [The *Moloney* guidelines] require a reference to probability. They also require an explanation that the greater the probability of a consequence the more likely it is that the consequence was foreseen and if that consequence was foreseen the greater the probability is that that consequence was also intended. ((1986) at 650)

With regard to the last sentence in this passage, the foresight of a highly probable consequence can only count as intended if foresight of a highly probable consequence is conceptually a constituent element of intention. That is the logic of Lord Scarman's position, but it is a logic to which he cannot admit because he wishes to follow the statement of the law in *Moloney*, where such a position was clearly rejected.[20]

### (b)   Hancock and Shankland's practical impact

If there is no reason *to* the position in *Hancock and Shankland*, is there any reason *for* it? Let us return to the example of the bomber. The prospect of political violence formed the backdrop to *Hyam* (1974), *Moloney* (recall the example of the bomb disposal expert), and also *Hancock and Shankland*. Lord Scarman spoke of –

... crimes of violence where the purpose is by open violence to protest, demonstrate, obstruct or frighten [which] are on the increase. Violence is used by some as a means of public communication. Inevitably there will be casualties; and inevitably death will on occasion result. ((1986) at 647)

It is in this context that Lord Scarman raises the question whether death arising as a side-effect should be murder or manslaughter. In a subsequent article, Lord Goff (1988) suggested that the current law of intention and murder may be too narrow to cover cases of violence that judges feel ought to be covered, and that therefore there is a need for a broader law. Whether intentionally or not, the reformulation of the guidelines in *Hancock and Shankland* does precisely this at the same time as paying lip service to a narrow concept of intention, respectful of a liberal, orthodox subjectivist standpoint. The law in *Moloney* coupled with these new guidelines might be said to have allowed the judges to have their principled cake and to eat it. The law is expressed in terms of virtual certainty while advice to the jury is premised on a kind of recklessness test.

This can be seen in the subsequent Court of Appeal judgment, *Nedrick*. There, Lord Lane followed *Moloney* in stating that the jury –

... are not entitled to infer the necessary intention unless they feel sure that death or serious bodily harm was a virtual certainty (barring some unforeseen intervention) as a result of the defendant's actions and that the defendant appreciated that such was the case. ((1986) at 1028)

But two paragraphs earlier, he says that if the defendant –

... thought that the risk to which he was exposing the person killed was only slight, then it may be easy for the jury to conclude that he did not intend to bring about the result. ((1986) at 1028)

On the law of oblique intention in *Moloney*, there is no possibility of such a defendant having the intention to kill, and no question for the jury, easy or hard, for degrees
of risk are irrelevant to the virtual certainty test. They are, however, quite relevant
to the *Hancock and Shankland* discussion of the *Moloney* guidelines,[21] and *Nedrick*'s
own formulation of the guideline questions invites the jury to consider –

(1) How *probable* was the consequence which resulted from the defendant's voluntary
    act?
(2) Did he foresee that consequence? ((1986) at 1028) (my emphasis)

Thus *Nedrick* completed a development of the law in which a disparity emerged
between the rule of law on indirect intention and the guidelines designed to aid juries
in applying the law. The law was based on orthodox subjectivist principles. What of
the guidelines? These reflect moral concerns about certain kinds of violence and, with
their broader approach, they reflect the concerns of the moral substantivists. We turn
now to the latest House of Lords case, *Woollin*, which updates the law and reveals
how the dispute between the two approaches to responsibility is now expressed.

### (iv)  The *Moloney–Woollin* axis

*(a)   Woollin and the parameters of indirect intention*

It is in this situation that the recent House of Lords case of *Woollin* (1998) makes its
appearance. *Woollin* seems at first sight to have resolved the lingering tension
between a law of virtual certainty and guidelines based on *Hyam*-style recklessness.
It does so by supporting the *Moloney* and *Nedrick* formulation of foresight of virtual
(previously moral) certainty. Of the guideline questions in *Nedrick* (above), Lord
Steyn politely but firmly states that it is 'unlikely, if ever, to be helpful to direct the
jury in terms of the two questions'. All that *Woollin* changes besides this is the
formulation in *Nedrick* that the jury is 'entitled to infer' intention. Henceforth, it is
said that the clearer 'entitled to find' should be used. The requirement of foresight
of 'virtual certainty (barring some unforeseen intervention)' is affirmed.

   *Woollin* seems therefore to heal an open sore in the law's reasoning by breaking
with the problematic guidelines. It appears to endorse an orthodox subjectivist
approach in line with the original intention of the law in *Moloney*. Against this,
however, a number of points should be noted. First, Lord Steyn in *Woollin* stops short
of over-ruling *Hyam*. While distinguishing that case from the law in *Moloney*, *Hancock
and Shankland* and *Nedrick*, he fails to acknowledge some of the *Hyam*-style errors in
these cases (see further Norrie, 1999, 533–5). To the contrary, he endorses some of
these formulations, at least by omission. Second, it is important to note the moral facts
in *Woollin*, which concerned a father who killed his child in circumstances that
suggested he had not previously harmed it. It was therefore a case like *Moloney* of
violence within a family, where a compassionate view might suggest the correct moral
label was manslaughter, not murder. Harder cases like those where an inherently
dangerous act is placed in the world, but it is not intended or foreseen as virtually
certain that a victim would be killed or injured, present a more difficult scenario for
judgment. Under the pre-*Woollin* cases, the judges preserved through the guidelines the
possibility of extending murder to those who acted with a 'wickedly reckless' disregard

for life, even if *the law* rejected the murder label in such cases. Whether intended or not, the pre-*Woollin* law permitted them to be principled orthodox subjectivists in law and moral substantivists (via the jury) in practice. That ambiguity seems now no longer to exist, but it should be noted that one judge in *Woollin*, Lord Hope, appeared to keep the flame alive. He seemed to think that the 'terrorist example' from *Moloney* should come within the law of murder. It is to include circumstances of killing exhibiting 'indiscriminate malice', which is to be inferred from the circumstances of the case. The broader, moral conception of mens rea for murder thus remains somewhat alive in *Woollin*, and it will be interesting to see if a subsequent case, another Mrs Hyam for example, persuades the judges to reconsider the broader version of the law.

### (b)    Woollin and the two approaches to intention

How does this development of the law relate to the conflict between the two approaches to intention, the orthodox subjectivist, and the morally substantive? The law's construction on orthodox subjectivist lines has been achieved by evading some of the tough, conflictual moral choices that it inevitably faces. As a result, moral issues that are not seemingly relevant to the law of intention emerge from beneath its surface to disrupt its calm, logical appearance. Moral substance will out. The conflict between the law and the guidelines in the post-*Moloney* case law can be seen as a tension between orthodox subjectivism in the law and substantive moralism percolating through the guidelines. The slacker formulation of the latter, with the address to the jury that it is for them to decide if the accused intended death or serious harm, became an invitation to it to use its moral 'common sense' to decide the issue regardless of the letter of the law. Cases of 'indiscriminate malice' could still be found to be murder despite their formal exclusion from the law. Sir Richard Buxton (1988, 484) described the law under *Hancock* and *Nedrick* as 'comparatively clear and simple' but added that it was based on an 'admittedly fragile equilibrium'. Such balance as the law had has proved fragile, and *Woollin* has confirmed as much by reverting to the orthodox subjectivist law and discarding the *Nedrick* guidelines. However, the underlying moral issues have not gone away, and cases of 'indiscriminate malice' may again re-open the path back to *Hyam*.

It is not that *Hyam*-style reasoning is in itself morally substantive, but rather that the foresight of probability approach admits more cases of indirectly intended death into the law of murder than does the foresight of virtual certainty test. It therefore provides the moral leeway argued for by the substantivists. Of course, were the law to return to *Hyam*, the problem would then arise as to what to do with situations which appear morally *not* to deserve the murder label, such as family killings like *Moloney* and *Woollin*. Sometimes substantive moral interpretation leads in one direction, sometimes another. The point is that the law's definition of indirect intention is captive to these behind-the-scenes pressures. It is in that sense that orthodox subjectivism, which dominates the law, needs morally substantive arguments at the same time as it eschews them.

### (c)    'Entitled to find' and the moral threshold

There is a second issue in *Woollin*, which returns us to our discussion of the relationship between motive and intention (above, pp 39–40). Having now considered the law of indirect intention, the anomalous nature of the argument in cases like *Steane*, *Gillick* and Dr Moor's case should now be clear. These were anomalous precisely because the possibility of an indirect intention formulation of the law was rejected. Yet *Woollin* seems to leave open the possibility of courts adopting the narrow, direct intent only approach in particular cases. Where a jury considers an accused foresaw death or serious injury in a murder case, it is 'entitled to find' he intended the result. If one is *entitled* to find a particular conclusion, it might be suggested that one does not have to, the word being permissive rather than obligatory in its implication. Thus in a case like *Steane* or *Gillick*, could a jury not choose to find the accused did *not* intend the criminal consequence, even if they found that the accused knew it was virtually certain to occur? They *could* (are 'entitled' to) find he intended, but do they have to?

Is there a rationale for such an approach? One (morally substantive) argument is that a person does not intend results foreseen as virtually certain where the result is no part of the overall moral design in her acting. There is a 'moral threshold' which separates the person off from results completely inimical to her purpose even if she foresaw them. An examiner marks a paper regardless of whether it will make the student deeply happy or unhappy. Even if she knows for sure that a fail will make the student miserable, she does not intend that consequence. It was no part of Steane's moral purpose to assist the enemy, or of the doctor to encourage unlawful sex, so they did not intend such results even if they anticipated them. Against this, it may be argued that such a view of intention strains the normal meaning of the term (which includes indirect intention). What happens in these cases is that a hidden moral defence of necessity emerges in the wrong place (Smith, 1987). The remedy is to develop more fully the defence of necessity, as is indeed now to an extent happening (see below, Chapter 8, pp 159–64). The response to this is that the 'moral threshold' argument rightly places the issue on a sound theoretical ground in the law of intention. Second, the limit on the law of necessity, that it is not available in murder cases, means that there will be situations which might be resolved by deploying the narrow intention approach. In the 'Herald of Free Enterprise' disaster, a man paralysed with fear blocked an escape ladder. He was pushed off with the result that he in all probability drowned. If the survivors were charged with murder, they could not, it seems, plead necessity, but a jury could find that their intention was not to kill, only to survive. *Woollin*'s 'entitlement' to find intention seems to permit this conclusion.

This is, however, a speculative argument, and must be read in the light of the recent Court of Appeal case of *Re A (children)* (2000), concerning the separation of conjoined twins leading to the inevitable death of one. There, it was held that on the law of intention, the doctors would be held to intend to kill the twin that would die since they would foresee her death as virtually certain to occur ((2000) at 1012, 1029). No mention was made of a 'moral threshold' or of the possibilities of 'entitled to find', nor was the possibility of a *Gillick* or *Steane* purpose based formulation considered. Instead the court opted for the defence of necessity, seeking to apply that defence very narrowly to the particular facts of the case (for further discussion, see below, p 163). However, it is worth noting that there was a subsidiary ground of appeal against permitting the operation under art 2 of the European Convention of Human Rights. Under art 2, the right to life is protected and it is stated that no one 'shall be deprived of life intentionally'. The argument was therefore made that under the law of intention, with its direct and indirect forms, Mary, the twin who was to die, would be intentionally deprived of life. The court had, after all, already stated as much itself. Now coming at the issue of intention from another direction, it changed its view. It held that the extended meaning of intention was 'not appropriate when determining whether a doctor who performed a separation operation . . . was intentionally killing the twin . . . to be sacrificed' ((2000) at 1050). 'Intention' was to be given its 'natural and ordinary meaning' which involved considering if 'the purpose of the prohibited action is to cause death' ((2000) at 1068). In deploying a direct intention only argument, the judges were acknowledging the moral threshold à la *Steane*. What they had denied, they now affirmed: moral substantivism will out.

## 4   CONCLUSION

If we draw together our discussion of the relationship between motive and intention (Section 2) and between direct and indirect intention (Section 3), we see that the law has three distinct definitions of intention. From *Steane* and *Gillick*, we see an interpretation of intention as involving only its direct form (aim or purpose). From the law in *Moloney*, *Nedrick* (but not their guidelines) and *Woollin*, we see it as involving both direct and indirect (foresight of virtual certainty) forms. From *Hyam* and the guideline discussion in *Moloney*, *Hancock and Shankland* and *Nedrick*, it embraces direct and indirect (foresight of high probability) intention. The last of these seems to be excluded from a statement of the present law, though it remains to be seen whether this will be a permanent position.

The common issue in all these discussions concerns the ability to base criminal responsibility's most central term on a psychological mental state which ignores the substantive moral issues which surround and inform it. The 'moral elbow room' in *Steane* and *Gillick* is needed to avoid convicting defendants who on the orthodox subjectivist reading of intention should be guilty of at least the indirect intention to commit the crime in question. The narrowing and broadening of indirect intention in the murder cases is likewise dictated by moral issues concerning the 'colour' of violence hidden behind the formal statement of the law. Whence comes this odd relationship between formal or technical legal forms of responsibility and substantive moral issues which are both excluded and determinative in the development of the law? How is it that the legal language of fault is subjected to this kind of moral ventriloquism?

The answer lies in the discussion of the law's psychological individualist form in the previous chapter (above, pp 24, 28–9). We are dealing here with the evolution of a particular legal model of responsibility that was devised to exclude or marginalise difficult or contested moral issues from the law and the courtroom. The problems of motive and intention, or direct and indirect intention, stem from this earlier period's separation of legal judgment from substantive moral issues. Since the technical approach to responsibility was founded on a desire to evade moral issues, it is not surprising that it has such difficulty in dealing with them when they arise today. Modern law is caught in a necessary, structural dynamic of excluding and re-admitting substantive moral issues into a technically conceived set of fault categories. The conflict between 'orthodox subjectivists' and 'moral substantivists' we have highlighted reflects this dynamic of inclusion and exclusion. This foundational dilemma of the modern law lies, I argue, at the root of Williams's view that English law lacks 'clear and consistent definitions of words expressing its basic concepts' (1983, 73).

# Chapter 4

# Recklessness

The existing variation in the meaning of recklessness is indefensible. (Smith and Hogan, 1999, 67)

In almost every case which I heard . . . litigants and witnesses, whether they lied or were mistaken, worked with the same moral and legal rules as the judges did. This is the mark of a homogeneous society; and it alone allows a satisfactory process of law. If the litigants have rules of rightdoing different from those of the judges, the judges can punish them, but not convict them. (Gluckman, 1963, 182)

## I  INTRODUCTION

Just as we have examined the contradictions and tensions within the law of intention, so we now repeat the task in relation to the other main form of mens rea, recklessness. Just as with intention, we will find that the law lacks 'clear and consistent definitions of words expressing its basic concepts' (Williams, 1983, 73). Indeed, if anything, the situation is worse in the law of recklessness because the contradictions are more visible.

Recklessness has two distinct and opposed meanings within the law. It can either involve doing an act and recognising that there is a risk that it may result in harm being caused or it can mean doing an act without recognising the risk where that risk would be obvious to a reasonable onlooker. The problem is that while most common law offences and their statutory successors can be committed with the first, narrower, mental state, only some can be committed according to both forms, and there is no rhyme or reason as to their employment. The following example highlights the problem:

If D takes an air rifle and, not even considering the possibility that it might be loaded (as is the fact), aims and fires it at P, breaking P's spectacles and destroying his eye, D will be liable for causing criminal damage to the spectacles but will not be criminally liable at all for the destruction of the eye. The law appears to give greater protection to spectacles than to eyes. (Smith and Hogan, 1999, 67)

D's conduct is likely to be reckless according to the definition of recklessness that does not require foresight of risk, but not on the narrower definition that does require it. While offences of criminal damage can be committed according to the broader definition, the offence of malicious wounding under s 20 of the Offences Against the Person Act 1861 requires actual foresight. The result is the kind of irrationality ably demonstrated in the example. The immediate cause of the problem is the definition of recklessness provided by Lord Diplock in the two cases of *Caldwell* (1981) and *Lawrence* (1981). Applied in a case of criminal damage, an accused is held to be reckless if, first, he does something which creates an obvious risk that property will be destroyed or damaged. Second, when he does it, he must either not have given any thought to the possibility of there being some risk or he must have recognised that there was a risk but gone on to take it.[1]

The opprobrium that this test occasioned (Williams, 1981; Syrota, 1982), and continues to occasion (Smith, 1991, 274; Smith and Hogan, 1999, 67), stemmed from the inclusion within the definition of recklessness of an *objective* alternative to the already existing *subjective* test of the accused's awareness of a risk. The *Caldwell/ Lawrence* test accounts as reckless not only the person who is aware of a possible risk, but also the person who had no awareness of that possibility, where the risk was obvious (*Caldwell*) or obvious and serious (*Lawrence*). This test accounts both the *advertent* and the *inadvertent* risktaker reckless. In *Caldwell*, this entailed a substantial challenge to, and departure from, a subjective concept of advertent recklessness.

What accounts for this opposition in the law? In our discussion of the law of intention, we saw that opposed versions of intention reflected underlying moral issues within the law that could be traced back to a primal split between motive and intention and the predominance of orthodox subjectivism. In considering reckless-ness, I argue that the law's subjectivist/objectivist division has a similar moral provenance. It is the historical product of the de-moralisation and decontextualis-ation of fault that occurred through the Enlightenment reform project. It was not an inevitable consequence of any process of legal judgment, but the actual product of a control process informed by liberal principle in a social order in conflict. Social conflict engendered a basic schizophrenia in the forms of judgment as to what it meant to be reckless.

In the next section, I do two things. First, I discuss in detail the state of the law after *Caldwell* and stress its inability to reconcile the subjectivist and objectivist strands that it contains (Section 2(i) and (ii)). Second, I then explore the character of subjectivism and objectivism in this area of law (Section 2(iii) to (v)). While the former employs a too narrow conception of individual responsibility, the latter involves an overbroad conception of social condemnation. There are fleeting indications in some judgments that the judges seek to find an intermediate path that would recognise responsibility in some but not all cases where there is no foresight of risk. The moral possibility, with at the same time the legal impossibility of this intermediate position, is central to my argument and I explore it through consid-eration of the work of Antony Duff in the third section. My argument will be that what is sought is a basis for judgment that synthesises individual fault and social condemnation, but that such a synthesis is impossible in a society based upon structural conflicts. In the fourth section, I argue that the result of this is that 'things fall apart' in the law of recklessness into, on the one hand, a too narrow form of (subjective) fault and, on the other, a too broad form of (objective) condemnation. The centre cannot hold, so we are left as a historical phenomenon with irreconcilable alternatives within the law.

## 2 SUBJECTIVISM AND OBJECTIVISM IN THE LAW OF RECKLESSNESS

### (i) The judgment in *Caldwell*

In order to explore the character of the law of recklessness, it will be helpful to consider four basic objections to *Caldwell*. The first concerns the manner in which the law was changed. Lord Diplock, who delivered the judgment in both *Caldwell* and *Lawrence*, was said to have ignored the 'intention of Parliament' whose reform of the law of criminal damage provided the opportunity for the case to be decided. In his dissenting judgment, Lord Edmund-Davies pointed out that the Criminal Damage Act 1971, the statute which gave rise to *Caldwell*, was in the main the work of the Law Commission, who in arguing for a modernisation of the law had specifically defined recklessness in its subjective form. The decision used a change in the form of the law to bring about a fundamental change in its substance, and one that went against the proposal of the initiating reform body. It has therefore been argued within the liberal discourse of the rule of law that Lord Diplock stepped outside the canons of legitimate judicial interpretation and did not properly attend to the 'rules of the legal game'. He did not heed MacCormick's injunction to use the standard rules of interpretation in order to bring about a change in the law that he (and the other judges who supported his judgment) thought desirable, but which was not sanctioned by the statute, properly construed.[2]

To ask why he should have done this brings us on to the second objection to the decision in *Caldwell*. Its effect is to make it easier to convict an individual because a jury will not, under the objective limb of the test, have to 'look into the accused's mind' in order to decide whether a risk was foreseen. Considerably more acts of damage potentially come within the purview of the criminal justice system, and it becomes easier for the prosecution to gain convictions. In his judgment, Lord Diplock spoke of what he called the 'fine and impractical' distinction between tests of advertence and inadvertence with which juries should not be required to wrestle. That distinction, however, had existed for at least a century, and it remains relevant and practical for many offences today. Nonetheless, without the barrier of having to consider if the accused foresaw the damage that his actions brought about, it becomes easier to obtain a conviction by simply asking the jury to consider whether a reasonable person would have foreseen the risk.[3]

The objection to this is again a liberal one. Not only does *Caldwell* open up the field of liability, but also, in conjunction with later decisions (*Elliot v C (a minor)* (1983); *Stephen Malcolm R* (1984)), it permits conviction where principles of subjective individual responsibility would otherwise deny it. *Caldwell* criminalises people unjustly, and offends against the principles of individual justice upon which the criminal law is supposedly based. Under the current law, the schizophrenic tramp who burns down a haystack (*Stephenson* (1979)), and the fourteen-year-old educationally subnormal girl who sets fire to a shed (*Elliott v C (a minor)* (1983)), can be convicted of acts of criminal damage. This is regardless of their inability, through no fault of their own, to match the standard of the reasonable person. Although there have been indications of a change of mind in the House of Lords (*R v Reid* (1992); cf Field and Lynn, 1993), it is sufficient that there is a risk of damage obvious to the reasonable person. That the accused could not attain the necessary standard of care in his conduct is rough luck.

A third objection to *Caldwell* stems from its disruption of a well-established order of forms of liability, based on the level of the accused's culpability. In this orthodox liberal account, intention, recklessness and negligence are ranked in order of blame-worthiness. After intention, the most culpable form of mens rea, comes recklessness. This entails awareness of a risk by the accused, and then, as a third form of mens rea for some offences only (most importantly, manslaughter), comes negligence (but only when it is serious enough to be described as 'gross': see Section 2(iv) below). Negligence involves a failure 'to exercise due caution, where the mind is not actively but negatively or passively at fault' (Williams, 1961, 100). It involves, in other words, inadvertence on the part of the accused. Recklessness and negligence are thus neatly divided in this account on the basis of the accused's awareness of a risk. The negligent actor is more properly not regarded as a criminal for most serious offences since everyone can make mistakes, and, if there is culpability, it is of a lesser kind than where a person recognises a risk of bringing about a criminal act yet goes on to take it. It was this division between reckless and negligent conduct that *Caldwell* threw into turmoil by rendering the inadvertent risktaker reckless for the purposes of the criminal law. In so doing, it not only undercut modern orthodoxy, it also threw into question the whole post-Enlightenment development of the criminal law, for the advertence–recklessness/inadvertence–negligence division had been establishing itself from the time of the Victorian Criminal Law Commissioners (1843, 23–6),[4] through Stephen (1883, II, 118–21, 122–23),[5] and Kenny (1902),[6] to the present. *Caldwell* undercut the modern development of the forms of liability within the law of mens rea, but because it could not at a stroke do away with everything that had gone before, it left the law in a state of confusion.

The fourth objection, adverted to in the introduction, is that as a result of *Caldwell* there now exist two competing tests of recklessness within the criminal law. For criminal damage offences, *Caldwell* makes it clear that it will suffice if the accused has failed to advert to an obvious risk. Later cases have established that it is to the reasonable person, sharing none of the characteristics of the accused, that the risk must be obvious (*Elliott v C (a minor)* (1983); *Stephen Malcolm R* (1984)). In the area of non-fatal offences against the person, the older test of advertent recklessness espoused in the case of *Cunningham* (1957) still has force (*Savage and Parmenter* (1991)). Other areas of law such as rape and involuntary manslaughter have also undergone periods of upheaval as a result of *Caldwell*.

The existence of these two tests has no rationale. The opportunity for augmenting the law with an objective test in *Caldwell* arose from the replacement of the concept of 'malice' in the old Malicious Damage Act 1861 with the modern concept of 'recklessness' in the Criminal Damage Act 1971. The objective meaning of recklessness under the 1971 Act was justified by the switch in terms (*Caldwell* (1981) at 965). Accordingly, under the Offences Against the Person Act 1861, which also employs the concept of malice, it was held that the decision in *Caldwell* could have no bearing on the older term where it still remained in operation (*W (a Minor) v Dolbey* (1983); *Savage and Parmenter* (1991)). The dilemma posed by the operation of the two tests of recklessness has emerged in other areas where case law has moved towards, and then away from, the objective test. Thus in relation to rape, an objective *Caldwell* test was applied in *Pigg* (1982),[7] but then apparently rejected in *Satnam and Kewal* (1984) where the requisite element of recklessness was said to exist if the accused 'could not care less whether [his victim] wanted to [have sex] or not, but pressed on regardless . . .' ((1983) at 155).[8] Similarly, in relation to the reckless commission of assaults not employing the term 'malice' to denote the mental element, a recent flurry of activity saw the House of Lords ultimately opting for a subjectivist approach to the basic requirement (*Savage and Parmenter* (1991); see Smith and Hogan, 1999, 407). Finally, in the law of manslaughter, *Caldwell* was applied in the case of *Seymour* (1983), but then repudiated in *Adomako* (1994), where a gross negligence test was revived to the exclusion of an objective reck-lessness test. It is thought that this in turn renews the existence of a subjective recklessness test where, for example, a defendant foresees death or serious injury as a probable consequence of his actions but not as a virtual certainty (Smith and Hogan, 1999, 377; Clarkson, 2000, 135).

## (ii)  Contradiction within *Caldwell*

This situation of conflict within the law, however, is not simply the product of a piece of opportunistic law making. It is the result of a deep tension within legal thinking about the character of recklessness, the roots of which can be seen within the *Caldwell* decision itself. For even in its own terms, *Caldwell* is not a satisfactory decision. An accused is reckless if –

> (1) he does an act which in fact creates an obvious risk that property will be destroyed or damaged and (2) when he does the act he either has not given any thought to the possibility of there being any such risk or has recognised that there was some risk involved and has none the less gone on to do it. ((1981) at 967)

In order to fall within this test, the accused must satisfy (1) and (2), falling under (2) within either the objective ('has not given any thought') or the subjective ('has recognised that there was some risk') limb of the test. The test is presented as a unity, but in fact does no more than bring together two tests that remain distinct in what they require. Where it is a matter of inadvertence, the risk foreseen by the reasonable person must be of a certain standard. It must be an 'obvious' risk of a criminal consequence, as *Caldwell* has it.[9] It would clearly be wrong to threaten to criminalise a person for any small risk that happens to attend his conduct. But where it is a matter of the accused being aware of a risk, there is no requirement that the risk be 'obvious', for where the accused deliberately runs even a small risk, the element of deliberation suffices to justify conviction for recklessness. Because the second limb of (2) remains a subjective test, it cannot properly be conjoined with the first part's 'obvious' or 'obvious and serious' requirement. Hence Lord Diplock talks of 'some risk' in *Caldwell* when he is considering the subjective use of the test, and not of an obvious risk as on its objective side (cf Smith, 1991, 273–4). Thus the first part of the *Caldwell* test which pertains to its objective limb is incompatible with the subjective limb of the second part. *Caldwell* conjoins but does not synthesise the objective and the subjective tests of recklessness.

The ultimate incompatibility of these two limbs of the test can be seen if we consider the so-called lacuna, or loophole, in *Caldwell* that emerges in *Chief Constable of Avon and Somerset v Shimmen* (1986) (see also *R v Reid* (1992)). *Caldwell* deals with both the person who does not foresee an obvious risk and the person who does foresee some risk and takes it. It might be thought therefore that it has covered all the possible ways, subjective or objective, in which a person might be reckless. But what of the person who recognises a risk (and therefore falls outside the objective test) and calculates his activity in such a way that, in his own mind, he rules out the possibility of the risk occurring (thereby falling outside the subjective test)? Shimmen was an exponent of the martial arts who sought to display his skill by kicking at, but not coming into contact with, a plate glass window. In the event, he broke the window but claimed that he 'had eliminated as much risk as possible by missing by two inches instead of two millimetres'. The court was able to seize on this explanation in order to claim that Shimmen had recognised the risk of damage, even if he thought he had minimised it, and was therefore guilty under the subjective limb of *Caldwell*. But they did not deny that another case might arise in which the accused claimed to have recognised a risk and to have completely ruled out in his mind the possibility of its occurrence, thereby falling under neither the subjective nor objective limbs of the test. While no such case has yet emerged, fact situations can be envisaged in which the loophole could be activated (see eg Smith and Hogan, 1999, 66 for discussion of the cases of *Crossman* (1986) and *Lamb* (1967)).

This loophole in *Caldwell* is important because it reveals the incompatibility of the subjective and objective tests sheltering under the same umbrella definition. The problem is that there is no real distinction between the person who consciously recognises a risk and rules it out (the potential Shimmen) and the person who firmly believes that there is no risk in what he is doing, and therefore does not conceive that there might be anything to which he might advert (cf Williams, 1988, 87–91; Birch, 1988). Life is composed of actions and activities that are negotiated with an unconscious confidence that they can be achieved without risk to self or others. Most people do not consciously advert to the possibility of risk because they resort all the time to systems of conduct that experience has taught them are safe. In the event, such belief may prove erroneous, but their error is no different from that of the person who does advert to a risk but mistakenly rules it out. There is in principle no difference between an action carried out *implicitly* under the assumption that it is safe, and where there is therefore no need to advert to the possibility of risk, and an action carried out after an *explicit* mental consideration that it is safe. Both involve the ruling out of risk, in the one case immediately and consciously, in the other by drawing upon a reservoir of past experience which is subconsciously applied to conduct. Yet the latter falls under the first limb of *Caldwell* and is reckless while the former comes within the loophole opened up by the availability of a subjectivist alternative in the second limb of the test.

Another way of putting the loophole problem is this:

> The person who, with gross negligence, fails to consider whether there is a risk is liable; but the person who considers whether there is a risk and, with gross negligence, decides there is none, is not liable. (Smith and Hogan, 1999, 67)

The first falls under the objective part of the rule in *Caldwell*, while the second relies on the existence of the subjective limb to manoeuvre into the loophole. Smith and Hogan argue that the law should return to the old subjectivist rule in *Cunningham*, thereby restoring the orthodox subjectivist category structure. Given the anomalies of the law, one can sympathise with this argument, but the question the orthodox subjectivists must confront is whether their approach adequately captures the moral nature of the fault the criminal law should penalise.

### (iii)   A limitation of the orthodox subjectivist approach

Thus far we have followed the orthodox subjectivists' objections to *Caldwell*, which are based upon the standpoint of advertence, and seen the way in which the advertence/inadvertence opposition works to promote inconsistency and incoherence in the law. Now, however, we need to consider in more detail the nature of subjectivist and objectivist accounts of recklessness, to see their limits and how they relate to each other. In this subsection, I deal with the subjectivist analysis, in the next, the objectivist account.

The orthodox subjectivist objects to the test of inadvertence because it fails to ground responsibility in what the accused knew at the time of his offence. In so doing, it disrupts a time-honoured gradation of fault and, in effect, makes negligent conduct reckless. But perhaps some forms of negligence can be regarded as culpable on a subjective test without there being advertence. If so, the old boundary between subjective advertent recklessness and objective inadvertent negligence would prove inadequate. Following Hart (1968, ch 6), Ashworth (1999, 197–200) argues that where a person has the capacity to take the care necessary to avoid a harm that a reasonable citizen would recognise, but fails to do so, he can be said to have been negligent in a manner that can be designated subjective. He may not have been aware of the risk but, so long as he possessed the capacity to be aware of it where a reasonable person would have been aware, that capacity safeguards against an indiscriminate charge of objectivism. Such a negligent person who fails to notice a high risk of harm may be more culpable than another person who knowingly takes a slight risk of the same harm.

Against the orthodox subjectivist, this argument seems right. The emphasis on the awareness of risk appears too narrow because it does not take into account another way in which people may be subjectively responsible for the acts they occasion, even if they remain unaware of the risk involved but have the capacity to be aware of them. Two points might be made against this revised subjectivism. The first, which I return to in the fourth section of the chapter, is simply to note that in the main the law has historically failed to incorporate this revisionist insight into its concepts of responsibility, preferring to develop on the basis of the advertence/inadvertence dichotomy. While this is hardly an argument, it is interesting to consider what lies behind this historical tendency to dichotomisation.

The second point, more substantially, is to note an area of difficulty for the revisionist account. If this form of fault is to be employed, it requires that the capacity test be supplemented by criteria to demarcate the boundaries of the harm and the risk necessary for fault. Ashworth stipulates that the harm must be 'great' and the risk must be 'obvious', but these are vague, inherently evaluative, terms, and historically the law has had great difficulty in putting flesh on them, as we shall see when we consider the development of 'gross negligence' manslaughter below. The orthodox subjectivist account may be too narrow, but it may be said to enjoy a degree of precision that tests based on inadvertent risktaking do not. The focus on what the individual actually foresaw, without reference to the evaluative questions of the greatness of the harm caused or the obviousness of the risk, anchors liability in a seemingly more straightforward question of fact about what the accused knew at the time of his acts. Questions of harm and obviousness of risk may be proper and relevant to arrive at a judgment of wrongdoing, but they could be said to involve much more contestable and indeterminate issues, issues which are occluded by the orthodox subjectivist approach. Deciding what went on in the accused's mind at the time of his act may not be easy, but it seems to produce a determinate answer: the accused was or was not aware of the risk. Deciding whether the risk was obvious or the harm great is a question with a more open quality, as we shall now see.

### (iv) A problem with the objectivist approach

*Caldwell* raised a furore because of its back-tracking on a subjectivist approach to responsibility in one area of the law where subjectivism was apparently well entrenched. Yet there was another area of law where objectivism was alive and well many years before *Caldwell*. In turning to the law of gross negligence manslaughter, we will be able to understand more clearly what is at stake for legal discourse in the subjectivist/objectivist controversy. The post-*Caldwell* decision in *Seymour* to turn reckless manslaughter into a crime of objective recklessness seemed to have excluded the need for an offence of gross negligence manslaughter. The two heads of liability were too close for both to be required. However, the subsequent case of *Adomako* (1994) 'disapplied' *Seymour* to reaffirm gross negligence manslaughter based on the older cases of *Bateman* (1925) and *Andrews* (1937). *Adomako* requires that there be a breach of a duty of care towards the victim (established by ordinary principles of negligence), which causes the victim's death, and which should be 'characterised as gross negligence and therefore a crime' (*Adomako* (1994) at 295). The problem with this approach, however, is to know what the term 'gross' means, for the test has been dogged by imprecision.

In *Bateman*, a test of 'gross negligence manslaughter' was used which distinguished criminal from civil liability not in terms of the accused's awareness of risk but in terms of the amount of negligence in his acts. The prosecution had to –

> . . . satisfy the jury that the negligence or incompetence of the accused went beyond a mere matter of compensation and showed such disregard for the life and safety of others as to amount to a crime against the State and conduct deserving punishment. ((1925) at 36)

The question of liability in *Bateman* is a matter for the jury, but the decision gives the jury no guidance as to how it should resolve the question of the amount or degree of negligence. They require a test as to when negligence becomes so gross that it is criminal, but to tell them to look for a degree of negligence which 'amount[s] to a crime against the State' is circular (cf Lord Mackay in *Adomako* (1994) at 296). Lord Hewart did provide a series of epithets ('culpable, criminal, gross, wicked, clear, complete') which could be attached to 'negligence' to denote the degree required for criminality, but these hardly helped without some qualitative definition of the required state, and this he was unable to give.

The problem lies with the vagueness of the central requirement of 'gross' negligence. The failure to produce a satisfactory definition meant that it was left to the jury to decide not only whether an individual was at fault for a crime, but also in effect to determine the content of the crime itself. 'No one', it was observed in one case, 'has been able to define where the dividing line is to be drawn' (*Tinline v White Cross Insurance* (1921) at 330) between ordinary and gross negligence. The jury is left with a 'discretion' (*Doherty* (1887) at 307) to establish what constitutes it, and judges are left to provide them with a set of factual or hypothetical examples as to where the line (the law) might be drawn.[10] Nor is the problem simply one of the 'quantity' of negligence, judged according to a common standard, for the issue of gross negligence is frequently a matter of the social perception of the 'quality' of what is done. Accordingly, there is ample room for evaluating the same or very similar conduct differently in different cases.[11]

This can be seen in some of the older cases of bad medical treatment, where the socio-political construction of the context of gross negligence is instrumental in determining the outcome. In *Williamson* ((1807) 3 C & P 635), a man-midwife delivering a baby tore away part of the uterus with the placenta, as a result of which the woman in childbirth died. The case report describes the defendant as one who was 'not a regularly educated accoucheur, but was . . . in the habit of acting as a midwife among the lower classes of people'. His error suggested a 'great want of anatomical knowledge', although other women whom he had assisted in delivery spoke of his kindness, skill and attention in delivering their babies. In directing the jury, Lord Ellenborough thought that the defendant, placed in a dangerous situation, had panicked, and observed that a finding of guilt would 'tend to encompass a most important and anxious profession with such dangers as would deter reflecting men from entering it'. Williamson was acquitted. In *Crick* ((1859) 1 F & F 519),[12] the same argument was used in the case of an irregular medical practitioner, while in *Spencer* ((1867) 525), a doctor who mistook strychnine for a tonic was found not guilty after Willes J told the jury that 'a blunder alone' was insufficient for criminal liability. In *Noakes* ((1866) 4 F & F 920), a chemist put a poison into the wrong bottle and a man then consumed it and died. The chemist was found not guilty, the judge having strongly put it to the jury that there was no case to answer on a charge of felony.

On the other side of the line, however, are cases like *Spiller* ((1832) 5 C & P 333). There the judge ruled that any person 'whether he be a regular or licensed medical man or not' who deals with life or health 'is bound to have competent skill to perform the task that he holds himself out to perform'. Similarly in *Markuss* ((1864) 4 F & F 356) (see also *Crook* (1859) 1 F & F 521, and *Burdee* (1916)), it was held that negligence might consist in using medicines of which the accused as an unqualified practitioner was ignorant. This line of argument constructs any intervention without a professional degree of skill as by itself criminally negligent, and is clearly contrastable with the alternative approach which states that mistakes made even by unqualified persons are not necessarily negligent for criminal purposes. These cases reveal that the business of establishing gross, criminal, negligence in relation to death was a matter of how the conduct was perceived and construed. There was no substantial difference between the quality of the act done in the different cases, so judgment boiled down to the employment by the jury (directed by the judge) of their 'discretion'.

This is also made apparent by comparing these medical cases with an employment case like *Benge* ((1865) 4 F & F 504). The accused had misread train times in the company timetable and had directed that a railway line should be taken up. There was a train crash and Benge, an employee of the company, was convicted of manslaughter. His primary mistake, which was adjudged criminal, was to misread the times of trains on a timetable, yet this was in substance no different from the kind of mistakes made by the chemist in *Noakes* and the doctor in *Spencer*. In another railway accident case, the judge summed up the problem for the jury in gross negligence situations thus:

> . . . what the prisoner must be found guilty of is gross negligence, or recklessly negligent conduct. However, the degree of care to be expected from a person, the want of which would be gross negligence or less than that, must in the necessity of things, which law cannot change, *have some relation to the subject and the consequences* . . . there must be a certain moral quality carried into the act for which the prisoner is made criminally responsible. (*Elliott* (1889) at 710) (emphasis added)

This is the problem for gross negligence: that there is nothing in the subjective mind of the individual that one can latch on to as the basis for responsibility. The judgment on the negligence is based upon observing the phenomenon and making a value-judgment on it. The vagueness of the objective test means that a judgment of something so ephemeral as a 'certain moral quality' in the negligence must inform the discretion that the jury have in determining the result in the case before them. Yet such a judgment is required in order to separate out cases of manslaughter from the many cases of death by accident or negligence that the criminal process does not want to prosecute.

Nor is this simply a problem in gross negligence, although it is particularly apparent there. It will arise in other situations where an objective test is used. Thus the rule in *Caldwell*, when it was applied to reckless manslaughter in *Seymour* (ie prior to *Adomako* (1994), generated the same problem in connection with the division within the law between two offences covering the same conduct, causing death by reckless driving[13] and reckless manslaughter where the latter is occasioned by driving a car. While the offences were ranked in terms of the severity of punishment (a maximum of five years for the driving offence, a maximum of life for manslaughter), they both involved the same elements of actus reus and mens rea. How, then, were they to be distinguished, so that prosecutors knew which offence they should prosecute, and juries whether they should convict? In *Seymour*, it was argued that the selection of one charge or the other must reflect the fact that –

> . . . there are degrees of turpitude which will vary according to the gravity of the risk created by the manner of the defendant's driving . . . [I]t will only be very rarely that it will be appropriate to charge 'motor manslaughter': that is where . . . the risk from a defendant's driving was very high. ((1983) at 1065)

Here we have the same problem of vagueness as arose with gross negligence manslaughter, this time couched in terms of 'degrees of turpitude'. Compare this with a subjective test, where the weight of the charge rests upon the state of mind of the accused. Take that away and the courts are left with a nebulous judgment of the extent of risk as perceived by a reasonable person. In *Seymour*, the court dealt with this by shifting the onus onto the prosecution to make the correct charge according to the facts of the case. It also recognised that it would be open to the jury to refuse to convict on an improperly brought charge. Thus the selection of the appropriate charge by the prosecution, and the decision whether or not to convict were based on an appreciation of the appropriate degree of 'turpitude', without further guidance from the law.[14]

Like the jury under the gross negligence test, the prosecutor under the objective recklessness test has a 'discretion'. Nor is this simply a result of the coincidence of two offences covering the same conduct, although that is what renders the example stark. The problem is a general one when using an objective test, because what constitutes an 'obvious' or 'obvious and serious' risk to a reasonable person remains a loose notion in relation to any offence, and so must incorporate a large amount of discretion to be exercised by the fact-finders within the criminal process.[15] The merit of the subjective approach is that, while it does not do away with discretion,[16] it provides a rule-defined empirical focus for the process of the criminal law, and it is this which makes it attractive for liberal subjectivist theorists. Without such a focus, as in the objective test, the jury and the prosecution are left with a much larger discretion than would otherwise be the case: a discretion, in effect, not to apply the law to individuals, but to make it in individual cases. The subjectivist approach provides a factual focus which seems to finesse this kind of problem.

## (v)   A 'third way'? Introducing 'practical indifference'

Here is the dilemma for the present law of recklessness. It consists of two incompatible approaches where neither by itself seems right. If the orthodox subjectivist approach is too narrow, ignoring the 'capacity' form of inadvertent subjectivity, the objectivist approach is too broad and indeterminate. It leaves the boundaries of the substantive law to be established in individual cases on the basis of value judgments about right and wrong. Here, opinions may differ and different social and political perceptions will be brought to bear. Is there a third way, based upon a concept of individual subjectivity that can go beyond advertence but which can at the same time establish determinate limits to the concept of recklessness/negligence that results?

One possibility, already adverted to (above, p 65), might be to employ a negligence or gross negligence test coupled with a subjective capacity requirement. However, such an approach does not satisfactorily evade the problem of vagueness inherent in the objective test. This is because the issue of capacity does not 'hook into' the determination of the obviousness or the seriousness of the harm done. It builds in a subjective filter for those who do not possess the normal capacity to respond to risks that they create, but it has nothing to say about the nature of the conduct that is to be criminalised. It grafts a subjective proviso on to a test that remains objective. It does not link the subjective culpability of the accused directly to the harm done, but rather establishes a ground for saying, negatively, that some persons cannot be so linked.

There is, however, perhaps the occasional hint of a third way in some of the gross negligence cases themselves, where a judgment appears tentatively to be reaching out across the great divide. In *Andrews v DPP* (1937), Lord Atkin followed the objective *Bateman* test for gross negligence manslaughter. However, he went on to talk of what he appeared to conceive of as a mental state involving a 'high degree of negligence' which he called 'reckless', but which involved '*an indifference to risk*' ((1937) at 583). This state of mind (if that is what it was) was contrasted with that of 'awareness of risk' so it involved neither simple objective risk nor a requirement of advertence. It appeared to exist somewhere between the orthodox subjective and the objective tests. Such comments were amplified in the more recent case of *Stone and Dobinson* (1977), where the Court of Appeal discussed the requirement of recklessness for the offence of manslaughter by omission. It implicitly rejected the need for advertence (the subjective approach) but accepted that 'mere inadvertence' was insufficient. It coupled together as the fault element a 'high degree of negligence' and (an inadvertent) *'indifference* to an obvious risk' ((1977) at 347) (emphasis added). To an orthodox subjectivist, such comments are opaque. How can one be indifferent to a risk of which one is unaware (cf Williams, 1978, 230; Smith and Hogan, 1999, 67)? Perhaps the courts were seeking to move beyond a too narrow subjectivist insistence on advertence without tumbling into an over-broad objectivist stance based purely on the grossness of the negligence involved. The concept of 'indifference' is inchoate and mysterious in these judgments, which are otherwise dominated by the orthodox dichotomy. What could it mean? One suggestion is that the judges are looking for a form of subjectivism that is evidenced not by one's *awareness* of a risk, but by one's *practical attitude* to it, as seen even in one's unconsciousness of it. That is the argument of one recent analysis (Duff, 1990), and if we now turn to it, we will see what it might entail. This will in turn help us to understand the historical and political limits upon the law's development, limits which, I shall eventually suggest, predicate and necessitate the current contradictory position.

## 3    RECKLESSNESS AS PRACTICAL INDIFFERENCE

Running against the objectivist thrust in the law of manslaughter, and the counterposed subjectivism of the orthodox theorists, I have suggested that there is a broader but inchoate subjectivist approach centred around the concept of 'indifference' within certain manslaughter cases. A similar point could be made in relation to the law of rape and indecent assault where the ideas of 'indifference' and a 'couldn't care less' attitude to the victim's consent have been attached to the language of recklessness (*Pigg* (1982); *Kimber* (1983); *Satnam and Kewal* (1983)). In this section, I turn to Duff's recent account of such an approach which I outline. I then consider if it can avoid, first, the objection of indeterminacy to the orthodox objectivist approach, and second, the orthodox subjectivist claim that subjectivism requires the existence of an actual state of mind to justify the name. I then go on to argue that it can meet these two problems, but only in certain crucial circumstances. My argument is that Duff has identified an important state of responsibility at the margin of the criminal law. The law needs that state, but cannot incorporate it fully in its categories.

### (i)    The concept of practical indifference

Duff argues that an actor need not be aware of a risk if his actions manifest a form of indifference or carelessness that can be characterised as callous (Duff, 1990, ch 7). It is the very fact of not consciously recognising some kinds of risk that constitutes a form of subjective recklessness. The bridegroom, for example, who misses his own wedding through forgetfulness is culpable even if he did not foresee that he might miss it. It is the forgetfulness in the context of such a mistake that constitutes a culpable form of *indifference*. This would, if it were carried into the legal sphere, be properly designated as reckless. A subjective element is present because we are concerned with the attitude of the accused and what it manifests and this can be evidenced as much by lack of awareness of risk as by its presence. Duff seeks to move us beyond the orthodox coupling of subjectivism and awareness of risk, while remaining himself a subjectivist.

A first illustration of this concept in the criminal law is drawn from a Scottish case in which two young men committed a violent robbery. One of them hit the victim so hard with a piece of wood that he killed him (*Miller and Denovan* (1960); see Gordon, 1978, 741). The argument is that such a killing is reckless even if the assailant 'is at the time so intent on his robbery (and so unconcerned about his victim's fate) that he does not notice the obvious risk to life which his action creates' (Duff, 1990, 158). One who mounts such an attack 'shows himself to be, in the very character of his action, reckless of his victim's life, whether he realises or not at the time that he might kill her'. What is revealed is a 'practical indifference' to the victim's interests:

> . . . [the] very failure to notice that risk displays just the kind of practical indifference which is [also] displayed in . . . conscious risk-taking. For if we ask *how* he could have failed to notice that risk, the answer must surely be that he did not notice it because he was indifferent to, or cared nothing for, his victim's life. (Duff, 1990, 162)

Such ignorance as Miller and Denovan showed in this case requires no element of conscious subjective awareness to be culpable. It is the very lack of awareness that is wrong, showing that one can indeed be subjectively indifferent to what one does not notice. One's attitude to an action, manifested in one's very lack of awareness of its effects, is as instructive as to one's state of mind as any conscious subjective choice one makes. Attitudes structure actions in their own way and can properly be said to be elements of a person's subjectivity even if there is no element of consciousness in existence.

But this developed form of inadvertent subjectivism should not be thought to be co-extensive with the existing objectivist law of recklessness, even if neither requires advertence for responsibility. *Caldwell* (with *Elliott v C*) establishes that a person is reckless if he falls short of the standard of care of the reasonable person. It is broader than both the orthodox subjectivist test and Duff's inadvertent subjectivism under which the question is whether the action manifested practical indifference. *Caldwell* fails to distinguish two groups of people that may inadvertently take risks: the subjectively 'stupid, or negligent, or thoughtless' (Duff, 1990, 164) and the subjectively *callous*. Both fail to see a risk, but only the latter can be held to have been practically indifferent in Duff's terms. A case where conduct would not be termed reckless according to his argument, but would on *Caldwell*, is *Faulkner* (1877). The defendant entered the spirit room on a ship in order to steal rum, lit a match to see what he was doing, and started a fire which destroyed the ship. The risk of fire would have been obvious both to the reasonable person and to Faulkner had he thought about it, but –

... if he was so intent on his theft that he did not notice that risk, he did not create that risk recklessly: he was grossly negligent, but his failure to notice the risk did not itself manifest a culpably reckless indifference to the harm which he risked causing. (Duff, 1990, 164–5)

Duff's account appears to offer a synthesis of the subjectivist and objectivist approaches outlined above, but we need to test it against the main issues within the two orthodox approaches (Sections 2(iii) and (iv) above). In relation to objectivism, does Duff provide us with a genuine means to differentiate a Caldwell or a Faulkner from a Miller and a Denovan? In relation to subjectivism, is his approach legitimately described as subjectivist?

## (ii)   Two questions about practical indifference

### (a)   Practical indifference and determinacy

Why do Miller and Denovan manifest practical indifference, while Faulkner does not? In both cases the accused are so intent on what they are doing (robbery, theft) that they do not notice the obvious risk to which their conduct gives rise. Why does the latter fall under the head of stupidity, negligence or thoughtlessness, but not the former? I suggest that Miller and Denovan's conduct could, on the evidence given by Duff, like Faulkner's, be read either way.[17] Is it not likely that one person's callousness will be another person's stupidity, negligence or thoughtlessness? Does Duff's account, as with 'gross' negligence, run the danger of indeterminacy because it is reliant upon competing socio-political constructions of the contours of fault?

Consider Duff's view that as between the actors in *Caldwell* and *Lawrence*, the latter's conduct reveals indifference, but the former's does not. Lawrence's actions, like Miller and Denovan's, displayed recklessness because to travel at high speed in a built up area could only reveal practical indifference to the safety of others. Caldwell in contrast 'intended only to damage property, not to cause injury: his intended action was not so closely related to the risk of death which it in fact created' (Duff, 1990, 166). Why so? Caldwell had set fire to an occupied hotel, and had in fact created a risk to its occupants. It is eminently arguable that his conduct did reveal practical indifference, at least as arguable the one way as the other.

A first argument against Duff's account, then, is that the concept of practical indifference rests upon an indeterminate conception such that one person's indifference will be another's negligence, stupidity or thoughtlessness. Like the division between negligence and gross negligence, there is nothing in the concept to help a jury make up its mind. It must ultimately be thrown back upon its own devices, on social and political interpretations of the events in order to find the law on the facts of the case before it. As in the old law of gross negligence, Duff recognises that the practical effects of his analysis will only become apparent after a 'detailed study of examples' (1990, 166)[18] but this is a necessary refuge for the discretionary value judgment masquerading as a rule based test. There may be a way around this problem in certain circumstances, to which we will turn below, but first, we must see how Duff fares in relation to the orthodox subjectivist position.

## (b) Is practical indifference subjective?

Duff recognises that what distinguishes the indifferent from the stupid, the thought-less and the negligent is the attitude of the interpretive audience to the conduct on display. It is the inference which 'we', the observers of events,[19] or the jury,[20] draw from the facts of the case which is relevant. This must be the case for, by definition, the attitude of practical indifference can, unlike a statement of intent or an acknowl-edgment of awareness of risk, *only* be established by the interpretation of an event. Given that the accused was by definition unaware of the risk, we have nothing to go on other than the pattern which the events reveal. But if the finding of practical indifference is founded upon the judgment not of the actor but of the onlooker, can it truly be said to be a form of *subjective* recklessness?

In the context of rape, Duff argues (1990, 169–70), that a mistaken belief in a woman's consent to intercourse may need to be reasonable before the accused can use it to deny a charge of reckless rape. The accused who acts with callous indifference as to his victim's state of mind, as evidenced in an unreasonable mistake as to her consent, should not be acquitted. Rape involves a 'serious attack on a woman's sexual interests and integrity' and the fault element can involve a disregard for these that is evinced by an 'utter practical indifference' to the woman's interests. This is present where the person is aware of a risk that the woman is not consenting but also where he has no such awareness but his actions display callous indifference. The latter is mistaken about 'something which is (which should be) essential to his intended action, since without her consent', he is engaged in a 'perverted, because non-consensual, distortion of that act'.[21] Further, he is mistaken about something that is entirely obvious 'which he must either fail to notice or radically misinterpret' (Duff, 1990, 169). This he could only do if he is ready to discount clear evidence to the contrary of his desires, perhaps because 'he has some general view about how willing women are to be forcibly seduced'. He thus treats the woman –

> . . . as a sexual object, rather than as an autonomous subject; and such an attitude, when it informs the commission of the actus reus of rape, should count as recklessness as to her consent. (Duff, 1990, 171)

The point is that the interpretation of conduct as revealing practical indifference in this example is based upon a value judgment as to the nature of the crime of rape, and what constitutes a reckless infringement of it. In order to agree with Duff, one has to accept his argument that women are not generally willing to be forcibly seduced, and that sex is a matter of deep emotional sharing rather than objectivised physical satisfaction. Yet Duff himself concedes that what is obvious to him and his (enlightened) reader may not be to one who 'has some general view about how willing women are to be forcibly seduced';[22] and we know that in our society, Duff's morally preferable model of heterosexual relations is not one about which there is popular consensus, or, indeed, consensus among practitioners of the criminal process (see Lacey and Wells, 1998, ch 4; Box, 1983, ch 4).

It is not a question of disagreeing with Duff on the merits of his substantive moral claim, but of noting that this is not a matter of consensus in a sexist society. The world ought to be as Duff wants it, but it is not. The 'we' who judge callous ignorance as to consent to be unreasonable cannot claim that our judgment is apolitical or universal. The attribution of responsibility on the basis of a conception of practical indifference therefore relies upon an interpretation of behaviour that may have nothing to do with the actual attitude of the defendant. It requires the imposition of an interpretation of behaviour from 'outside'. It is practical indifference as interpreted objectively by an audience, and having no necessary subjective link with the mind of the accused. The accused may well not share Duff's interpretive stance, yet may be judged guilty on his account. It may be right to argue politically that the law ought to promote Duff's enlightened values through the imposition of a reasonableness requirement. It should not, however, be represented as a form of subjectivism, for the actor and the audience do not share in this case the same interpretive framework, and that is the crucial matter. Duff recognises the issue, but thinks he can have it both ways. His approach –

> ... still makes criminal liability properly 'subjective': for [the accused's] recklessness consists in his own practical attitude of indifference to the woman's interests ...

But he concedes that:

> The judgment that he is reckless depends, of course, on an 'objective' judgment of the reasonableness of his beliefs and conduct. (Duff, 1990, 172)

Duff's account of the nature of rape and the evaluation of the attitudes of perpetrators requires an interpretation of reasonable sexual conduct. To impose that interpretation on the actual attitudes of actual sexual assailants may be politically acceptable but cannot meaningfully be said to be anything to do with their actual subjectivity. They do not share a common view of what constitutes reasonable sexual conduct. Thus a second criticism of the concept of practical indifference is that in social situations where there are conflicting beliefs about the rightness and wrongness of actions, the description of the practical indifference test as subjective is invalid.


### (iii)  The political limits of practical indifference

To grasp the significance of Duff's argument and these objections to it, it is first of all important to see that 'practical indifference' is not *always* incompatible with a subjectivist account of responsibility. We have already seen (above, p 65) that it is possible to identify a concept of negligence compatible with subjectivism, which would add to the objective requirement of a reasonable standard of care an additional subjective element of personal capacity to reach the required standard (Hart, 1968, ch 6; Ashworth, 1999, 197–200). This involves a conception of the actor possessing latent forms of knowledge and skill which could and should have been applied in a particular case, but were not (Duff, 1990, 159–60). If subjectivism can be extended in this way to justify a kind of negligence, it can also be extended to recklessness in the situation of callous indifference suggested by Duff – on one condition. That is that we build into this definition of indifference–recklessness a parallel subjective requirement that the accused was capable of exercising a less callous, more reflective, approach to his actions than he revealed at the time of the crime. This would enable him at a later date to acknowledge the practical indifference evidenced by his earlier actions. Such a requirement would involve *both* a latent capacity for sensitivity or compassion on the part of the accused *and*, importantly, shared moral and political values between the accused and his audience with regard to his criminal conduct. Without that, the accused could not be expected to recognise that his act reflected callousness. We would have to know both that the accused could have acted in a less indifferent fashion, and, as a prerequisite for this, that he recognised that the value judgments implicit in his actions were wrong. The second element is crucial because without it, there is no genuinely subjective requirement, only an objective reading into conduct of an attitude that was not in fact there.

The example of reckless driving (see note 13) is a good one here, for it is an area where a significant proportion of the population, including those convicted of the offence, would agree that in general such driving was in principle wrong. If such driving was done by a person who had the capacity to drive better, and who shared the view that driving with callous indifference to others was in general wrong, his actions could be said to reveal an attitude of practical indifference. We could therefore say both that the person's general attitude to the offence committed is the same as that of the interpretive audience, and that he had the capacity to have behaved with greater care and without practical indifference. All would be agreed that his conduct was in the appropriate case callous rather than thoughtless, negligent or stupid. It would be the evaluative consensus between actor and audience that would allow us to say that the accused's attitude had on an occasion revealed practical indifference. Without that, the audience would be imposing an understanding onto the accused's 'attitudinal profile' that did not exist, and therefore could not be said to be using a subjectivist test in its approach to his responsibility.

This question of agreement between the audience of judgment and the accused is also the key to the other problem of indeterminacy in Duff's argument. Just as agreement fixes the proper boundaries of subjectivism, so it fixes the actual boundaries of practical indifference in individual cases and avoids the charge that there is no real conceptual basis to the distinction between callousness and stupidity, negligence and thoughtlessness. A comparison with the orthodox subjectivist position is instructive. In that approach, the actual awareness of risk anchors the legal categories against an otherwise indeterminate judgment as to the grossness of a risk. In Duff's case, the recognition of callousness by the accused would distinguish his conduct from the merely stupid, negligent and thoughtless in a way that is not possible so long as the interpretation of conduct remains a matter for the shifting perceptions of the social audience.

Duff is right to push for a category of inadvertent practical indifference as a legitimate element of subjectivism, but wrong to extend it to situations in which the judgmental audience and the accused do not share a value consensus. Without that, the subjective element cannot exist. He is also right to maintain that it is possible to distinguish stupid from callous behaviour, but wrong to think that there is any way of anchoring such judgments, of giving the difference any measure of determinacy, without 'fixing' them through an agreement between audience and actor. But then we begin to see that the underlying conceptual substratum, the real basis of subjective responsibility and determinate judgment around an inadvertent subjectivist position, ie *when subjectivism is pushed to its proper limit*, is the existence of a political consensus between actor and community. It is only where there is agreement between actor and audience that the category of individual subjective recklessness can operate in its fullest form.

Duff has convincingly shown that the orthodox subjectivist/objectivist dichotomy provides an incomplete account of the grounds for subjective judgment of wrongdoing because it is based on the requirement or absence of advertence. Conduct can be inadvertent but reckless in the sense of practical indifference or callousness. If that is what the judges were striving to say in *Andrews v DPP* and *Stone and Dobinson* or the sexual assault cases (above, pp 69–70), they were right to do so. However, the existential basis for this extended subjective, *inadvertent* recklessness has to be a political consensus between judge, jury and accused, which does not necessarily exist. Duff shows us what is wrong with the orthodox liberal subjectivist account of legal responsibility, but he leaves us with a question: can the law live with his solution?

## 4　THE HISTORICAL ROOTS OF RECKLESSNESS

We have seen that there is an impasse in the current debate on recklessness. On the one hand we have a cognitive test advanced by the orthodox subjectivists that cannot do the whole job of describing the mental state that is known as recklessness. On the other hand, we have a revised theory that attempts to construct a more complete concept of recklessness through the idea of 'practical indifference', but which, in reaching beyond the advertence test is in danger of sliding into indeterminacy, and therefore unworkability from the law's point of view. Because it relies upon a political assessment of recklessness, it requires the existence of a social consensus to work. In this section, I argue that the dilemma represented by these two approaches is a reversal of an historical debate that occurred at the beginning of the modern criminal law. In constructing a modern rational approach to law, the aim was to narrow down the definition of recklessness, and *exclude* the broader approach that is favoured by the modern moral substantivists. In following through their argument, we will be able to understand more of what is at stake in the current debate.

### (i)　'Factual' versus 'moral' recklessness

The Victorian Criminal Law Commissioners considered the issue of recklessness in the context of the doctrine of implied malice (as it then was) in the law of murder. In effect, this was the kind of situation we have examined in cases like *Miller and Denovan* and, had people in the hotel died in the fire he started, *Caldwell*. Their target was the eighteenth century lawyer Sir Michael Foster who had stated that implied malice existed where death was attended 'with such circumstances as are the ordinary symptoms of a wicked, depraved, and malignant spirit'. Put differently, it consisted 'of a heart regardless of social duty and fatally bent upon mischief' (1839, xxiii). What does this mean? For the Commissioners, it means a 'disregard of life manifested by exposing life to peril' (1839, xxiv), but this broad, interpretive approach to malice (note the similarity to Duff's practical indifference) is rejected and immediately reduced to a question of subjective advertence:

It is the *wilful exposure* of life to peril that constitutes the crime . . . Where the offender does an act attended with manifest danger to life wilfully, that is with knowledge of the consequences, he may properly be said to have the mens mala, or heart bent upon mischief . . . [I]mplied malice . . . means nothing more than the state or disposition of the offender's mind when he wilfully does an act likely to kill or wilfully intends to put life in peril . . . (1839, xxiv) (emphasis in original)

Advertence is the sole requirement for recklessness, for they go on to say that 'No facts or symptoms evidencing brutality or malignity of mind could possibly be material to the inquiry, except so far as they tended to show the wilful intention to occasion the risk'. When the mental state was proved, the offence would be complete. Thus the move is from a broad evaluative account of recklessness to a narrower awareness based account. A profound change was occurring in the law of this period, and one that has remained crucial to the law today. Behind it, there lay an important functional and institutional reason. In Foster's account, the vague moralism of mens mala meant that the law was left uncertain in individual cases, without 'any precise and definite rules' (1839, xxiv). The use of metaphorical description within the law meant that 'in several instances offenders have escaped punishment from inability on the part of the court to decide as questions of law what ought to have been decided by juries as matters of fact' (1839, xxvii). The Commissioners made it clear that the emphasis on advertence in the law of implied malice was a means of positivising, de-moralising and thereby rendering certain the law of recklessness with regard to homicide:

> The vicious want of social affection is but an inference from the wilful exposure of life to peril. The law ought, therefore, to be founded on the original test, not on a mere inference from it as to the want of human feeling and a heartless indifference to human suffering. If the proper test and criterion be referred to, not directly, but circuitously only, there is a greater danger of error and uncertainty in its application; and what is still more important, the conclusion, which is properly one of fact, becomes matter of law, and as such is sometimes involved in doubt, which would have been avoided by treating the question as one of fact. (1843, 24)

A factual approach to recklessness is preferable to an evaluative approach that leaves the content of the law at large in the community. As with the separation of motive and intention, the aim of the factualisation of the subjective test was to take politics out of the law. The liberal subjectivist test was narrowed precisely to exclude the kind of arguments that Duff would admit. This was at the cost of a fuller mode of judgment of the rights and wrongs of risk-taking conduct, as Duff's argument makes clear. But his more sophisticated approach to judgments of recklessness is too substantively open for a system that wants to exclude politics from the courtroom.

### (ii) The roots of orthodox subjectivism

The subjectivism–advertence/objectivism–inadvertence dichotomy which runs through the law of recklessness, historically and in the present, is challenged by the argument for practical indifference at a fundamental level. It is not just a question of putting forward a different and improved account of recklessness but of raising the deepest questions about the nature of the law of criminal responsibility. Historically, there developed a concept of recklessness that was designed to secure the Enlightenment value of certainty, and, in order to do so, the law had to be shorn of the elements of value-judgment. This was achieved by focusing on the factual question of awareness of risk, and abstracting that question from the broader contextual, moral and political question of evaluation of risk. The advertence/inadvertence dichotomy secured a subjective conception of recklessness in which the question to be asked of the accused was the purely factual one 'did he foresee the risk?' On the other hand, this too narrow subjectivism was counterbalanced, on the objective side, by too broad a law of gross negligence in relation to manslaughter. Usually, negligence did not appear in the criminal picture because of the dominance of the subjective test, but in this area, where it could not be excluded because of the seriousness of the offence, it took a wholly objective form. Advertent subjectivism, with its emphasis on awareness of risk and its exclusion of callous indifference, was counterposed to inadvertent objectivism with its outright denial of the relevance of awareness of risk. This gave rise to a need to divide criminal from non-criminal conduct according to a discretionary, indeterminate concept such as 'gross' negligence.

The too narrow form of subjectivism, countered by the too broad form of objectivism, was an historical product of the post-Enlightenment criminal lawyers' attempt to depoliticise, positivise and factualise the law in order to ensure certainty of legal rule. The emphasis on awareness of risk in recklessness immediately drew the line between recklessness and negligence on the basis of lack of awareness. Thus the Criminal Law Commissioners identified alongside recklessness a lesser fault category. This involved 'the want of consideration, the omission to exercise that degree of vigilance to acquire the knowledge of danger, and found upon it those measures of precaution which prudent men from reasonable regard to the safety of human life would exert and adopt' (1839, xxv). In other words, they identified inadvertent negligence.

The practical indifference test disrupts this historical project by asserting that to be reckless can involve more than a state of awareness of a risk. One can be reckless by displaying in one's conduct a practical indifference or callousness that may not invoke awareness, but does involve a subjective attitude. This seems to be right, but it shows that the concept of recklessness is not just a mental state that can be anchored in the individual in abstraction from the broader social context in which he operates. To be reckless in this sense entails a socio-political value judgment about what constitutes callousness, and, for it to be properly subjective, an ex post facto agreement between audience and actor that his conduct did indeed reveal callousness and not just thoughtlessness, negligence or stupidity. Practical indifference brings politics back into the law by showing that recklessness is, in each case, a matter of individual and socio-political judgment. Such judgments change over time and reflect developments in the society of which they are a part, particularly as these are influenced by dominant ideological currents which enjoy power in society. They are also inherently conflictual with regard to the subject matter of the criminal law.

Thus what is practical indifference in relation to sexuality depends upon what you think about sexual relations, and the same could be said about practical indifference in the work environment, or in relation to crimes of disorder and violence generally. Were practical indifference to be incorporated into the law of recklessness, it would have the same effect as introducing morally substantive judgment into the law of intention (above, Chapter 3), or broader conceptions of involuntariness or duty into the law of acts and omissions (see below, Chapter 6). Such concepts tend to destabilise the law because they reveal that the business of attributing responsibility to individuals requires the recognition of political value conflict. The law always wishes to deny this in connection with its core concepts of responsibility in order to preserve its self-image of being a fundamentally apolitical phenomenon. The liberal legal project of the early nineteenth century, within which legal discourse still operates, was based squarely on this denial of political difference.

### (iii)  An objection: the 'objective' question in orthodox subjectivism

Against this, it may be argued that I have misrepresented the law of orthodox subjective recklessness by describing it as purely factual. There is also a political and evaluative question, recognised by the subjectivist, of the reasonableness of the risk taken. The objection is valid in the sense that, indeed, the political question is there in the orthodox subjectivist account, but the interesting issue is how it is dealt with. In doctrine, it is stipulated that, in contrast to the factual question of subjective awareness, the political question of the reasonableness of the risk taken is to be objectively decided and without reference to the views of the accused at all. In practice, because of this, the question has been marginalised. There is no case law upon it, and in its place there are offered some anodyne examples with which everyone could agree.[23] Smith and Hogan state the law as follows:

> Whether it is justifiable to take a risk depends on the social value of the activity involved relative to the probability and the gravity of the harm which might be caused. (Smith and Hogan, 1999, 61)

It may seem obvious that this should be so, but it must be remembered that there are many activities in the modern world which involve taking risks with others' lives or safety so that the justifiability of risk must often be a significant issue. The annual statistics for deaths on the roads and in factories, which far exceed the number of deaths for which charges for homicide are brought, reveal that there are a substantial number of risks that are regarded as socially justified. Such risks are often taken by people with a high profile of ideological respectability and in ways that are ideologically constructed as justified.[24] Thus 'evaluations of the reasonability of risks taken by transport operators may go some way to explaining the rarity of prosecutions following large-scale transportation disasters' (Ashworth, 1999, 185). The objective question of justifiability of risk is not normally a problem for the law because a whole process of filtering out what are seen as justifiable risks has already taken place.

This process of social construction of what is dangerous, which excludes the political issues from the courtroom, is completed inside the courtroom by the objective test of justifiability of a risk. This leaves it impossible for the defendant to raise his subjective value position in the same way as *Caldwell* leaves it impossible for him to raise his subjective perception of the facts. There is a process of exclusion of politically contentious questions and arguments from the courtroom. It begins in the wider political and ideological environment, filters into the decisions of the personnel of the criminal justice system who bring cases to court, informs the perspectives of adjudicators in the courts, and finally enters into the very bones of the substantive criminal law. If taken seriously within the law, Duff's account would require the reversal of that process of exclusion, and would challenge the political certitude in decision-making that goes with it. This is hardly likely to recommend it to those charged with reform of the criminal law, yet Duff's argument, it must be said, is morally important and builds upon interstitial developments in the case law.

## 5   CONCLUSION

The narrow subjectivism of the criminal law is an historical achievement of liberal legalism that revisionist, morally contextualised subjectivism threatens to undermine by 'bringing politics back in'. That is the ultimate problem that revisionists face in arguing for a change in the orthodox advertent–subjectivist/inadvertent–objectivist dichotomy within the law. The orthodox position was an historical attempt to exclude what the revisionists wish to include. But the revisionists are ultimately right because to be a risktaker *is* something that combines individual and collective judgment about what is legitimate conduct. The law cannot embrace this synthesis because of its pre-emptive exclusion of politics from its discourse. The upshot of this is a legal doctrine that is out of balance with itself and contradictory in its operation. Its too narrow advertent subjectivism attracts an overly broad inadvertent objectivism as its other side. Instead of a proper synthesis, the law is made up of juxtaposed slabs of the subjective and the objective which threaten to undermine each other at every turn. The current *Cunningham/Caldwell* dichotomy at the core of the doctrine of recklessness illustrates the point amply. I prefaced this chapter with Max Gluckman's perhaps idealised observation of adjudication in an African tribe. Gluckman emphasises the significance of a consensual bond between ruler and ruled, without which a person may be punished but not judged. Western liberalism posits the image of a homogeneous society; but its forms of control were built on the basis of a highly conflictual social order and had to be shaped to take account of this. A concept like recklessness, when used properly, can unite the individual and the social in a moral judgment of what risks are and are not permissible, and how people should or should not address themselves to them. Without homogeneity, however, a society based upon fundamental social conflicts must seek ways of making its judgments on individuals while cutting out the element of moral and political evaluation of conduct. The latter can only lead to political contestation within the law itself. The result is the narrow subjectivism and overbroad objectivism that we have discussed. Duff's account of practical indifference begins to show what a genuine moral community-based conception of recklessness could include.[25] The problem with his account is that he seeks to apply it to a society and legal order in which such a community does not exist. The subjectivist/objectivist dichotomy in modern criminal doctrine is the historical product of a broken society.

# Chapter 5

# Strict and corporate liability

In general, the authorities on strict liability are so conflicting that it is impossible to abstract any coherent principle on when this form of liability arises and when it does not. A particular proposition affirming strict liability can almost always be matched by its contradictory affirming fault liability. The result is that in the absence of express words in the statute judges can generally attach any fault element to it that they please, or refuse to attach any fault element; and they can always find some apparent authority or argument for what they propose to do. (Williams, 1983, 934)

. . . this great redistribution of illegalities was even to be expressed through a specialisation of the legal circuits: for illegalities of property – for theft – there were the ordinary courts and punishments: for the illegalities of rights . . . special legal institutions applied with transactions, accommodations, reduced fines, etc. (Foucault, 1979, 87)

In a world where the actual and symbolic interconnectedness of human action can be denied and where the faces of victims are unseen until it is too late, almost anything becomes permissible. (Jackall, in Hills, 1987, 198)

## I   INTRODUCTION

The basic categories of the criminal law are informed by an abstract form of individualism which developed in the nineteenth century in order to control primarily working-class deviance through a legal form that gave formal respect to the individual. A general sphere of individual justice mediated, controlled and masked social relations that were inherently conflictual and inequitable, but this was only possible on two conditions. First, the categories embodying individual justice had to be shorn sufficiently of social content so that it was impossible for the individual to appear as anything other than a 'universal' individual. Only abstract human characteristics such as intentionality (see above, Chapter 3), 'factual' recklessness (see above, Chapter 4), voluntariness and rationality (see below, Chapters 6, 9) could be relied upon in the courtroom. Personal circumstances, and mental aspects linked to circumstances such as motive, were closely confined (see above, Chapter 3; below, Chapter 8). More broadly, any claims that could introduce an element of politics into the courtroom were excluded so far as possible. This was, and is, the structural tendency within the law's general principles, yet the legal doctrine that was achieved through this process remained political precisely in its silences about individual personality and political dispute. Most signally, it was political in its focus upon the crimes of individuals primarily drawn from the lower social classes.

The second condition was precisely that it was necessary to maintain the illusion that socially dangerous and unacceptable activity was predominantly the province of the lower orders. This was, and is, achieved by a variety of ideological mechanisms in society that legitimate the present order of things, but it was also done through the criminal process itself, by virtue of a number of administrative, judicial and doctrinal mechanisms that maintained the vision of crime as a matter of individual-on-individual violence or property interference. One result of this is that corporate criminality is usually seen either as not criminal at all, or as a lesser form of criminality properly regulated by a regime of minor offences on the edge of the criminal law proper. For many years, criminologists have challenged the law's attitude to corporate deviance (Sutherland, 1949; Lacey and Wells, 1998, ch 5). However, it is only in recent times and after a spate of major disasters, involving large-scale death and clear evidence of corporate wrongdoing, that the criminal law has been forced to consider how it should deal with this phenomenon – one for which, functionally, it was not primarily intended.

Such consideration immediately faces two inherent problems that are the product of the process of historical development described above. The first is that the criminal law was *in its form* developed to deal with individuals, not forms of social organisation such as the corporation, so that its categories are unadapted to the particular ways in which corporations arrange their activities. The second, tied to the first, is that the criminal law ideologically was never thought to be an appropriate mechanism for dealing with 'respectable' corporate criminals. On both a political-ideological and a formal juridical level, corporate criminality and the standard categories of the criminal law do not fit. Yet, measured in the same scales, the wrongs that corporations do are every bit as deadly, and often more so, than those done by individuals, and there appears to be an increase in social awareness of this. The law's responses to corporate deviance are caught in this tension between a need to act and a historical and ideological tendency, instantiated through the legal categories themselves, not to.

There are two primary ways of dealing with corporate deviance within the criminal law. The first is through the strict liability offence which operates on the basis of a *differentiation* between corporate and individual deviance. Yet there is no basis in the quality of the harm done for such differentiation, only a political-ideological belief that those who commit corporate crimes are more respectable than those who commit other kinds. There exists only a sociological distinction, so that the problem for the legal categories is to maintain a distinction without a difference. In the process, the legal doctrine is forced to reveal the essentially political nature of its resolute claim to be apolitical.

The second is through a process of *assimilation* in which the corporate deviant is taken (infrequently, it must be said) to be a 'real' criminal, with only the smallest adaptations necessary within the standard doctrinal categories. Here the problem is that these individualist categories will not do the work. They need to be expanded to take into account the various ways in which corporate deviance is socially organised within the corporation. Then the problem is that, in pushing out the limits of the individualistic legal form, a very definite social and political content is admitted into the law. Alternatively, the source of the deviance evaporates into the social environment in such a way that even an expanded concept of individual responsibility cannot 'catch' the problem. Pushed hard enough, the legal form evaporates before the reality of a society organised and premised on legitimised forms of violence.

Either way, the law cannot win. In both the moment of differentiation and the moment of assimilation required by corporate deviance, the political character and historical limits of the legal form are laid bare.

## 2   DIFFERENTIATION: STRICT LIABILITY

### (i)   Introduction

As the quotation from Williams at the head of this chapter makes clear, the topic of strict liability is a difficult and confusing one from the point of view of legal logic. There are some offences, described as 'technical' or 'regulatory' in which the general rule that mens rea is required for the completion of an offence does not hold.[1] While the strict liability offence can often be identified sociologically, attempts to comprehend the distinction from a legal point of view are fraught with difficulty.

The doctrinal categories adopted to differentiate the strict liability offence do not work. In *Alphacell v Woodward* (1972), offences under the Rivers (Prevention of Pollution) Act 1951 were held to be strict because they were 'not criminal in any real sense, but acts which in the public interest are prohibited under penalty'. This description (from *Sherras v De Rutzen* (1895)), together with the observation that it was 'of the utmost public importance that our rivers should not be polluted' ((1972) at 490), were deemed sufficient by Lord Salmon to determine the status of the offences. However, broadly speaking, all offences are acts which are in the public interest prohibited under penalty, and the seriousness of the damage hardly speaks for or against strict liability. Consider also Lord Diplock's less than illuminating distinction in the modern case of *Sweet v Parsley* between 'penal provisions . . . of general application to the conduct of ordinary citizens in the course of their everyday life' and 'the regulation of particular activity involving danger to public health, safety or morals, in which citizens have a choice whether they participate or not' ((1969) at 362). It is very difficult to see any conceptual substance here. Similarly, the description of such offences as 'public welfare' offences does not help since all offences are designed to protect such welfare, and words like 'technical' or 'regulatory' are too indeterminate to do definitional work. The addition of the Latin tags 'malum in se' ('real crime') and 'malum prohibitum' ('quasi-crime') are equally unhelpful without some further definitional substance (cf Williams, 1983, 936).

Orthodox discussions of this topic are frequently confused by false assumptions which confirm the existing division between forms of liability and obscure its social basis. The first of these is a picture of regulatory offences as being composed of minor breaches of regulations. Williams' main illustration of a strict liability offence is a case of milk adulteration, a case of 'small social harm' (1983, 931), which he uses to argue for the development of a negligence requirement to weaken the strictness of liability. The 'ideology of triviality'[2] revealed in this view is supported by the example of certain kinds of strict liability offences such as those concerning the maintenance of working tail-lights on cars. However, even Williams's discussion of the milk adulteration case underplays the serious problems of food tampering that occurred in the nineteenth century and which legislation was sought to cure (Paulus, 1975). Beyond that, Williams makes no mention of the many situations in which the social harm connected with strict liability offences is serious indeed. Deaths and serious injuries in factories, on railways, ferries and elsewhere can all result from the breach of regulatory offences.[3]

The second assumption concerns the ideology of individual justice which, it is said, is undermined ('jettisoned in favour of raison d'État': Williams, 1983, 933) by strict liability offences. These are presented as aberrations in the historical development of the law (cf Nelken, 1987), which moved towards individual responsibility in the first half of the nineteenth century. Williams indicates that the offences which were developed in the second half of that century were 'social' offences, but offers no further explanation. There is perhaps a superficially attractive distinction between individually *assumed* and socially *imposed* responsibility, but it obscures as much as it reveals, for all individual responsibility is for social harms, and all social responsibilities are imposed upon natural or artificial individuals. We need to ask some more fundamental questions about the changed and changing social and political functions of the criminal law, and the way that these shape the legal forms that are brought into being to mediate social conflict. In particular, we need to ask how the different social statuses of the individual, generally lower class, criminal and the entrepreneurial or corporate, generally middle class or white collar, criminal generate differences in the function and content, and thence the *forms* of regulation.

The third assumption is a naive faith in the morality of the entrepreneur which takes him to be an ideal legal subject rather than a profit-seeking economic actor. Strict liability is 'apt to create a burning sense of grievance and a loss of confidence in the administration of law'. Even for trading concerns, says Williams (1983, 931), 'the result of a rule disregarding fault may be that business men come to regard fines as part of their overhead costs . . . [the businessman] may adopt a cynical and self-interested attitude . . .' This comment precisely inverts the relationship between strict liability and fault as it emerged in the nineteenth century. In the prototypical Factories Acts of this period, one of the principal reasons for adopting strict liability offences was that businessmen already had a cynical disregard for the law. It is business that structures law, not the other way round.

Legal distinctions that will not hold anything in their grasp, the false assumption that strict liability offences owe their difference to the relative unimportance of the conduct they prohibit, and the insistence that the measuring stick against such offences is a principle of individual responsibility – these are the parameters within which the subject is discussed. Through an historical analysis of the way in which strict liability offences emerged, and a comparison with the way in which the standard criminal offences developed, we will understand the social functions that underlie the otherwise incomprehensible doctrinal division between 'real' and 'quasi'-crimes, or 'technical', 'welfare' offences. It was, I shall argue, social and political factors in the development of British capitalism which generated these different forms of law, and spawned a legal discourse that was inherently contradictory.

### (ii) The ideological and practical context of the strict liability offence

There is a well-known history of the concept of strict liability that owes nothing to the work of doctrinal scholars, and to which they largely remain blind. This history, which deals with the genesis of various strict liability offences in the nineteenth century is an invaluable contribution to our understanding of these concepts today. It reveals that strict liability offences, with their ambiguous relationship with the standard doctrinal categories, emerged like 'normal' crime out of a particular social and historical period but with different results. Of particular value here is the work of Carson[4] in connection with the emergence and enforcement of the Factories Acts, the early statutes that regulated the conditions of labour in the United Kingdom. Although these statutes have been repealed in favour of later generations of regulatory laws, they remain essential to an understanding of the concept of strict liability. They established a pattern that has remained in existence to this day, a pattern that in particular reveals the *sociological* ambiguity of the concept of employer-criminality. It is this that underlies the *legal* ambiguity of strict liability.

The Factories Acts were among the first to forge the concept of strict liability. It was out of the experience of the first factories inspectors that the call for such an approach to criminal law emerged. Historically, the Factories Acts were the product of a variety of causes all rooted in the development of early industrial capitalism. There was pressure for their creation both from labour and from the most advanced capitalist employers who, expressing humanitarian motives, felt keenly the competition of less highly capitalised employers using sweated labour in the place of capital investment. In order to reap the benefits of their investment, the major capitalists sought regulation of the work practices of their smaller competitors. To this systemic pressure for the regulation of working hours and of female and child labour, there were added certain features that militated against a strict and effective regulation. The first of these was that even the employers in favour of reform were engaged in systematic breach of the regulations that were introduced. Breaches of the Acts were endemic to the entire productive system of Victorian capitalism so that prosecution of lawbreakers had of necessity to be selective, and factories inspectors were required to criminalise what was normal within the factory system. Furthermore, they were required to criminalise a body of men not on the periphery of moral life, such as displaced or poverty-stricken workers, but men who were at the centre of the emerging political and social order (cf Turk, 1969). Practically, this was expressed in the manning of the magistrates' bench by men of the same class and interests as the inspectors were required to prosecute.

The structural location of the wrongdoer led to the adoption of a strategy of last resort prosecution after a process of persuasion and explanation had proved futile. The inspectors resolved the contradictions of their policing role by presenting themselves as friends and advisers of the employer, with prosecution only once friendship and advice had yielded no success. They opted for a strategy that stressed the blameworthiness of the employer who was ultimately prosecuted, but, paradoxically, they did this at the same time as they were arguing for the removal of mens rea requirements from the law itself. There were two main reasons for this. The first and primary one was that the inspectors' ability to prosecute factory owners with any degree of success was undermined by the need to attribute fault to these respected members of the community before a bench composed of their peers. Magistrates refused to convict their own kind of criminal offences. A second subsidiary reason concerned the form of work organisation under the factory system. It was too easy for the owner to deny all knowledge of wrongdoing, particularly when he could show that the fault lay (as was often the case, at least in direct terms) with one of his employees who had subcontracted child labour outwith the terms of the law. The problem stemmed from the particularly social and interconnected nature of work organisation, something to which we will refer in our discussion of corporate criminal liability. This practical problem of proof merged with the general ideological problem of prosecuting factory owners to produce the idea of strict liability. The presentation of the offence as 'regulatory' or 'strict' permitted the subtle negotiation of the criminal label that would have ensued had mens rea been proved. These were not 'real' criminal offences. Thus mens rea was removed from the definition of the offence but inserted into the prosecution practices of the inspectors. This was a means of managing the reality of endemic criminality (too many potential prosecutions), of side-stepping the ideological conflicts inherent in dealing with respectable members of the community as criminals, and of ultimately gaining a minimal number of successful prosecutions.

The inspectors' strategy combined political and ideological considerations, relating to the moral position of the target criminal population, and practical considerations relating to the nature of the labour process as an organised, socially co-ordinated system. It was out of this particular history that the concept of strict liability emerged, generating the purely doctrinal arguments about the difference between 'real' and 'quasi'-crimes, or 'technical' and 'regulatory' offences. The origin of this differentiation lies not in the (inadequate) legal distinctions but in the historical development of the factory system. Industrial capitalism established a system of social classes that required different forms of regulation on different sides of the social divide. On the one side, it generated a system of individual responsibility that would in principle respect the freedom of the worker as an abstract individual, at the same time as it sought to control the crime that labour's social position generated. On the other side, it required a system of consultation and a level of regulation that would at least *appear* to control the most visible excesses of the system and those who held power within it.[5]

It is as difficult to imagine a *general* system of law enforcement of the lower social classes based upon advice, consultation and warning as it is to imagine an orthodox label of guilt being imposed on factory owners by a system of vigorous policing. The difficulty emerges from the different social functions of the legal forms, not from an a priori system of legal classification. Strict liability emerged as a doctrinal concept, first, out of the ambiguity of policing respectable men, and second, in the context of the organisational institution of the factory. From its early beginnings, it has mushroomed in the twentieth century as a result of the increase in state intervention and social regulation of industry and commerce, and has also expanded into other areas where respectable people commit crimes, like road traffic offences (see Lacey and Wells, 1998, 496–502). But its starting point was the nineteenth century desire to provide some mode of regulation, however ineffective, of respectable men.

### (iii)    Strict liability and 'real' crime: a presumption of mens rea?

There is what one might call a category failure in this area of legal doctrine. As Williams observes, for every precedent that explains strict liability, another can be found which confounds it. But category failure is an effect, not a cause. More deeply, it is an inability among lawyers and legal academics to recognise that the problems stem from the socio-political location of different groups of offenders within the system, and the nature of what is to be regulated. This is a necessary inability, because the presentation of law as a universal and formal discourse must exclude the possibility that the legal categories are the product of a prior process of socio-political differentiation. Real social differences must be absorbed within the law's abstract and general terms, but the social conflicts that the legal categories both mediate and elide do not go away, they return to generate an impasse in criminal doctrine. This is seen in those cases where a statute appears to legislate for strict liability, but the courts wish to interpret it as entailing a presumption of mens rea. Given that the real social basis for the distinction between the two types of offence cannot be admitted, on what basis is the court able to distinguish such a case from the run of strict liability offences, where no such presumption is accepted?

One of the central themes of this book is that the distinction between 'law' and 'morality' was an historically and politically motivated development that permitted both the legitimation of the law and the exclusion of alternative, critical viewpoints on the nature of social order. Legal doctrine seeks to marginalise and seal itself off from moral or, more broadly, socio-political judgments.[6] It seeks to pretend that the realm of law enjoys independence from the realm of political value-judgment. Once within the charmed circle of the law, morally substantive judgment is excluded. The law is a realm of homogeneous concepts that are cut off from the outside world of morality and politics by both techniques of legal argumentation (which are value-neutral) and by the abstract nature of its concepts (act, intent, recklessness, and so on). But this cutting-off of the law is something, we have seen, that itself had to be achieved through social and political struggle, resulting in an intellectual process of forced juridical abstraction: law cannot be hermetically sealed off from social conflict and political ideology.

It is this problem of artificially separating law from politics and morality that constitutes the difficulty underlying the famous late nineteenth century strict liability cases of *R v Prince* and *R v Tolson*. The essential problem in these cases was that while strict liability offences had emerged to regulate business interests, contemporary statutes dealing with 'individual' or 'real' crime had also created offences while apparently omitting to stipulate a required mental element. The judges therefore had to consider whether these offences, which through careless drafting had fallen on the wrong side of the sociological divide, were offences of strict liability, and if they were not, how to distinguish them from the 'genuine' strict liability offences. Why should statutory offences which appeared identical be read differently so as sometimes to include, sometimes to exclude mens rea? The judges remain silent on the questions of power and status that provide the real distinction, but in seeking a legal solution, trip over their own previously declared repudiation of the significance of morality to the criminal law.

In *Prince*, the defendant was convicted of the offence of 'unlawfully taking an unmarried girl under the age of sixteen years out of the possession' of her father (under the now repealed Offences Against the Person Act 1861, s 55), although he had reasonably believed her to be eighteen. His conviction was upheld on appeal by a majority of fifteen judges to one. Eight of the judges supported Blackburn J's view that 'the intention of the Legislature' should be read literally to require that liability be strict and that there should be no presumption of mens rea. Six of the majority however agreed with Bramwell B that the central issue was not the strict construction of the clause but that the accused had done 'wrong', even if he had not acted illegally: 'The act forbidden is wrong in itself, if without lawful cause. I do not say illegal, but wrong.' Even without illegality, there was a basic underlying moral wrong (an intrinsic wrong, a wrong in itself) that the accused had undertaken, and it was this which justified punishment, giving as they saw it 'full scope to the doctrine of the mens rea' ((1875) at 142).[7]

From the tenor of the judgments in *Prince*, it appears that the judges felt little sympathy for the defendant, and accordingly, the argument for a literal interpretation fused with the argument for moral guilt to produce an almost unanimous conviction. This left the judges in a cleft stick, however, in a case that was similar, at least in formal legal terms – the case of *Tolson* (1889).[8] In this case of bigamy, it appears that the majority felt sympathy for the accused as a deserted woman who reasonably believed her first husband to be dead, but had married again within the seven year period stipulated as providing an excuse under the statute.[9] Yet her offence was expressed as a strict one,[10] and the majority in *Prince* had held that in such a case an offence should be interpreted literally. How then could *Tolson* be distinguished from *Prince*?

One way of so doing would have been to have taken the two positions in *Prince* and turned the minority's moral guilt argument *against* the literal strict liability argument, to have argued that Mrs Tolson had done no wrong. However, in the most significant judgment, Stephen developed an important and general analysis which excluded this possibility. There was, he said, a general presumption of mens rea. However, the phrase 'non est reus, nisi mens sit rea' could be misleading if it were taken to imply a general *moral* state of a 'guilty mind', rather than a number of *technical*, varying legal rules required to constitute different criminal offences. Most importantly, it could suggest to a non-legal mind 'that by the law of England no act is a crime which is done from laudable motives, in other words, that immorality is essential to crime' (Tolson (1889) at 644). Stephen asserts against this view the need for a separation of morality from law in a way that Bramwell B's judgment in *Prince* had denied.[11] In that *particular* case, conflating legal and moral guilt (as perceived by Victorian judges) combined to confirm the conviction. But Stephen, more circumspectly, argues for the *general* political uncertainty of the law if moral claims are allowed to supplement legal ones. The requirement of immorality –

> . . . is a topic frequently insisted upon in reference to political offences, and it was urged in a recent notorious case of abduction, in which it was contended that motives said to be laudable were an excuse for the abduction of a child from its parents. (*Tolson* (1889) at 644)

We have seen how, in relation to intention and recklessness, the lawyers of the 1830s and 1840s had aimed at a separation of law and morality in order to avoid acquittal of those who could claim a good motive or excuse for their crimes (see above,

Chapters 3 and 4). At the end of the century, there were still judges willing to stand on morality where it led to the *conviction* of the accused,[12] but Stephen's judgment cogently points out the risks they run, and that they cannot have it both ways. However, his important argument leaves the criminal law with an essentially modern problem. If law is positivised and separated from morality, what is the basis for going beyond the letter of an apparently strict liability statute in order to establish a presumption of mens rea in some but not other cases? If it relies upon technical and formal concepts as expressed in standard sources, what is the licence for saying sometimes that these are sufficient, but sometimes that they are not? Must judges interpret literally the statutes that appear to express strict liability? If not, what is their licence for asserting a presumption of mens rea in some but not other cases?

In *Tolson*, having argued that the question of the morality of the mind of the accused is irrelevant to mens rea, Stephen finds a way to avoid the conclusion to which his own argument takes him. He claims that Tolson can be distinguished from Prince on the basis of the difference in the 'intention of parliament' in the two cases. While immorality is irrelevant as regards the mental state of the accused, it is central to determining what parliament intended. The remarriage of widows was 'not in the smallest degree immoral', whereas the Legislature had clearly 'meant seducers and abductors to act at their peril' (*Tolson* (1889) at 648). Having excluded the question of morality as a subjective question concerning the accused's mind, Stephen is quite happy to allow it back in as the basis for a political 'fix' of the distinction between *Tolson* and *Prince*.[13] The 'intention of the Legislature' is no more than a construction of the judges, for no reference is actually made to evidence of what parliament did intend. For this reason, a minority of five judges felt perfectly able to construe that intention in the opposite direction, by revealing the potential immoral abuses to which an acquittal of Mrs Tolson could lead.

The larger problem behind these cases was the existence of a sociological division between crimes committed by individual, normally but not exclusively working-class, criminals and 'organisational' middle-class criminals. The style of enforcement of the latter generated the strict liability form. In *Prince* and *Tolson*, however, 'individual' crimes were expressed in strict liability terms, leaving the judges with a problem: should they as good legal positivists follow the law, or should they find a way around it? What way around it was available to them given that they could not openly admit the sociological dimension to the distinction that Prince and Tolson had both 'by accident' fallen foul of? Wills J scouts the issue in euphemistic terms in *Tolson*. Affirming a general presumption of mens rea, he concedes that this is not an inflexible rule, and that there is indeed a large body of what he calls 'municipal' law which does not require it. Such law, on the face of it, looks no different from 'normal' legal provisions, so how to distinguish it?

> If identical language may thus be legitimately construed in two opposite senses, and is sometimes held to imply that there is not an offence when the guilty mind is absent, it is obvious that assistance must be sought aliunde, and that all circumstances must be taken into consideration which tend to show that the one construction or the other is reasonable . . . (*Tolson* (1889) at 636)

'Reasonableness' is plainly a wild card in this pack, but it has not been substantially improved on by later generations of lawyers. Among the factors which Wills J argues should be taken into account is the question of the moral seriousness of the crime and its penalty and the *immorality* of the criminal. Penal servitude 'seems properly reserved for those who have transgressed morally as well as unintentionally done something prohibited by law', to those who have a 'tainted mind' (*Tolson* (1889) at 638, 640). The language is similar to that of Baron Bramwell in *Prince*, to whom Wills is drawn in order to explicate the decision to exonerate Mrs Tolson and to distinguish 'municipal offences'. But his return to an undifferentiated moral-legal concept of the guilty mind stands opposed to Stephen's argument differentiating legal from moral guilt. The latter's position in turn, however, is hardly satisfactory, setting up a division between two types of offence distinguished on the basis of their supposed moral value according to the 'intention of Parliament'. Such a position gains little acceptance in a criminal law that proclaims its positive and secular character.

Morality has been excluded as a supplement to legal responsibility in order to carry through the project of depoliticising and positivising mens rea, begun in the early part of the century. But it then has to be re-introduced to explain why the formal letter of the law does not apply in relation to some, but not other, offences. This helps us understand why a judge in a modern case should argue that offences of strict liability 'are only quasi-criminal offences' in which 'it does not really offend the ordinary man's sense of justice that moral guilt is not of the essence of the offence'. They are not 'truly criminal' (*Warner v Metropolitan Police Comr* (1968) at 360), and equally why such distinctions should cut so little ice. The judges are driven to distinctions that make no real sense within a 'technical' modern law, because the real ideological and social basis of the distinction that informs their practice is one that cannot be officially conceded.

Some strict liability offences may be regarded as genuinely trivial and excluded from the full panoply of legal doctrine for that reason. However, the process that says that breaches of factory or transport regulations, leading to serious injuries or deaths, are not so serious as to be treated according to standard criminal provisions with serious legal penalties, is a socio-political, value-laden judgment. It cannot simply be passed off under the cover of 'quasi-criminality', mala prohibita, or the non-moral, 'technical' or 'regulatory' character of the offence. The continuing hints at a deeper morality and the reliance on an ideology of triviality are necessary to explain a difference in legal applications that cannot be explained in legal terms. That is because the difference has its source in the social and political nature of wrongdoing, a difference that dare not speak its name, and that the law would deny in order to maintain its formal existence (cf Fish, 1993).

## (iv) Conclusion

It is possible to pass off cases like *Tolson* and *Prince* simply as cases where the judges' perception of the morality of the accused played a larger part than it should. Prince was a 'wicked seducer' of a girl in the 'possession' of her father, and doubtless some of the judges had in their time been the respectable Victorian fathers of young girls. Tolson on the other hand was a deserted wife, wronged by the spouse who later became her accuser. Perhaps she was 'fragrant'. There is an interesting parallel here with the two leading modern strict liability cases of *Warner* and *Sweet v Parsley*. Warner's story was that he was unknowingly in possession of dangerous drugs in a container that had been left for him in a café. It was not believed by the jury at his trial. He appealed on the basis that the offence with which he was charged required mens rea. This was turned down by virtue of a highly artificial definition of the meaning of 'possession' that created a measure of strict liability within the offence.[14] The general atmosphere of 'moral panic' about drug-taking in 1968 reared its head with one judge claiming that to require mens rea would be to establish a 'drug pedlar's charter' (*Warner* (1968)). In contrast, the defendant in *Sweet v Parsley* was an apparently innocent sub-letter of a country farmhouse to what Lord Reid described as members of the 'beatnik fraternity'. She had been charged with an offence of 'being concerned in the management of premises used for the purpose of smoking cannabis'. Behind her claim of ignorance of what was going on and assertion of the need for mens rea, there rested a large group of 'respectable' managers of various premises who would potentially be liable if the offence was regarded as strict. 'Policy', as well as 'individual justice', suggested elimination of the element of strict liability in this particular offence.[15] Whereas *Prince* and *Tolson* key into the late Victorian social and political concerns about sexual morality, *Warner* and *Sweet v Parsley* are linked to later political concerns about youth and drugs (Young, 1971).[16]

However, it should be noted that moral value-judgments structure the law on strict liability in two different ways. First, the concept of a legal system employing 'politically neutral' general concepts like mens rea entails an attempt to exclude political and moral issues in favour of technical and formal legal categories. Politics and morality are excluded from the law ('the division between law and morals'), but only superficially so. They have to be reincorporated to explain why it is that some offences are real crimes and some are not. Secondly, more narrowly, individual cases are swayed one way or the other on the issue of strict liability depending upon the judges' predilections in matters of personal morality. In cases like *Prince*, *Tolson*, *Warner* and *Sweet v Parsley*, it is not suggested that these offences are 'merely regulatory', and so the arguments in them for strict liability or mens rea represent particular judicial value-judgments in individual cases.

This means that even cases which appear to be resolved on straightforward grounds of principle give rise to a question of socio-political or moral interpretation. The recent House of Lords case *B v DPP* (2000) is such a case. It concerned the offence of inciting a child under 14 to commit an act of gross indecency (contrary to the Indecency with Children Act 1960, s 1), and the question whether an honest belief that the child was 14 or over could negate liability. While falling under a different statute, the case exhibited parallels with *Prince*. However, the House held, in a unanimous decision, that a presumption of mens rea should apply and further, that the requirement in *Tolson* that the defendant's mistake be reasonable should also not apply. An honest mistake as to age would suffice.

The case is a triumph for subjectivist principle. Prince's case is described by Lord Steyn as a 'relic from an age dead and gone' ((2000) at 471), while Lord Nicholls imports the requirement of honest mistake into strict liability cases via *DPP v Morgan* and its progeny. The decision is described by Smith as one 'where the House hit the jackpot' and a 'good start to the new millennium' (Smith, 2000a, 405). Now followed in *R v K* (2001), *B v DPP* should still be treated with some care. As regards the presumption of mens rea, the lead judgment speaks of 'the established common law presumption that a mental element ... is an essential ingredient', but immediately qualifies this: 'unless Parliament has indicated a contrary intention either expressly or by necessary implication' ((2000) at 455). These words show the House holding on to the possibility of discarding the presumption according to their construction of Parliament's intention in other cases. So what encouraged the House so strongly to invoke the presumption of mens rea in *B v DPP* against previous authority? We could contextualise the decision by considering Horder's analysis of what was at stake in this area of the law. The incitement to indecency by a 15-year-old boy of a 13-year-old girl on the top deck of a bus should be 'properly regarded as tolerable, as one of life's vicissitudes' (Horder, 2001, 17) and therefore as at least permissible and non-criminal. Horder emphasises neither the cognitive elements which go to produce the decision on mens rea nor the subjectivist principle which underlie them, but the substantive moral context within which a person acts. This is not the reasoning the judges adopt in *B v DPP*, but it is surely plausible that their unanimous resort to subjectivist principle was underpinned sotto voce by a Horder-style analysis of the moral borders of the criminal sanction. This is another example of the process of intermixing morally substantive and orthodox subjectivist categories to produce a legal decision, though on its face, it looks just like an affirmation of orthodox subjectivism.

Judicial politics operate at two levels. They work, first, at the general level of reflecting the sociological division between the crimes of the powerful and the crimes of the ordinary individual in judgments about what constitutes a strict liability offence. Second, they operate at the specific level of criminalising or declining to criminalise forms of individual conduct through manipulation of the presumption of mens rea. The ultimate basis of strict liability is a judicial, and more broadly societal, perception of who the 'real criminals' are and it is this that informs the hazy distinctions between 'real' and 'quasi'-crime which bedevil the law in this area. Differentiation within the law fails because the need for it relies on a pre-existing societal differentiation that the law must deny in order to protect its universalistic and formalistic self-image.

## 3   ASSIMILATION: CORPORATE LIABILITY

### (i)   Introduction

The same factors that give rise to the ambiguities of strict liability are present in relation to the question whether or not a corporation can be guilty of committing a 'real' crime, and in particular, whether it can possess mens rea. While that question in principle has been answered in the affirmative in Britain for a number of years (*ICR Haulage* (1944); *Tesco Supermarkets Ltd v Nattrass* (1971)),[17] it was necessary in the more recent prosecution of the P & O company following the Zeebrugge ferry disaster to establish that a corporation could be guilty of the crime of manslaughter (*R v Coroner for East Kent, ex p Spooner* (1987); *P & O Ferries (Dover) Ltd* (1990)). The initial problem is that of seeing an actor or actors at the 'moral centre' of the community as a criminal. To prosecute a company for manslaughter is to perceive the 'captains of industry' upon whom, it is said, we rely for our economic wellbeing, as reckless or grossly negligent killers. In 1978, the Ford motor company was prosecuted in the United States for the manslaughter of three teenage girls burned when the petrol tank of their Pinto car caught fire in a minor accident. It had been revealed that the company had known that the Pinto's design was faulty but had decided not to instigate a recall because an actuarial calculation indicated that it would be more costly to do so than to meet damage claims resulting from accidents. Tracing changing perceptions, Swigert and Farrell (1980–1) reveal how companies became candidates for a criminal label only as their conduct came to be seen as calculated and unrepentant, and their acts as life-threatening to individuals (see also on the *Pinto* case Cullen et al, 1984; Dowie, 1987). This involved a shift from the prevailing perception that corporate crime involved a diffuse, non-personal harm to 'society in general' to recognition that a company was actually harming individuals in that society. Yet corporate violence has just as (if not more) serious an effect on individuals as does interpersonal violence,[18] so that the different treatment is a matter of socio-political construction and of how labels of criminality come to be conferred on some but not on others.

There is, however, a deeper problem with the nature of the concept of criminal responsibility. It is suggested that, even if a change in the political environment meant that there was more pressure to prosecute corporations, this would not necessarily lead to convictions in appropriate cases. The reason for this is that historically, criminal responsibility was established as the ideological mechanism whereby the punishment and control of individual human actors would be sanctioned. Mens rea is not only individualistic in that it fails to contextualise how individuals operate. In focusing fault attribution on individuals, it fails to provide an appropriate mechanism for attributing fault to complex social organisations such as corporations. Designed to isolate the individual from his social context and thereby to criminalise him, the basic principles of the criminal law necessarily find it hard to encapsulate the ideas of social and organisational complexity required by an understanding of the modern corporation (cf Moran, 1992). In the area of corporate liability, we confront the limits of the forms of the criminal law in a different but equally fundamental way.

### (ii)    Conflating individual and corporate fault: the identity doctrine

The established doctrine of corporate liability specifically identifies corporate mens rea with individual mens rea by founding the former upon the mental state of those individuals who control the company. Where those at the head of the company, acting on behalf of it, have a guilty mind, there is a direct transfer of that state of mind to the company itself:

> A living person has a mind which can have knowledge or intention or be negligent and he has hands to carry out his intentions. A corporation has none of these; it must act through living persons, though not always one or the same person. Then the person who acts is not speaking or acting for the company. He is acting as the company and his mind which directs his acts is the mind of the company . . . If it is a guilty mind then that guilt is the guilt of the company. (*Tesco v Nattrass* (1971) at 153)

This raises three problems for the orthodox approach which are connected to the social and collective nature of modern corporate agency. First, *Tesco* makes clear that it is only those who represent the 'head' of the company whose mental state can be identified with that of the company. Those who are its 'hands' do not act on its behalf for the purposes of criminal liability. But the head and hands analogy is loose and metaphorical rather than conceptually substantive,[19] and to the extent that it does any analytical work, it tends to restrict corporate liability to a very high level within the company. Thus in *Tesco*, the branch manager of a supermarket was held not to act for the company, or to have been delegated so to act by the company's board. In a corporate world increasingly dominated by conglomerates and big chain stores, the identification doctrine sets criminal liability in a way that denies the extensive delegation required to make the large, decentralised firm work.

The problem was addressed to some extent in the Privy Council case of *Meridian Global Funds Management Asia Ltd v Securities Commission* (1995), where senior personnel of an investment company acquired shares without notifying the Securities Commission of New Zealand, as they were required by law to do. They acted with the company's authority, but without its board or managing director's knowledge of their failure to notify. Lord Hoffmann framed the question to be asked in a *purposive* way: 'Whose act (or knowledge, or state of mind) was for this purpose intended to count as the act etc of the company?' (*Meridian* (1995) at 507). He answered that it was 'Surely the person who, with the authority of the company, acquired the relevant interest' for otherwise 'the policy of the Act would be defeated' (*Meridian* (1995) at 511). Lord Hoffmann stressed a realistic and flexible approach in which 'not every rule has to be forced into the same formula'. He sought (depending on how one looks at it) either to extend identification doctrine in order to reflect modern realities, or to move beyond it to a new species of 'personal liability'. The latter position was argued for by the Crown in the corporate manslaughter case of *A-G's Reference (No 2 of 1999)* (2000), but was rejected by the Court of Appeal. *Meridian*'s novelty was accordingly marginalised, and it was taken to be a reaffirmation of identification theory ((2000) at 102, per Rose LJ).

Second, interpreted narrowly, the identity theory fails to recognise the diffuse nature of responsibility in the corporation wherein a number of people at the top of an organisation may be severally responsible for acts of contributory negligence or recklessness. This, it was argued in the *P & O* case, means that corporate fault should be judged as the result of the aggregation of such contributory acts and omissions. In *R v Coroner for East Kent, ex p Spooner*, however, Bingham LJ rejected this:

> I do not think the aggregation argument assists the applicants. A case against a personal defendant cannot be fortified by evidence against another defendant. The case against a corporation can only be made by evidence properly addressed to showing guilt on the part of the corporation as such. ((1989) at 16)

The analogy with individual liability is evident here, but the assumption that this is the correct analogy remains unexplained. The argument consequently begs the question because the issue to be resolved is precisely how guilt on the part of the corporation should be established (cf Field and Jorg, 1991, 161).

Third, the identity theory cannot take into account significant elements of corporate fault which may be manifested in the conduct of the company's 'hands', but for which it is the company that is nonetheless to blame. In the formal investigation held into the capsizing of the *Herald of Free Enterprise* at Zeebrugge, Sheen J found the following:

At first sight the faults which led to this disaster were the . . . errors of omission on the part of the Master, the Chief Officer and the assistant bosun, and also the failure by Captain Kirby to issue and enforce clear orders. But a full investigation into the circumstances of the disaster leads inexorably to the conclusion that the underlying or cardinal faults lay higher up in the Company. The Board of Directors did not appreciate their responsibility for the safe management of their ships. They did not apply their minds to the question: What orders should be given for the safety of our ships? The directors did not have any proper comprehension of what their duties were. There appears to have been a lack of thought about the way in which the *Herald* ought to have been organised for the Dover/Zeebrugge run. All concerned in management, from the members of the Board of Directors down to the junior superintendents, were guilty of fault in that all must be regarded as sharing responsibility for the failure of management. From top to bottom the body corporate was infected with the disease of sloppiness. (Sheen, 1987, para 14.1)

The Sheen Report illustrates graphically how the negligence of the 'hands' should be put together with that of the 'head' in order to reveal a full picture of a corporation's criminal fault. Negligence on the ship's deck may itself be evidence of corporate fault because it reveals the failure of the company properly to structure and co-ordinate its responsibilities. The acts of individuals operating within an overall organisational structure are conditioned by the nature of that structure. If the issue is that of the liability of the organisation, the assessment of its culpability should depend not upon an analogy with what it is not (an individual or individuals acting on its behalf). Rather, it should stem from what it is, a collective structure which conditions the conduct of agents within it. The effect of deploying the identity doctrine in the area of corporate manslaughter has been that it has only been possible to convict small companies where the 'directing mind' was closely involved in the events leading to the death (*OLL Ltd and Kite* (1994)). Prosecutions against large operators have failed, as in the *P & O* case (Wells, 2001, 107–111), or that of Great Western Trains for deaths in the Southall rail crash of 1997 (*A-G's Reference (No 2 of 1999)* (2000)).

### (iii)   The responsibility of an organisation: aggregation and beyond

*(a)   Aggregation*

A new approach to corporate criminal liability was mooted in the *P & O* case through the concept of the aggregation of fault. Aggregation, however, presents a problem. While it correctly recognises that the harm produced by a corporation can involve the combined activities of a number of persons, it fails to specify what it is that unifies those activities so as to justify attributing responsibility to the corporation. It fragments the concept of the 'directing mind', in order to reflect the way in which corporate *harm* occurs, but it fails to explain why corporate *responsibility* should be based thereon. The idea of the 'directing mind' 'works' precisely because it analogises corporate with individual human activity. But if that analogy is rejected, then it is not clear what unifies aggregated actions to make them the actions of a company. In the human analogy, the directing mind controls the actions of its limbs, unifying and 'assuming' responsibility for them. With corporate aggregation, however, the corporate equivalent of a unifying mind is denied in order to reflect the diffuse character of the harm done (cf Lederman, 1985, 305–7). What is needed is some non-anthropomorphic principle that can work, as it were, behind aggregation to unite the actions of the different members of a company, and this has been sought by some in the concept of the corporation's *organisational structure*.

### (b) An organisational approach

Such an approach seeks to move beyond both the individualism of the identity doctrine and the diffusion of that individualism in the aggregation approach, and to establish the responsibility of the company in creating an organisational environment that may be unsafe, inefficient, and therefore criminally dangerous. It suggests that behind the evidence of negligence or recklessness scattered throughout the company, deeper questions about the nature of corporate organisation must be asked in order to establish the corporation's responsibility. For example, it would be necessary to establish criteria for attributing fault for the 'disease of sloppiness' in the *P & O* case in terms of the company's organisational or systemic failures.

Peter French has suggested in this vein that the organisational equivalent of individual intentionality should be found in the Corporation's Internal Decision Structure, which should be examined in determining the fault of a corporation (French, 1984, chs 3, 4). It is the procedures and policies of the corporation as developed in and through the 'CID Structure' that permit us to talk of an organisational equivalent to individual intentions: 'Corporate agency resides in the possibility of CID Structure licensed redescription of events as corporate intentional' (French, 1984, 47). In the spirit of this argument, Field and Jorg have argued for what they call 'organisational criteria' for corporate liability. In particular, they argue that a company should be open to criminal liability where it has manifested an 'acceptance' of the possibility of harmful consequences stemming from the actions of its operatives, and where it had the 'power' to do something about them. There is, in other words, a set of criteria of fault in the corporate context that exists behind the standard individualistic criteria of fault operated by the criminal law, and Field and Jorg attack the narrow, humanistic individualism of the traditional doctrinal categories (1991, 159–60).

### (c) Problems with the organisational approach

While such an approach represents an advance on the identity and aggregation doctrines in terms of its ability to reflect the socially organised reality of the corporation, the search for organisational criteria runs up against some serious problems of its own. Evaluations of whether a company either had the power to change a practice, or could be said to have accepted it, quickly become political questions. As regards the power to change a practice, Field and Jorg acknowledge that an appropriate approach to such a question depends upon 'corporate realities'. If the working of a corporation leads to accidents which 'could have been prevented by readily available safety measures, by changing the general practices and procedures of the corporation or by installing new safety devices, that corporation may be said to have the power to eliminate the risks' (Field and Jorg, 1991, 166). But what constitutes a 'readily available' safety measure would be a crucial definitional question, as would the issue of the relative costliness and facility of installing new safety devices.

For example, the debate after Zeebrugge centred on the level of investment needed to make ferries more safe. The modifications required to stabilise 'roll-on, roll off' ferries involved major structural adjustments to a ship's hull, costing considerable amounts of money. The newest generation of ferries had safety features far in advance of those previously available, so that their introduction immediately altered the balance of the debate as to what standards a ferry company had the capacity to meet. On the other hand, the Department of Transport argued that tougher standards could and should be enacted, but also that foreign competition made this impractical.[20] In light of this, how and where should the lines be drawn in the criminal case based upon a company's power to do other than it did in a shifting socio-economic environment? At bottom, these are questions of business strategy which can only be resolved in the context of judgment about a competitive economic environment.

In the case of British Rail's responsibility for the lax safety leading to the Clapham rail disaster in 1989, investment proposals in BR had had to be sponsored by one of its business sections; and safety investment, not being directly related to profitability, was a low priority. There was an organisational disincentive to safety investment although BR had formally forbidden the wiring practices that led to the accident. Did fault then lie with BR for structuring their operations, as exhorted by the government of the day, in a profit-led direction? According to the company's Director of Operations, there was a 'change in railway culture' during this period. This was not something for which the company was itself responsible; rather it responded to the government-led ideology of the enterprise culture, leading to the downplay of safety measures (see Field and Jorg, 1991). In the light of more recent post-BR disasters, it is plain that this kind of question remains relevant.

Similar arguments can be made about whether a company 'accepts' dangers arising from its operations. British Rail had forbidden electricians from wiring in unsafe ways; but in the organisational climate in which they were operating, their general way of organising their activities generated precisely the unsafe practices they had formally prohibited. Had they then 'accepted' those practices? Field and Jorg argue that acceptance depends upon routine tolerance as much as positive recognition and endorsement of a state of affairs, but ultimately the question can only be answered according to political criteria, with an evaluation based upon one's belief in the proper limits on economic activity. Field and Jorg acknowledge that their approach –

> . . . will sometimes pose difficult questions about corporate response to an external environment, for example from competition within a market economy or changes in levels of state funding or state priorities. Any value judgments about corporate behaviour have to be made in the light of such external contexts. (Field and Jorg, 1991, 170)[21]

These 'external contexts' are precisely the real contexts within which corporate organisations conduct their business. Given that market economic policies have become the dominant ideology within the state itself, a criminal law that failed to isolate the issue of criminal fault from the hegemonic, political morality of the day would surely be doomed to fail before it started. This would be even more the case if the state itself was directly implicated in the encouragement of lax standards by failure properly to regulate industry. The Department of Transport, for example, had important regulatory responsibilities in relation to both shipping and the railways. Did it perform its duties properly in relation to the recent spate of tragic cases? Questions of the power to change, or the 'acceptance' of, unsafe practices would hardly leave the state itself untouched.

### (d) Law reform proposals

In the light of these possible problems with an organisational approach, it is interesting to consider the Law Commission's proposal for a new offence of corporate killing (Law Commission, 1996). This proposal combines a modernised version of the gross negligence manslaughter test with an organisational approach to corporate fault. Under a draft Bill, clause 4 states:

> 4(1) A corporation is guilty of corporate killing if –
> (a) a management failure by the corporation is the cause or one of the causes of a person's death; and
> (b) that failure constitutes conduct falling far below what can reasonably be expected of the corporation in the circumstances.

Clause (4(2)) goes on to define 'management failure':

> (a) There is a management failure by the company if the way in which its activities are managed or organised fails to ensure the health and safety of persons employed in or affected by those activities; and
> (b) Such a failure may be regarded as a cause of a person's death notwithstanding that the immediate cause is the act or omission of an individual.

The interesting question may be whether the concept of 'management failure' represents an opportunity for, or another barrier to, the successful prosecution of large companies. It is plainly meant to allow a court to look behind the immediate causes of a death to underlying organisational causes without at the same time requiring identification of deaths with the mental states of the highest officers of the company. If implemented, would there be 'management failure' in an individual company where a whole system, say the transport system, was in crisis? What or who constitutes the 'management' which 'fails' in that situation? What would a management be required to know or anticipate before it could be said to have failed (cf Wells, 2001, 125–6)? The operation of this concept would be likely to generate disputes linked to the issues discussed in the previous subsections. It is worth raising Smith's objection that a distinct offence of corporate killing is unnecessary given the rediscovery of gross negligence manslaughter in *Adomako* (1994). Gross negligence manslaughter may avoid the weakness in the identification theory, that it requires proof of a mental state at the top of the company. Gross negligence is 'concerned with conduct, not states of mind' so that the question in manslaughter is 'did the conduct of the defendant deviate so far from the standard required as to deserve condemnation as manslaughter?' (Smith, 2000b, 478). There seems no reason in principle why a jury should not answer this question as easily of a company as of an individual. If so, the concept of management failure is rendered unnecessary by virtue of the rough and ready quality of the gross negligence manslaughter test, a test which is already part of the law. We saw in Chapter 4 how gross negligence manslaughter can be criticised for both its objective and its indeterminate character (above, pp 66–8). Paradoxically, it is just these aspects that make it a possible way forward in the area of corporate manslaughter.

### (e)  Conclusion

In the early articles on corporate criminal liability, it was objected that a corporation could not be criminally liable because a fictional entity could not possess the moral guilt required by the criminal law. The argument of Stephen that criminal fault entailed a technical and positive mens rea was dutifully wheeled out to squash that particular canard.[22] But in assimilating corporate fault to the technical and individualist doctrine that developed in the nineteenth century, a largely inappropriate legal form was imposed upon an essentially conflictual and politically controversial area of the law. In a world in which disasters have begun to transform public awareness of the nature of the corporation, attempts to render the law's form more appropriate to the nature of corporate organisation raise the political and moral questions that remain comfortably obscured by the individualistic identification doctrine. In attempting to reveal the internal connectedness of disparate agency within the corporate structure, such accounts reveal at the same time the outward connections between the corporation and the world of economic competition. Those who, like Milton Friedman, endorse the morality of the enterprise culture, deny responsibility for anything other than the making of profits:

> There is one and only one social responsibility of business – to use its resources and engage in activities designed to increase its profits so long as it stays within the rules of the game . . . [and] engages in open and free competition, without deception or fraud . . . Few trends could so thoroughly undermine the very foundations of our free society as the acceptance by corporate officials of a social responsibility other than that to make as much money for their stockholders as possible. (Quoted in Hills, 1987, 199)

The key question in seeking to expand corporate liability is what the 'rules of the game' are, but a model of laisser faire economic competition and co-ordination would draw the lines quite differently from an interventionist approach stressing social responsibility and protection. What companies can and cannot do to increase safety is a value-laden question, answered according to one's political viewpoint. In such an environment, firm doctrinal rules become an impossibility. The identification doctrine does not accurately capture (if it can be captured) the nature of corporate responsibility. Its very lack of realism, tied to the individualism of mens rea, is precisely what maintains the appearance of a narrow, 'apolitical', technical doctrine of the law removed from political judgments about the nature of fault in a social world dominated by economic calculation. To attack the law's historical achievement of a discourse rooted in an abstract, positive and depoliticised individualism is to open the doors once more to the big moral and political questions of right and wrong in a society where such questions are inherently contestable.

To say this is not in itself to oppose the opening up of such doors, merely to reveal the pressure pushing from the other side against opening them. It is to indicate the nature of the issues that are at stake behind the veil of reform talk about individualist and organisational criteria. The individualist approach also involves a political stance, but its merit from a conservative point of view is its location in a discourse that has achieved the singular feat of appearing apolitical.

### (iv) Responsibility, social complexity and the corporate form

We have seen that an evaluation of the corporation's internal mode of organisation could not be made in isolation from the external social environment in which it operates. Identification of the organisational structure as what unifies corporate activities and justifies the attribution of fault to the corporation immediately opens up the question of the relationship between the internal organisation of the corporation (what makes it a 'corporate individual') and the external environment (its social context). Expanding the legal form breaks down the decontextualisation achieved by the orthodox mens rea and identification doctrines. The social character of corporate organisation, and the problems this poses for attempts to attribute fault and punishment to corporations, is also seen in relation to the issue of the social *complexity* of modern economic organisation. This is both in terms of the inter-connection of companies, and the broad co-ordinative roles they play in society as a whole. The former leads to potential problems with regard to corporate *responsibility*, while the latter leads to problems with regard to corporate *punishment*.

### (a) Economic integration and corporate responsibility

The modern corporation is organised within what Collins (1990) calls a 'complex pattern of economic integration'.[23] Those nominally in charge of a company (those who normally would be regarded as its 'head' in legal doctrine) may in fact have little control over its activities for a number of reasons. By virtue of complex systems of company ownership within a conglomerate financial structure, of relationships of contracting and sub-contracting with dependent ancillary com-panies, and of positions of strong influence enjoyed by partial, non-controlling owners or third parties such as banks, the locus of actual responsibility for a criminal act may reside far away from the formal head of a particular company, *even if* he is himself an immediately responsible agent.

The point is that the reality of interlocking corporate units, in which actual control is quite different from legal control, means that the concept of an individual corporation's responsibility fails to correspond to the nature of corporate inter-connection. It would be possible because of this interconnection for companies to shield themselves from responsibility for their actions by setting up or contracting with subsidiary companies whose responsibility it is to carry out potentially criminal activities. It is said in America that companies appoint senior personnel as pre-emptive scapegoats in order to evade opprobrium falling on the company as a whole (the 'Company Vice-President responsible for going to jail'). One individual carrying the responsibility for fault permits business to proceed as usual. Should corporate liability ever be developed more expansively by the courts, such a strategy might not be so effective, for the fault of the senior executive might be too readily identified with that of the company. At such a point, the sensible thing for a company to do would be to establish or engage with a separate corporate entity in order more completely to avoid identification between its acts, omissions and ensuing crimes.[24]

One reason given by the families of those killed in the Piper Alpha disaster for abandoning their attempt to mount a private prosecution against the oil rig company was its sale by the parent company, Occidental (Wells, 2001, 160). The ability of companies to disaggregate, to dissolve or to reconstitute themselves makes the question of responsibility harder to resolve both in theory and in practice.

### (b)    Social co-ordination and corporate punishment

The second issue concerns the dualistic nature of the corporate entity. From the legal point of view, the company is a corporate agency, organised to produce effects within the world. From the social point of view, it is an artificial representation of the interests of those who invest in it (in the case of a private company) or those on behalf of whom it operates (in the case of a public utility). From this second point of view, the corporate body is no more than the juridical form utilised to organise the production of goods, services, profits and employment. To punish a corporation is, because of this dualism, to affect both the company as a corporate actor and at the same time all those persons who as investors, employees, and consumers are the living human beings within the company's orbit. The corporate form focuses our attentions on the agency of the company itself, but the company is at the same time a means of organising a wide variety of social needs and functions. The ultimate recipient of the penal sanction, 'behind' the corporate form, is a group of individuals who may have little or nothing to do with the wrong that has occurred (cf Coffee, 1981).

The joint stock company socialises the productive and wealth-extracting processes of the capitalist labour process, in a way that diffuses the impact of penalising a company. It makes it impossible to punish a juridical artifice without at the same time penalising a wide variety of social actors – shareholders, workers, consumers – in relation to whom the limited liability company stands as a kind of artificial representative. To identify and punish the 'corporate individual' in this context is to address a legal form which hardly approximates to the reality of corporate organisation in society. We may say that the shareholders, for example, bear the risk of their investment, but do we say the same for the workers, consumers and others who may in practice be affected by the effective punishment of a company? Because of this, there is an in-built limitation on the typical corporate punishment, the fine, that Fisse describes as the 'deterrence trap'.[25] Economic deterrence required to match wrongdoing may exceed the company's ability to pay, eventually driving it to the wall. Such a result affects society as a whole, not just the company and its shareholders.

One response to this problem is to consider forms of non-financial sanction. If fines hurt too much, then other punishments less potentially damaging to the corporation can be considered. Proposals include the use of 'equity fines' or stock dilution, in which shares in the company are issued to the state in place of monetary fines, enforced adverse publicity, community service, and corporate probation orders or punitive injunctions focused on restructuring the firm's internal organisation (Coffee, 1981; Fisse, 1990). Box (1983, ch 2) has suggested nationalisation of the company for limited periods of time with public appointed directors, community service and compensation orders. These different suggestions provide a number of alternative ways of punishing the criminal corporation in ways that accentuate either the non-financial sanctioning possibilities, or the potential to establish mechanisms for the reform of the internal structures of the corporation, but they contain two problems.

The first concerns the possible effectiveness of non-financial sanctions upon organisations geared to the making of profits. The cynical view would be to suggest that if it isn't hurting the corporation in its pocket, it isn't hurting it at all. It might be suggested that 'brass-necked' corporations are unlikely to feel terribly embarrassed by adverse publicity unless it affects, say, consumer attitudes to their product. But Fisse suggests that such publicity might act to 'shame' the corporation and diminish corporate prestige. He may be correct to say that the top officials of some corporations are embarrassed by adverse publicity, even if it does not affect company sales, but the question really is how serious a sanction this can be when weighed against the *primary* economic motivations of the corporation. This and other non-financial sanctions can only have secondary effects if they do not affect the company's primary motivation, so that their ability to supplement the financial sanction is strictly limited. Yet proposals like these stem from the already recognised inadequacy of the financial sanctions themselves as a result of the 'deterrence trap'.

The 'deterrence trap' provokes thoughts on alternative sanctions to increase punishment, yet the alternatives generally appear as lesser sanctions when measured against the corporation's primary aim. Such sanctions do not side-step the basic problem of the financial sanction. Since corporations are at bottom concerned with profitability, punishment will only have serious effects to the extent that corporations' transaction costs, and therefore their balance sheets, are affected by alternative sanctions. But then the alternative sanction is simply an alternative to the monetary fine, and subject to the original objection. If it is to work, the alternative sanction has to hurt; but if it hurts, it must affect transaction costs, having the same deleterious effect as the financial sanction.

The second problem concerns the attempt to use sanctions to restructure the company's working practices and safety mechanisms. Coffee has suggested that courts appoint management-consulting firms or business school teams 'to determine if inadequate internal reporting or information flow' contributed to crime (1981, 448–55). He notes, however, that such a disposal would interfere with managerial autonomy and that any attempts to legislate would be resisted by corporations. Further, Coffee suggests that such probation orders would have to be court-administered, for regulatory agencies which might otherwise be involved 'can be lobbied, and their willingness to pursue corporate misbehaviour waxes and wanes . . . with the tide of political changes'. But the same would be true of 'management consulting firms' and 'business school academics' appointed by the court, Coffee's own preferred solution (cf Fisse and Braithwaite, 1988).

The problem with such an approach is that it affects the control of the company. It therefore steers the criminal justice system into a political conflict with the economic ideology of laisser faire. Fisse and Braithwaite (1988, 501–2) concede that the 'dominant impact of probation or punitive injunctions would be interference with managerial power and prestige, not exaction of cash or dilution of the value of shares'. They add, however, that the main question is whether they could be used without 'subjecting corporations to inefficient and excessively intrusive governmental intervention'. Such a system might be more costly than a system of fines, and they suggest that sentencing criteria 'should be devised so as to maximise freedom of enterprise in compliance systems'. Thus what is proposed is a system that will be costly, and which will buy legitimacy at the expense of not being too interventionist. It will rely on the self-activity of the criminal corporation and the understanding of the business community as to what is feasible. Such an approach based upon co-operation and consultancy appears to have much in common with the ways in which ineffectual statutory bodies like the factories inspectorate operate. Yet the focus on corporate crime in recent years stems precisely from a *dissatisfaction* with such approaches (see Carson, 1970, and the discussion above, Section 2).

There are stronger versions of this restructuring argument, such as Box's proposal that criminal corporations should be nationalised and then reformed. However, whether it is a stronger or weaker version, the basic problem remains of confronting the political and economic power of a dominant interest group in society. Box's politically corporatist restructuring sanction is in many ways the most interesting, but the open grasp of the nettle of politics both reveals the extent of the issues at stake and suggests the likelihood of success. The deepest problem for both the 'minimalist' and the 'maximalist' (and to which their different approaches are a response) is that of the size and strength of modern corporate power. This means that alternative sanctions will either gain acceptance at the cost of ineffectiveness, or not gain acceptance at all this side of a social revolution.

Further, the dominance of corporate power in the nation state has to be placed alongside the effects of the internationalisation of capital, which impart to the idea of the successful control of the major transnational corporations a utopian quality. Corporations will either bargain organisational régimes to suit themselves or relocate elsewhere (Carson, 1981). The control of organisational crime will be at the cost of unemployment and relocation of corporate violence to third world countries with more pliant régimes (Box, 1983, 78). Were such sanctions ever to be introduced, the smaller, nationally based corporations would at best be caught by such arrangements. The big fish would swim free, made all the more competitive by the lower 'transaction costs' resulting from their ability to evade sanctions and the travails of their national competitors.

The issue of sanctioning corporations takes us far from the calm, apparently apolitical, waters of the national criminal justice system. That system was designed functionally to control 'natural' individuals, wrenched from the social context of their crime. To try to transfer those forms from the political context of control of the lower social classes ('street crime') to that of control of an organisational élite ('suite crime') is to ignore the basic differences in content, purpose and function of the criminal law. These impose serious limitations on the possibilities for sanctioning corporations through it. That is not to say the effort should not be made, only that one should be sanguine about the limits of what can be achieved (cf the ambivalent conclusions to Wells 2001, 164–8).

## 4 CONCLUSION

The standard mens rea doctrine of the criminal law is a singularly inappropriate form with which to organise the control of the corporation. Yet corporations are responsible amongst other things for acts of violence that in their potential scope and impact far outweigh the effects of similar culpable acts performed by individuals. It is not unnatural in such a situation to wish to criminalise the malefactor, be it a natural or artificial person. Militating against this are two crucial differences between the natural and the corporate person. First, there is the actual difference between a human and a corporate individual. The former is *relatively* easily represented within doctrine, since agency is immediately located within a single person who can be treated in isolation from the social relations of which he is a part. The latter is different, being a work of juridical artifice which stands in the place of a set of social processes of production, labour, profit-making and exchange. To locate responsibility in a company is to locate it in an irreducibly social phenomenon. The individual agent, it is true, is also irreducibly social in its being but it differs from the corporation in having a naturally individuated basis, the human being. The form of the juridical individual maps onto the actual human individual in a way that it cannot with the corporation. Look behind the corporation and all that can be seen is a social process, not an actual human being.

The second issue concerns the irreducibly political nature of judgments about corporate agency, and the way that these cannot be represented within doctrine because of the social nature of corporate activity. With the human individual, the law has managed the clever trick of representing essentially political acts as depoliticised crimes, recognised under criteria that appear universal and apolitical. The technical doctrine of mens rea is crucial in conferring liability on individuals without apparent recourse to the moral and political grounds for action. But this achievement of an apparently depoliticised legal form is called into question by the nature of corporate deviance, in the realms of both strict and corporate criminal liability.

With regard to strict liability, the morally central character of the employer-criminal coupled with the practical problems of establishing guilt within the manufactory process conduced to the establishment of a guilt-free form of liability. This was in large part a directly political and ideological result of the position of the employer within the social order. But how could this be admitted in the context of a doctrine that was consciously attempting to rule out moral and political considerations within the law? The only solution was to attempt to find technical legal justifications for treating the two kinds of offence differently. That has proved impossible, so we are left with vague explanations concerning the nature of 'regulatory offences' and 'real crimes'. These are plainly inadequate, so that occasionally judges let the cat out of the bag by conceding, like Lord Reid, that the issue is ultimately morally evaluative. In reality the legal category follows the moral and political standing of the malefactor rather than the malefaction, as the law would like it to be seen. The political nature of the treatment of the employers undermines the pretence that the employees are being dealt with according to an apolitical, universal legal doctrine. The problem of defining strict liability in relation to the crimes of the powerful undermines the attempt to depoliticise liability for the crimes of the powerless.

With regard to corporate criminal liability, there is an attempt (exceptionally: most of the actual criminal work, to the extent that it is done, uses offences of strict liability) to apply the individualistic mens rea doctrine to the corporation. But the effects are equally problematic. The social nature of corporate production, both as a matter of internal company organisation and as a matter of the relationship with the external environment, makes it clear that violence and other forms of damage carried out within our society cannot be comprehended within an individualistic form. Nor can the issue of formal harm be separated from a political debate about the nature of wrongdoing. If a company's grossly inadequate safety standards lead to death and injury, is that a matter for liability, or simply a regrettable fact of life in a world of profit-driven motivation? The answer to that question can only be political, but it is precisely the connection between crime and politics that the criminal law has sought to obscure in relation to 'ordinary' crime for a hundred and fifty years. Once again, the crimes of the powerful and the way they are treated cast a powerful, critical light on the crimes of the powerless and how they are treated.

The form of the legal individual at the heart of the traditional criminal law doctrine is clearly exposed as a political artifice by the attempts to *differentiate*, in the case of strict liability, the deviant acts of the corporation from those of the ordinary offender. Differentiating the two reveals that forms of deviance comparable in their effects, for example violence in the factory through unsafe machinery and violence on the streets amongst individuals, can only be treated differently by affirming the relative social and political acceptability of some forms of violence but not others. Differentiation exposes the historical and political character of the apolitical juridical individual.

Attempts to *assimilate* the criminal liability of the corporation and the individual also reveal very clearly the limits of legal individualism as a form of mediation of social control processes. Even if corporate criminality is designated as 'really criminal', there remains the problem of encapsulating forms of deviance that involve widespread social interconnectedness within an individualistic form. Corporate violence is the outcome of processes of social organisation in a way that individual violence is not. A straightforward imposition of legal individualism, for example, the 'head and hands' doctrine, is consequently inappropriate. But attempts to extend the legal form to cover the company both expose the underlying political nature of the definition of deviance, and lead us to see that major kinds of violence are organised socially, inherent in socially legitimate networks, and uncatchable within traditional legal forms. Changing these forms leads to an open confrontation of the nature of violence in our society, and makes us consider anew the zeal with which society pursues conventional crime.[26] Assimilation, like differentiation, exposes the historical and political character of the 'apolitical' juridical individual. If the law assimilates, in corporate criminal liability, it reveals the actual socio-political control functions that rest behind its individualistic forms, for élite criminality cannot be conceptualised within them. If the law differentiates, in strict liability, the control function is again exposed, for it is impossible to explain in formal terms what the difference is. The socio-politics of corporate deviance drives a wedge between the criminal law's form and its content. It undermines any attempts to give that law determinate form, and all conceptual solidity 'melts into air'.

# Part III

# Actus reus

# Chapter 6

# Acts and omissions

... it is apparent that the category of involuntary acts is very limited. (*Bratty* (1961) at 533, per Lord Denning)

... findings of voluntariness or involuntariness ... are policy based determinations and only superficially findings of legal fact ... The concepts of choice, waiver, consent, etc, the key operative concepts ... are highly subject to conscious and unconscious manipulation. (Vandervort, 1987, 217)

A sees B drowning and is able to save him by holding out his hand. A abstains from doing so in order that B may be drowned, and B is drowned. A has committed no offence. (Stephen, 1887, Art 212)

[Modern society] almost covets its sense of being disturbed at the disintegrating ties of community. It is simply shocking that someone would see an accident victim and fail to render aid. It is 'morally self-evident' that some cases of failing to avert harm should be treated as homicidal. (Fletcher, 1978, 633–4)

## I   INTRODUCTION

Criminal lawyers work towards a system of rules that is intended to be formal, technical, consistent in principle, and to do justice to individuals. This discourse is always under threat because it is built on concepts that enforce exclusions: the competing politics of non-élite groups, the social context of criminal activity, and the political perceptions of the élite group itself. The principles of responsibility upon which the criminal law is based are given their particular shape by what is excluded from the subjective assessment of fault, and by the political interventions of the social élite charged with their development. That which is excluded, the subterranean forces of the political and the ideological, continually irrupts within the law, unsettling its formal appearance of consistency and disturbing its conceptual categories. In this and the following chapter, I explore the working out of this contradictory process in relation to the primary elements of actus reus: acts, omissions and causes. In all three areas, I will argue that the fundamental issue is the construction of the abstract individual in legal doctrine. I will note that that construction operates differently as between acts and omissions, and acts and causes for reasons that concern the functional operation of the different concepts within the social and legal context.

Acts, omissions and causes represent the bedrock of the law of actus reus. Like mens rea, actus reus is not a tightly defined concept but rather a loose 'common denominator' which denotes the requirement that every crime requires an external element. Accordingly, it is best described negatively:

> All that can be said, without exception, is that a crime requires some external state of affairs that can be categorised as criminal. What goes on inside a man's head is never enough in itself to constitute a crime. (Williams, 1983, 146)

This formulation indicates an immediate point of connection between the common law and the positive side of liberal values, for it is made clear that it is no crime to think criminal thoughts.[1] Against this, it must be pointed out that the practical impact of this libertarian stance is blunted by the wide way in which the law draws certain criminal categories, such as conspiracy (Williams, 1983, 146–7; Spicer, 1981). However, the aim of this chapter is to probe the philosophical principles underlying the law of acts, and this takes us away from the practical question of whether thoughts need to be translated into actions and into the mirror question of whether actions have to be accompanied by thoughts.

## (i)   Acts

The law of actus reus has as its central requirement that acts must be carried out *voluntarily*. In the next section, I argue that there is a close parallel between the way that voluntariness is constructed in the law of acts and the way that motive and intention are divided in the law of intention. In relation to acts, a narrow physical conception of the nature of involuntariness squeezes out subjective excuses based upon a broader moral conception which might incorporate the social context of action. The *physical* conception operates as a 'technical' criterion for judging conduct involuntary, because it excludes all considerations other than the abstract and general issue of whether or not the act was a conscious one. It therefore parallels the technical conception of intention, which artificially separates out the question of *how* an intention is formed from the question of *why* it is formed. The *moral* conception of involuntariness, on the other hand, opens up questions about the social context in which actions are formed and in which broader judgments, about whether the accused could have helped doing what he did, become relevant. The exclusion of this conception, which is potentially more political in its effect, parallels the exclusion of motive from the law of intent.

Furthermore, there is a second form of exclusion at work within the law of voluntary acts. This second form of exclusion operates by imposing particularly tight limits on the conditions under which even a physically involuntary act can be claimed. Paradoxically, one of the ways in which this is done is by suspending the technical conception of an involuntary act by an argument from what can be called *moral voluntariness*. The argument is that even if an act is physically involuntary, in the technical sense described, the law is able to deny the relevance of that involuntariness in favour of a significant episode of prior fault. Having excluded the broader moral involuntariness in order to secure a narrow conception of physical involuntariness, the law then undermines its own narrow technical concept by means of a renewed commitment to a moral conception. The *exclusion* of moral involuntariness has the effect of narrowing and de-moralising the subjective fault category, in order to hold the line against the introduction of politics into a defence. The *inclusion* of moral voluntariness 'at the other end' has the effect of re-moralising that category with the effect of securing convictions in situations where the judges believe that control must be affirmed, and application of the technical test might secure an acquittal. The resultant to-and-froing in the cases has a close parallel with what we have witnessed in the law of intention.

## (ii)   Omissions

While the first quotation at the head of the chapter indicates that the law is extremely broad in relation to the concept of a voluntary act, the third indicates that it is extremely narrow in relation to the concept of a criminal omission. The nature of the law of omissions, and the reason for its narrowness are considered in the second main section of the chapter. It will be argued that the law's shape is determined in both contexts by a narrow, individualist focus, although this affects the two areas differently because of the difference in content and practical function of the two concepts.

In relation to omissions, a narrow conception of omission operates not to extend liability but to restrict it. The reason for this is to draw a line between the omissions of the 'criminal few' and the 'virtuous many'. It is in the nature of the concept of an omission that it is very hard to draw a line between the kind of omissions that ordinary citizens in a Western society are responsible for every day, and the omissions of those that the state would wish to criminalise. In a world in which 'structural' or economic injustice and violence associated with poverty and discrimination prevail with consequences in terms of loss of life and serious injury to body and mind, it is necessary to draw a tight line around criminal omissions. Their scope is narrowly fixed by virtue of the use of a 'contractual' model which affirms the existence of a duty to act only where a prior commitment has been declared. In the process, certain 'obvious' duty situations, such as that of easy rescue described above by Stephen, get lost. In exploring the reasoning behind this problem, and the alternative view provided by a communitarian model of social responsibility, we are able to see the underlying socio-political and theoretical character of the law in this area.

A criminal act already designates a criminal actor, while a failure to act fails to differentiate immediately the one the state wishes to criminalise from the many it does not. The law's solution is to draw the line by means of a narrow individualism which *excludes* a broad band of 'normal' respectable omitters, just as a parallel narrow individualism in relation to the voluntariness of acts *includes* a wide sweep of criminal actors.

## 2   ACTS

The liberal philosophy which underlies the criminal law requires that an act be voluntary. Where an individual acts unconsciously or consciously but by reflex (see the examples in Hart, 1968, 95–6), 'there is not "really" a human action at all and certainly nothing for which anyone should be made criminally responsible' even if liability is 'strict' (Hart, 1968, 107). There is a distinction between doing something and having something happen to one, 'and this distinction is a basic postulate of a moral view of human behaviour' (Williams, 1983, 148; cf Moore, 1984). To act involuntarily is not to act at all, but what is meant by 'involuntary' in this context?

## (i)   Conflicting conceptions of voluntariness

### (a)   Physical involuntariness versus moral involuntariness

In his *Lectures on Jurisprudence* (1869, I, 427), John Austin, who was also a Criminal Law Commissioner, wrote that 'the only objects which can be called acts, are consequences of Volitions. A voluntary movement of my body, or a movement which follows a volition, is an act.' 'Volitions' he defines as 'desires of those bodily movements which immediately follow our desires of them' (1869, I, 426). Thus a voluntary act entails a bodily movement (most basically, some kind of muscular contraction) which is accompanied by a desire for such a movement or contraction. The volition that accompanies the movement is sometimes attributed to 'the will' as a separate mental phenomenon, but Austin argues that there is no such thing apart from the existence of the volitions that make the movement voluntary.

Austin's account is written in the shadow of the early liberal philosophy of action of Hobbes (whom he cites as a marginal note), so that the connections in this area of the law between legal concept and liberal theory are direct and manifest.[2] Since Austin's time, the formulation of the issue has changed, but not in a way that radically affects its character. Hart has objected that it is artificial to break down the components of voluntary acts and claim that people desire muscular contractions. Rather they 'desire to do some action (eg hit someone) which *involves* muscular contractions' (1968, 103). Human action can only properly be described at the level of human beliefs about, and consciousness of, action. Refusing to reduce it to the pseudo-scientific level of a desire for muscular contractions, Hart maintains the importance of conscious control in agency: 'the controlling agency is not a desire for muscular movements but the mind of a man bent on some conscious action' (Hart, 1968, 106).

It is this conception of physical voluntariness and involuntariness with which the law primarily operates. However, elsewhere Hart has also described another potentially more expansive *moral* conception which stresses the connection between voluntariness and 'universal ideas of fairness or justice'. More specifically he argues that 'unless a man has the capacity and a fair opportunity or chance to adjust his behaviour to the law its penalties ought not to be applied to him' (Hart, 1968, 181). Similarly, in the context of voluntariness in the law of causation, he writes of 'a conception of a human agent as being most free when he is placed in circumstances which give him a fair opportunity to exercise normal mental and physical powers and he does exercise them without pressure from others' (Hart and Honoré, 1985, 138), and of the need for a 'free, deliberate and informed act or omission of a human being' (Hart and Honoré, 1985, 136).[3] These conditions for voluntary action are less atomised and potentially more 'contextual' than under the test of consciousness.

Agency is located in a broader moral and social environment, in the situation in which the person acts. This requires consideration of the degree of deliberation and information, and whether there was a fair opportunity to exercise the normal basic powers of control that go into individual acts.

While the law has generally recognised that physical involuntariness operates to repudiate the existence of an act,[4] its reaction to moral involuntariness has always been lukewarm. The paradigm reaction is that of Stephen who drew a clear line between what he called cases of 'compulsion' (duress, necessity, and marital coercion: Stephen, 1883, II, 105–10) and situations of involuntariness. People who acted under compulsion operated in situations where they could not act freely, yet they acted voluntarily. He endorses the narrow physical concept of involuntariness. This leads him to argue that 'a criminal walking to execution is under compulsion if any man can be said to be so, but his motions are just as much voluntary actions as if he were to leave his place of confinement and regain his liberty' (1883, II, 102). But is not the person walking to the gallows, in a perhaps slightly different sense, *also* acting involuntarily? Stephen makes explicit the distinction between physical and moral involuntariness, but in a language that indicates their similarity:

> The importance of rightly understanding the nature of voluntary actions consists in the light which it throws on the nature of compulsion, and so on the law relating to it, and on the reasons on which it is founded . . . [T]he first point to be observed is that there is no opposition between voluntary action and action under compulsion. The opposite to voluntary action is involuntary action, but the very strongest forms of compulsion do not exclude voluntary action . . . Freedom is opposed to compulsion as voluntary is to involuntary. A man is free when he can do what he likes; in other words, when he is not compelled to do what he dislikes . . . but whether a man is free or under compulsion he is equally a voluntary agent, and choice and volition equally enter into and regulate all his voluntary actions. (1883, II, 101–2)

We can recognise the line Stephen seeks to draw between involuntariness in the narrow physical sense, and compulsion as a broader conception of human unfreedom. But his distinction between physical unconsciousness as a denial of *voluntariness* and a broader form of compulsion as a denial of *freedom* makes little sense in terms of the construction of fault. The result is to marginalise a broader conception of involuntariness in favour of a narrower one. This division has remained central to the criminal law, in which the broader conception is hived off into a separate category of excuse (duress, necessity: see below, Chapter 8) in certain narrowly defined circumstances. While it rests uncomfortably with the main doctrines of act and mind, it provides a safety valve in extreme cases, as well as a form of 'conceptual sealant' to prevent the leakage of questions about the context and value of conduct into the primary mechanisms of fault attribution. A broad, moral concept of involuntariness would challenge the idea of individual responsibility in a way that the narrow conception of physical involuntariness cannot. It would allow a variety of excuses concerning the reasons why people commit crimes to infiltrate the concept of an act. Thus in the Canadian case of *Perka* (1984), Dickson J recognises the overlap between these two concepts of voluntariness. Speaking of a 'conceptual link between necessity as an excuse and the familiar criminal law requirement that . . . actions constituting the actus reus of an offence must be voluntary', he continues:

Literally, this voluntariness requirement simply refers to the need that the prohibited physical acts must have been under the conscious control of the actor. Without such control, there is, for purposes of the criminal law, no act. The excuse of necessity does not go to voluntariness in this sense ... Realistically, however, his act in the necessity situation is not a 'voluntary' one. His 'choice' to break the law is no true choice at all; it is remorselessly compelled by normal human instincts. This sort of involuntariness is often described as 'moral or normative involuntariness'. ((1984) at 14–15)

But Dickson J also recognises the dangers inherent in permitting moral involuntariness into the criminal law. To do so would be to admit discussion of social and political factors into the court, requiring judgment to be made of individual conduct in its context. This would lead courts to make judgments of those contexts, while overriding the technical fact of guilt as established by the doctrine of actus reus. To 'hold that ostensibly illegal acts can be validated on the basis of their expediency' (or some 'higher social value') would politicise the law, requiring courts 'to second-guess the legislature and to assess the relative merits of social policies'. From this point, it is but a short step to consideration of the effects of bad social background and deprivation on the voluntary character of conduct. Such a leakage would fundamentally undermine the fault attribution process (cf Fletcher, 1978, 798–807; for a critique of his and similar accounts, see Norrie, 1991, 154–9). However Dickson J contrasts the danger of permitting politics to enter at large into the criminal law through actus reus with 'the *residual* defence of necessity' which, because it is marginalised and 'conceptualised as an "excuse", is . . . *much less open to criticism*' ((1984) at 14) (emphasis added). The defences of duress and necessity represent both a danger and a safety valve for legal doctrine. Judges will be keen not to allow these defences to get out of hand, as this would include and excuse too much otherwise criminal conduct. But by marginalising the discussion of moral voluntariness through giving it its own definitional box, the doctrine can at the same time keep the broader concept carefully under wraps. By categorising it in opposition to actus reus, the distance between individual fault and social context is maintained.

This argument concerning the social and political relationship between actus reus and the excuses ties in with the discussion of the relationship between intention, motive and sentencing in Chapter 3, and of necessity and duress in Chapter 8. The deep conceptual structure of the criminal law is based upon a process of social exclusion, a denial and containment of the social and political nature of criminality. Far from being the abstract theoretical building blocks of an apolitical system, the form these concepts take is wholly implicated in the socio-political strategy of modern Western society. The division between physical and moral involuntariness, like that between intention and motive, is necessary in a world in which defences to crime based upon moral involuntariness or motive could all too readily be made on the basis of social environment or background.

### (b)    Physical involuntariness *versus* moral voluntariness

Before moving to consider the ways in which the law concerning physical involuntariness has been developed, it is worth considering a second and quite different way in which the morality of an act affects the question of voluntariness, this time in the work of the Criminal Law Commissioners. Incapacity brought about by *voluntary intoxication* will not excuse criminal conduct:

The well-established rule of the English law that intoxication, if voluntary, shall afford no excuse in favour of the accused, rests in part on grounds of policy. It is *necessary* to exclude the plea . . . To admit it would be attended with fatal consequences to society. The pretence would be constantly resorted to as a cloak for committing the most horrible outrages with impunity . . . The legislator is under the necessity of treating every such act as wilful, by disregarding the plea of temporary incapacity . . . [as] incapacity voluntarily occasioned . . . (Criminal Law Commissioners, 1843, 19–20)

There are three positions mixed into this argument. These are (1) that social control requires the denial of the defence of incapacity to the person voluntarily intoxicated, but the rule rests on this only 'in part'; (2) that the intoxication will not excuse if it is voluntary; and the third, implicit, argument is that, (3) but for these grounds of policy and principle, the accused *would* have a claim that his act was not 'wilful'. The determinative argument is the second, concerning voluntariness. The accused may act involuntarily when he is intoxicated, but his action will still be culpable if it is the result of a *prior voluntary act* of getting drunk. That prior act is physically voluntary, although it is not the conscious act with which the accused is charged. It cannot therefore in its *physical* aspect take the place of the unconsciously committed crime. It can, however, take its place as a form of *moral* voluntariness, that is a form of culpability that does not rest on the existence of consciousness per se, but a broader normative form of fault involved in the act of getting drunk.[5] We shall see how this conception of moral voluntariness operates in the next section.

## (ii)  Limiting involuntariness

### (a)  The requirement of unconsciousness

If the central focus of the law is upon physical involuntariness, the situations in which such involuntariness may be claimed are tightly circumscribed. This is seen in the requirement that for an unconscious act to be involuntary, it must be totally so. In *Broome v Perkins* (1987), a man was held not to be in an automatous state throughout a car journey if, from time to time, he was apparently able to regain consciousness sufficiently to control his car, veering away from vehicles to avoid a collision. Similarly, in *A-G's Reference (No 2 of 1992)* (1993), the Court of Appeal held that a lorry driver driving in a trance-like condition (known as 'driving without awareness') brought on by the repetitive nature of motorway travel did not do so involuntarily. It is in connection with the defence of automatism that the question of involuntariness has most frequently been raised, and it is made clear that the automaton must not just lack control but be unconscious. Thus in *Bratty*, Lord Denning held that 'simply because the doer could not control his impulse . . . does not render his act involuntary' ((1961) at 532). *Bratty* was a case of a psychiatrically attested 'irresistible impulse' which combined consciousness with lack of control (see further, below, Chapter 9). If a person knows what he is doing, it matters not that he cannot resist doing it under the law of voluntary acts.

This decision chimes well with the older case of *Chetwynd* in which an argument in favour of automatism in the case of a 'split personality' was rejected, Scrutton J observing pithily that 'in his opinion Dr Jekyll would have been hanged for the murder that Mr Hyde committed, if it were proved that Mr Hyde knew what he was doing' (Williams, 1961, 487).⁶ In such cases, there is clear ground for argument that, even if the accused was conscious, the kind of deeper moral consideration of individual culpability that goes into establishing fault in the case of voluntary intoxication ought to operate against fault where the conscious act is underpinned by a pathological mental condition; yet the law cleaves single-mindedly here to the exclusive significance of the physical involuntariness test.

Similarly, crimes committed by conscious persons driven by addiction to drugs or alcohol are regarded as voluntary. The artificiality that this entails can be seen from American cases which first opened up the question of involuntariness in this area, and then quickly closed it down again. In *Robinson v California* (1962) (discussed in Fletcher, 1978, 426–33), it was accepted that an offence of being 'addicted to the use of narcotics' wrongly penalises a condition that the accused has no power to control. In *Powell v State of Texas* (1968), however, it was sought to extend this view to a situation of 'being found in a state of intoxication in any public place', but *Robinson* was distinguished. The court in effect drew a line between a specific offence criminalising addiction and the commission of offences which result from that addiction, between punishing a status and punishing the manifestations of that status. The problem that this artificial restriction upon the law⁷ seeks to address is not hard to guess at in light of the social problems in the United States associated with drug addiction. Unless *Powell* could be distinguished, *Robinson* threatened to open up a potential defence to a large and highly significant class of offenders.⁸

It is probably significant that there is no similar jurisprudence in this country, yet the resulting denial of the defence of involuntariness to a particular class of persons is clear. The contradiction between principle and policy created by the addict is articulated by Gordon (1978, 413):

> The addict creates a special problem. Although his drinking would probably be held by a court to be voluntary, there is much to be said for the view that since it is compulsive and the result of a mental illness – alcoholism – it should be regarded as involuntary . . . It is probably inevitable that the law should treat the addict as a voluntary drinker – the idea even of a sudden irresistible impulse is a difficult one for the law to accept, and the addict's impulse is constant and recurring.

Gordon adds that, whether voluntary or not, the addict should receive special treatment within a detoxification unit, if not within the law. It is precisely the need for treatment as a disposal of the court that belies the denial of involuntariness in such a case.

### (b)    Intoxication, physical involuntariness and moral voluntariness

The old argument suggested by the Criminal Law Commissioners, that the moral culpability in the act of getting intoxicated can take the place of the voluntariness required for an actus reus, undercuts the technical requirement that there should be a legally specified act. It constructs the fault element not out of the material that the law has cut for itself, but out of a form of moralism that a modern technical system of rules applied to practical acts and intentions ought not to permit. Yet this argument has been developed in modern times, and in a way that threatens to backfire on the law's original aim.

Two avenues were open to the courts in developing the law of intoxicated involuntariness. The first was to adopt the Commissioners' first argument that, as a matter of simple 'policy', drug induced automatism will not lead to a finding of physical involuntariness. The nature of crime as a social problem is such that the logic of individual responsibility must simply be excluded. But such a 'policy' rule might be too strict, and might lead to the exclusion of some people whose intoxication lacked 'real' fault. Besides, it might be embarrassing to proclaim the policy rule too openly in a system supposedly based on principles of individual fault.[9] The second avenue is to marry the dictates of policy to an argument from individual fault that would both legitimate the requirements of policy and permit the recognition of some cases of intoxicated automatism where the accused was considered not to be at fault while denying it to others. But in developing a concept of self-induced intoxication to legitimate the general exclusion of the defence, while permitting it for a worthy minority, what would happen if a member of the unworthy majority should seek to claim it? How is the line between minority and majority to be policed in terms of the concept of prior moral fault?

Even where an act is unconscious, ie physically involuntary, the courts will not recognise it if it results from self-induced intoxication. In *Lipman* (1969), the accused strangled his girlfriend while under the drug induced hallucination that he was fighting a serpent. The decision, while based on the law of manslaughter, appears to have operated on the assumption that a claim of involuntariness would not be available. The later case of *Quick* (1973) interprets it as one of self-induced incapacity which cannot excuse. *Quick* was a case of 'non-insane' automatism caused by the improper taking of insulin by a diabetic (see below, p 180 for discussion of the distinction between 'insane' and 'non-insane automatism'). Lord Justice Lawton argued that a self-induced incapacity, or one which could have reasonably been foreseen as the result of improperly taking prescribed drugs (by, for example, mixing them with alcohol, or not taking regular meals with insulin), may not excuse. On the other hand, his argument indicated by implication that where there was no fault in the taking of the drug, the accused might be relieved of responsibility. The issue of fault shifted from the intoxicated condition of the offender to the circumstances in which he became intoxicated.

Quick's appeal was allowed on the basis that the jury had not been allowed to hear his account of the circumstances of his becoming intoxicated, though the general tenor of Lord Justice Lawton's judgment is one that focuses on the potential fault implicit in his actions. Quick is portrayed as a probably self-induced (therefore at fault) automaton acquitted on a technical issue. In the subsequent case of *Bailey* (1983), the defendant had failed to take food properly with his doses of insulin, and claimed that he had hit his victim with an iron bar while in an automatous condition. The court developed the idea that in such circumstances, it should not be assumed that the person in question was necessarily at fault as one whose automatism was self-induced. The question was whether the accused appreciated the risk that his failure to take food might lead to aggressive, uncontrollable conduct. While it was common knowledge that those who take alcohol or dangerous drugs may become aggressive or dangerous, the same could not conclusively be said of the diabetic who fails to take food after an insulin injection. The test was one of 'subjective reckless-ness', whether it was shown that the accused knew that his action or inaction was likely to make him aggressive. The concept of subjective recklessness here functions as a more sophisticated modern counterpart to the Criminal Law Commissioners' old idea of a moral fault based upon the voluntary consumption of alcohol. It is the conscious risk-taking *in relation to the drug*, not in relation to the crime, that is relevant: legal fault is constructed out of the prior culpable act, or denied because there was none.

But *Bailey* begins to open a gap in the law because if the prohibition of an intoxication-related defence on policy grounds is rationalised by an argument of prior fault, such an argument can be seen to cut two ways. From being in the first instance a means of rationalising the *exclusion* of a defence, the prior fault ground becomes a way of arguing that there should be a defence if one was *not* at fault in becoming intoxicated. In *Hardie* (1984), the accused argued that his acts were the product of taking, without prescription, old stock of valium which he believed would have, and which he intended to have, a soporific effect. The court held that the self-induced intoxication rule would apply to exclude evidence of lack of mens rea or of automatism only if the accused foresaw a risk when he took the drug. There was no evidence of either individual or general knowledge that the drug would have the effect it did, and although taken deliberately, valium was 'wholly different in kind from drugs which are liable to cause unpredictability or aggressiveness' ((1984) at 853).

The prospect emerges of an unstable distinction being drawn between different classes of drugs. If the issue remains one of the foresight of risk in taking a drug, then there is in principle no reason why this should not undermine the fundamental denial of the automatism defence in 'straightforward' cases of intoxication by alcohol or other drug. *Bailey* speaks of a 'conclusive presumption' against the admission of proof of intoxication in the case of alcohol or dangerous drugs, but this distinction, on the basis of the 'social colour' of the drugs used, is an extremely difficult one to police. Where a person argues, for example, that he has always taken half a bottle of whisky or ten pints of beer in order to calm his nerves, and in twenty years it has always had that effect, it seems hard to blame him when on one occasion things turn out differently, while excusing someone like Hardie.

The tension is seen in *Allen* (1988) where the accused had drunk home-made wine, believing it to be much weaker in alcohol content than it turned out to be. The court upheld his conviction, arguing that the strength of the alcohol, and his belief about it, was irrelevant to his fault. Yet if *Hardie* and *Bailey* are to be accepted, why was Allen's lack of foresight not? The answer would appear to be that home-made alcohol is to be treated in a different way from other drugs like the valium in *Hardie*. If this is so, then the line is being drawn not according to fault, but according to a straight-forward policy judgment that some kinds of drug-taking will not be tolerated while others will. The prior fault requirement, in other words, has had the reverse effect to that which was originally intended, opening up the possibility of using intoxication as an excuse. When this runs up against a potentially non-culpable but otherwise standard drunkenness case, the moral voluntariness rationalisation, which evolved to legitimate the policy prohibition against the excuse of intoxicated involuntariness, now runs in the opposite direction. The judges are forced to beat a hasty retreat to the basic unmediated policy stance. The problem, however, is rooted in the attempt by the judges to have their cake and eat it. They wish to maintain the appearance of a technical, amoral conception of criminal law through actus reus, but to rationalise derogations from their own conception through a moralistic doctrine when it suits them. Such moralism can then backfire, as it threatened to in *Allen*.

## (c)  Denying involuntariness in situational liability cases

This same issue of what I have called 'moral voluntariness', the placing of a prior culpable act in the stead of the act required for the actus reus of the offence, also emerges in relation to so-called 'situational liability'. In *Larsonneur* (1933), a French woman was required to leave the United Kingdom by a certain date. She did so, taking the ferry to the Irish Free State. A month later, she was ordered to be deported from Ireland and placed on a ferry back to England by the Irish police. On arriving in England, she was charged with an offence of being 'found within the United Kingdom' contrary to a Government order. She had been deported against her will, and found herself in a situation entirely of others' making. It has been argued that there was no voluntary act on her part (Clarkson and Keating, 1998, 101), yet her conviction was upheld on appeal. Hall describes the case as 'reach[ing] the ultimate peak of arbitrary injustice' (quoted in Williams, 1961, 11), but its spirit has been followed in the case of *Winzar* (1983). The police were called to remove a drunk from a hospital, and took him to their car parked on the road outside. The accused was later convicted of an offence of being found drunk on the highway, when his being on the highway was something over which he had no control. These cases attract widespread condemnation because, it is argued, they reveal no voluntary act on the part of the accused.

Two points can be made about this. The first is to recall Stephen's example of the man walking to the scaffold, and to say that Larsonneur in fact did act voluntarily. The legal category of an involuntary act is sufficiently *narrow* to exclude her situation, so that, if the case is to be criticised, it is the basic doctrine of voluntariness that must be addressed, and not one exception to it. The second is to argue, as has been done in relation to *Larsonneur*, that there was a prior fault in her conduct leading up to her deportation to Ireland. She placed herself in the position where she would be in danger of being deported by the Irish authorities (Lanham, 1976). In Winzar's case, similarly, there was prior fault in getting drunk and finding himself in an obnoxious condition in the hospital, invoking a police intervention.

The fault to be discovered in these cases is only tangentially related to the offence with which the accused is charged, but if a broader moral fault is to be admitted in the intoxication cases, there is no reason why it should not be employed in other cases too. The problem with this line of argument is that once the game of opening up the time frame to past culpable acts is started, there is in principle no end (cf Kelman, 1981). One can continue going back into the accused's history to find the original voluntary act that set the rest of his conduct in motion and blame him for that,[10] but then the technical concept of actus reus becomes a fraud, a mere bagatelle, too obviously introduced or excluded to suit the perceptions of right and wrong of the judiciary.

For that reason, judges must limit their employment of the moral voluntariness doctrine and, if they do use it, need to appear to pay lip service to the technical doctrine even as they discard it. An illustration of this process is provided by the Australian case of *Ryan v R* (1967). In the course of an armed robbery, Ryan was surprised by a sudden movement of his victim. His defence claimed that in a reflex action caused by the shock of the movement, he squeezed the trigger of his gun, killing the man. As his action was a reflex one, it was not voluntary. Rejecting this argument for the majority, Windeyer J affirmed that even on the defence's claim, there was a voluntary act in the technical sense and he used a 'moral voluntariness' argument to construct it. He argued that if a 'fully conscious man who has put himself in a situation in which he has his finger on the trigger' experiences a sudden apprehension of danger and pulls it, death is 'a consequence probable and fore-seeable of a conscious apprehension of danger, and *in that sense* a voluntary act' ((1967) at 245) (emphasis added).[11] Thus the prior moral fault of putting oneself in the situation of danger was argued to directly satisfy the requirement of a voluntary act, overriding the need to consider the claim that the pulling of the trigger was in fact reflexive. One can see what the judge is doing in this case, but it is not clear, in doctrinal terms that he should be able to do it.

### (iii)   Conclusion

The Hobbesian heritage within liberal theory provided the law with a ready-made abstract physical conception of voluntary individual agency. This proved an ideal basis for a technical concept of actus reus which could hold the line of liability on the basis of a narrow 'value-free' concept of voluntariness. To this end, it excluded the broader claims associated with the idea of moral involuntariness, shifting them into the exceptional box of excuses, and thereby delimiting the opportunities that an accused person would have for claiming that his acts were involuntary. In order to increase the opportunities for convicting an accused person, however, the judges have themselves eroded the technical doctrine at 'the other end' through their use of an ideology of 'moral voluntariness', although this has to an extent backfired on them.

As with the law of intention, one has the sense here of a complex formal dance around a set of categories that construct individuals in different ways so as to secure conviction, and that it is this aim, rather than the prescribed form of the dance, that is determinative. It is not, however, that the dance steps are 'free'; they have a complex logic that corresponds to certain abstract qualities associated with human life. In order to understand the dance, one has both to grasp its formal structure and realise that a self-centred choreographer will at regular intervals switch the steps without having properly calculated the effect, or notified the dancers. This necessi-tates a certain amount of 'improvisation' on the floor, and it becomes appropriate to savour stylistic qualities of quick-footedness as well as the dance's more formal properties.

## 3   OMISSIONS

Anglo-American criminal law operates with an extremely narrow conception of those situations in which an omission can take the place of an act as the basis for criminal liability. The purpose of this second main section is, through an analysis of the law and theory of omissions, to understand why this should be. I begin by outlining how one can compare and contrast acts and omissions through the concept of causation, and then proceed to show why it is necessary to establish a duty requirement as the basis for omissions liability. Thereafter, I examine the particular way that the duty requirement has been constructed historically, and examine a modern communitarian critique of it. In so doing, I identify both the negative, (literally) anti-social, and the positive sides of liberal legalism in this area of the law.

### (i)   Constructing the concept of an omission

An omission can be described as a negative act, a description which indicates that omissions are in their essence similar to rather than different from acts. Omissions can be conscious decisions either not to do something, or to do something other than the thing that is not done (Honderich, 1980, ch 2, 62–3). Either way, to describe a failure to act is as much to describe a practical orientation to the world as is the description of an act. A failure to act is not 'just nothing', it is as much a description of what happened as an act itself so that 'negative statements like "he did not pull the signal" are ways of describing the world, just as affirmative statements are' (Hart and Honoré, 1985, 38). It is true, as Hart and Honoré's claim suggests, that an omission is likely to be described in a negative rather than a positive way, but this is only an empirical difference. It does not lead to a different evaluation of omissions and acts because both sorts of occurrences can be given both negative and positive descriptions (Honderich, 1980, 64–7).

Furthermore, omissions can be as much the cause of an event as acts. An omission can serve just as well as an act as a necessary and sufficient condition for any particular outcome (Honderich, 1980, 67–70). Honderich's conclusion is that acts and omissions cannot generally be distinguished as the basis for a difference in their rightness (Honderich, 1980, 80–9). But this then leaves the major question as to why in law omissions should be treated so differently from acts. If, in terms of a judgment of culpability, they cannot be distinguished, why are they distinguished legally?

Part of an answer is provided by considering their empirical difference. Omissions differ from acts in that we look for a connection between what a person did *not* do and a result. Omissions may be as causally efficacious as acts, but their identification is not so easy. It is true that the process of constructing an act as the cause of an event involves an evaluative process, as our discussion of the character of voluntariness makes clear (and see also Chapter 7 on causation, below). With omissions, there is a double indeterminacy in that we construct a causal relationship between a result and something that was *not* done. Many things are not done by many people, whereas acts are done by individually identifiable people.[12] It is therefore necessary to attribute the responsibility for an omission to an individual or individuals on the basis not of what was done, but in terms of a relationship giving rise to the *need* for an act.

There is considerable overlap here between the concept of an omission, and the concept of a cause, which we treat in detail in the following chapter. It is however helpful to turn here pre-emptively to the causation analysis of Hart and Honoré and their discussion of the concept of an omission (1985, 37–8). A central theme of their analysis of causation, with implications for their account of omissions, concerns what is and is not understood as 'normal' in society. Normal conditions and causes are those which do not 'make a difference' in commonsensical terms to causal chains. They are those conditions and causes given to human beings as standard features of the natural and social environment. The existence of oxygen in the air necessary to a fire, for example, is not seen as a significant cause of the fire when compared to the act of the individual who sets fire to material with a match. The 'normal' condition or cause in human affairs may, however, also be social, an 'artefact of human habit, custom, or convention'. Human beings have discovered that nature can be just as harmful when they do not intervene as when they do, and have therefore 'developed customary techniques, procedures, and routines to counteract such harm' (1985, 37). Social inventions or discoveries, like umbrellas to keep off the rain and inoculation against disease, protect people. When these become the norm in a society, their non-availability becomes the cause of the relevant harm in the popular perception.

By extension from this analysis of the role of the 'normal' in the construction of social causes, an *omission* in human conduct may be identified when there is a failure to act in conformity with an expected or required norm. If I park my car on a steep hill, and leave the handbrake off so that it rolls down the hill and crashes into another, the cause of the crash will be attributed to my omission rather than to the steepness of the hill. It is a normal expectation that people parking a car on a hill will apply their handbrake (see Leavens, 1988, 573). Where social techniques or routines have evolved and become established, they become 'a second "nature" and so a second "norm"'. It is the failure to implement a recognised technique or routine which will be seen as the cause of whatever results.[13] Omissions arise out of situations where a person fails to act where it would be 'normal' so to do.

Although such a causation analysis can be seen to lie at the back of the law of omissions, responsibility has traditionally been formulated not in causal terms, but in terms of the pre-existence of a *duty to act* in certain defined circumstances. What is the relationship between causation and the duty to act? Leavens (1988) has argued that causation is both necessary and sufficient to establish the existence of an omission in relation to a criminal result. The additional concept of a duty is unnecessary because the language of causation can do all the work. He argues that a concept of 'but for' (factual) causation, on to which is grafted a 'proximate cause' requirement (understood in terms of what is normal or expected), is all that is needed.[14] All omitters are 'but for' causers of the harm, but 'only those individuals whose failure to act is inconsistent with the common expectation that they will prevent a particular harm can be said to cause that harm. Other omitters, however culpable from a moral standpoint, are merely observers, not causers, of the harm' (Leavens, 1988, 576–7). In seeing what is wrong with this argument,[15] we can appreciate why a duty requirement exists, and the nature of the particular dilemma that faces the law of omissions. Two situations illuminate the issues.

### (a)   The drowning infant/stranger

Take an expanded version of Stephen's illustration quoted at the head of this chapter. An infant drowns in a pool when she could have been saved either by a parent, by the child's sitter, or by a passing stranger without danger or inconvenience in each case. In relation to the parent and the sitter, Leavens argues (1988, 577–8) that their conduct naturally violates our expectation that they should save the child, and that therefore they have omitted so to do. The passing stranger, he suggests, and this is generally believed to be the law's position too, is in a different position. While we may agree that 'even a bystander is morally obligated to try to save the child', it is not our expectation that he will, perhaps because of 'the notions of individual freedom and autonomy that pervade our society'. Without 'a special relationship, each person is responsible for his own welfare, and thus a person's decision to "mind his own business" cannot be said to affect the welfare of others'. Leavens goes on to say, however, that our 'value judgments' may change so that in a possible future time, the stranger may be held to have omitted.

Two comments are elicited by this. The first is that it is as arguable that most people would *not* have the expectation that the passing stranger would pass the infant by. Our commonsensical, and that is the criterion for omission on the Leavens/Hart-Honoré analysis, judgment would be that it was an omission so to do. The law's failure to punish such an omission is commonly not defended in terms of the legitimacy of the omission on grounds of respect for individual autonomy, but in terms of some other consequence that is avoided by keeping the law narrow. Typically, the argument concerns the inability to draw lines between the case of easy rescue at no cost, and the more difficult case in which it is envisaged that one person must give up virtually all that he has in order to save as many as possible by his sacrifice.[16] It is commonly not argued that the easy rescue case is defensible in terms of what is socially proper or expected.

In other words, the easy rescue case drives a wedge between the commonsense expectation or evaluation of what constitutes an omission, and the law's conception of the same. But this then leaves a question. If we agree that the stranger-bystander is obligated to act, why do we need, as Leavens suggests, an evolution in social values in order to uphold the omission in law? The values are already there, the problem is that the law does not embrace them. A direct reduction of omission construction *in law* to the 'normative causation' analysis will not work, for there is a significant gap between the two.

The second point enlarges this first. It concerns the conflict in moral values operating in society, and the existence of values that do uphold the right not to intervene alongside values of social solidarity that demand intervention. These values of individual autonomy and freedom conflict with the claim that a person should assist his fellow human being. In other words, there are *competing* moral values at play – those that say that people ought to intervene in the stranger situation, and those that say they do not have to. One set of values extols a narrow individualism, the other stresses a more rounded doctrine of social responsibility. We can now see why it is wrong to reduce the analysis of omissions to those of causes, by-passing the concept of duty. The latter concept provides for a socio-political 'fixing' of those omissions that are held to be criminal around a *particular* conception of what is to be expected of the individual in the Anglo-American social context, in a situation of *competing* conceptions.

### (b)   Killing and letting die

There is a longstanding distinction made in the medical treatment of patients between acting in a way that hastens (causes) the death of a patient and failing to act through the withdrawal of treatment. While the former is forbidden as a crime, the latter may be permitted as a non-criminal omission. The distinction has been recognised in cases involving the non-treatment of handicapped new-born babies (*Re B (a minor)* (1981); *Arthur* (1981)) and in the House of Lords case of *Airedale NHS Trust v Bland* (1993). Where a young man had been in a 'persistent vegetative state' for three-and-a-half years, doctors could discontinue treatment because their duty to treat extended only to situations where it would 'confer some benefit on the patient'. There was no duty 'where a large body of informed and responsible medical opinion was to the effect that no benefit at all would be conferred by its continuance' ((1993) at 858).

The decision relies on the distinction between a (permissible) omission and an (impermissible) act, but the House acknowledges a difficulty. It would 'appear to be almost irrational' to make it 'lawful to allow a patient to die slowly, though painlessly, over a period of weeks from lack of food, but unlawful to produce his immediate death by lethal objection, thereby saving his family from yet another ordeal' ((1993) at 885). One can develop hypothetical illustrations to show that the relied upon distinction easily collapses in the hospital context (Smith and Hogan, 1999, 49), testifying to the equal causal efficacy of omissions and acts. Their *separation*, however, in collaboration with a duty analysis permits a form of 'passive euthanasia' (Lacey and Wells, 1998, 481–2) in a situation where its active form would not be tolerated. To those who believe in the sanctity of life, killing by omission is no different from active killing. To those who follow secular opinion, a moral distinction has to be made between killing and letting die. Distinguishing act and omission and developing the duty analysis allows this to happen in a way that simple reliance on a causal analysis would not.

These two illustrations help us see why the duty analysis is important. It pins down exactly which moral conceptions of conduct will inform the criminal law of omissions where the causal analysis is open to competing views. This leaves us with the question how the law has in fact shaped the duty requirement and how that affects the law of criminal omissions. The starting-point of the Anglo-American criminal law has been a *narrowing down* of the categories of legal omission by relating them to the classical liberal ideology of moral individualism. This forecloses broader conceptions of the relationship between people such as would be entailed by a model based upon an idea of social responsibility.[17] The law instantiates a *particular* normative conception of the relationship between individuals, one which excludes broader conceptions through the use of the duty concept. The drowning infant by-passed by the stranger is the most noteworthy victim of this ideological foreclosure of the category of criminal omissions. It is the duty requirement based upon narrow, laisser faire individualist grounds that makes this possible.

## (ii) Juridifying the concept of an omission

The climate in which the early discussion of the scope of the law of omissions developed was one of political liberalism and economic laisser faire. In his famous note on the Indian Penal Code, Macauley (1898, 109–15) insisted that a clear line should be drawn between the arresting of acts of positive harm, which was the law's business, and the encouragement of acts of positive good, which was not. An individual was only responsible to another individual to the extent that he had voluntarily entered into legally recognised transactions with him. Beyond such voluntary transactions, there existed only a more or less strongly felt sense of morality which may move the individual to act, but need not. In relation to a beggar, the rich man owes only a moral duty, but nothing more, because the two parties have no actual relationship with each other. Macauley does not recognise the interconnection between wealth and poverty, the ways in which the rich acquire wealth at the expense of the poor.[18] The economic environment is regarded as a datum of human existence, not a product of social relations. It is true that Macauley recognises the 'too lenient' character of his rule, but he argues that 'we do not think it can be made more severe, without disturbing the whole order of society' (1898, 113).

Macauley's political and economic liberalism put a philosophic gloss on a sordid state of affairs. The present law of omissions with its narrow confines has its roots in the nineteenth century's stubborn refusal to imagine relations and duties between people save on the narrow basis of a cash or contractual nexus. This is seen even in relation to the most 'natural' social duty that can be imagined, that of a parent to a child. It is usually assumed that this duty is so obvious as to be 'commonsensical' (Ashworth, 1989, 441) yet Glazebrook (1960) has shown how the nineteenth-century jurists sought in vain for any legal basis for the duty of a parent to care for a child. The only source for a parental duty was to be found in the poor laws. These were concerned not with the enforcement of parental duty as such, but with allocating financial burdens away from the parish and onto parents of sufficient means. There was no developed legal duty imposed on a parent in relation to a child.

The suggestion of such a 'common law duty' probably arose to explain what would otherwise have been an 'inexplicable lacuna in the law' (Glazebrook, 1960, 396), and even when such a duty was identified, it was often applied in a very restrictive fashion (1960, 399–403). It may well have been the case that judges were reluctant to convict poor mothers for the deaths of children they could not support at a time when infant life was regarded as cheap (Rose, 1986). Nonetheless, the existence of a narrow, laisser faire doctrine of omission endorsed the view that infant life among the poor *was* cheap, and not necessarily to be protected by too much stress on 'natural' parental duties. The hard fact was that beggars died, and so did infants: legal duties should certainly not be made out of the former circumstance, and only reluctantly out of the latter.

The primary juridical basis for the existence of a duty to act was the concept of a contract. This was compatible with the doctrine of laisser faire: indeed it was central to it, because it based liability on the individual's prior consensual act, and it remains today the most important foundation of the law of omissions. Initially, duties arising out of a contract were identified in the old master-and-servant relationship. Where it was expressly stated in a contract that a master had undertaken to provide necessaries to a servant, he could be prosecuted for neglect, although this provision was as restrictively interpreted as possible (Glazebrook, 1960, 396–401). In the late nineteenth century, the law developed the contractual analysis beyond master and servant into other relationships where an implied or explicit contract could be established, in order to found a duty of care. The most important case was that of *Instan* (1893), which despite its moral rhetoric should not be interpreted as giving rise to a dramatic change in the law. In his judgment, Lord Coleridge expressed the duty of a niece to look after her aunt in broad moral terms,[19] but the niece's conduct was immoral because she failed to provide food for her aunt 'which was paid for by the deceased's own money for the purpose of the maintenance of herself and the prisoner' ((1893) at 454).[20] This was therefore a case where the accused had implicitly undertaken to look after the aunt in return for her own keep. *Instan* remains a case based on the old contractual analogy.[21] The actual requirements for a contract may not have been present, but the underlying model of an obligation, voluntarily undertaken, remained in place.[22]

The contract not only remained a central element in these cases extending liability, it was also a potent concept for developing the law to situations where the contractual relationship was not with the victim but with an employer to perform a task, such as minding a railway gate (*Pittwood* (1902)). Glazebrook points out that the value in legal principle of founding criminal liability upon a contract to which the victim may be in every way a stranger is questionable (1960, 406). Yet the late nineteenth-century cases which arose from the transformation of the means of communication brought about by trains, trams and the like threw up situations where employee negligence called out to judicial ears for criminal sanctions. The contract of employment provided at a pinch the juridical basis upon which to proceed. The increased reliance on mass communications meant more people being placed in positions of responsibility for the safety of others. This was an example of what Hughes calls the 'growing interdependence in modern society' (Hughes, 1958, 634), but this development was not matched by a developing legal consciousness, so that the old narrow individualistic concepts had to be deployed, whether appropriate or not. The individualistic contract was both the natural (in legal terms) and unnatural (in social terms) basis for extending the legal duty of care in a changing world, one in which interconnectedness invoked some extension of social regulation.

### (iii)  Abstract right and social need

In the late twentieth century, the law on omissions remains circumscribed by the legal concepts of the early nineteenth. The 'modern consciousness of interdependence' has had some effect through statutory interventions in areas where the concept of a contract could provide little assistance, but where modern notions of the need for community supervision of individual actions was deemed necessary. Thus the increasing supervision of children and childcare has led to the creation of offences of omission with regard to the maintenance (Children and Young Persons Act 1933, s 1)[23] and education (Education Act 1944, s 39) of children, and the coming of the motor car has led to a wide variety of regulatory offences including that of failing to report an accident causing damage or injury within twenty-four hours of its occurrence (Road Traffic Act 1972, s 25(2)). The concept of the 'interventionist state' has led more broadly to the creation of 'elaborate statutory scheme[s] of regulation of industry or commerce' (Ashworth, 1999, 47). Yet such modern 'welfare' or 'regulatory' offences have not affected the general common law attitude to the idea of duty of care. On the other hand the individualism from the contractual context has found a new outlet in the doctrine that where an individual brings about a dangerous situation by a prior act, he is under a duty of care to deal with it. The emphasis on the existence of a prior act in such a formulation reflects the individualist assumption that individuals bring responsibilities on themselves by their own acts freely undertaken. In cases such as *Miller* (1983),[24] all that has been changed is the nature of this 'undertaking'.

We are, however, left with a doctrine on omissions that remains narrow, and circumscribed by the old liberal ideology. The inability of this form adequately to embody social concepts of care is particularly seen in the modern case of *Stone and*

*Dobinson* (1977). The defendants were the brother of a mentally ill woman, who lodged in his house, and his common law wife. They made ineffectual efforts to get assistance to the victim, who suffered from anorexia, and she died. They were tried for, and convicted of, manslaughter. The conviction rested upon the requirement of a duty of care towards the dead woman. With regard to the brother, Stone, the court held that 'whether [deceased] was a lodger or not she was a blood relation of the appellant ... she was occupying a room in his house'; while Dobinson 'had undertaken the duty of trying to wash her, of taking such food to her as she required', adding that this 'was *not* a situation analogous to the drowning stranger. They *did* make efforts to care.'

There are two arguments here, one concerning blood relationships, the other the undertaking of a duty of care. As regards the former, the court states the law more broadly than it has ever been stated, without authority, and without any consideration for the breadth of the rule they have created.[25] As for the latter, the argument rests on a play on the concept of an undertaking. Dobinson had, as a matter of fact, 'undertaken' certain actions on the deceased's behalf, but there was no evidence that she had made an undertaking to perform such tasks as she performed. There is a slide in the judgment between 'undertaking' in a practical and in a 'contractual' sense (cf Glazebrook, 1960, 409; Williams, 1983, 262–6).[26] The problem for the judges was that as they dwelt upon the tragic condition of the sister, rotting alive in Stone's house, they had no real basis in law for establishing a duty to act in the case of either defendant. The laisser faire, contractualist basis of the law had to be manipulated into action in relation to Dobinson, while the underdeveloped conception of a duty of blood relatives, which had previously been restrictively applied, was pressed into service in relation to Stone.

The judges had only two choices: to allow the accuseds' appeal on the basis of the existing, narrowly constituted, legal doctrine, or to uphold the conviction on the basis that they had done wrong, even if the legal concepts did not make it clear why. They were caught, in the terms of the quotations at the head of the chapter, between the 'moral shock' to which Fletcher refers, and Stephen's sanguine appraisal of the individualist limits of the law.

In the light of *Stone and Dobinson*, how might an English court deal today with the locus classicus of laisser faire individualism, the United States case of *People v Beardsley* (1907)? A man was found to have no duty of care to his mistress where she took a fatal drugs dose in a hotel room with him. It has been suggested that a broader duty ground of 'interdependence ... from shared family life or close communal living' (Clarkson and Keating, 1998, 107; Fletcher, 1978, 613) would lead to a different result today. The case of *Khan and Khan* (1998), however, gives pause for thought. The defendants had supplied heroin to a 15-year-old acting as a prostitute for them. It was probably the first time she had used it, she took double the normal amount, and went into a coma. The defendants left her without medical help, returning the following day to find her dead and disposing of the body.

The case turned on the different kinds of involuntary manslaughter. The Court of Appeal observed, however, that to 'extend a duty to summon medical assistance to a drug dealer who supplies heroin to a person who subsequently dies would enlarge the class of persons to whom, on previous authority, such a duty may be owed'. They added that it 'may be correct that such a duty does arise' ((1998) at 831). It is thus acknowledged that the law does not cover such a case and, tentatively, that it should.

On what basis? It is unlikely to be on the ground of 'interdependence', which is too broad and nebulous. More likely is a building out from the idea of an implicit undertaking of a duty to act, for example, by joint engagement in a dangerous activity (Smith and Hogan, 1999, 48), or perhaps through an extension of the prior dangerous act doctrine (*Miller* (1983)). Either approach, as *Khan and Khan* suggests, would take the law beyond its present parameters. Until that happens, the position in *People v Beardsley* appears to reflect the English law of the 21st century.

### (iv)    Beyond individualism?

It has been argued that the law of omissions should be extended to include situations of 'easy rescue' on the basis of a communitarian ideology of criminal responsibility. This is in opposition to the narrow individualist approach which underlines the existing law.[27] There are certain duties of citizenship which extend beyond those responsibilities that one has voluntarily undertaken on the basis of a contractual analogy. These derive from the social responsibility that comes from living in a community with others.[28] What would be the effect upon the law of developing the duty to act in this way?

### (a)    The line drawing problem

The essential problem with such an extension was put by Macauley in his notes to the Indian Penal Code 150 years ago. Where a duty exists on the basis of the existing civil or criminal law, as for example between a gaoler and a prisoner, or a nurse and an infant, an omission causing death will be criminal. Where, however, the relationship has no pre-existing legal basis, there is no duty to act. A man is not a murderer because he omitted to relieve a beggar even if there was the clearest proof that the beggar's death resulted from the omission. A surgeon is no murderer for refusing to go from Calcutta to Meerut to perform an operation, even if he is the only surgeon in India who could perform it and the patient will otherwise die. The surgeon could find himself in an 'easy rescue' situation where he will suffer no personal danger or financial loss, but if he nonetheless chooses to travel to England, or to await the arrival of his family by the next ship, he has committed no crime. If one were to punish the surgeon for not carrying out the operation, it would be inconsistent not to punish the rich man should he refuse to disburse the smallest sum to save a beggar. There is no way to draw the line between duties owed, so one must hold fast to a pre-existing legal relationship, criminal or civil, as the basis for a duty.

Macauley acknowledges the narrowness of this approach but thinks it unavoidable:

> We are sensible that in some of the cases which we have put, our rule may appear too lenient; but we do not think it can be made more severe without disturbing the whole order of society . . . [W]e are unable to see where, if we make such a man legally punishable, we can draw the line. If the rich man who refuses to save a beggar's life at the cost of a little copper is a murderer, is the poor man just one degree above beggary also to be a murderer if he omits to invite the beggar to partake his hard-earned rice? (1898, 113–14)

How are the lines to be drawn so as to include some of these broader duties but not others? Feinberg has suggested that one should draw the line at 'clear cases of opportunity to rescue with no unreasonable risk, cost or inconvenience whatever' (1984, 155–6). He admits that drawing a line between 'no unreasonable risk' and 'reasonable risk' would be problematic.[29] Feinberg suggests that 'careful drafts-manship of statutes' could help, but concedes that such statutes would in reality be relatively vague. The problem with the line Feinberg seeks to draw is seen in that he suggests that a person at the edge of a swimming pool would be duty bound to rescue a child in difficulties, but not one 100 or 200 yards away. Fairly quickly, the argument returns to Macauley's example of the surgeon who will not travel to Meerut.[30] Ultimately the matter would be left to the discretion of prosecutors, judges and juries because the line could only be expressed in 'relatively vague terms'.

Perhaps, however, this is not so important because the law frequently gives discretion to decision-makers and fact-finders in the criminal process through the criterion of reasonableness, in cases, for example, of provocation or self defence (Feinberg, 1984, 157). There is a difference, however, in that these are situations in which the criminal act, together with the basic form of the relevant defence, are already constituted by the law. In these situations, actors within the criminal process are told by the law what the offence is, and then asked to decide whether an individual's conduct comes within it. In the case of omission liability, the reason-ableness requirement is linked to the determination of the actual crime itself. The constitution of the actus reus would be at large, for actors within the process to determine. The particular indeterminacy of the omission concept emerges specifically when the definition of duty is not tied to a pre-existing contractual or quasi-contractual relationship. The vagueness is in the constitution of the offence itself.[31]

This issue of line-drawing can be put in another way. In Chapter 4 (pp 72–6), we examined the problem of indeterminacy in relation to the development of a syn-thesised concept of recklessness. There we noted that the move from the orthodox subjectivist approach to a developed form of subjectivism uniting the judgment of the individual and community could not occur in a conflictual society where there was no broad agreement about the way people should behave in particular contexts. The result was an indeterminacy of judgment that had to be short-circuited by the factualisation of recklessness through the adoption of a narrower form of subjec-tivism. The same problem of indeterminacy arises if the law follows the demand to move beyond individualism in the area of omissions. Reviewing the question of relationship duties, and touching upon some of the issues concerning blood ties and proximity of accommodation raised by *Stone and Dobinson* and *People v Beardsley* (1907), Ashworth raises the question whether –

> . . . there is any defensible line which can be drawn short of a duty of common humanity owed to any person who is seen or known to be in need of urgent assistance – a form of legally-enforced social responsibility which might require anyone to spend time and money in helping any person who came destitute to his or her doorstep . . . (1989, 442)

The issue is not just one of drawing a line, but of *competing* definitions of what duties are owed by people to each other, and this is an issue that the law of omissions short-circuits by tying duties to a laisser faire, individualist model. Without that, it would be impossible to arrive at an agreed solution: the foreclosure achieved by individualism is necessary in the same way that it is necessary for subjective individualism to pre-empt a broader concept of recklessness.[32]

A second suggestion from Feinberg exposes the covertly political nature of this enterprise of line-drawing through the 'juridicalisation' of omissions. He proposes that the duty line should be drawn not so much by law, but through the design of social institutions (the law, the welfare state). The law should impose duties in relation to the 'random and unpredictable emergencies of life that require time and effort, rather than money, from chance passers-by'. No one should be charged with a beggar's death 'since agencies of the state will not permit the beggar to die in any case' (sic) (Feinberg, 1984, 158). The obvious response to this is the empirical one that we are perhaps not so far from Macauley's India in the West than we were two decades ago when Feinberg wrote. Even if we pay our taxes, we know that the gap between rich and poor, and the declining level of the officially set revenue duties, means that our omissions are not covered by the state's welfare umbrella. To pigeonhole the duty to rectify social omissions by advocacy of a welfare state, while leaving a narrow definition of omissions to work in relation to the criminal law, has a certain cogency to it. It reflects the institutional design of a society in which a public welfare net is (or was) employed to catch the least well-off. The case of *Stone and Dobinson*, for example, cried out for a proper *social* intervention to protect both the accused and their 'victim'. Sidelining the interconnections between wealth and poverty through the design of political institutions, however, only affirms the argument that the construction and delimitation of duties to act within the criminal law is itself a highly political act.

Yet this argument has a particular persuasiveness in that the politically constructed limits of the law are presented in a form that appears apolitical. By reflecting the underlying ideological logic and structure of laisser faire individualism in Western societies, and basing the responsibility for omissions upon the prior assumed duties of self-interested individuals, the liberal model occludes the social and economic relations which underlie the apparently 'simple' and apolitical matter of individual free choice. The resulting division of private responsibility and public duty makes perfect sense, but only because it reflects a particular historical way of organising the production and distribution of wealth that leaves some to beg and others to enjoy the well-earned fruits of their labour in peace.

### (b) Specific duties of citizenship?

Finally, in considering the relationship between the individualist approach and its communitarian critique, I wish to emphasise and affirm the 'other side', the positive aspect, of liberal individualism. In Chapter 2 (see pp 28–30; also below, pp 223–5), I argued that the abstract individualist model is a double-edged sword. On the one hand, it is a form of oppression because it excludes from sight the social realities which underlie criminality by virtue of a model of individual responsibility. We have seen how the law of omissions operates in its own way to achieve this exclusion. On the other hand, it is at the same time a defence of individual right, albeit in narrow individualistic terms. Both sides of this contradictory phenomenon must be included in any analysis of the criminal law.

It is easy, in the light of the foregoing discussion, to conclude that, as between the individualist model of duty and the 'social responsibility' model adopted by recent writers within a communitarian perspective, it is morally or politically better to side with the latter against the former. But this may not be so, for the latter may have authoritarian implications that cut across the positive side of the liberal model. Ashworth, for example, argues for the adoption of a duty to take reasonable steps towards law enforcement alongside the duty to assist a stranger on the ground of 'each citizen's obligations towards other citizens and towards the community as a whole' (1989, 454). Such a positive duty sounds unexceptionable, until one views it in the light of the old debate about negative and positive liberty (Berlin, 1958), and then considers the libertarian objection that it would 'turn us all by force of law into subsidiary policemen and tell-tales' (Williams, 1991, 90). Viewed thus, responsibilities to the community take on a sinister, authoritarian colour, in contrast to which the narrow individualism of the orthodox liberal approach appears benign. For example, the French Penal Code (Article 223) imposes duties of easy rescue and crime prevention on its citizens, duties that were first imposed in 1941 under Nazi occupation. Doubtless, these laws were formulated and applied differently before and after 1945 (Ashworth and Steiner, 1990), but it gives pause for thought to recognise the initial provenance of, particularly, the duty to prevent crime provision.

Modern communitarian theory starts from the concept of social responsibility, and works towards individual duties, while the traditional liberal approach works in the opposite direction. To impose a communitarian perspective on to the actual working of the criminal justice system would be to circumvent the defensive individualistic side of the traditional liberal approach.[33] Even if carried out with good intentions, an authoritarian element is implicit in the communitarian approach, so one should be careful about assuming that a critique of one approach necessarily means an endorsement of its opposite. In a world without political and social conflict, where communitarian ideas could not become the legitimating basis for authoritarian regimes reflecting powerful minority interests, one might endorse a broad concept of social responsibility.

Until then, one should be aware of all the nuances of the models that are available in our conflictual society, and consider where a commitment to one or another takes us. In light of drowning stranger and dying mistress scenarios, the idea of a duty of easy rescue seems attractive. A limited statutory offence might seem more appropriate in some such cases than a prosecution for manslaughter. Against this, such provisions shift the fulcrum in the relationship between the individual and the state and generate civil liberties issues in authoritarian times. One should certainly distinguish duties of easy rescue and crime prevention (cf Ashworth, 1999, 50). The general point is that one should be aware of the political and ideological limits and effects of the different concepts that are available, and strive to grasp them in their complexity. The way to do this is to understand the two-sided character of legal individualism. On the one side, it establishes a form of respect for the individual against the commands and desires of an authoritarian state. On the other side, it stands as a mystifying representation of underlying social relations. Any understanding of the criminal law must reflect, where relevant, both aspects – the libertarian and the mystificatory – of liberal legalism (cf Norrie, 1991, ch 9).

## 4    CONCLUSION

In this chapter, we have examined two central elements of the law of actus reus. These elements appear in most criminal law texts as essentially unconnected, or as united only by a basic fact of human life: that human beings both act and omit to act. I have tried to show that one fundamental point of connection within the law is pro- vided by the concept of the abstract juridical individual. This is employed both to construct individual fault in the law of acts, and to delimit the boundaries of fault in relation to the law of omissions.

The concept of a voluntary act designates the central element of agency required to accompany the different mental states required to constitute crime. As with the law of intention, the form of agency has been stripped down to the most basic component of individual life: to a narrow, technical form of individuality which excludes the possibility of a broader moral or socio-political content being expressed through it. At the same time as individuality is decontextualised, a moral 'super individualism' is permitted through the back door to disrupt the law's technical form. This happens because the aim is to intensify the law's potential for fault attribution, although not, as we saw, without paradoxical results. The dialectic of legal technicality and moral judgment to which this gives rise is conditioned by the interplay between liberal ideology and the law's control functions as perceived by the judges.

The concept of an omission fulfils a different function in the law from that of a voluntary act because of its peculiar character. The law must not only construct the individual in particular ways in order to attribute fault, it must also construct the concept of an omission in order to delimit the boundaries of fault. Omissions do not attach to actors in the way that acts do, so there is a double work of construction required of the law's ideology of individualism. It is essentially the free individual of the law of contract, as developed and analogised, who plays the part of setting the boundaries of the law. Without the prior commitment associated with the free assumption of a duty, there can in general be no criminal omission.

Such an approach constructs the law of omissions on a model of laisser faire ideology which denies any interconnectedness between people beyond that of the market and its analogues. For anyone who wishes to argue for a broader range of duties, the issue may be posed in terms of their imposition on top of individualistic relations, as in the case of positive and particular statutory interventions. Alternatively, it may be in terms of the philosophical development of the individual's duties beyond the 'safe', and apparently apolitical, context provided by his/her own prior acts or undertakings. The result of the law's laisser faire ideology is society's 'shock', as Fletcher puts it, at its failure to criminalise acts that are 'self-evidently' wrong. That failure, however, is historical and structural, and attempts to develop the law run immediately into the well-rehearsed counter-arguments of the libertarian side of liberal individualism.

Thus in both acts and omissions, we see the deployment of the law's abstract individualistic categories, but to different ends. In the case of acts, the end is the securing of individual fault in relation to conduct that the state wishes to criminalise, while avoiding leakage into the system of other accounts of why people commit crimes, or what it means to act voluntarily. In the case of omissions, the aim is the circumscription of the realm of criminal acts so as to avoid leakage from the realm of 'normal' omissions that could occur in a society based upon self-interest, wealth and poverty. There must be a law of omissions, because there are some omissions that the state does wish to criminalise. This category must, however, be defined so as to avoid political debates within the law as to the rights and wrongs of acting or not acting, or political and moral questions about the distribution of wealth, power and responsibility in society. The law of acts secures liability for a particular group of individuals, while the law of omissions ensures that the boundaries of liability will not become extended to cover other groups who are not constructed as criminal by the dominant ideology. The narrow individualism of the law of voluntary acts excludes the social context in order to convict those who are considered socially deviant. The narrow individualism of the law of omissions excludes the social context in order to draw a tight line around those whose conduct has already been constructed as deviant by the state and its various actors.

# Chapter 7

# Causation

[T]he principles [of causation] to be found in the common law . . . are reasonably well settled and can be stated quite shortly. (The Law Commission, 1989, 188)

. . . hitherto the judges have made little progress in establishing [the] principles [of imputation] . . . (Williams, 1983, 382)

## I  INTRODUCTION

A central feature of actus reus is that the accused's act or omission must have caused a result which is the object of a criminal charge. At one level the issue is the relatively straightforward one of whether an act or omission is *in fact* causally connected with a result (*White* (1910)), but there remains the further question as to whether or not the one will be imputed as a cause of the other *in law*. Thus, under the old rule in murder that death must ensue within a year and a day of an assault, an assault outwith that period could be the factual cause of death, but not its legal cause (*Dyson* (1908)). That rule has now been abolished (Law Reform (Year and a Day Rule) Act 1996) but where an injury resulting in death occurred more than three years previously, the Attorney-General must now agree to a prosecution. This substitutes administrative discretion for legal rule but still indicates there are non-factual considerations relevant to the constitution of legal cause. The distinction between cause in fact and in law can be expressed using a variety of terms:

> The but for cause is sometimes referred to as the factual cause, or the de facto cause, or the scientific cause. The important thing is to distinguish it from cause in another sense, the 'imputable' (or 'legal' or 'effective' or 'direct' or 'proximate') cause . . . (Williams, 1983, 381)

The essential reason for differentiating factual and legal causation parallels the position in omissions, where a duty requirement imposes a set of limits upon what would otherwise be a politically contestable and indeterminate process of fault attribution. The underlying nexus in the law of omissions that required foreclosing was that provided by causation, and the construction of causal sequences in the law of causation itself is an equally open and potentially conflictual task. The essential problem is that of anchoring responsibility for causation in individuals in the context of causal sequences that predate and postdate individual agency. Why focus on what *this* person did given that his actions were part of a causal chain that both preceded what he did, and continued after his actions? The question of *preceding* cause is primarily answered in the law by the doctrine of voluntary acts, analysed in the previous chapter. A special significance is attached to such acts which operate as both 'a barrier and a goal in tracing back causes' (Hart and Honoré, 1985, 44). The difficult question of *antecedent* or *supervening* cause, is the particular focus of this chapter. As we shall see, the concept of a voluntary act plays its part here too, though it is constructed in a way that differs significantly from its construction in the law of voluntary acts.

The two quotations at the head of this chapter both relate to the law of supervening cause. What happened between 1983 and 1989 to occasion the turnaround in the fortunes of the criminal law's conception of causation? The answer is nothing, and the argument of this chapter will be that Williams's assessment of the position is much closer to the mark than that of the Law Commission. As a result, the Law Commission's own analysis, restating the common law, only succeeds in replicating its confusions (for comments, see Williams, 1989; Clarkson and Keating, 1990, 430). To take the discussion of the victim's refusal of a life-saving blood transfusion, one of two crucial examples on supervening cause,[1] the Commission's argument does not properly support the conclusion advanced, that an original assailant has caused ensuing death. It is argued that the refusal is not sufficient in itself to be the legal cause of death, even if it is unforeseen and not reasonably foreseeable (Law Commission, 1989, 188). While it is obvious that a refusal to accept blood can only form part of a causal sequence leading to death where some prior act has occasioned a serious condition of bleeding, so that the refusal by itself can never be the sufficient cause of death, this is an observation concerning *factual*,[2] not legal, causation, and does not address the question of whether the causation is to be imputed to the accused *in law*. What if the victim refused the transfusion out of spite for the accused? Would the Law Commission still maintain that the assailant had caused the death, given that the wound would remain a necessary condition, and the refusal could still not be said to be sufficient to cause death? Some indication of what might be the relevant means for breaking the factual chain of causation in such a case is necessary in order to distinguish, for example, the religious from the spiteful victim, but the Law Commission do not provide it.[3]

I suggest that in this example the problem is that the Law Commission has sought to restate the common law principles as they emerge from the leading cases, believing them to be essentially adequate. In so doing, however, they can only incorporate the tensions and contradictions that exist within the law. In relation to causation, as elsewhere in the criminal law, the traditional approach of lawyers and academics has been to seek to resolve what are seen as essentially superficial problems of legal doctrine by engaging in deeper conceptual rationalisation of the legal concepts. The outstanding illustration of this in causation is Hart and Honoré (1985) and it is their account that I focus on in this chapter. However, I will argue that, for all its analytical sophistication, the authors are unable to provide a sound philosophical basis for the criminal law of causation. A critical reading of their analysis and the leading cases is required to explain, if not to rationalise, the problems of the law in this area.

## 2   A CRITICAL APPROACH TO CAUSATION

The nature and limits of the doctrine of causation and the issues that are at stake within it can be grasped by historically tracing a significant American debate about the nature of causation in the law of tort that occurred at the end of the nineteenth century. This concerned the decline of what was known as the 'objective theory of causation', an approach that was popular because of its individualist emphasis on the existence of one 'natural' cause for every event that occurs (Horwitz, 1982). Such a belief made it possible to assert individual liability for torts and to locate the law of tort firmly within the area of private law, but it came increasingly under attack from both the Millian doctrine of the multiplicity of causes and the legal doctrine of foreseeability. The leading proponent of this theory, Wharton, argued that the idea of a multiplicity of causes would lead to a selection of the legal cause of the tort on anti-capitalist grounds,[4] and he also opposed the growth of a foreseeability doctrine on related grounds. The growth of modern industry carried with it certain inherent risks to life and limb, so that statistically, it was foreseeable that a certain number of injuries would result. Again, it would be the capitalist who would bear the financial brunt. Beyond that, the recognition of the multiplicity of causes and the inter-connection between the nature of the society and the incidence of injury called into question the whole concept of tort as an individualistic, private law concept. If the objective theory were abandoned, did not the future lie in private and public insurance, and the severing of the question of injury from the concepts of cause and fault?[5] These individualistic doctrines were threatened by theories of causation which dissolved agency within a socialised conception of harm and its redress.

This analysis is highly suggestive for thinking about causation in criminal law. As in tort, the emphasis is upon individual responsibility, and the question is always one of attributing causation to a particular actor: why *this* individual should be said to have been the cause of a particular injury or other effect, and not another. In tort law, the early confidence in an objective doctrine of causation gave way to a realist scepticism about the possibility of separating out 'cause in law' from 'cause in fact' on rational grounds. Concepts such as 'proximity/remoteness' and foreseeability became seen as no more than rationalisations of decisions taken on other grounds. In the absence of genuine concepts, and in an industrial-political world that was 'tortogenic', decisions about fault could only reflect the interests of powerful social agents in the society at large.

The same could be said of criminal law. Crime is a social phenomenon that, particularly as it is processed by the state, is primarily the product of particular socio-economic contexts and classes.[6] The question suggested by Horwitz's account of the debate in tort for the criminal law is this: in a society that is as much criminogenic as 'tortogenic', is it possible genuinely to 'fix' individual responsibility through a conceptually adequate concept of causation? Or is the establishment of causal responsibility simply a political act dressed up in mystifying conceptual language?

A large part of the answer to these questions was supplied in the previous chapter, where it was argued that the social context of individual agency was excluded from the law's consideration by the construction of a very narrow conception of involuntary agency, and a concomitantly broad conception of volun-tariness. The conceptual language mystifies, but it does so because it is practical and efficacious, and because it cleaves to its own narrowly individual logic, albeit a logic that contains significant flaws and occlusions. So effective is this language, that it has established a relatively firm barrier against the opening up of the broader questions raised in the law of tort in the area of criminal liability.[7] But there is one area where the legal realist, policy-oriented critique comes to bear within the criminal law, and that is the area of supervening cause. It is all very well to trace causal responsibility back to an individual, but, looking forward from the individual's act to the intervention of subsequent further acts and causes, at what point does the law cease to impute causation? In this context the law is dealing with causal sequences which frequently *begin* with a criminal act (eg an assault) and end with a further (potentially) criminal consequence (eg a death). How do the legal concepts rationalise the imputation or non-imputation of causal responsibility for the further consequence in light of a new causal intervention? In this area, the realist critique of the law of causal imputation still threatens the ideology that criminal doctrine is founded on sound principles, and we turn now to Hart and Honoré's sophisticated attempt to defend that ideology.

## 3 LIBERAL PRINCIPLES FOR THE IMPUTATION OF CAUSATION

Rooted in a liberal individualist analysis of human agency, Hart and Honoré extol 'the distinctive form which the legal control of conduct takes'. Its value lies in 'its primary appeal to individuals as intelligent beings who are assumed to have the capacity to control their conduct'. Deferring its sanction until such an appeal has been revealed as ineffective by the occurrence of crime, criminal law is a 'form of control that invites the subject's obedience and so, by preserving the possibility of disobeying, maximises freedom within the framework of coercive sanctions' (Hart and Honoré, 1985, lxxix).[8] This liberal theory of the maximisation of individual freedom requires a recognition of the role of individuals as causal actors within the world, whose voluntary interventions 'make a difference' (cf Williams, 1989; Kadish, 1985, 329–36).

In the situation of supervening cause, the central notion is of something which interferes with or intervenes in the course of events which would otherwise occur. Human beings are able to manipulate things, to move and change them, so that where an individual has acted, he is said to have caused any changes that occur, and responsibility for the changes can be imputed to him (Hart and Honoré, 1985, 28–32). However, individuals become implicated in sequences of events, in chains of causes in ways that do not always permit us to impute responsibility. Where an *abnormal contingency* occurs after the act of an individual, or where there is a third party *voluntary intervention*, we no longer impute causal responsibility to the first actor. The intervention of an abnormal contingency reduces the agency of the first actor to that of a background factor: it is the abnormal contingency which now 'makes the difference' (1985, 33–41).

Similarly, the intervention of a third party voluntary act breaks the causal connection between the result and the first actor, for human agency has a special significance and finality to it (1985, 41–4). Once we have a voluntary human act, we do not continue to trace back the causal enquiry beyond it: it operates as both 'a barrier and a goal in tracing back causes' (1985, 44). Hart and Honoré argue that where there is a 'free, deliberate and informed act or omission of a human being' intervening in a causal sequence, the initial causal chain is negated (1985, 136). They operate with 'a conception of a human agent as being most free when he is placed in circumstances which give him a fair opportunity to exercise normal mental and physical powers and he does not exercise them without pressure from others' (1985, 138; cf above, p 112).

Hart and Honoré's position is most plausible where they draw their examples from situations in which an individual, isolated and alone, acts to bring about some effect in nature, for example, the lighting of a spark which sets a forest on fire. But even here, the picture that is presented is one-sided, for we are told nothing about the conditions in which the act occurs, or how it is perceived.

This becomes clear in the crucial distinction they draw between abnormal and normal conditions. An individual is only the moral/legal cause of those events in the world that are accompanied by the normal range of attendant conditions. Where an abnormal condition ensues, it becomes the cause in place of the human intervention, which in turn becomes an antecedent condition to the abnormal element. The problem is that what is normal and what is abnormal, what is cause and what is condition, is a matter of judgment and perspective. To use one of the authors' own (slightly modified) examples (1985, 35), the effect of a famine in a third world country might appear to a peasant as the consequence of drought, and to a relief agency as the result of the inefficiency and corruption of government. To a charity activist, it would be seen as the product of the meanness of the industrialised countries, and to a radical as the effect of economic underdevelopment resulting from neo-liberal economics. All these different factors could be singled out as the cause, with the others regarded as the background conditions; each could be presented as the factor which 'makes the difference'. Hart and Honoré acknowledge that 'the distinction between cause and condition may be drawn in different ways in one and the same case according to the context' (1985, 37). But if the 'normal' is contingent and subject to development and change according to context, it is a weak, potentially unstable, foundation for legal and moral judgments. Individual responsibility ultimately relies upon a variable evaluation of what is 'normal' in social life.

A good illustration is provided by Lord Scarman (1981) in his report into English inner city riots in the early 1980s. Speaking of the events leading to a particular riot, he stated that –

Deeper causes undoubtedly existed, and must be probed: but the immediate cause of Saturday's events was a spontaneous combustion set off by the spark of one particular incident. (1981, 37)

Which factor 'makes the difference', the 'deeper causes' or the 'immediate cause'? If those 'deeper causes' (relating to poor social environment, racial discrimination, police harassment) are part of the 'normal' conditions of life in late twentieth-century England, are they *for that reason* excluded from our account of what caused the riot? It would perhaps be convenient for the law, with its emphasis on the individual, if they were. Elsewhere in his report, Lord Scarman did draw a distinction between the 'causes' and the 'conditions' of the riots (1981, 16). This was shortly before he argued that the *conditions* of young black people cannot exclude their guilt for grave criminal offences which, as causal agents, they have committed (1981, 14). If Hart and Honoré are correct to say it is all a matter of perspective, the example of the Scarman Report reveals that there are competing political views to that of the law.[9]

Second, there is the question of the law's use of the concept of voluntariness. On the face of it, the idea of a new intervening voluntary act by a third party possesses a measure of solidity that the distinction between the normal and the abnormal does not. However, this is illusory since it all depends on how one defines 'voluntary'. Only a voluntary act will break the causal chain, so the act of a third party may not break the chain if it is adjudged 'involuntary'. Hart and Honoré concede that there are narrower and broader uses of the terminology (1985, 138), and much hinges upon their notion of what constitutes a 'fair choice'. This, they say, 'depends in part on what conduct is regarded from a moral or legal point of view as reasonable in the circumstances', an issue that 'raises questions of legal policy' (1985, 42; cf Stapleton, 1988, 124).

This becomes apparent in their discussion of situations which are not regarded as voluntary by the law. These include, in addition to the more obvious situations of unconsciousness and physical duress, the policy-influenced situations of preservation of property, safeguarding of rights and interests, including economic interests, and the carrying out of legal and even moral obligations (1985, 142–62). All may be regarded as situations in which an individual did not act voluntarily. Just how broad the concept of the involuntary may go becomes apparent when the authors are discussing legal obligation:

> In ordinary speech we recognise that even a social obligation restricts our freedom, so that if I have accepted an invitation to dine with you I am 'not free' to dine with anyone else. So too in the law. (1985, 138)[10]

With such wide notions of what might constitute involuntariness, the hope that the voluntary intervention of a third party might draw a line across a causal chain in a principled manner is impossible. The definition is too flexible, too open to broad and narrow interpretations of what the term means.

What is voluntary may be subject to a more or less individualistic interpretation. If it is a matter of looking at whether an individual was conscious when he acted, this is a narrow focus on the individual and his mental state. If, on the other hand, it is a question of examining social or legal obligations, this locates the individual in a network of social relations and understandings, and presents a broad view of the voluntary/involuntary line. From this latter, more social view, rooting the individual in a context of interpersonal relations,[11] it is questionable just what significance the voluntariness of human agency should have (see further Norrie, 2000, chs 1, 9).

Hart and Honoré's argument is that voluntary human agency has a special finality about it. While we may look for reasons why a poisoner did what he did in terms of motives like greed or revenge, we do not regard his motive as the cause of death, although we may consider it the cause of his action. The example is perhaps tendentious,[12] but the main point is that it draws upon the illustration of an isolated, asocial individual, alone with his private emotions, and does not locate individual agency in its broader context. A good counter-example is provided by J B Priestley's play, *An Inspector Calls*. The author persuades us to look behind the 'voluntary' act of the young woman's suicide to the conduct of the various members of the well-to-do family, who each in their own way have contributed to the girl's decision to take her life. Priestley forces the family to see that each of its members has in his or her own way caused the girl's death. They cannot conceal behind the girl's 'voluntary' act their own causal roles stemming from the interconnectedness of relations between rich and poor. It is this which ensures that any focus on individual agency can only be falsely narrow. The girl's suicide is 'voluntary', but it is still caused by the acts of the family, so that no special finality is given to her actions. 'Voluntariness' loses its special character when a broader view of events and actions is taken.

Hart and Honoré's analysis is neatly dovetailed with the individualism of the law, and it is this that provides its strength and its weakness. Its strength is its ability to rationalise the way in which judges do talk about causation in the criminal law, and to give effective expression to the concepts that are implicit and explicit in their judgments in a way that the policy reductionist critique (above, p 136) cannot. For the reductionist, judicial distinctions are a veneer for decisions that can only be based upon policy grounds, for there is no plausibly effective language of causation (other than basic sine qua non) in a world where causation is everywhere. Hart and Honoré reflect the individualist logic of the law which stipulates that individuals are practical actors, who effectively act upon the world and are producers of causes and consequences by their acts. Their weakness lies in their inability, like the law, to produce a synthesised conception of the relationship between individual agency and social and political structures. Because of this, the strength of their concepts, based upon the individualist model, ebbs away when confronted with the broader context within which individuals operate. Thus individuals are held to be the causes until something abnormal intervenes, but what is abnormal depends upon social perception, and therefore upon a socio-political label being stuck upon it. Similarly, causation stretches as far as the new voluntary act of a third party, but what is meant by voluntary can be as narrow or as broad as one likes, depending upon how much one is prepared to recognise the social character of the lives of individuals.

My argument is that it is this limited, unsynthesised individualism in the law's causation analysis that makes it rely on 'policy' to draw the lines for it. The causation analysis is both genuine and operative in legal decision-making and fundamentally flawed by its focus primarily on individuals in abstraction from social relations. Although she mistakes the part for the whole, it is this flawing that gives the policy-reductionist an entrée, and which, we shall see, undercuts the rationality of the law. Hart and Honoré's analysis is a paradigmatic, if late, expression of Enlightenment thought. Rooted in the philosophy of Hume and Mill (Hart and Honoré, 1985, ch 1), it rests in the first instance upon the analysis of the individual, engaging with other individuals and with nature as a self-contained monad, capable of producing effects in the world as a cause in him/herself. This is the law's approach too, but what is missing from both is any recognition of the way in which individual agency is fundamentally constructed and constituted within pre-existing social relations. When Hart and Honoré or the law open up this relationship, they undermine their own premises, and must resort to a political 'fix' to establish the causal relationship. It is the gap between the individual and the social that hounds the case law on causation.

## 4 ANALYSING THE CAUSATION CASES

The focus upon the individualism of the causal connection means that the language of causation in the criminal law is always artificially foreclosed by concepts that lack a valid theoretical grounding. In addition to the concepts of normal and abnormal, voluntary and involuntary, vague notions of 'reasonable' and 'unreasonable' and of 'natural' and 'unnatural' conduct have to be drafted in to decide the causal issue in a way that lacks rigour and generates contradiction as cases go in different directions. Thus, it is a 'foolish' or a 'daft' act of the victim that constitutes a supervening cause, an 'unreasonable' act that negates causal connection, while it is a 'natural' act that maintains the causal chain (Hart and Honoré, 1985, 327, 331–6, 342).[13] The language of causation is employed but it can never do the whole job; it requires political judgments to shut down or open up the grounds of causation in each case.

### (i) The intervention of a new voluntary act

Because of the two-sided nature of actions as both individual and social, what appears from one point of view as a voluntary act can from another point of view appear involuntary, and vice versa. Much depends upon the focus of the enquiry (cf Kelman, 1981, 640–2). The more narrowly one analyses the various actions and actors, the more likely it is that they will appear to be discrete, self-contained and autonomous phenomena. The more broadly one examines the facts, however, locating what happened within the wider context, the less an act is likely to appear voluntary. For example, Hart and Honoré discuss the American case of *State v Preslar* (1885) (1985, 326–7) as one in which the language of voluntariness was determinative. A wife was beaten by her husband, and left the family home with her child to walk to her father's house. Two hundred yards from the latter's home, she lay down, stating she did not wish to continue until morning, and died of exposure. Hart and Honoré, following the logic of the court, argue that 'since the wife had exposed herself without necessity and there were circumstances showing deliberation in her leaving home', her actions were to be treated as 'fully voluntary' (1985, 327).

If, as seems likely, the woman's acts were connected with the treatment she had received from her husband, the decision to leave the home, deliberated upon or not, could easily be construed as part of a scenario relating to self-preservation, an accepted ground for negating the voluntariness of an act,[14] and thereby extending the causal chain. Deliberation in itself counts for nothing if one considers the context within which the deliberation takes place. The basic facts do not determine the authors' conclusion.

Similarly, in *Carbo v State* (1908) (1985, 327), the defendant had created a risk of an explosion, about which a fireman ignored a warning. Entering the building, the latter was killed, but his 'foolish' act in so entering was held to be a supervening voluntary act. Again, an alternative account is available, in which the acts of brave firemen, often at risk of personal injury, are construed as the conscientious actions of employees fulfilling their obligations, and as such involuntary. As Hart and Honoré point out themselves, in the law of tort, precisely such a narrative operates in order to permit employees working in dangerous conditions to gain damages for injuries received (1985, 147). Again in tort, where a rescuer acts from either legal or moral obligation, even in a way that is 'unreasonably brave', the existence of the obligation removes the voluntary aspect of her actions (1985, 148). The alternative scenario is readily available.[15]

*Carbo* can also be contrasted with *State v Leopold* (1929) (1985, 333), where the accused was convicted of murder when the tenant of a house which had been set alight by the accused sent his sons into the building in order to recover property. The sons died in the fire. In this case, it was held to be 'natural' to recover property in this way, and there was therefore no voluntary act on the part of the victims. But it appears quite reckless, indeed 'unnatural', to put the value of property above the value of one's children's lives. It is 'foolish' to re-enter a burning building, so that the ground for saying that Leopold caused the death is contingent on the way in which one interprets the facts.

Nor is it simply a matter of how one frames the incident in question: it also depends upon a perception of what is and is not reasonable conduct within an incident. This is seen in particular in the cases where it is alleged that self-preservation negates the voluntariness of an action. To construe the actions of a woman as involuntary where minor sexual molestation in a moving car leads her to jump out to her injury (*Roberts* (1971)) or even death (*People v Goodman* (1943)), it is necessary to empathise with the alarm experienced by women in such situations. It is only if the victim does something 'daft' that her act is regarded as voluntary (Hart and Honoré, 1985, 331), but 'daft' is what 'daft' does.[16]

There is something odd in the idea that the test of a new intervening act is that it is 'not so daft as to make it . . . voluntary' (*Williams and Davis* (1992) at 8). Also, 'daftness' is to take account of the capacities of the victim. In *Corbett* (1996), a mentally handicapped man with a drink problem who had been drinking all day was assaulted. He fled, fell in the gutter and was killed by a passing car. The defendant's appeal was dismissed because the victim's conduct was foreseeable given that he was 'immensely drunk'. To break the causal chain, the victim's reaction would have had to be 'daft' in the circumstances. What made his reaction not 'daft' in law was the fact that he was 'daft' through drink and handicap on the day he died.

Similarly, in *Dear* (1996), the victim had been slashed following allegations that he had sexually abused the defendant's child. Two days later, the victim died either as a result of re-opening the wounds or failing to take steps to staunch them when they re-opened themselves. The defendant argued that this amounted to a new intervening act of suicide. The court held that, whatever the deceased's contribution, it was irrelevant provided that the initial wound was an operating and significant cause of death. Even if the victim had treated himself with gross negligence, it would be irrelevant to causation. It would be a 'retrograde step' if 'the rules which the concepts of novus actus interveniens and foreseeability did or should play in causation were to invade the criminal law' ((1996) at 595). This argument simply repudiates the need for analysis of causal principle.

The role of policy in structuring the perceptions and establishing the breadth of the frame of analysis is perhaps most clearly seen where police officers kill third parties in attempts to control armed individuals, and causal responsibility is imputed to the latter.[17] In a number of American cases, this has happened and is explained by Hart and Honoré, under the two heads of self-preservation and legal duty, as cases where the officers have acted involuntarily (1985, 331–2, 334).[18] This leads to what the authors concede is the counter-intuitive result that where an armed criminal is killed by a police officer, he can be said to have committed suicide (1985, 332, 334). On the other hand in the case of *Commonwealth v Moore* (1904) (1985, 334) it was held that a rioter was not causally responsible for the death of a bystander shot by a soldier quelling the riot, though presumably an alternative conclusion was available.

The irreducibly political content of these decisions can be seen by comparing *Pagett* (1983) (see note 18) with the Northern Irish case of *Brown* (1973). The latter is a self defence rather than causation case in which the defendant shot and killed a police officer, arguing in his defence that he fired his gun only because he believed, mistakenly as it turned out, that the police officer was 'unjustifiably or unwarrantably' going to kill him. The court held that this defence was unsound because 'the law throws, without any such refined reservations, a protecting mantle over persons preventing or assisting in preventing crime' ((1973) at 109–10). If self defence is not available in this situation for the policy reason given, then the argument on the ground of causation, that the accused's act of self-preservation was involuntary so that the policeman caused his own death, is unlikely to get off the ground. Yet the only difference, it seems, between this case and the others is the political one of who is wearing the 'protective mantle' of a uniform. In *Pagett*, for example, the police may have killed the victim, yet their acting reasonably for the purpose of self-preservation and in pursuit of a legal duty meant that Pagett was held to have caused the death (cf Clarkson and Keating, 1998, 459–60).

Finally, there is *Blaue*, a case in which a young woman died from stab wounds having refused a blood transfusion because it was against her beliefs as a Jehovah's Witness. Hart and Honoré argue that the refusal did not break the causal connection, despite the fact that it was deliberate (cf *State v Preslar* (1885)), because the holding of such a belief is involuntary:

> . . . the question to be decided is whether the decision to refuse treatment is not merely deliberate and informed (as it clearly was in the *Blaue* case) but also a free one. In view of the high value attached in our society to matters of conscience, the victim, though free to accept any belief she wished, is not thereafter free to abandon her chosen belief merely because she finds herself in a situation in which her life may otherwise be in danger. So it was not her free act to refuse a transfusion. (1985, 361)

Hart and Honoré suggest this as a more compelling argument than the 'take the victim as you find her' argument (discussed below) used by the court. They add that 'An element of legal policy certainly enters into such a judgment', but this is an unnecessary claim for them to make given that their definition of voluntariness is sufficiently broad to include moral obligation as a negating factor (1985, 335). Why not simply argue that the case illustrates their argument on the broad causal principle? The answer possibly lies in the fact that in a secular society the contentious character of the assertion that religious persons are bound by their beliefs so that their actions are involuntary is clear. It is not that the sense of 'involuntary' cannot be understood here, but rather that there is equal recognition of a sense in which those who take on moral commitments can equally well be said to have acted and to be continuing to act voluntarily. Here, different possible definitions of 'voluntary' are so near the surface of the argument, too obviously available in a secular society, for the claim that the victim in *Blaue* had 'really' acted involuntarily readily to hold sway.[19] Perhaps for this reason, Hart and Honoré concede against their *own* very broad analysis of involuntariness, that the decision involves a determinative element of policy. In doing so, they are only making explicit in *Blaue* what is implicit in the other cases: that policy is ultimately determinative in a causal analysis caught within the duality of human action as an individual and social phenomenon. The duality ultimately requires for its resolution reference to some extrinsic element such as 'policy'. Without this, it can only rely on fudge words which evade the conflict in a non-rational manner.

## (ii) The intervention of an abnormal occurrence

Where a causative event occurs contemporaneously with or subsequent to the act of the accused that can be described as coincidental, it breaks the causal chain. A coincidental event is marked by four features: it is very unlikely (it is abnormal) by ordinary standards; it is significant or important; it occurs without human contrivance; it is independent of the other relevant act or event (Hart and Honoré, 1985, 78). Such a coincidental event 'makes the difference' and therefore breaks the causal chain. However, the question of normality and abnormality implicit in this definition requires a contextual selection of the appropriate focus to be adopted before a result can be obtained in a particular case, ie requires that the issue of causation be fixed by 'policy' grounds external to the analysis. More seriously, there are rules in this area in which a socio-political judgment does not *complete* the individualist analysis of causation but goes further and undermines it.

### (a)   The medical treatment cases

Like the other major textbook writers, Hart and Honoré treat these cases as a separate group, to some extent autonomously of the general principles they have elaborated. Yet the empirical location of a set of cases ought not to disturb the conceptual analysis, if the latter is valid. In *Jordan* (1956), the victim died after receiving treatment that was described by a medical witness as 'palpably wrong', and which was administered after the accused's stab wounds had mainly healed. The court held that death that ensued from 'normal' medical treatment would not interrupt the causal chain, but that the treatment in this case was not normal. While they did not directly define abnormal treatment, they explained the term by referring to the 'two separate and independent features of [the] treatment [which] were, in the opinion of the doctors, palpably wrong'. The inference appears to be that treatment that is either negligent or grossly negligent (it is not clear which), will break the causal chain, and this fits with the Hart and Honoré analysis of normality and abnormality.

Hart and Honoré do not, however, claim the decision as support for their own view, despite its apparent closeness conceptually, for they must also explain the subsequent case of *Smith* (1959), in which the court isolated the earlier decision, calling it 'a very particular case depending upon its exact facts'. In this case, the victim died as a result of stab wounds compounded by medical treatment that was described as 'thoroughly bad', where, with proper treatment, he had a 75 per cent chance of recovery. The appellant's conviction of murder was, however, upheld on the basis that –

... if at the time of death the original wound is still an operating and a substantial cause, then the death can properly be said to be the result of the wound, albeit that some other cause of death is also operating. Only if it can be said that the original wounding is merely the setting in which another cause operates can it be said that the death does not result from the wound. Putting it in another way, only if the second cause is so overwhelming as to make the original wound merely part of the history can it be said that the death does not flow from the wound. (*Smith* (1959) at 198)

This decision employs the kind of soft metaphorical language beloved by the policy reductionists, and which Hart and Honoré sought to replace with something conceptually harder. It makes no reference to the test of abnormality which they had suggested was a way of distinguishing cases where a new intervening act would break the causal chain. Within that context, the fact that a wound is still 'an operating and substantial cause' is relevant but inconclusive,[20] for the question should be whether the intervening cause 'makes the difference' to the outcome. Smith's victim was given 'thoroughly bad' (surely a synonym for 'palpably wrong') treatment and had a 75 per cent chance of recovery. It is hard not to say that the treatment 'made the difference' if the test of abnormality is applied, yet *Smith* is entirely against *Jordan*.

The counter-argument is that the wound in *Smith* remained an operating cause, whereas in *Jordan*, it was more or less repaired, no longer operative and therefore only the setting in which maltreatment occurred. This argument only holds on a failure to see the facts in *Jordan* broadly enough, for it was still the accused's actions that landed his victim in the hospital, and that led him to be treated in the way that turned out to be palpably wrong. The victim in *Jordan* was only in hospital receiving treatment as a result of the assault by the accused. He was only treated because of the existence of the original wound. Even if the wound had virtually healed, it was still the reason why, and the *only* reason why, the victim was treated. It therefore remained an operating and substantial cause of the treatment. Thus his actions could be said to be a substantial cause of death as in *Smith*, the only difference being that one must look at the former case in a broader focus in order to see it.

Part of the problem here concerns the meaning of an 'abnormal' course of treatment in such cases. It is one thing to fill this concept out with a description of medical treatment that is (grossly) negligent, for then one can point to the intervention of the actions of another individual who is blamed (the doctor) in place of the accused. But if we take into account the broader context in which negligent conduct occurs, it becomes difficult to apportion blame to individuals at all. In *Smith*, there is evidence of the poor medical provisions available to soldiers in a peace-time medical station in Germany. There were no facilities, for example, for blood transfusion, which would have been, in the court's words, 'the best possible treatment'. In their discussion of what constitutes 'the abnormal' in human affairs, Hart and Honoré point out (1985, 35–8) that this can change when our perceptions of what is acceptable and unacceptable in society's provision for dealing with particular problems change.[21] From this point of view, one possible causal 'bottom line', nowhere canvassed in the cases, might be the inadequacy of the state in its provision of medical facilities for soldiers overseas. The response to this is likely to be that no individual should be able to renounce his causal responsibility by so 'passing the buck'. One might, however, point out that the only difference between Jack abroad and Jill at home, both involved in assaults, is that Jill's victim survives because of the availability of proper medical support. Jack's murder conviction rests on happenstance of time and place, and the causation 'principle' applied is ultimately a matter of bad luck for the accused.[22] If these matters were to be canvassed in a subsequent criminal case, they could only be resolved by a political prise de position as to what was to be regarded as the normal and abnormal in the state's running of medical affairs.

Another part of the problem in *Smith* is that, as with the 'eggshell skull' rule discussed below, judicial policy does not so much complete the causal analysis as undercut it. The retreat to the 'substantial cause' argument plus the isolation (not, note, the overruling) of *Jordan* are means to allocate responsibility by ducking the question of the relevance of a new intervening abnormal act. In *Smith*, the court evade consideration of the intervening act doctrine entirely, preferring comfortably vague terms like 'substantial cause' in place of a straight confrontation of the argument raised by *Jordan*. Because they do this, they are forced to distinguish the earlier case as a particular one decided on its facts, which is not to distinguish it at all.

To return at this point to the Law Commission and their discussion of medical negligence, we are told that maltreatment is unlikely but not unforeseeable, and is not, save in an exceptional case, sufficient in itself to cause death (1989, 156).[23] But no analysis is provided of what the 'exceptional case' might be and what would distinguish it from the normal case. The argument again rests upon the concept of the sufficiency of the maltreatment by itself, and therefore on the concept of an 'operating and substantial cause' of death, but this language suffers from the same problem as talk of 'remote' or 'proximate' cause. It is too vague to do anything other than allow courts and juries a free hand in deciding cases.[24] It is also inadequate, as Hart and Honoré point out, for it fails to specify when intervening maltreatment *could* amount to a supervening cause (1985, 361; see quote at note 20). The Law Commission's discussion, like Hart and Honoré's, reflects the two cases of *Smith* and *Jordan*. These cases have never been satisfactorily reconciled, so that the sense in which the wound in the one case remained 'operating and substantial' but not in the other depends, as I have argued, on the way in which one looks at the facts.

The more recent medical maltreatment case of *Cheshire* (1991) reflects the same problem. There, the Court of Appeal held that the accused's acts 'need not be the sole cause or even the main cause of death' so long as they 'contributed significantly'. Where there is medical negligence in treatment, even as the 'immediate cause of death', it will only break the causal chain if it was 'so independent, and in itself so potent in causing death' as to be a supervening act. What makes an act 'so independent' or 'so potent'? Where medical staff are involved, 'it will only be in the most extraordinary and unusual case that treatment can be said to be so independent' ((1991) at 677). Yet *Cheshire* was arguably just such a case. The defendant had shot the deceased in the leg and abdomen (the anatomy is important). As part of the treatment, the hospital had attached a tube to his windpipe to aid breathing. Two months later, when the wounds were no longer life-threatening, a reaction to the tube in the windpipe set in. Despite clear signs of this, the hospital did nothing and the victim/patient died.

The time lag, the process of healing the original wounds and the anatomical distance between the wounds and how death was caused suggested a *Jordan* rather than a *Smith* scenario. Of course, it can always be argued that a victim in hospital is there as a result of the initial injury. The possibility of the argument going either way is seen in the competing accounts of death from expert witnesses on both sides. The defence expert stated that 'the cause of death was the failure to recognise the reason for his sudden onset and continued breathlessness ... the severe respiratory obstruction', placing causal responsibility with the authorities. The pathologist for the Crown said death was 'due to a condition which was produced as a result of treatment to provide an artificial airway in the treatment of gunshot wounds of the abdomen and leg'. He elided the anatomical gap by declaring that the cause of death was 'cardio-respiratory arrest due to gunshot wounds of the abdomen and leg' ((1991) at 672). Which story is right?

Returning to the legal argument in *Cheshire*, one might say that it points to the need for a high level of negligence before the causal chain will be broken by medical maltreatment. Smith and Hogan (1999, 344) suggest the negligence should be gross. Yet the facts of *Cheshire* together with the requirement of 'extraordinariness' suggests a degree of closed-mindedness to the possibility of a new intervening act in cases of this kind. Like the police in *Brown*, medical staff seem to enjoy a 'protecting mantle' in these cases.

## (b) The 'eggshell skull' case

One particular problem stems from the 'take the victim as you find him' rule that operates in most legal systems. In the classic death from an eggshell skull case, it could be argued that the particular physical character of the victim is coincidental on the Hart and Honoré criteria, and therefore the accused should not be said to have caused the death. It is after all very unlikely that a victim will have a very thin skull, it is very significant, it occurs without contrivance, and it is independent of the accused's acts. Hart and Honoré, however, argue that the rule is a legitimate one:

> An abnormal *condition existing at the time* of a human intervention is distinguished both by ordinary thought and, with a striking consistency, by most legal systems from an abnormal event or conjunction of *events subsequent to that intervention*; the former, unlike the latter, are not ranked as coincidences or 'extraneous' causes when the consequences of intervention come to be traced ... *The scope of the principle which thus distinguishes contemporaneous abnormal conditions from subsequent events is unclear*; but at least where a human being initiates some physical change in a thing, animal, or person, abnormal physical states of the object affected, existing at the time, are ranked as part of the circumstances in which the cause 'operates'. In the familiar controlling imagery these are part of 'the stage already set' before the 'intervention'. (1985, 79–80) (emphasis added)

Note first that the distinction drawn between conditions present *at the time* and *subsequent* circumstances or events is irrelevant since a coincidence may occur, on the author's own definition (1985, 77–8), contemporaneously with the act of the accused. It may, however, be argued that a condition like the eggshell skull gains its significance from the fact not that it is contemporaneous with the act of assault, but from the fact that it pre-exists the act in question: it is part of 'the stage already set', as Hart and Honoré put it.

If this is the genuine ground for the distinction, it too is inadequate, because, as the authors themselves acknowledge, the issue still has to be faced as to whether or not the pre-existing condition is normal or abnormal (1985, 33–5). A condition is irrelevant to causal attribution *where it is a 'mere' condition, that is, one that is 'present both in the case of the disaster and of normal functioning'*, or is a 'normal feature . . . of the thing in question' (1985, 34). The 'mere' condition is the one that does not 'make the difference' (1985, 35) between the accident and things going on as usual. But in the eggshell skull case, it is indeed the existence of the exceptionally thin skull that makes the difference between the 'normal' assault and its 'abnormal' result, the death. It is not a 'normal feature' of the skull, and it is not present in both the 'normal functioning' case and the disaster case. It most certainly does 'make the difference'.

It is not surprising that the precise scope of the abnormal physical condition rule is not clear, for it cuts across the basic principle that Hart and Honoré propose. Of course, the assault that occasions death in the eggshell skull case is a causa sine qua non, but for the authors to claim that 'ordinary thought' would not regard the physical characteristics of the victim as a coincidence is both highly questionable psychologically,[25] and wrong on their own analysis. There is not even here the respite of arguing that the case may look differently from different perspectives. What we have is a rule of judicial policy, one of the most firm and well-known of causal rules, that cuts across and cuts down an attempt to advance rational grounds for causal distinctions on an individualist basis.[26]

## (c)    The regulatory context

The role of the abnormal condition in breaking the causal chain has recently been considered in the House of Lords in *Environment Agency v Empress Car Company Ltd* (1999). There, the House had to determine whether a company had caused a leak of pollution when an unknown third party had opened a tap. On its face, a third party intervention suggests a new intervening act, but the House found the company to have caused the leak. Lord Hoffmann used the 'common-sense distinction' between acts and events which are 'abnormal and extraordinary' and those which are 'in the generality a normal and familiar fact of life' ((1999) at 34). Since there is 'nothing extraordinary or abnormal about leaky pipes or lagoons' or about 'ordinary vandalism', one does not say about any of these 'that was an extraordinary coincidence, which negatived the causal connection' and caused the pollution (ibid).

As in the medical maltreatment cases, one can see how the argument could have gone either way in this case. Lord Hoffmann, however, has another argument up his sleeve. It is the policy based observation that 'common sense answers to questions of causation will differ according to the purpose for which the question is asked' ((1999) at 29). One needs to know the 'purpose and scope of the rule' ((1999) at 31) in order to decide causation issues under it. For a strict liability offence, causation is broadly stated to include all 'normal' kinds of pollution, including those where 'ordinary vandals', though not 'terrorists' ((1999) at 34), cause it. What counts as a normal condition, and therefore is to be budgeted for by the company under pollution legislation, is decided in a broad purposive way. Whether this is a different approach to interpreting legal cause as a result of the specific regulatory context, or whether such a 'purposive' approach is always implicitly on offer in the law of causation, is considered in the Conclusion, below.

## 5 CONCLUSION

The individualism of the causal analysis reflects the individualism of legal practice and the problems associated with it. The causal responsibility of the individual rests, first, on a concept of *voluntariness* which cannot be easily pinned down, since broader and narrower concepts of voluntariness are possible in a situation of individual and social contextualisation of action. Second, it involves a concept of actions 'making the difference' by virtue of a socio-political ('policy') conception of what is normal and abnormal. Legal individualism requires supplementation by purposive 'policy' readings, to reach decisions in individual cases, and this leads to a case law which is essentially unstable and irrational.

There is an additional problem that emerges from this unstable interface of policy and principle. It is the ability of policy arguments to 'break free' from their attachment to principle, to move from being supplements to inchoate principles to determinative arguments in their own right. The *Empress Car Company* case is unusual in that it involved a regulatory strict liability offence, but Lord Hoffmann's judgment reveals much about the underlying problem. Causation issues 'often arise for the purpose of attributing responsibility to someone'. If a man forgets to take his radio out of his car and it is stolen, who caused the damage? If a thief is on trial 'so that the question is whether he is criminally responsible, then obviously the answer is that he caused the damage'. However, in the context 'of an inquiry into the owner's blameworthiness under a non-legal, common-sense duty to take reasonable care of one's own possessions, one would say that his carelessness caused the loss of the radio' ((1999) at 29).

How far should one read these comments about the functional and purposive character of enquiry into the nature of criminal causation? Is the context of the criminal trial determinative of the *answer* to the causation question a priori, or is the purposive analysis itself controlled by grounds of principle? Hart and Honoré insist it is, but it is debatable if the law genuinely reflects their argument. When it comes to potential supervening causes, the law's position seems in some situations to be one of unalloyed 'purposiveness'. There is a criminal, and the purpose of the causation rules is, quite simply, to attribute responsibility to him. It is no answer to say that there is a supervening cause where that cause involves the police, the medical services, or physical or psychological characteristics of the victim. The context of the criminal on trial determines the result regardless of Hart and Honoré's common-sense principles. Policy does not so much complete as override principle.

Finally, it is worth comparing the law of supervening cause with the law of acts and omissions. In the law of acts, the concept of involuntariness is closed down so as to exclude the *moral* conception of involuntariness (above, pp 112–14). With causes, it is opened up, causing particular problems of indeterminacy in this area. With omissions, the external limits of duty are narrowly and specifically set, whereas in supervening cause, the line is drawn (in the Hart and Honoré analysis) by the inherently vague concept of what is normal or abnormal. Why should the concepts of act and omission be set so narrowly and precisely, while the parallel concepts in the law of causation are by comparison broad and vague? The answer lies in the functional context, which determines the form of the law. The narrowness of involuntariness in the law of acts excludes excuses and strengthens fault attribution, while the narrowness of the duty requirement in omissions focuses fault attribution on a pre-selected criminal group while excluding 'respectable' omitters.

In the area of supervening cause, the law is concerned primarily with the linkage of already constituted criminal acts to further, more serious, criminal results. But for a broad conception of involuntariness or a vague and malleable conception of abnormality, these might be said not to be caused by the accused. In this context, the social control interest of the judges encourages an approach which stretches causal connection as far as individualistic logic will allow, and beyond. Thus, whereas the law of acts excludes issues of moral involuntariness concerning the acts of the *accused*, the law of causation opens its arms wide to moral involuntariness involving the acts of the *victim*. The function remains the same in the two areas of law, but the form changes. A narrow conception of involuntariness in the general law of acts and a broad conception in the law of acts negativing causation *both* strengthen the fault attribution process. The difference in approaches in the two areas is striking and inexplicable in formal logical terms. It is explicable in terms of the political shaping of the individualistic logic of fault to the end of criminal conviction.

Similarly, if we compare the narrowing of the causation analysis in the law of omissions through the use of the duty concept with the broad character of the normal/abnormal criterion in the law of causation, a flexibility is present in the latter. This does not exist in the former area, where the aim is the *exclusion* of types of fault from the criminal process. As a result, the problem of indeterminacy that emerges from a broadening of the duty requirement in the law of omissions (above, pp 128–30) looms large in the area of causation because of the flexibility of the concepts deployed to achieve conviction. Even here, however, within an approach that gives maximum room for manoeuvre, the eggshell skull or medical maltreatment cases indicate that the judges will not necessarily regard themselves as constrained by causal principle.

# Part IV

# Defences

# Chapter 8

# Necessity and duress

The point is simply that the criminal law should express the way we live. Our culture is built on the assumption that, absent valid claims of excuse, we are accountable for what we do. If that cultural presupposition should someday prove to be empirically false, there will be far more radical changes in our way of life than those expressed in the criminal law. (Fletcher, 1978, 801–2)

Blackstone shared his contemporaries' view that much criminal activity resulted from social conditions . . . Characteristically, however, he shied away from the conclusion that poverty or exposure to vice and evil companions stripped one of a truly free will. That conclusion (for which he provided no logical rebuttal) he regarded as dangerous to the public order. Poverty, he asserted, ought not to ground a defence of involuntarism or of necessity, especially in cases of theft of food or clothing . . . (Green, 1985, 296)

## I   INTRODUCTION

The contradictory impulses behind the criminal law are nowhere better illustrated than in the area of excuses and, in particular, in the two parallel defences of necessity and duress. Paradox reigns here in abundance. We have a well recognised defence of duress, but the judges cannot make up their minds as to whether it ought to be allowed for all crimes. The House of Lords has taken the unusual step of overruling itself on this question. At the same time, they express unease as to why there should be such a defence at all: duress 'is difficult to rationalise or explain by reference to any coherent principle of jurisprudence' (*Howe* (1987) at 783) (see also *Lynch* (1975) at 679). Why should the defence of duress cause such problems for criminal law theory?

With regard to necessity, things are, if anything, worse. While such a defence is recognised in particular situations, the judges have not endorsed any general acceptance. The alternative view that there is a general defence of necessity must contend with the strange peculiarity of the doctrine, that is, 'the difficulty or impossibility of formulating it with any approach to precision' (Williams, 1961, 728).[1] Yet, as Cross put it, the defences are so similar that to provide for a defence of duress while excluding one of necessity represents 'the apotheosis of absurdity' (Cross, 1978, 377). Lord Hailsham confirmed as much when he described duress as 'only that species of the genus of necessity which is caused by wrongful threats' (*Howe* (1987) at 777). Recent activity in the Court of Appeal confirms the similarity of one form of necessity (now termed 'duress of circumstances': *Conway* (1988); *Martin* (1989); *Pommell* (1995); *Abdul-Hussain* (1999)) to duress itself ('duress by threats'). A defence of necessity in medical cases has also emerged in recent years (*Gillick v West Norfolk and Wisbech Area Health Authority* (1986); *F v West Berkshire Health Authority* (1989); *Re A (children)* (2000)). Still, duress and necessity, the twin defences, have generally been treated in quite different ways.

Behind the compromise and slippery logic of the duress cases and the strong opposition, until recently, to the necessity defence there lie important pulls of judicial policy on legal doctrine, but the necessity and duress situations also raise deeper questions about the validity of the legal approach to blaming individuals. What is the character of legal guilt? To what extent does it match our understanding of how individuals act in society? The quotation from Fletcher at the head of the chapter (which refers to the issues raised by the law in this area) suggests a comfortable partnership between legal categories and social assumptions. But I shall argue that a thorough investigation of the necessity and duress cases raises fundamental problems in connection with the law's 'cultural presuppositions'.

The chapter is divided into three main sections. In the first two, we examine the basic arguments behind the necessity and duress defences, identifying the main points of conflict within them and indicating the deeper theoretical issues involved. In a final section, we then look at these more fundamental questions.


## 2 NECESSITY

An initial problem faced in discussing necessity concerns the character of the defence as either a justification or excuse. Viewed as a justification, necessity is understood as involving a choice between two evils in which the accused's act is held not to be wrong where the lesser evil is selected. The choice is justified, so no wrong act has been done. A utilitarian calculus brought into play sanctions the act in question. From this perspective, necessity would justify the killing of one person to save two, but not the killing of two to save one. In the latter situation, the balance of utility is in favour of the saving of two lives against the loss of one. As an excuse, the choice between evils is in principle irrelevant because the focus moves from the question of the value of the act to the position, condition or circumstances of the actor and their effect on his culpability. If the actor was compelled by circumstances beyond control to perform a killing, it does not logically matter whether one person or two (or more) were killed. The focus is not on the utility of the act but the plight of the actor, who does not say that no wrong was done, only that he ought to be excused from conviction or punishment for it.

Commentators differ in their emphasis on these two approaches to necessity. Williams analyses the defence as essentially one of justification, but adds a form of necessity (compulsion of circumstances) to his account of duress which is excuse based (1983, 597, 634–5). Compulsion of circumstances, because it can be analogised with duress, is included in the Criminal Code Bill, but the development of a lesser evils approach is left to the judiciary to clarify as they see fit (Law Commission, 1989, 228, 231). While some American commentators have supported the distinction

(Fletcher, 1978, ch 10), others have questioned its value in theory and in practice (Hall, 1976; Greenawalt, 1986; Gur-Arye, 1986). Fletcher argues that necessity necessarily involves both approaches, for some situations can only be understood in the context of excuse, others only in that of justification. However, the examples that he gives of situations that can only be understood as involving justification are not so clear-cut (Fletcher, 1974, 1274–8).[2] He may, however, be correct at a deeper level in that it may be that some defences necessarily incorporate both justificatory and excusatory elements, as is the case with provocation (Ashworth, 1976; Horder, 1992).

The matter cannot be resolved here. There is, on the one hand, a tendency in the modern law to prefer excusatory to justificatory argument (Norrie, 2001). Necessity qua excuse therefore more easily fits the logic of the law as it stands because it assimilates 'duress of circumstances' to the excuse of 'duress by threats'. On the other hand, the cases of medical necessity, discussed below, have been cast in a justificatory framework. The discussion here therefore reflects without fully explaining the changing patterns of thinking in the law.[3]

### (i) Necessity's ambiguous history

A brief historical survey reveals that the necessity defence has always been regarded with ambivalence by lawyers. In the sixteenth century, it was argued that a distinction could be drawn between a breach of the letter and of the spirit of the law. The former breach could 'give way to some acts and things done against the words of the same laws . . . where the words of them are broken to avoid greater inconveniences, or through necessity, or by compulsion . . .' (*Reniger v Fogossa* (1552)) (see Smith and Hogan, 1988, 223 for a fuller account). In 1630, Bacon identified situations of hunger, of drowning persons fighting for a plank and of escapes from a burning jail as ones where no crime was committed on account of necessity (Glazebrook, 1972, 110–11). Hale, however (1736, 1, 54), with whom Blackstone agreed, stated that theft 'being under necessity for want of victuals or clothes' was still a felony (see generally Glazebrook, 1972; Fletcher, 1978, 822–3). The political issues behind the defence, which echoed through the courtroom again in the 1971 civil case of *London Borough of Southwark v Williams* (1971) (see below, p 159), were to the fore in Hale's account. He observed that a defence of necessity would render private property insecure, and that no true necessity situation could emerge because of the poor laws. At the same time, he rebuked those who claimed that there was a necessity defence for thereby advising 'apprentices and servants to rob their masters'.

In the early nineteenth century, the Criminal Law Commissioners admitted a defence of necessity to homicide (1839, xxi; 1843, 227). The Commissioners of 1846 rejected it in their Second Report, holding that it was better to opt for the administrative solution of convicting and leaving the individual to the mercy of the Crown. Otherwise the law risked the possibility that individuals would 'overrate the danger to which they are exposed, and . . . place too low an estimate on the life of another when placed in the balance against prospect of additional safety to themselves' (1846, 36). In this they followed the Indian Law Commissioners (1898, 61) who, recognising the impossibility of deterrence and the consequent wrongness of punishment in necessity situations, nonetheless argued that instances could not be defined in advance and must be left to governmental discretion in prosecution and punishment.

The ambivalence towards the defence is also seen in Stephen's work. Writing of compulsion by threats, he argued that since criminal law was 'itself a system of compulsion in the widest scale', it was 'at the moment when temptation to crime is strongest that the law should speak most clearly and emphatically . . .' (1883, II, 107). Yet writing of compulsion by necessity, Stephen changed his tune. He argued that 'it is just possible to imagine cases in which the expediency of breaking the law is so overwhelmingly great that people may be justified in breaking it' (1883, II, 109). He added, however, like the Indian Law Commissioners, that such cases could not be settled beforehand. He provided no sound basis for his differential approach to the two forms of compulsion.

The historical background then is one of a partial and hesitant recognition of the potential effects of necessity on legal guilt weighed against the political and social implications of permitting it as a legal defence. Individual justice is weighed against social consequence, and found wanting. This combination of factors is seen in the most famous necessity case, to which we now turn.

### (ii)    Judgment and context: the case of *Dudley and Stephens*

In *Dudley and Stephens* (1881–5), the defendants had killed and partially consumed an ailing cabin boy having been shipwrecked at sea for eighteen days and without food and water for seven and five respectively. At their trial, the jury found that they 'probably would not have survived' and would within four days have died ((1881–5 at 62). After some procedural legerdemain (Simpson, 1986, 218–23), it was held by the Court of the Queen's Bench Division that the accused were not entitled to the defence of necessity but were guilty of murder and they were therefore sentenced to death. This sentence was later commuted to six months' imprisonment without hard labour.

In general, the reasoning in the case conflates questions of justification and excuse. At one point, Lord Coleridge stated that the killing must be murder unless it 'can be *justified* by some well-recognised *excuse* admitted by the law' ((1881–5) at 67) (emphasis added). Fletcher has contended that the argument of the court rests on justification (1974, 1282).[4] Yet the crucial issue of principle raised by Lord Coleridge both at the beginning and towards the end of the judgment, when considering the circumstances of the case, concerns not whether the act was justified but whether a man has the right 'to declare temptation to be an excuse' ((1881–5) at 68). The prisoners were 'subject to terrible temptation and to sufferings which might break down the bodily power of the strongest man, and try the conscience of the best' ((1881–5) at 63). He concludes by stressing 'how terrible the temptation was, how awful the suffering, how hard in such trials to keep the judgment straight and the conduct pure' ((1881–5) at 67). These observations all relate to the terrible position of the accused, not the justifiability of their acts. It is true that in discussing the authorities, Lord Coleridge returns repeatedly to the question of justification. It is also true that he discusses the decision to select the cabin boy in terms of a choice that could not be justified, but his analysis of the actual plight of the accused is in terms of the extreme difficulties they faced in resisting temptation, a matter of excuse.

Dudley and Stephens, however, were not to be allowed the defence of necessity. Having recognised the plight of the men, Lord Coleridge's tone shifts significantly. His comments on the temptation suffered by the accused possess a compassionate 'there but for the grace of God go I' tone. We are all human beings, he suggests: who could not sympathise with the accused's plight? This 'morality of equals', however, is then rejected in favour of an absolutist, authoritarian moral tone demanding self-sacrifice in the name of principle. In war, 'it is a man's duty not to live, but to die', and we are reminded of the 'Great Example' which in a Christian country 'we profess to follow'. Judges are often 'compelled [sic!] to set up standards we cannot reach ourselves and to lay down rules which we could not ourselves satisfy. But a man has no right to declare temptation to be an excuse' ((1881–5) at 67–8). Lord Coleridge expresses compassion for the accused in terms of a morality that recognises normal human standards of conduct, but he nonetheless condemns them in terms of an Old Testament morality for their lack, not of normal human standards, but of heroism.

These are the main arguments, but behind these shifts in moral gear there is a narrower but without doubt significant utilitarian consideration. Like the 1846 Commissioners, Lord Coleridge is concerned that if the principle of necessity were to be admitted, it 'might be made the legal cloke for unbridled passion and atrocious crime' ((1881–5) at 67). Dudley and Stephens must be condemned *both* for their lack of heroism *and* to secure the greater social good. To admit the defence would be to open the door to great and terrible crime, a 'cannibal's charter' perhaps. Thus arguments of moral principle and utility both cancel out moral compassion and the excuse of necessity.

There is however paradox in this grandiloquence. What Lord Coleridge takes with one hand he returns with the other. Dudley and Stephens must be condemned, but at the same time he recommends 'to the Sovereign to exercise that prerogative of mercy which the Constitution has entrusted to the hands fittest to dispense it' ((1881–5) at 67). The two men were reluctantly (Simpson, 1986, 239) condemned to death but then had their sentences commuted to six months' imprisonment without hard labour. Who could this judgment satisfy? If no man had the right to declare temptation to be an excuse, why the heavy hint about mercy? If an example had to be made, did it not need to be carried out? Such a token sentence is surely itself in danger of becoming (on the judge's logic) the 'Legal cloke for unbridled passion and atrocious crime'. Simpson (1986, 255) in fact tells us that the impact of the case upon the seafaring communities was to confirm that survival cannibalism *was* acceptable. As Fletcher puts it, there is 'something inescapably odd about a court's simultaneously affirming a conviction and recommending clemency' (1974, 1283; cf Fletcher, 1978, 824). The implication is that the court did not mean what it said, and one is left to ask why they should have arrived at the position they did.

The consistent inconsistency of the lawyers on necessity reflects conflicts between and within the two central theoretical justifications of punishment in the criminal law. Within a retributive philosophical perspective, the primary element is that which leads to a theory of excuse through a morality which stresses respect for the choice of individuals caught in a maelstrom of circumstances. Retributivism suggests a morality of equality between judge and judged and it is this which exists in tension with the sense of divine retribution and sacrifice ultimately called for by Lord Coleridge. This latter element was not originally a part of retributive morality, although it became a significant element in such thinking towards the end of the nineteenth century. To the individualistic, Enlightenment inspired respect for the individual, it opposed an authoritarian negation of individual right in favour of a greater moral purpose (Norrie, 1991, ch 5).

Opposed also to this Enlightenment-derived respect for the individual is another, utilitarian, morality which again renounces the individual, this time as a sacrifice for the social good. This second element emerges from a conflict that exists within utilitarian thought itself. One side of utilitarianism holds that since no individual can be deterred by fear of punishment in face of the circumstances confronting him, any such punishment is 'useless cruelty' and 'clear evil' (Macauley, 1898, 57). But the theory is then turned on its head. The individual concerned may not be deterred, but the rest of society, beholding the terrible example of punishment in such circumstances, may be the *more* persuaded to follow the law and the more likely to avoid getting themselves into situations of necessity. As a system of individual deterrence along the lines initially conceived by Bentham, the limits of deterrence play a role in restricting punishment. As a system of State punishment, promoting the good of society as a whole, the individual is no more than an exploitable unit, a means to a greater end (cf Fletcher, 1978, 823 and, below, pp 205–7). The unsatisfactory compromise evident in the conviction and sentence of Dudley and Stephens reflects a conflation of these different and conflicting moral logics. But we then need to ask how it was that these different logics should have merged in the case of *Dudley and Stephens*.

These theories of morality and utility come together in the context of a judgment upon the seafaring practice of the nineteenth century. As regards utilitarianism, there is a tension within the theory between the reflection of individual self-interest and the embodiment of the 'greatest happiness of the greatest number'. This tension emerges in *Dudley and Stephens* in the context of a perceived need to declare a legal prohibition on survival cannibalism (the 'legal cloke' argument), while recognising the implausibility of expecting any deterrent effect in the individual case through punishment of such a crime. Hence the sentence of death and the heavy hint as to the appropriateness of mercy. Similarly, with moral retributivism, we see a morality of individual right and equality stress compassion for common humanity and fellow-feeling, but the moral ideology operates in a world in which common humanity was put through the mangle of social difference. What did judges of the Queen's Bench Division really know of the plight of shipwrecked and starving people, or of the judgment of the seafaring communities on such situations? In the nineteenth-century world of the sailing ships, survival cannibalism was a not uncommon phenomenon sanctioned by the custom and morality of the sea. Public attitudes to the particular plight of Dudley and Stephens were 'all one way' in favour of the accused (Simpson, 1986, ch 5). By contrast it was only among the literate upper classes that there was support for the prosecution, with the Home Secretary agreeing to it to negate 'the popular idea that Dudley was a hero'. Even the dead boy's family bore no ill will to the two accused (Simpson, 1986, 87–9).

To the morality of the judges was opposed the morality of the people. For the former, common humanity was rejected in favour of a heroic standard of resistance; for the latter, the two men were, if anything, heroes for doing what had to be done in a hostile environment.[5] At the very least their plight should have been recognised and their 'crimes' exculpated. Their ultimately lenient treatment again reflected a compromise, this time a political one, between 'official morality' and public sentiment around these two different moral standpoints.[6]

*Dudley and Stephens* is a classic illustration of the interface between legal discourse and social reality. On the one hand, we have a judiciary and state bureaucracy drawn from the upper ranks of the social order, well-heeled and therefore able to cultivate and proselytise refined manners and morals (cf Chase, 1985, 1253). On the other hand, we see a social audience of poor sea-faring folk for whom ill-paid and hazardous work on the sailing ships just kept body and soul together. The two groups meet and clash in the political forum of the courtroom around the defence of necessity. The antithesis that is produced by their conflicting views is 'dialectical'. It was the sacrifices made by, and the profits to be got from, the work of these men that maintained the ship-owners, the social cousins of the men on the judicial bench, as wealthy and morally upstanding members of the community. It was because men like Dudley and Stephens went to sea at great risk to themselves that men like Lord Coleridge could sit in judgment on them when things went wrong.[7]

There was candour in Lord Coleridge's observation that the judges were compelled 'to set up standards we cannot reach ourselves, and to lay down rules which we could not ourselves satisfy'. But there was no accompanying recognition that the chance of a Lord Coleridge finding himself in the position of a Dudley or Stephens was infinitesimal, or that it was because the latter did what they did that the former could sit in comfortable judgment over them. Such a social arrangement did not exclude the possibility of fellow-feeling, but it did impose political limits upon its practical operation.

## (iii)  The re-emergence of necessity

### (a)  Necessity as Pandora's Box

There is also a deeper level of difficulty associated with the necessity defence, one that goes beyond its ability to excite clashing philosophical viewpoints on the theory of punishment. The rationale of necessity as excuse[8] operates as a door between the individual and the context within which he operates. A claim of necessity relates conduct to grounds of action that go beyond the simple individual decision to do something. In so doing, it provides the basis for an alternative, politically substantive, account of 'the facts' to enter the courtroom and to challenge the law's formalistic defence of the political and economic status quo.[9]

In the relatively recent civil case of *London Borough of Southwark v Williams* (1971), Lord Denning repeats some of the arguments we have examined in the older authorities. The case involved two families forced through homelessness to squat in empty council property. One family, including a five-year-old child and a baby aged five months, were forced to walk the streets of London in September 1970. For three days they were homeless, apart from one night when they were taken in by a stranger. In desperation they effected an illegal entry into derelict property. The judges extended their fellow-feeling for the families' plight but weighed this against the legal rights and wrongs of the situation. Lord Denning, expressing the 'greatest sympathy' ((1971) at 177)[10] for the families, proceeded to quote Hale at them and continued:

If homelessness were once admitted as a defence to trespass, no-one's house could be safe. Necessity would open a door which no man could shut . . . The plea would be an excuse for all sorts of wrongdoing. So the courts must for the sake of law and order take a stand. They must refuse to admit the plea of necessity to the hungry and the homeless; and trust that their distress will be relieved by the charitable and the good. ((1971) at 179)

This is Lord Coleridge's 'legal cloke' again. Doubtless, if it had been a criminal case, Lord Denning would have made noises about the need for discretion in prosecution and merciful sentencing in such cases.[11] It is the old story of 'jam yesterday, jam tomorrow, but never jam today' (Wells, 1985, 472). But what is apparent from his judgment, and the alignment of his position with that of Hale, is the potential for the necessity defence to open up the link between crime against private property and a social context of homelessness and hunger.

To see how this comes about, it is worth considering again the Canadian case of *Perka v R* (1984). There it was held that compulsion of circumstances renders conduct *morally involuntary*, and is to be excused out of respect for individual autonomy. The court locates its decision within the extended form of moral involuntariness that we identified in Chapter 6 (above, p 114).[12] Noting that the voluntariness requirement of actus reus only requires that the accused be in conscious control of his acts (physically voluntary), and that conduct under necessity involves such control, Dickson J observes that –

Realistically, however, his act is not a 'voluntary' one. His 'choice' to break the law is no true choice at all; it is remorselessly compelled by normal human instincts. This sort of involuntariness is often described as 'moral or normative involuntariness'. ((1986) at 15)

But there remains a conflict. The law may accept the evidence of human weakness and need and incorporate it into its doctrine. To the extent that it does this, however, it risks eroding protection of private property rights. In *Perka*, Dickson J states that 'involuntariness is measured on the basis of society's expectation of appropriate and normal resistance to pressure' ((1986) at 22). But who or what is 'society'? In *Dudley and Stephens*, the views of society were split along identifiable lines of class. The same would be true with regard to homelessness. What is regarded as 'appropriate' or 'normal' conduct from the perspective of the hungry or the homeless might be rather different from that of a Lord Denning. The law may either recognise the social consequences for individuals of a world of rich and poor and incorporate such recognition through a socially centred exculpation such as necessity (cf Vandervort, 1987, 220), or it may insist that individuals are responsible in order to protect the status quo. It cannot do both, and the significance of the necessity defence is that it permits an opening for the former approach, one which the law has historically turned its back on.

One can therefore call the necessity defence a 'Trojan Horse' (Bannister and Milovanovic, 1990), or a 'Pandora's Box' for the law. Into it are concentrated a variety of causes and explanations for criminal behaviour that the law normally seeks to exclude. Beyond the excuse of dire social need, it has the potential to open up a whole area of political controversy for the law because it allows broader accounts and contextualisations of agency to be raised in the courtroom. In the United States, the necessity defence has been used to challenge political choices made by the state concerning the support of Apartheid, intervention in Central

America, and nuclear power and weaponry (Bannister and Milovanovic, 1990; Levitin, 1987).

The seemingly remote connection between necessity and agency described in such cases may make it hard to imagine how the law could be invoked. The existence of a necessity defence nonetheless allowed the defendants the legal space to make their case before a jury, with the chance of appealing to their broader sense of justice. Links were also made between United States policy and the deaths abroad of innocent people at the hands of death squads and terror groups, and between the conscientious breaking of the law and the influence of such protests on government policy. In this way, law breaking in the United States was connected with the protection of human life in the foreign country, life which was in imminent danger. Bannister and Milovanovic comment that while the object of the defendants' actions was often hundreds or thousands of miles away, trial courts 'recognised the harm as imminent and greater than the injury committed by the defendants' actions' (Bannister and Milovanovic, 1990, 187).

In England, necessity has been used in recent years by peace protesters, environmental campaigners and users of cannabis for medical purposes (Berlins and Dyer, 2001). In 1996, two women charged with £1.5m criminal damage to a fighter plane used necessity to secure an acquittal. The plane was destined for Indonesia where it was said it would be used against the East Timorese, contrary to international law. In 2001, the same defence was successful for defendants charged with conspiracy to cause criminal damage to a nuclear submarine. Similarly, Greenpeace activists charged with destroying genetically modified crops used the necessity defence permitted under the Criminal Damage Act 1971 to secure an acquittal in 2000. Section 5(2)(b) permits destruction of property to protect other property where there is an 'immediate need of protection' and the means adopted are reasonable. In a number of cases, magistrates and juries have also acquitted users and suppliers of cannabis where the drug has been used to alleviate chronic medical conditions. In all these cases, necessity operates to permit alternative political, ethical, economic and moral arguments to confront the formal logic of the law. Resting on a concept of moral involuntariness, it opens up the grounds upon which a defendant can say 'I could do no other'. For this reason, the law has traditionally fought shy of it.[13]

## (b) Duress of circumstances

In the light of the foregoing, it is perhaps surprising that the courts have been prepared in recent years to introduce a defence of necessity under cover of 'duress of circumstances'. One has to understand the two-sided nature of the defence to see how this could happen. Necessity can appear as the gateway to anarchy:

> No system of positive law can recognise any principle which would entitle a person to violate the law because on his view the law conflicted with some higher social value. (Dickson J in *Perka* (1984), quoted in *Pommell* (1995) at 614)

But also as the necessary, just addition to positive law:

> If Anne Frank had stolen a car to escape from Amsterdam and been charged with theft, the tenets of English law would not, in our judgment, have denied her a defence of duress of

circumstances, on the ground that she should have waited for the Gestapo's knock on the door. (*R v Abdul-Hussain* (1999) at 571)

The second quotation comes from a case of aircraft hijacking where the defendants sought to evade deportation to Iraq, where there lives would be at risk. To do justice to the hijackers, the Court of Appeal acknowledged the defence of necessity (qua duress of circumstances), but they also opened up the quandary for the law identified by Dickson J in *Perka*.

This tension underlying necessity accounts for its covert development under another name. In *Conway* (1988), the Court of Appeal noted that it was unclear whether there was a general defence of necessity but argued that 'to admit a defence of 'duress of circumstances' is a logical consequence of the existence of the defence of duress'. (They added, however, that this 'does no more than recognise that duress is an example of necessity' ((1988) at 1029)). The early cases were all in the area of defences to driving offences, but any thought that the defence was to be restricted to this area was repudiated in *Pommell*, a case of unlawful possession of a firearm. There, the Court of Appeal observed that the defence, 'being closely related to the defence of duress by threats, appears to be general, applying to all crimes except murder, attempted murder and some forms of treason' ((1995) at 615). *Abdul-Hussain* confirms the point.

This is a fascinating and potentially far-reaching development in the law. Its impact will depend on the extent to which the judges restrict its application to tightly controlled circumstances, as in the recent law of duress (below, pp 168–71). In *Pommell*, the limit concerned how soon a defendant must desist from committing the offence. When would a reasonable person have known the duress had ceased? In *Abdul-Hussain*, it was held that the threat to life had to be 'imminent', but not necessarily the more proximate 'immediate'. Behind these limits, there still lurks the question whether necessity qua duress of circumstances will open a door which, in Lord Denning's words, 'no man could shut'. Commenting on how lines would be drawn to avoid the 'lawlessness' that Lord Denning fears in the homelessness situation, Smith and Hogan suggest a distinction. A line could be drawn between taking of food or entry onto property where this was necessary to prevent death or serious injury through starvation or cold, and situations where the aim was merely 'to prevent hunger, or the discomforts of cold or homelessness' (1999, 247). The distinction would be virtually impossible to maintain, as well as unedifying and embarrassing for the courts to operate. One could imagine, for example, the testimony of a group like Shelter on the connection between homelessness and life chances, or of doctors on the connection between hunger and personal injury. At some point a defence of 'duress of circumstances' is likely to raise substantive political issues, even if, as Smith and Hogan argue, its existence makes sense in terms of legal principle.

### (c)  Medical necessity

A further development in recent years has been the recognition of a form of necessity as a defence for doctors who might otherwise be regarded as having assaulted or killed a patient. In *F v West Berkshire Health Authority* (1989), the House of Lords held that doctors could operate to sterilise a 36-year-old, mentally handicapped, woman without her consent on the ground of necessity. Lord Goff claimed that the existence of a 'common law . . . principle of necessity . . . is not in doubt' ((1989) at 1084). Yet, as we have seen, the judges have been extremely reluctant to admit such a principle. In the case of the conjoined twins, *Re A (children)* (2000), Brooke LJ observed that the doctrine was obscure and had 'featured . . . seldom in our case law'. Lord Goff had, indeed, been instrumental in giving it a 'new lease of life' ((2000) at 1032) in *F v West Berkshire Health Authority.*

What are the limits of this reborn necessity? It appears to go further than necessity qua duress of circumstances. It does not rely upon the existence of an emergency (*F v West Berkshire Health Authority* (1989) at 565), and it involves a choice of evils analysis in which the chosen act is regarded as justified rather than excused (*Re A (children)* (2000) at 1048). *Re A* also suggests that this kind of necessity extends to cover cases which would otherwise be murder. In this, it comes into conflict with both *Dudley and Stephens* and the duress case of *R v Howe* (see below). Considering these cases, Brooke LJ observes that neither 'had in mind a situation in which a court was invited to sanction a defence (or justification) of necessity on facts comparable to those' in *Re A*. That is true but legal rules by their nature migrate across fact situations.

Both Brooke and Ward LJJ were at pains to emphasise the exceptional character of *Re A*. Ward LJ stipulated that the case is authority only for the 'unique circumstances' that –

> . . . it must be impossible to preserve the life of X without bringing about the death of Y, that Y by his very continued existence will inevitably bring about the death of X within a short period of time, and that X is capable of living an independent life but Y is incapable . . . of viable independent existence. ((2000) at 1018)

This is the narrower of two formulae for restricting necessity in murder cases. Compare it with Brooke LJ's view that for necessity –

> (i) the act is needed to avoid inevitable and irreparable evil; (ii) no more should be done than is reasonably necessary for the purpose to be achieved; and (iii) the evil inflicted must not be disproportionate . . . ((2000) at 1052)

The third condition mentioned by Ward LJ might be construed as relevant only to the conjoined twins situation. Otherwise there is little here to restrict the application of necessity only to medical cases like *Re A*. Brooke LJ gives examples of rightful non-medical situations for applying a necessity defence (two mountaineers dangling from a rope, pushing the fear-paralysed man off the ladder on the sinking ferry: (2000) at 1041–3). Medical necessity is opening a door that *Dudley and Stephens* and *Howe* had sought firmly to shut.

Finally, *Re A (children)* is important for its revelation of the underlying links between offence and defence in the criminal law. In Chapter 3, we saw how the law of intention operates as a barrier to considering the broader moral issues in the law. There, we saw how the judges in *Re A* had argued for the defence of necessity because they held that on the law of intention the doctors would otherwise be guilty of murder (above, p 57). Yet, there is an argument on the law of intention for saying that, where a consequence of an intended action crosses a moral threshold, it is not intended, even if it is foreseen as virtually certain to happen. (This is akin to the moral doctrine of 'double effect' which received judicial recognition in *Airedale NHS Trust v Bland* (1993) at 868. It was, however, rejected in *Re A* ((2000) at 1012, 1030) on the questionable ground that it could not operate where the unintended effect was the death of another). The value of having a defence like necessity is that it operates as a moral safety valve. While defending the seemingly neutral terms of the 'definition of the offence' (mens rea plus actus reus), the law can pigeonhole the awkward moral cases. On a *moral* analysis of intention, this is not a necessary move. The law's problem, given its structure, becomes one of controlling the flow of moral 'steam' through the valve. We have already seen how applying the law of necessity in *Re A* evolves the defence to a level where it conflicts with existing authorities on murder.

## 3  DURESS

Because the judges have until recently maintained a consistent policy stance against accepting the principle of necessity, the contradictory attitudes depicted in the previous section have remained at the (enlarging) margin of the criminal law. The same is not so with duress, which, either as duress of threats or now of circumstances, acts as a full defence to all crimes except murder, attempted murder and treason (Smith and Hogan, 1999, 233). Duress is constituted by a threat or danger of death or serious injury to oneself, one's near family, or perhaps simply to another, but not to property. It must be 'imminent', but not necessarily 'immediate' and the response 'reasonable and proportionate' (*Abdul-Hussain* (1999)). The threat may operate despite the ability to seek police help (*Hudson and Taylor* (1971)), though it will cease to operate when it is reasonable to desist from committing the crime (*Pommell* (1995)). In judging the efficacy of the threat, it can be coupled with other non-qualifying threats, for example to reveal the defendant's homosexuality, as part of a cumulative pressure (*Valderrama-Vega* (1985); but cf *Ortiz* (1986)).

There has been considerable litigation in recent years, particularly around the question of the availability of the defence to those charged in cases of murder. The result of this has been that the potential for conflict within compulsion excuses has been actualised in a series of cases which have moved first in one direction, then in another. In *Howe* (1987), we saw the House of Lords overruling their earlier decision in *Lynch* (1975) on the basis of a change of mind about the acceptability of the duress defence. This cannot simply be explained in relation to the contrasting circumstances and plights of the accused in the different cases, although these may have played their part.[14] Beyond differing factual situations, it is necessary to examine the availability of the competing and conflicting viewpoints accessible to the judges on the subject of duress. In examining these in the context of judicial pronouncements of the law, we can confirm the argument of the last section concerning the anomalous and problematic nature of the duress and necessity defences.

### (i)  Conflicting positions in the recent murder cases

In *Lynch*, it was decided by a House of Lords majority of three to two that threats of death or serious injury could excuse participation by an aider or abettor to the crime of murder. In legal language recognised (at the time) as archaic, a 'principal in the second degree' to murder was held to be able to use the duress defence, although the question of whether or not an actual killer (the 'principal in the first degree') could was left open.[15] Two years later, in the case of *Abbott* (1977),[16] it was held that a principal in the first degree could not use the defence. The decision was literally one of life and death for the accused, since the death sentence still operated in Trinidad and Tobago, and Abbott was executed.

The radical distinction in treatment between principals in the first and the second degree occasioned considerable debate. In *Howe*, the most recent duress-murder case, the House of Lords conceded that the distinction between degrees of involvement was untenable. In *Abbott*, the majority had claimed that they accepted the binding authority of *Lynch* but this acceptance was only verbal since they by-passed its substance. This led the minority to state that 'the majority opinion of their Lordships amounts, in effect, to side-stepping the decision in *Lynch* and, even were that constitutionally appropriate, to do it without advancing cogent grounds' ((1977) at 772).[17] The volte face in *Howe* vindicated retrospectively Lord Edmund-Davies's strongly worded criticism in *Abbott*. It was necessary to 'either move forward and affirm the view of the minority in *Abbott* that duress is available as a defence to murder generally'. Alternatively, the court should 'depart from Lynch's case and restore the law as it was generally accepted . . . whereby duress was not a defence available to any party otherwise guilty of murder' (Lord Bridge in *Howe* (1987) at 784). It was the latter course that the judges took.

What lay behind the anomalies of *Abbott* and the about-turn of *Howe*? The main arguments in *Lynch*, *Abbott* and *Howe* have a familiar ring to them after examining *R v Dudley and Stephens*. On the side of moral principle, we find a strong 'there but for the grace of God go I' position amongst the majority in *Lynch*, and an equally strong morality of heroism in Lord Hailsham's judgment in *Howe*. On the side of raison d'état and the need to sacrifice individual justice for the social good, there is the argument of Lord Simon as one of the minority in *Lynch* and that of Lord Salmon for the majority in *Abbott*. For the judges in favour of denial of the defence, the consoling carrot of administrative mitigation is dangled by the minority in *Lynch*, the majority in *Abbott* and in all three of the main judgments in *Howe*. What is interesting in examining the arguments in detail is the inherently contradictory nature of both the main positions.

## (ii) The conflict within the basic arguments

I will focus primarily on *Lynch* since the arguments of principle are most developed there. The starting point was a conception of the defence which, it was acknowledged, made it hard to slot it into the standard legal categories. Legal responsibility rests upon the twin concepts of mens rea and actus reus. In duress situations, the accused acts intentionally and voluntarily, thereby complying with the standard requirements for liability. If duress is to exculpate, it is therefore necessary to see it as something on top of and overriding the act and intention. It is, in Lord Wilberforce's words –

    . . . something which is superimposed upon the other ingredients which by themselves would make up an offence, ie upon act and intention. 'Coactus volui' sums up the combination: the victim completes the act and knows that he is doing so; but the addition of the element of duress prevents the law from treating what he has done as a crime. ((1975) at 679–80)

This, the standard, explanation (Williams, 1961, 751; Williams, 1983, 624–5; Smith and Hogan, 1999, 231–2) was accepted by four of the five judges in *Lynch*.[18] It places duress in an anomalous situation, and is the reason why, it has been said, 'attempts to cram the defence into legal pigeonholes have failed in the past' (Wasik, 1977, 456).[19] Duress sits uncomfortably with the standard doctrines of act and intention. It draws upon the anomalous concept (in legal terms) of moral involuntariness to explain how a person who 'was as cool as a cucumber under pressure' (Ashworth, 1999, 231) can still have a defence to a serious crime (cf Smith and Hogan, 1999, 232. Ashworth (ibid) is in fact sceptical about the concept).

If there is agreement that duress has an essentially anomalous character, there has been disagreement about what to do about it. The majority in *Lynch* argued that where the will was overborne by duress, it would be unjust to the individual to convict him. Conviction involves criminal stigmatisation of a faultless individual that the soothing tongue of mitigation cannot remove. Mitigation, commented Lord Edmund-Davies ironically, 'at least makes for neatness. No matter how terrifying the circumstances which have impelled a man (and, indeed, which might have impelled *most* men) to transgress the criminal law, he must be convicted . . . The trouble about such neatness is that it may work intolerable injustice in individual cases . . .' ((1975) at 707). In language reminiscent of the compassion expressed by Lord Coleridge in *Dudley and Stephens*, Lord Morris spoke of the need of 'any rational system of law [to] take fully into account the standards of honest and reasonable men'. It should pay heed to 'the miserable agonising plight' of the accused, and not expect in 'the calm of the court-room measures of fortitude or of heroic behaviour' ((1975) at 670).

For the majority in *Lynch*, justice to the individual must be done by excusing him for his crime, but it is important to consider the counter-argument of Lord Simon. Part of his stance is standardly utilitarian in the Stephen mould. He argues that criminal law is itself a system of threats not to be withdrawn in the face of counter-threats. He raises Lord Coleridge's 'legal cloke' argument in the shape of the danger that the defence might be 'a charter for terrorists, gang-leaders and kidnappers' who could confer immunity on their subordinates by threat of death ((1975) at 688). But Lord Simon also advances an important new reductio argument. Duress affects neither act nor intention. It affects the motive behind act and intention by imposing extreme fear upon the individual. It is the fear of death or serious injury to self or family which 'overbears' the will, and the test is whether in fact the will has been overborne.[20] However, the fear affecting motive in duress situations is no different from any number of fears that individuals may possess and which may lead them to act in criminal ways. Why, then, permit one kind of fear to possess a peculiar and anomalous position within the criminal law, when all these other fears, which may be equally potent, only go to mitigation of the crime? Admit one, admit all, or exclude one, exclude all. Do not mix these two logically tenable options:

. . . a threat to property may, in certain circumstances, be as potent in overbearing the actor's wish not to perform the prohibited act as a threat of physical harm. For example, the threat may be to burn down his house unless the householder merely keeps watch against interruption while a crime is committed. Or a fugitive from justice may say, 'I have it in my power to make your son bankrupt. You can avoid that merely by driving me to the airport.' Would not many ordinary people yield to such threats, and act contrary to their wish not to perform an action prohibited by law? . . . Faced with anomaly and uncertainty, may it not be that a narrow, arbitrary and anomalous defence of duress, negativing the crime, is *far less acceptable in practice and far less justifiable in juristic theory* than a broadly based plea which mitigates the penalty? ((1975) at 686–7) (emphasis added) [21]

If doing justice to individuals involves recognising their motives in acting in the duress situation, why does the law not recognise their motives in all those other contexts in which crimes are committed? But if the logic of duress were extended, how much of the standard legal model of individual responsibility would be left standing? Williams has written that 'Fear of violence does not differ in kind from fear of economic ills, fear of displeasing others, or any other determinant of choice, it would be inconvenient to regard a particular type of motive as negativing will' (1961, 751).[22] Why then, Lord Simon would ask, regard a particular type of motive as negativing responsibility, conviction and punishment? On the basis of the standard divisions of the law, this question has some force. We could, however, turn it around and ask why the law should in general operate with a model of individual responsibility which ignores the crucial role of motive in determining conduct. Analysis of the duress defence raises in a very sharp way the question of what the law means when it claims to do justice to individuals. If 'doing justice' to a Lynch means taking into account his motives, it is unclear why 'doing justice' to everyone else means ignoring theirs.[23]

While Lord Simon brings out the conflict in the argument of the majority in *Lynch*, there is equally one in his own position (which was later to inform the majority view in *Abbott*). It is one we are familiar with from *Dudley and Stephens*. It is necessary, both to affirm the law and to deny a charter for terrorists and other criminals, that those who commit crimes under duress should be convicted.[24] If this works injustice for individuals, this can be countered by mitigation in punishment. But, as we have seen, if the aim is to deter, then mitigation of punishment should not be allowed. Indeed the aim of deterrence, of placing a counter-threat against the terrorist's threat, would tend to be met by *increasing*, not decreasing, the punishment. Mitigation and deterrence are in conflict with each other. On the other hand, if the aim of mitigation is to recognise guiltlessness, why convict at all? If the alternatives of non-prosecution, pardon, discharge or minimal sentence are all possibilities, what is the aim or value of a conviction?[25] The mitigation lobby want to have it both ways.

Mitigation is a way of encouraging substantial discretion in the system at the prosecutorial, sentencing and post-sentencing stages and undermining the ideology of the rule of law (cf above, pp 44–6). Legal justice in the liberal conception is concerned with doing justice according to rules, and not leaving matters in the hands of participants within the system. Mitigation amounts to an abdication of the law's self-claimed responsibility to govern human conduct by rules. In place of laws which state the extent and limits of the duress defence, Lord Simon wishes to give judges, prosecution and state officials discretionary powers to allocate punishments in ways unregulated by law. The conflicts in *Lynch* are forced on the judges by the contradiction within a system based on individual fault attribution where for once the judgment of fault is socially contextualised, and where an overall desire for social control is balanced against a requirement of individual fault.

In *Howe*,[26] the House of Lords have followed Lord Simon's suggestions with regard to the crime of murder, and in so doing have produced a position on duress that is unlikely to be satisfactory. The decision to exclude murder cases from the ambit of duress does not do away with the anomalies produced by the decisions in *Lynch* and *Abbott*: it entrenches them at a different level. Criminal law is based on general rules, so that offence and defence categories cannot be unreflectively partitioned without serious gaps in the law's logic opening up. Duress remains a full defence to a charge of causing grievous bodily harm with intent under the Offences Against the Person Act 1861, s 18. If the victim of the assault later dies, the accused has, in the absence of other issues such as provocation or diminished responsibility, no defence to a charge of murder. The contingency of whether death occurs radically affects the accused's culpability.

Similarly, if duress is unavailable in murder cases, it is still apparently available in manslaughter cases. Availability of the defence accordingly depends upon the knife-edged boundary between these two offences, a boundary which, as we saw in Chapter 3, is both opaque and subject to shifts over time (see Milgate, 1988, 74). The decision in *Gotts* (1992) to exclude the defence in cases of attempted murder removes the anomaly as between that crime and murder. It instates another tension in the law as between attempted murder and wounding with intent, which can be established on facts that are substantially the same (see Lord Keith at 834).

Nor does *Howe* avoid the deeper issues of principle raised by the duress defence. According to Lord Hailsham, the law should set 'a standard of conduct which ordinary men and women are expected to observe' and the ordinary person is 'capable of heroism'. Duress is a refuge for 'the coward and the poltroon' ((1987) at 780). To save one's own life by sacrificing that of another or others is cowardly and poltroon-like. But where does heroism lie when the choice is between death of a stranger and the death of oneself *and* one's immediate family? Lord Hailsham's identification of surrender to duress and cowardliness fails to address the question.[27] It is possible to imagine duress situations such as that involving the death of one in exchange for the lives of many where the present limit on the defence would seem immoral. It is not impossible that a future case would re-open the trajectory of the law begun by *Lynch* and blocked by the subsequent cases. *Re A (children)* (above, p 163) is also relevant, though its impact is likely to be minimised by reference to its 'very unusual circumstances'.

## (iii)  Further limits

I have argued that the moral claims invoked in necessity and duress situations present the law with both a cogent demand to honour them and a fear that, if honoured, they will undermine the law. One result of this is that the courts have developed a number of ways of seeking to limit the application of the defence. This, however, tends to produce further anomaly in the law.

### (a)  Mistake of duress

First, there is the issue of mistake of duress. Where an individual misperceives the situation he is in, he is judged not on the facts as he saw them, including any mistake he has made, but on the facts as they would have been perceived by a reasonable person. The test is 'was the defendant, or may he have been, impelled to act as he did because, as a result of what he reasonably believed [the person making the threats] had said or done, he had good cause to fear . . . serious physical injury?' (*Graham* (1982) at 806; approved in *Howe*). This test reveals the law's inconsistency on matters of mistake. It should be compared with the earlier mistake/ mens rea case of *Morgan* (1976) and the later self defence cases of *Gladstone Williams* (1983) and *Beckford* (1987). The choice between a subjective and an objective rule of law is probably rooted in the judges' mistrust of the jury.[28] Individual right is surrendered in favour of social control, but inconsistently because of the so-called 'inexorable logic' which *Morgan* brings to bear in other areas of the law of mistake (cf Norrie, 2000, 181–7).

### (b) Standard of resistance

Second, there is the question of the standard of fortitude expected of the defendant. By *Graham* ((1982) at 806, approved in *Howe*) an objective element is imported into the analysis. The test is whether 'a sober person of reasonable firmness, sharing the characteristics of the defendant' would have responded in the same way as the defendant. The stipulation that what is required is 'the self-control reasonably to be expected of the ordinary citizen in his situation' juxtaposes an abstract standard of conduct and agency (the reasonable, ordinary citizen) and the position of an actual, situated, individual. Again, the subjective/objective controversy is evident, although in this case in a more piquant form. Graham lived in what was described by Lord Lane in the Court of Appeal as a 'bizarre ménage à trois' with his wife and his male lover. He suffered from an anxiety state for which he was prescribed tranquillisers. The jury would in effect be asked in this case to put itself in the defendant's shoes and decide how a 'reasonable, anxious bisexual man' would respond to duress. The test is nonsensical. It stems from admixing recognition of the relevance of subjective characteristics with the desire to control the admission of too much individuality into the law. Again, mistrust of the jury's ability to detect a bogus use of the defence probably lies behind the brain-teaser it is set.

As with the provocation test (*Camplin* (1978)) on which *Graham* is based, a number of Court of Appeal cases have sought to clarify the extent to which characteristics can subjectivise the reasonableness test. In *Emery* (1992), the court held that an expert account of a condition of dependent helplessness would be relevant to the objective test. *Hegarty* (1994) in contrast held that medical evidence of emotional instability and a 'grossly elevated neurotic state' were inadmissible. An attempt to impose order on which characteristics should be admissible was made in *Bowen* (1996). There it was held that (1) the 'mere fact' that the accused is more pliable, vulnerable or timid does not amount to a characteristic. However, (2) categories such as age, sex, pregnancy, serious physical disability or a recognised mental illness or psychiatric condition would be admissible. As regards mental conditions, the court (3) drew a further distinction. Psychiatric evidence showing the accused was suffering from 'some mental illness, mental impairment or recognised psychiatric condition' which made him more susceptible was admissible. A doctor's opinion, however, that an accused not suffering from such a recognised illness was 'especially timid, suggestible or vulnerable to pressure' ((1996) at 844) would not suffice. The aim here is to restrict the use of characteristics to a 'recognised psychiatric condition'. What is excluded is a lesser psychological condition which leads to vulnerability, to which a practitioner could nonetheless attest. The court also held (4) that characteristics due to self-induced abuse by alcohol, drugs or glue-sniffing could not be relevant.

The *Bowen* formula is problematic on two grounds. First, its exclusion of forms of addictive abuse is an exclusion of what could on medical grounds be characterised precisely as a 'recognised psychiatric condition' (Buchanan and Virgo, 1999, 529). It is consistent with the general legal attitude to 'self-induced' conditions (see above, pp 115–18), but that is not to say that it is morally realistic. It is also inconsistent with developments in the law of provocation, which is similarly formulated, but where addiction is relevant (*Morhall* (1995); *Smith* (2000)). Second, the distinction developed in (3) is one without a difference. Psychiatric 'conditions' lack the degree of formality that can distinguish them from the lesser conditions to which doctors would also testify. Psychiatric classification rests on the grouping of symptoms and signs in a fluid and 'atheoretical' way. This makes it hard to draw a line around a group of behaviours that are specifically the domain of psychiatry. The legal approach 'begs the question of why some personality traits merit the title of recognised psychiatric condition and others do not' (Buchanan and Virgo, 1999, 528–9). The law seeks to use psychiatry to control subjectivisation of the law, but in a typically legalistic way which does not conform with the psychiatric approach.

## (c)    Self-induced duress

Third, there is the situation where the accused brings duress on himself through his voluntary participation in an organisation or gang at an earlier stage. In *Fitzpatrick* (1977), the accused had joined the IRA in Northern Ireland at the age of nineteen, believing that civil war was imminent. He was charged with murder and armed robbery. In his defence, he argued that he had sought to withdraw before the robbery, but had been forced to participate by threats. His defence of duress was excluded on the ground that he had voluntarily exposed himself to the illegal compulsion. In *Sharp* (1987), the defendant participated in a number of armed robberies, but claimed that he acted under duress during the last one. Where he had 'voluntarily and with knowledge of its nature, joined a criminal organisation or gang which he knew might bring pressure on him to commit an offence and was an active member when he was put under such pressure, he cannot avail himself of the defence' ((1987) at 861).

The 'active member' requirement narrows the application of *Fitzpatrick*, where the defendant had previously sought to leave. Similarly, the 'knowledge of nature' formula was applied in *Shepherd* (1987) to permit a claim of duress to one who had joined a gang of shoplifters and then come under threat of violence. Two later cases are hard to reconcile. In *Lewis* (1992), the defendant refused to testify against a fellow armed robber and was charged with contempt of court. He had been attacked in prison by this man prior to the trial and was terrified of him. Despite his knowledge of the violence of his colleague, it was held that duress should have been left to the jury since the link between the agreed acts of violence and the duress was remote. In *Ali* (1995), by contrast, the defendant was linked by drug dealing to a man whom he knew to be violent. He owed him money and was forced to repay by committing a robbery on threat of death. The court held that the crux of the case was knowledge 'of either a violent nature to the gang . . . or a violent disposition in the person . . . involved' ((1995) at 303). Both Lewis and Ali knew that their association was with a 'man of violence', yet in one case but not the other an element of remoteness was introduced.

The question still remains whether 'self-induced duress' is a valid limit on the availability of the defence. *Shepherd* refers dismissively to the would-be criminal whose nerve fails and who then seeks, but is unqualified, to use the duress defence. What, however, of the person who genuinely withdraws from a criminal enterprise? Under the law of complicity, it is possible for a participant to a crime to withdraw, even during its commission, though at that stage, the withdrawal must be of a highly 'effective' character (*Becerra and Cooper* (1976) at 219). If one can 'reinstate one's innocence' in such a situation, why should it then be compromised by the actions of one's erstwhile co-participant, over which one has no control? If one can withdraw from a violent crime committed with a colleague, why can one not withdraw from a violent criminal colleague?

The exclusion is in line with other exclusions in the law where an accused brings a condition upon himself, and is subject to the same criticisms.[29] There is an empirical difference between a person who has been involved in an organisation and sought to leave and a person who has never had such involvement. The legal decision to withhold the defence from the former is, however, only possible because of an unconscious shift in the discourse. A concept of 'moral voluntariness' such as that used in the law of acts (see above, pp 115–20) is employed at the earlier stage of joining the organisation, to evade the claim of moral involuntariness at the later, and directly relevant, stage of the commission of the crime. The switching from a discourse of morally involuntary conduct to one of a 'super-individualist' moral voluntarism is carried out unreflectively within the law.[30] Its functional purpose is to limit the use of a defence to defendants who might qualify for it in law, but not be regarded morally to 'deserve' it.


## 4 CONCLUSION

We saw in Chapter 1 that one of the claims to legitimacy made on behalf of criminal law is that it respects and does justice to individuals by punishing them only for their voluntary acts. In the language of retributive philosophy, the individual brings punishment upon himself by the acts he voluntarily undertakes. There are, however, directly political as well as ideological limits to this respect for individuals. The political limits are seen in the ambivalence of the judiciary towards the necessity defence and the about-turn on the application of the duress defence in murder cases. Individual justice confronts political utility in both situations, with the latter imposing limits on the former. The judges shift in these situations from their position as guardians of a logic of individual right to that of being, in Glanville Williams's term (1983, 144), a 'State instrumentality'.

More deeply, there is an ideological limitation on the claim of individual justice which is implicit in Vining's observation (above, Chapter 1) that the law does not know real individuals at all, only abstract images of the individual which populate our thought in the stead of real human beings. The criminal law's currency of judgment is that of a set of lowest common denominators. All human beings perform conscious acts and do so intentionally. That much is true, and there is logic in the law's denial of responsibility to those who, because of mental illness or other similar factor, lack voluntariness (narrowly conceived) or intentionality. But such an approach misses the social context that makes individual life possible, and by which individual actions are, save in situations of actual cognitive or volitional breakdown, mediated and conditioned. There is no getting away from our existence in families, neighbourhoods, environments, social classes and politics. It is these contexts that deal us the cards which we play more or less effectively. Human beings, it is true, are not reducible to the contexts within which they operate, but nor are they or their actions intelligible without them. This basic truth of the duality of human life, as both individual and social (Norrie, 1996, 2000), is ignored by a practice and philosophy of legal judgment in which context is always regarded as extrinsic to agency. Even where it is admitted, it is as a secondary and exceptional phenomenon added on to the judgment of conduct 'from the outside'. The law focuses its attention on an isolated homunculus, an individual without past or future, a solitary atom capable of acts and intentions and responsible for them. Even if he cannot choose a particular act, he can choose a previous act which takes its place.

A striking illustration comes from the United States. The major cities there have been gripped by an epidemic of drug abuse, which acts as the seedbed of a great volume of crime (including many 'orthodox' duress situations brought about by gang war). The response of the authorities is to erode civil liberties and to convict large numbers of young people in the inner-city areas. This in turn leads to more and worse violence, as in the Los Angeles riots of 1992. As one economist points out, however, the real backdrop to this criminal inflation is the decline in the social and economic infrastructure in the inner city areas, and what this means for 'choice':

> Revisiting Watts nearly a generation after a famous pioneering study of its problems, UCLA industrial relations economist Paul Bullock discovered that conditions had grown far worse since 1965. At the core of community despair was endemic youth unemployment. Bullock observed that the only rational option open to youth – at least in the neo-classical sense of individual economic choice – was to sell drugs. Indeed as power resources in the community have generally declined, ghetto youth, refusing simply to become 'expendable', have regrouped around the one social organisation that seems to give them clout: the street gang. (Davies with Ruddick, 1988, 51–2) [31]

There is a social world 'out there' which rarely finds its way into the courtroom. If judges are concerned about 'charters for terrorists, gangleaders and kidnappers', these are not simply the product of wicked individuals exploiting the law. They are the product of structural and systemic forces, which the law with its individualist focus ignores. [32]

The significance of the duress and necessity defences is that they begin to open up this otherwise hidden world *within legal discourse*. Such situations are in one sense highly unusual and idiosyncratic. They involve a kind of threat that most will never experience. But the fear that stems from such situations is qualitatively no different from a range of other fears which may be equally efficacious for the 'ordinary reasonable man'. These include, in Williams' account, 'fear of economic ills, fear of displeasing others, or any other determinant of choice'. Whether it be a gangleader, someone using violence for political ends, convicts threatening a prisoner with homosexual rape (Vandervort, 1987, 212–13), people stealing out of hunger or breaking into property because they are homeless, or simply living life in 'the ghetto' with no legitimate options, the contexts are all clearly social, and not easily differentiable. It is this which gives Lord Simon's argument in *Lynch* its cogency when he argues that the law ought to ignore the constraining context of duress, but in so doing, he must deny the concept of individual justice in its extended morally involuntary form.

Imagine a newspaper picture of a major social event such as a riot in which a mass of people stand on a street and throw stones at another group of people (a police force, an army, an opposing group). The picture is in sharp detail and shows the faces and bodily postures of those concerned. Along with the picture goes the kind of standard text of the better newspapers which explains the sequence of events that occurred, and then proceeds to analyse those events in terms of a series of causes and effects of which they are a part. On another page in the same newspaper is an editorial column which addresses the political and social options and structures available to solve the problems of rioting. Now go back to the picture, draw a ring around one stone throwing individual and cut it out. That is effectively what the law does. It is only interested in *this* individual performing *these* acts at *this* time. Everything else, which gives what the individual did meaning, and without which he would not have acted, is irrelevant. But this is the way it has to be if responsibility is to be imputed purely and simply to the individual.

Legal individualism is one-sided and decontextualised, and this has crucial implications for our understanding of legal justice. For Hart (1968, 22), justice requires that the law 'adjusts the competing claims of human beings [by] treat[ing] all alike as persons by attaching special significance to human voluntary action'. There is at the same time more and less truth in this than Hart realises. The law does indeed treat 'all alike as persons', for it is only by decontextualising individual actions that the multifarious real differences between individuals in society can be ignored. It is only in terms of an abstract category of legal personhood that human beings who are essentially different in terms of background and biography can be treated as the same. Similarly, the law does indeed attach a 'special significance to human voluntary action': the capacity to be at fault for acting in social contexts that are not of one's making. This ideological process of decontextualisation, as we have seen, is deeply political, for it enables fault attribution to take place while silencing the opposing political and ideological reasons that individuals would give for their actions if they could. Necessity and duress are significant precisely because they push at the line between context and agency. In Chapter 6 (p 114), it was argued that the law permits these defences as a kind of safety valve or sealed box to take the pressure off the narrow paradigm of physical involuntariness with which it standardly operates. We have seen, however, how the law seeks to limit the size and content of this box, lest when opening the lid, it turn out to be veritably Pandora's.

# Chapter 9

# Insanity and diminished responsibility

[T]he M'Naghten test is based on an entirely obsolete and misleading conception of the nature of insanity. (Royal Commission on Capital Punishment, 1949–53, 80)

The insanity defence holds a special fascination because it appears (falsely) to be a limited technical issue . . . The point is that the technical issue keeps slipping away, since the real issue is to make decisions about how to distribute power. (Smith, 1981, 172)

## I  INTRODUCTION

In this chapter, we consider the general defence of insanity which is available in relation to all crimes, and the additional partial defence of diminished responsibility, which is available only to reduce a murder charge to manslaughter. It is widely accepted that the law in this area is inadequate (see eg the Committee on Mentally Abnormal Offenders, 1975, 217–19). The general defence is too narrow in its test for insanity and too broad in terms of its concept of disease. The result of this is that many defendants whom most people would regard as insane cannot use the defence, while some whom most would regard as perfectly sane are forced to use it if they want to deny responsibility for a crime. For the former group, the additional partial defence of diminished responsibility operates, but only to scale murder down to manslaughter. For the latter group, it is sometimes better to plead guilty to the charge than to have one's physical condition (for example, epilepsy: *Sullivan* (1983); or diabetes: *Hennessy* (1989)) forced into the law's pigeonhole of insanity.

There have been many attempts to reform the law to produce a workable defence of insanity, but these have yet to be acted upon. Indeed, despite sustained criticism and suggestions for change, famous trials of the 1980s[1] revealed a clear tendency to retrench the law around the traditional, much criticised rules. On the surface, what is at stake in these cases is the question of fairness to the accused and how one draws the lines in order to reflect individual responsibility. The issue falls squarely within the orthodox liberal account of doing justice to individuals, and reflects the underlying link between responsibility in law and in morality. Liberal and legal ideology feed into and draw from each other:

We are speaking, therefore, of responsibility in the sense of moral or legal accountability. A person is *morally* responsible if he can justly be blamed and perhaps punished when he does wrong. We do not regard a dog as responsible, or a babe in arms, or a gibbering lunatic. On much the same principle they are not regarded as *legally* responsible, ie legally liable to punishment through the agency of the courts. (Williams, 1983, 640)

The concept of insanity appears to fit neatly into a liberal framework. The insane person is morally, therefore legally, irresponsible for his acts, and unpunishable. The criticism is that the law's outmoded narrowness stems from a judicial over-sensitivity to the needs of social protection which should be corrected by reform in favour of the accused (see eg Ashworth, 1999, 215–7). What is not recognised is how the traditional views about insanity are *ideologically* entrenched within legal discourse, so that much more rides on the issue than a measure of enlightened liberal reform. At stake is a particular legal way of seeing the social world and the human beings that populate it that is both powerful, and odd. While the insanity rules are outmoded, it is not just inertia that keeps them in place.

The power is seen in the high profile courtroom battles to affirm or deny the legal categories in light of the presumptions of another profession, that of psychiatry. Both lawyers and psychiatrists have professional vested interests in holding up their view of the world as natural and right. Both would like to claim the 'turf', the expertise, to explain insanity as a technical concept within their particular vocabularies. Yet both are open to serious critical challenge. What is interesting is that these two powerful professional groups possess views which are in important ways conflicting and incompatible, and which may come into conflict when the psychiatrist confronts the lawyer as an expert witness.

The oddity is illustrated, for example, in the report of the trial of Mark Chapman, who, in 1981, changed his mind and pleaded guilty to the murder of John Lennon. His reason, he told his lawyer, was that God had commanded him and this had been confirmed in religious literature he read. His lawyer is reported as having advised him to stick to his original plea but stated that 'when God told him to plead guilty . . . I was effectively removed from the decision-making process', adding that 'there is no doubt in my mind that he is insane' (*Times*, 23 June 1981). After a delay of an hour because 'the judge wanted to assure himself that Mr Chapman knew what he was doing', it was decided that the change was made 'knowingly and intelligently'. The Assistant District Attorney commented that the accused had made 'a knowing, intelligent and voluntary waiver of his right to trial'.

Thus educated people could claim that a waiver of trial was 'knowing and intelligent' on the basis of sudden messages from God confirmed by holy readings. This suggests a continuity of thought between the lawyer and the further fringes of religious thought rather than the connection with good common sense that is normally asserted. Nor is such a view atypical. Peter Sutcliffe (see below, pp 187, 192–3) was held to be responsible and convicted of murder despite receiving divine instructions to kill his victims. It was not a question of whether or not such voices were believed, but that they were insufficient to mount a defence of insanity *even if they were believed.*[2]

Together with the longevity and stubborn resistance to change shown by the legal categories, these comments suggest that we should look deeper into the legal discourse and its conflict with psychiatry. At play, I shall argue, is not a technical issue of law reform but a question of how the power to define and control bizarre conduct is exercised in our society by competing professional groups, with results that are often in themselves somewhat bizarre. In the next section, we examine the historical emergence of a legal ideology of individual responsibility, which is contrasted with a conflicting medical-psychiatric account of madness. In the following two sections, we then look at the current law on insanity and diminished responsibility and proposals for reform in the light of the enduring conflict between these two models of human conduct. In the fifth section, we note, in addition to the ideological conflicts between law and psychiatry, an enduring *agreement* between the two sides that the problem of madness is an individual phenomenon. This underlying consensus helps to cement a practical but not always stable alliance between the two professions, while obscuring the social issues which underlie the problems of madness.

## 2   LAW AGAINST PSYCHIATRY: THE SOCIAL CONTROL OF MADNESS

We have seen in previous chapters how the social conflicts of the nineteenth century were marginalised by the development of legal categories which excluded the political nature of private property and much of the violence that it occasioned. From rules protecting the social interests of some, the law became seen as a universal form of social mediation on the basis of its rational, de-moralised individualism (see Chapters 3–6, 8).

### (i)   Law's rational subject

The reasoning individual legal subject, located within a world of universal legal rights, protected by the rule of law, was a powerful mechanism of ideological legitimation in Victorian England, as indeed it remains today. The concept of the rational legal subject, pursuing his interests and responsible for his actions, necessarily established a barrier beyond which responsibility could not go in the case of those who were not rational. The presence of rationality presupposed the possibility of its opposite, the existence of irrationality. As Erskine put it in the landmark trial of *Hadfield* in 1800:

> It is agreed by all jurists, and is established by the law of this and every country, that it is the REASON OF MAN which makes him accountable for his actions; *and that the deprivation of reason acquits him of crime.* This principle is indisputable . . . ((1800) at 1309–10) (emphasis added); quoted in Gordon, 1978, 348).[3]

The law accordingly had to develop a concept of insanity, and it naturally did this in accordance with its conception of the individual as a reasoning being. The legal approach to insanity concerned a test for the absence of rational intelligence within the human mind. Eventually this emerged as the M'Naghten Rules of 1843, which remain the basis of the law today, and which we discuss below.

### (ii)   The asylum and psychiatry

Before doing so, however, it is necessary to note the existence of another approach to insanity that began to develop in the eighteenth and early nineteenth centuries.

When the old Western feudal societies began to break up through the dispossession of the peasantry and the growth of the towns, there developed a period of intense social disruption. This was met in part by the strategy of what Foucault calls the 'Great Confinement' (Foucault, 1965; Hirst and Woolley 1982; but cf Porter, 1987). In this time, marginalised members of those social classes experiencing the greatest dislocation were to be contained and disciplined in a variety of 'houses of correction'. Amongst these marginal people were the mad, who in the less ordered conditions of feudal life had been permitted more of an existence at large in society. From this time on, they would be contained in places of confinement. During the period of the Enlightenment, which followed that of the Great Confinement, these places of containment of the mad were transformed into 'the asylum'. From this institutional foundation, there was derived the alienist's corpus of knowledge. This led in turn to the establishment of a new profession of psychiatry, a group of medical practitioners whose authority was based on their special position in relation to the mad.

Society charged these early practitioners of psychiatry with certain control responsibilities in relation to the insane, and these were institutionalised within a legal framework (Unsworth, 1987; Smith, 1981, chs 1, 2, pp 69–70). The early psychiatrists were thus given a certain measure of social legitimacy and a professional standing they were keen to defend and develop. At the same time the potential for a boundary dispute between law and psychiatry was established. Both insane and non-insane people could break the law, but the law would wish to exclude the insane from punishment on the basis of their irrationality, sending them as a consequence to the asylum rather than the prison. The psychiatrists in the asylum, on the other hand, were committed to accepting the insane, but expected and sought to be accorded a certain status in the courtroom as experts upon the nature of the problem they were uniquely positioned to study, and expected to contain.

To begin with, this did not present much of a problem because the earliest psychiatric approaches adopted a conception of treatment as involving individual moral reform through the promotion of rational self-governance, and thus were not far removed from the law's own ideas on human conduct. As the nineteenth century progressed, however, psychiatry increasingly drew upon a natural scientific methodology and a medical model of illness in order to explain the incidence and aetiology of insanity. Insanity came increasingly to be seen as a product of disease located in the brain which caused the mad behaviour. Following their methodology to its natural conclusion, psychiatrists then argued that the 'truth' of insanity lay not in its empirical manifestation, in conduct displaying an obvious lack of reason, but in the underlying causal mechanisms to be found in the brain.

It was this move in thinking that caused the break with law. The ultimate locus of insanity was not in its psychological manifestation but in underlying organic causes. It therefore became possible to conceive of forms of insanity which left the 'surface' areas of the psyche, for example the reasoning faculty, relatively unaffected while attacking the 'deeper' elements of the will or the emotions. A lack of reason became one, but only one, *symptom* of an underlying, causal, mental illness. A man could as a result appear quite rational but still be insane. The crucial innovative concept, a lucid form of madness, was described by the French alienist Pinel as manie sans délire (mania without delusion).[4] In this account, insanity did not affect the cognitive processes so much as the volitional (the will) or the emotional.

A man might know that he was doing wrong but be unable to stop himself (volitional insanity), or believe that he was not bound by the normal rules of society (emotional insanity).

## (iii)   Conflicting views of crime

At stake in this developing conflict in diagnosis were two competing ways of understanding human behaviour, and beyond that, two conflicting social ideologies as to the forms through which power should be exercised in society. For the lawyers, a society of rational individuals with a propensity for evil was held in check by a firm penal code which punished the wrongdoer for purposes of deterrence and justice. The law symbolised both the defence of order against anarchy (the utilitarian premise) and the moral rightness of giving the criminal his due through the punishment (the retributive premise). The crucial element in this conjunction of utilitarian and retributive goals was that the guilty should not escape the sanction of the law. Deterrence and desert both required that crimes should be punished. This was especially the case in relation to the most symbolic of punishments, the death penalty for murder. In the execution of the murderer, the law revealed its steadfast and implacable opposition to the worst of crimes. In connection with the most serious of punishments, where the law displayed its most trenchant power and threat, there could be no question of the accused evading his just deserts.

For the psychiatric profession on the other hand, as it developed its own viewpoint on insane criminality, the conception of mental disease and its effects on conduct went much further than the law allowed. Insanity was not to be viewed 'metaphysically' as a question of the lack of reason, but as a matter of physiological causation. The development of medical science in turn suggested a new technological approach to social order, in which the problems of crime would be solved not by the punishment of an individual who could not help himself, but by isolating and treating the causes of crime within the psyche. The aim was not expiation but prevention and cure, and the old punitive ideology was anathematised as irrational, ineffective, and unjust. To punish people for what they could not help, when help was available, was cruel and immoral. A different methodology enjoying a different mode of legitimation, the scientific treatment of the weak and the sick, was deployed.

The conflict between these two different ideologies was seen primarily in the capital murder case. Insanity was in the majority of cases used as a defence of last resort to evade the gallows. The psychiatrists both rejected the law's analysis of insanity and believed that its narrowness led to the inexcusable possibility of executing those who were genuinely insane. Capital cases therefore presented a dramatic forum for the clash of these two distinct accounts not just of insanity, but of the broader moral and legal order within which insanity occurred and was to be understood. On the one side were the psychiatrists striving for recognition of their views in a highly public forum, convinced of the backwardness of legal ideas of morality, and seeking to save the accused person from execution. On the other side were the lawyers operating their rationalistic categories, convinced of the symbolic rightness of their view of the world and of the value of the death penalty. They were therefore opposed to what they saw as special pleading on behalf of sane people who deserved to be hanged but might 'get off' if the psychiatrists had their way.

Thus what appears on the surface as a technical question of different definitions of insanity has its roots in a much deeper question involving the nature of the social and legal order and the power to define and shape a central institutional form of social control. Psychiatrists did not just disagree with lawyers, they threatened to 'relocate the symbols of the moral order' by abolishing evil and retribution (Smith, 1981, 33, 74). Lawyers for their part 'jealously guarded the discourse in which human action was a proper object of judgment' (Smith, 1981, 75). It is striking to compare the relationship between law and psychiatry in the different areas of civil commitment, where an alliance was strong, and criminal law, where the lawyers refused to move away from the juridical conception of individual responsibility.[5] This differential approach can only be understood in terms of what was ideologically at stake for the law and the state through the use of the legal categories. While the abolition of capital punishment has taken some of the urgency out of the conflict (in Britain, but not the United States), the opposition of the two standpoints, together with the ways they collaborate, remain the key to an understanding of the law today.

## 3   BETWEEN LAW AND PSYCHIATRY: THE LEGAL DEFENCES

In this section, we examine the legal rules on insanity and diminished responsibility. It is argued that they have emerged out of the continuing interplay between the legal and psychiatric accounts of human conduct.

### (i)   Insanity

The legal test for insanity is contained within the M'Naghten Rules of 1843. Daniel M'Naghten had shot and killed a man, believing him to be the Home Secretary of the day, Sir Robert Peel. Medical evidence had indicated that he had acted under the 'morbid delusion' that he was being persecuted by the police on instructions from the Tory Party, and that such a delusion could mean that his acts were outside his control. Despite these delusions, there was no evidence that M'Naghten did not know what he was doing in firing the gun, or that he did not know it was wrong. The delusions did not affect his rationality on these matters or his ability to form the intentions to plan and commit the crime. Along with the contemporaneous case of *Oxford* (1840), M'Naghten's acquittal caused political concern. It was linked in the mind of the establishment with Chartist disorder (Quen, 1968), and even occasioned the Queen to express her misgivings.[6] As a result, the judges proceeded to formulate a set of rules to govern the legal definition of insanity. The central elements were:

> . . . every man is to be presumed to be sane, and to possess a sufficient degree of reason to be responsible for his crimes . . . [T]o establish a defence on the grounds of insanity it must be clearly proved that, at the time of the committing of the act, the party accused was labouring under such a defect of reason, from disease of the mind, as not to know the nature and quality of the act he was doing; or, if he did know it, that he did not know he was doing what was wrong. (*M'Naghten's Case* (1843) at 210)

The Rules have been criticised as being, at one level, too broad in their application, and at another level, too narrow. In both circumstances, the ability of lawyers to create their own definitions in the face of both the professional opinions of psychiatrists, and a measure of common sense, is notable.

### (a) The breadth of the Rules: 'disease of the mind'

The breadth of the rules is seen in the definition of what constitutes a disease of the mind. Relatively recent cases have established that any medical condition affecting the mind and 'internal' to the accused constitutes such a disease. Thus in *Kemp* (1956), it was held that a disease affecting the mind, arteriosclerosis, was as much a disease of the mind as a clearly mental disease such as schizophrenia. The definition was extended further in *Bratty* (1961) where Lord Denning stated that 'any mental disorder which has manifested itself in violence and is prone to recur is a disease of the mind' ((1961) at 534). The definition is oriented to the practical goal of social control rather than the accurate use of language, as Denning's further comments make clear.[7] In *Burgess* (1991), the functional character of the concept was extended where a sleepwalker who assaulted a friend was held to suffer from a disease of the mind. The causes of sleepwalking were 'internal' and it did not matter if it would not recur, it was still a 'disease of the mind'. A similarly broad approach is seen in *Sullivan* (1983):

> If the effect of a disease is to impair [the] faculties [of reason, memory and understanding] so severely . . . it matters not whether the aetiology of the impairment is organic, as in epilepsy, or functional, or whether the impairment itself is permanent or is transient and intermittent, provided that it subsisted at the time of commission of the act. ((1983) at 677)

Lord Diplock underlines the pragmatic intention behind this wide definition by linking it to the requirements of social control.[8] The effect of this has been in practice to deny the defence of automatism (above, Chapter 6, pp 115–16) to epileptics, sleepwalkers and to some, but not all, diabetics. With regard to the latter, where the unconscious state results from a natural build-up of the blood-sugar level (hyper-glycaemia), perhaps through a failure to take insulin, the automatism is a result of an internal, organic, condition and is therefore classed as 'insane' on the *Sullivan* test. Where the unconscious state is caused by an overdose of insulin (hypoglycaemia), however, this is regarded as an 'external' element, and therefore the automatism is 'non-insane'. Thus it matters whether the accused's automatism was the product of a failure to take insulin, or a failure to take the proper amount. The absurdity of this consequence of the 'internal'/'external' distinction results from allowing the concept of disease of the mind to overspill any reasonable, definitional limit in the interest of what is regarded as necessary for social control.

### (b) The narrowness of the Rules: the two cognitive tests

The narrowness of the Rules is seen in their cognitivism, which denies any other forms of insanity, such as the volitional, as well as requiring judge and jury to pick and choose between delusions. In the first limb of the Rules, the accused must not know the nature and quality of his act. A nurse who puts a baby on the fire thinking it is a log, the killing of a human being under the delusion that one is crushing an ant, 'the madman who cuts a woman's throat under the idea that he was cutting a loaf of bread' (Kenny's illustration, quoted in Smith and Hogan, 1988, 192). These are all illustrations of delusions that fall within the test because there is a qualitative difference between what the accused thinks he is doing and what he is actually doing. It matters under this test precisely what the delusion is. The belief that one is an avenging angel sent by God to kill prostitutes may be delusional, but it will not fall within this limb of the test because the accused appreciates the nature of his acts (the putting to death of other human beings). The delusion must be directly related to the quality of the criminal act.

The Rules are unsatisfactory because they make courts draw lines between delusions. They purposely expressed a form of insanity based on the exclusion of all rational elements, for the absence of mental reason was to be the sole basis for irresponsibility in law. The consequence was that reason could be 'divided up' and judges could pick and choose between varieties of unreason to suit their rationalistic test. This was possible because the legal test did not have to be directly related to an underlying concept of mental disease, save as a limiting element to exclude, for example, the drunk (who might want to claim temporary insanity) from trying to use the defence. This is seen in particular in the judges' answer to the fourth question put in M'Naghten's case concerning a delusion as to some facts, but a measure of reason in relation to others. They argued that responsibility would depend upon treating the facts with respect to which the delusion existed as if they were real. If the accused killed under a delusion of injury to his character or fortune, he would be responsible because the delusion would not affect the overall wrongfulness of his conduct as an otherwise rational person.

The judges could not see that a 'partial delusion' obliquely, or not at all, related to the crime could inform its commission just as much as a more total delusion about the nature and quality of the act. For the psychiatrist, elements of reason and unreason could exist in the same mind, because these would be articulated by the underlying mental disease into a form of insanity in which elements of rationality and irrationality coexisted. A 'monomaniacal' obsession, apparently contained and partial, could totally govern a person's life. For the lawyer, on the other hand, because the focus was purely on the surface functioning of the mind and what it knew, any partial rational ability left to the accused was evidence that he was partially sane. When the psychiatrist spoke of 'partial insanity', he meant to indicate that 'many lunatics were not totally abnormal' (Smith, 1981, 37) while still remaining insane. For lawyers, with their narrower frame of reference, the term indicated that the individual was partly sane (cf Stephen, 1883, II, 161–2).

Similar points can be made in relation to the second limb of the Rules which permit the accused to show that he did not know that he was doing wrong. Here the law is specific that 'wrong' means against the law, rather than morally wrong, again forcing the jury to pick and choose between delusions (*Windle* (1952)).[9] It is no defence to say that the accused heard voices from God, for as one judge glibly put it, 'the mere fact that a man thinks he is John the Baptist does not entitle him to kill his mother' (quoted in Smith and Hogan, 1999, 204). Presumably, however, it would in principle make a difference whether the divine message was a direct instruction to bypass the law of the land in favour of a higher law, or whether it advised the insane person that the law of the land had in fact been suspended for him. In the latter situation, he would not believe he was breaking the law. This is an absurd distinction for the law to draw. It is evaded in practice by a tendency among psychiatrists to blur their account of what the defendant in fact knew (Mackay, 1995, 104).

These problems with the Rules have been widely discussed. The Royal Commission (1949–53), as we have seen, described the M'Naghten test as 'obsolete and misleading', for insanity 'does not only, or primarily affect the cognitive or intellectual faculties, but affects the whole personality of the patient, including both the will and the emotions'. An insane person, they added, may both know the nature and quality of his act and that it is wrong by law, but yet commit it as a result of mental disease. The M'Naghten Rules, 150 years old and still going strong, steadfastly refuse to countenance such a possibility.

To understand why the M'Naghten Rules should have been interpreted broadly on the concept of mental disease but narrowly on the cognitive tests, it is necessary to see the functional role that these two different aspects of the Rules play within the criminal process. The concept of mental disease has evolved in relation to the defence of automatism and the requirement of voluntariness in relation to acts. The consequence of establishing that a criminal act was involuntary is that the accused is entitled to an acquittal. However, the effect of finding that his acts were the product of an insane form of automatism is that he becomes subject to the power of the court to detain him on account of his insanity.

A broad definition of mental disease opens up the possibilities for the court to order a form of social control where the alternative, under a finding of non-insane automatism, is that the accused walks free. (It also has had the effect in practice of channelling the accused into a plea of guilty rather than accept the stigma of a label of insanity, and the possible consequences that might follow.) The cognitive tests, on the other hand, operate where the alternative to a finding of criminal insanity is one of criminal responsibility, either full or diminished. Where the choice is between freedom for the accused and the possibility of his control by psychiatry, the courts err in favour of the latter. Where it is between a finding of legal guilt or psychiatric control, they err in favour of the former, in part for the reasons of ideology outlined above.

## (ii) Diminished responsibility

The Rules have resisted a number of attempts at reform. One partial reform, which permits their worst consequences to be ameliorated, is the mitigatory defence of diminished responsibility under the Homicide Act 1957, s 2(1). A successful plea reduces murder to a form of voluntary manslaughter.

### (a) Meaning of terms

Section 2(1) is expressed as follows:

> Where a person kills . . . he shall not be convicted of murder if he was suffering from such abnormality of mind (whether arising from a condition of arrested or retarded development of mind or any inherent causes or induced by disease or injury) as substantially impaired his mental responsibility for his acts and omissions in doing . . . the killing.

There are two requirements under the section. The defendant must first have been suffering from an 'abnormality of mind', which, second, 'substantially impaired his mental responsibility for the killing'. In *Byrne* (1960), the broader concept of 'abnormality of mind' was contrasted with the narrower 'defect of reason' under M'Naghten. It is –

> . . . wide enough to cover the mind's activities in all its aspects, not only the perception of physical acts and matters, and the ability to form a rational judgment as to whether an act is right or wrong, but also the ability to exercise will-power to control his physical acts in accordance with that rational judgment. (*Byrne* (1960) at 4)

This formulation covers a number of conditions. It includes, for example, volitional states of insanity such as 'irresistible impulse' as well as cognitive states. In *Sanderson* (1993), the bracketed causal terms in s 2(1) were explained. 'Any inherent causes' covered 'functional' mental illnesses such as the paranoid psychosis from which the defendant suffered. The phrase 'induced by disease or injury' referred to 'organic or physical injury or disease of the body including the brain' ((1994) at 336).

While 'abnormality of mind' draws upon a psychiatric view of the causes of mental illness, it is hitched to a moral-legal judgment as to whether the abnormality 'substantially impaired responsibility'. This is fundamentally a question for the jury, to be assessed according to their understanding of the defendant's actions and situation.

### (b) Conflict and co-operation in the law

The law is essentially based on a conflict between two discourses. While 'abnormality of mind' requires the testimony of psychiatrists (although it is not a proper psychiatric concept), 'substantial impairment of mental responsibility' requires the moral judgment of the jury, and there is in logic no way of inferring the one from the other. Within the scientific discourse of the psychiatrist, mental conditions can be studied to reveal the relationship between abnormality of mind and the propensity to crime as a matter of cause and effect. The question of the mental responsibility of the accused raises a metaphysical question of the freedom of the will which scientific discourse does not recognise and cannot answer (*Sparks* (1964)). The question, for example, whether the accused suffered an irresistible impulse or simply failed to resist it, is a non-question for psychiatric discourse. It is therefore not one that its testimony can illuminate.[10] For the psychiatrist, 'irresistible impulse' is the product of mental disease, and the person experiencing it is caused to act as he does. For some lawyers, however, with their mentalistic conception of human conduct, there is always a suspicion that the accused has simply declined to resist a particular impulse.[11] One judge described it as a 'fantastic theory . . . which if it were to become part of our criminal law, would be merely subversive' (*Kopsch* (1925) at 50).[12] The law is a system of deterrents, and the proper answer to such an impulse is a sufficiently strong deterrent to counter its alleged irresistibility.[13]

Nonetheless, the criticisms of the M'Naghten Rules and the official recognition of other forms of insanity by the Royal Commission on Capital Punishment eventually led to the partial acceptance of psychiatric concepts through the 1957 Act, albeit on the law's terms. In *Byrne* (1960), Lord Parker explained that the mental state caught by the section is not a form of full insanity, as the psychiatric view implies, but rather a 'partial insanity or being on the border-line of insanity'.[14] This language has been disapproved where a depressive condition is involved. Such a mental state can found a defence, but it is not bordering on insanity, and it would therefore mislead a jury to use these terms (*Seers* (1984)). Nonetheless, the description shows how the law justifies the *mitigation* of punishment, for the accused is *partially sane* in legal terms. Lord Parker also acknowledged that the term 'abnormality of mind' in the section could include situations both of inability to exercise will-power to control physical acts (the psychiatric premise) and situations of difficulty in so doing (the legal premise).[15] But if the accused was unable to control his acts (the former category), there is no reason not to acquit him as insane rather than to mitigate his punishment,[16] other than that the existing insanity rules do not allow it. Thus conflicts remain.

Nonetheless, in practice, s 2 operates as a means of avoiding a conviction for murder and the compulsory life sentence that accompanies it. In its early years, it operated as a means to avoid the death penalty. Nowadays, it has eclipsed the use of the insanity defence in homicide cases. Faced with mandatory indefinite hospitalisation on an insanity plea to murder (Criminal Procedure (Insanity and Unfitness to Plead) Act 1991), mentally disordered killers who fall under M'Naghten, as well as those who do not, are encouraged to plead diminished responsibility (Mackay, 2000, 59). It also covers a variety of different situations, ranging from the mentally ill person who would be adjudged insane on a broader legal test than that allowed by M'Naghten, to the mercy killer,[17] whose mental condition may have been affected by the illness of a loved one but who could not be said to be insane at all. The defence intermingles scientific and metaphysical discourses in a way that produces an amelioration of the law's narrowness but on the basis of an intellectual muddle and compromise. As Ashworth (1999, 288) puts it, lawyers and doctors have approached the test with a 'compassionate pragmatism rather than with the rarefied verbal analysis too frequently encountered in English criminal law'. One person's 'rarefied verbal analysis', however, is another's technical precision in the use of legal terms.[18]

Certainly, under the surface of agreement, there is scope for dispute. In *Sanderson* (1993), the question for the jury was whether a paranoid psychosis would count as an abnormality of mind. It was held that the defendant's appeal could succeed only if it were accepted that his mental state stemmed from an inherent cause related to childhood abuse, which was exacerbated in his case by drug addiction. If the jury thought the paranoid psychosis was the result of drug-taking alone, without additional underlying cause, the defendant would not have a defence. This is in line with the general attitude taken by the courts to matters of alcohol and drug abuse. In *Tandy* (1989), for example, it was held that chronic alcoholism could found a diminished responsibility defence, but only if it removed any element of voluntary choice. There had to be an underlying brain injury resulting in gross impairment of judgment and emotional response. These decisions insist on underlying causes for existing mental problems before diminished responsibility will be permitted.

Where, however, does this leave the depressed mercy killer (of which there were 22 between 1982 and 1991: Mackay, 2000, 79) who also gets to use the diminished responsibility defence? Such a person typically will not be able to point to an underlying condition, but is reacting depressively to the unhappiness of the situation.

To the extent that a case like *Sanderson* probes the limits of abnormality of mind, to that extent, it threatens the 'compassionate pragmatism' of the defence. Given the competing theoretical discourses and the compromise to which the section gives expression, the defence *could* work only if both sides adopt a pragmatic attitude and keep the law vague.

Finally, it is worth noting the limitation that the defence is only available to mitigate murder. If Byrne, the sexually psychopathic killer had committed a serious sexual assault, he would have had no mitigatory defence to compensate for the narrowness of M'Naghten. Is this explicable? If diminished responsibility were regarded as simply a way of extending justice to those mentally disordered offenders excluded by M'Naghten, it could surely be argued that it should be applicable to more than just one offence. If, however, diminished responsibility is seen as peculiarly balanced between a number of vectors of policy, principle and understanding, this is not so obvious. These include mitigation specifically of the death penalty/life sentence for murder and accommodating the different views of lawyers and psychiatrists in relation to those who kill. They also involve extending legal recognition of mental disorder beyond even its psychiatric bounds where killings attract compassion. The diminished responsibility defence fills a very particular niche in the criminal law. We return to its working in Section 5, below.


## 4   LAW AND PSYCHIATRY IN CONFLICT: THE POLITICS OF LAW REFORM

In this section I focus on the process of reform in this country and, to a certain extent, in the United States in the 1980s, and its implications both for the law and for the analysis of this chapter. My argument will be that this reform process can only be understood in terms of the political and intellectual conflicts between doctors and lawyers in the context of broader political developments. In order to understand the reform process, however, it is also necessary to recognise that in addition to the deep conflict between the two professions, there are also important points of compromise and co-operation. Practically, law and psychiatry participate from day to day in a more or less firm strategic alliance to share power in a situation where both sides' views enjoy a measure of legitimacy.

Especially from the late nineteenth century, there has been a continued recognition by the state of the role of psychiatry in the social control and care of mentally disturbed persons. In the beginning, psychiatry had to fight hard for acceptance of its perspective, and the battles around the definition of insanity reflect this. However, since in particular the endorsement of the welfare state, psychiatry has enjoyed a substantial degree of legitimacy. This is reflected in the existence, for example, of the plea of diminished responsibility, which allows a partnership and compromise between the two disciplines to be expressed within the law itself.[19] As we have seen, the terms of the 1957 Act exhibit the conflict between the two discourses, a tension which is overcome in practice by the pragmatic co-operation of both sides. The compromises are reached, however, pragmatically at the level of social politics (cf Smith, 1985), and not at the level of substantive agreement about the nature of insanity and how it should be understood. The way to grasp the process of law reform in this area is therefore to keep in mind the residual conflicts that underlie the superficial partnership between the two protagonists.

## (i)  The post-Hinckley debate in the United States

In the United States, this is particularly clear because in the 1950s and 1960s, a psychiatric definition of insanity made more legal headway than it did in Britain. Under the rule in *Durham* (1954), the court formulated a 'product' test for insanity which required the defence only to show that the accused's conduct was caused by the mental disorder from which he suffered, without reference to any legal test of responsibility along the lines of M'Naghten. In addition to *Durham*, the United States also proceeded much further in terms of its recognition of the old lawyer's bugbear of 'irresistible impulse'.[20] For the psychiatric profession, these tests embodied a more appropriate means for allocating responsibility because they permitted a direct 'scientific' account of the accused's conduct to be delivered in cause and effect terms in the courtroom, unencumbered by old-fashioned and ultimately metaphysical tests of responsibility. *Durham* addressed the underlying causes of mentally disordered crime rather than dealing with what might only be certain symptoms of a disorder. It dealt concretely with the disordered subjectivity of the accused, and therefore was from the psychiatrists' viewpoint more just and understanding.

For lawyers, however, *Durham* represented a threat to the very notion of individual justice according to law. First, it took the decision out of the hands of both the law and the jury by making the question of insanity a matter for psychiatry alone. The law was side-lined and the jury left with no real decision on the accused's responsibility. Lawyers further argued that the psychiatric approach to crime seriously threatened the liberty of the individual, who was no longer regarded as a person with rights but as an object of control according to scientific techniques. The retributive theory of punishment underlying the law posited an intervention in the individual's life only on the basis of a prior wrong act. The responsible individual was protected from absolute power by the law, and subject to psychiatric intervention only in extreme circumstances, such as those posited by the M'Naghten Rules. Psychiatry legitimated a group of experts whose superior knowledge placed them above the law and the layperson (the juror), and legitimated interventions in the lives of individuals that could potentially extend far beyond the normal reach of the law.[21] Psychiatry threatened the liberal conception of the rule of law.

Second, the product test threatened to open the door to a host of other experts on human behaviour who could testify that crime was the product of a variety of individual and also social factors beyond the control of the accused. The psychiatrists' scientific operating assumption of a universal *determinism* threatened, it seemed, to engulf the law's assumptions of free will and responsibility. The implications would be felt across the whole area of criminal conduct, and not just in relation to insanity. If insane people were caused to commit crimes on the determinist model, then so too were sane people in their decisions to engage or not in criminal conduct.[22] Scientific determinism was not a theory about insanity, it was a general theory about human conduct.[23] Psychiatry threatened the liberal conception of the responsible subject.

A third remaining objection is the old one that psychiatry leads to a potential slacking of deterrence and social control by allowing people to 'get off ' by pleading insanity. This complaint enjoyed renewed vigour among conservatives in the United States after the acquittal of John Hinckley for the attempted assassination of Ronald Reagan, on the ground that it was tantamount to letting him off. Psychiatry threatened the efficacy of the liberal system of crime and punishment (Simon and Aaronson, 1988).

In these three criticisms of psychiatry, it is interesting to note the convergence in the late 1970s and early 1980s of liberal and conservative critiques of the psychiatric approach, both stemming from the idea of the free legal individual. The liberal wants to defend the individual against the power of the psychiatrist, whereas the conservative wants to defend society against people escaping their just deserts. Both, however, want to affirm the narrow legal approach to insanity in order to pursue these differing ends.[24] This backlash against the broad definitions of insanity, in a number of states, led to a number of different reforms. In some, the insanity defence was abolished in favour of the sole use of a mens rea test. In others, it was returned to a M'Naghten style cognitivist test. In yet others, a conceptually flimsy but politically astute 'guilty but mentally ill' alternative to the insanity verdict was created.[25] Uniting the conservative political concerns of the United States in the 1980s with the liberal criticisms of the 1970s, the law/psychiatry boundary was renegotiated in favour of a more punitive, law-dominant, response to criminals with mental problems.

## (ii)  Reform proposals in England and Wales

In England and Wales, the relationship between law and psychiatry has remained more stable, but only, one suspects, because psychiatry has always been kept more at bay. The dramatic and public falling out between the professions in the case of Peter Sutcliffe (1981) revealed the underlying conflicts to be as virulent as ever if the political compromise were suspended. The prosecution initially agreed, in the light of unanimous psychiatric evidence, to accept a plea of diminished responsibility. The judge, however, refused to accept this and required the issues to be put to a jury, at which point the prosecution had to reverse their original standpoint and challenge the evidence they had initially been prepared to accept. Two central elements in the prosecution's case then became the claim that Sutcliffe had allegedly 'comforted' his wife with the assurance that he would plead diminished responsibility and be out in ten years, and that the psychiatrists had been tricked by a man whose actions were devious and rational. Having been prepared to accept the psychiatric evidence, the prosecution then mounted an all-out assault on the psychiatrists' interpretation of Sutcliffe's conduct, often suggesting an explanation of it in diametrically opposite terms.[26] For the psychiatrist, Sutcliffe's cunning, premeditation and determination not to be caught were classic symptoms of paranoid schizophrenia. For the prosecution, they were evidence of his responsibility, control and capacity for calculation (Bennett-Levy, 1981).

Equally significant has been the fate of the Butler Report (Committee on Mentally Abnormal Offenders, 1975), which has remained shelved since its publication. Butler proposed a new special verdict of 'not guilty on evidence of mental disorder'. The first limb of the new defence operated where the accused did not have the necessary mens rea for the crime, and was suffering from mental disorder at the time. Under the second limb, a person could claim the defence where he was suffering at the time from severe mental illness or severe subnormality. One stumbling block for the new defence is this second limb which involves 'a major change of principle in that there need be no causal connection between the abnormality and the commission of the criminal act' (Smith and Hogan, 1999, 209). The lawyer's objection to this is that the accused could be suffering from a severe mental disorder, but his crime might still be the product of normal intellectual processes, and therefore properly the subject of conviction and punishment. The Committee conceded the theoretical possibility of this occurring, but found it difficult to imagine it happening in practice. At heart, the concern here hinges around the old conflict between lawyers and psychiatrists. For the former, the accused might be suffering from a severe mental illness, but still retain a residue of responsibility for his actions; for the latter, the medical condition is definitive of the person in *all* his actions.[27]

The draft Criminal Code Bill of the Law Commission continues in the same vein by providing that a person may be found 'not guilty on evidence of mental disorder' in the following circumstances (clause 35(1)):

> A mental disorder verdict shall be returned if the defendant is proved to have committed an offence but it is proved on the balance of probabilities . . . that he was at the time suffering from severe mental illness or severe mental handicap.

'Severe mental illness' is constituted by a number of different characteristics including 'lasting impairment of intellectual functions', 'lasting alteration of mood [involving delusion]', persecutory, jealous or grandiose delusional beliefs, 'delusional misinterpretation of events' and 'thinking so disordered as to prevent reasonable appraisal of the defendant's situation' (clause 34). 'Severe mental handicap' means 'arrested or incomplete development of mind' and includes 'severe impairment of intelligence and social functioning'. The Commissioners, like their legal forebears, the judges in M'Naghten, take the problem of partial illness and continuing responsibility seriously,[28] stipulating (clause 35(2)) that the mental disorder defence will not operate where –

> . . . the court or jury is satisfied beyond reasonable doubt that the offence was not attributable to the severe mental illness or severe mental handicap.

In this apparently innocuous clause, there lurks the germ of the old law/psychiatry conflict, unresolved. The accused may be only partially insane, and therefore partially rational; his conduct, if it stems from the rational aspect of his mind, may be perfectly responsible even if he suffers from a serious mental disorder. Drawing in the main clause upon a medical definition of insanity similar to that in Butler, this simple sub-clause re-introduces the old legal concerns. Under the original Butler test, Sutcliffe would almost certainly have been found not guilty (Mackay, 1987); with clause 35(2), the possibility in such a case of an open power struggle in the courts between lawyers and psychiatrists would remain.

## 5   LAW AND PSYCHIATRY COMBINED: THE DECONTEXTUALISATION OF MADNESS

It is possible for anyone in our society to develop the symptoms of madness, whatever they may be. Nonetheless, there is evidence that the distribution of the varying forms of madness, together with the likelihood that one will be classified as mad, is affected by key social variables such as class, race and sex (see Hill (1983) for a review of the literature). Mad behaviour which results in the commission of crime is, like non-mad crime, a social phenomenon tied to wealth and power, and to the unequal distribution of life-chances between rich and poor, black and white, male and female. An unequal society allocates the power to people to be or not to be in control of their lives, or to have them controlled by others, in a differential fashion. One critic of psychiatry has put it thus:

> Poverty is not so much a matter of possession [of wealth] in itself, but of a more subtle and significant affair: power. The poor have no control over the events in their lives . . . I have come to see that all psychotic episodes are brutal parables of power. The content of delusions, the shards of disconnected thought, the seemingly senseless rage, the gesticulations and posturing, the whole crazy show revolves around issues of power and control . . .
>
> Major studies at the Maudsley Hospital in London over the last two decades have shown that just prior to a person's having a schizophrenic episode, there was an increased frequency of adverse life events . . . There is a limit to what people can stand. Madness has not been consigned to humanity by providence. It is an artefact of society's power arrangements . . . Whatever madness is, it is deeply rooted in social and sexual inequality. (Drummond, 1980; quoted in Hill, 1983, 259–60) [29]

Legal discourse is about the decontextualising of social acts and the individualising of social conduct. The legal test for insanity, with its emphasis on the presence or absence of reason, is no different from the law of intention or recklessness in this regard. It disregards the circumstances in which madness occurs; in particular, the way in which society 'drives people crazy'. Just as the separation of motive from intention removes action from its context, so too does the narrow rationalism of the M'Naghten test withdraw the individual from the social conditions of his madness.

In contrast to the law, the psychiatrist's broader typology better reflects the variety of forms that madness takes in modern society. However, in order to understand how the law's decontextualisation strategy works in this area, it is necessary to highlight a theoretical congruence, not conflict, between the work of the lawyer and the psychiatrist. Theoretically, psychiatry, like law, decontextualises social agency, in its case by locating the problem of insanity in the constitution of the individual. Medical discourse hides the social significance of madness by portraying it in terms of *individual* mental illness. This ignores the deep social significance of insane crime, as Smith makes clear in relation to the nineteenth-century cases:

> . . . crimes clearly conveyed [social] meanings. For example, Forrester killed his children when financially distressed, Townley murdered his fiancée because he considered her 'his property', Brixey killed her employer's child to preserve its innocence, and Oxford shot at the Queen. To say that these crimes were 'caused' by insanity was to restrict their meaning. (Smith, 1981, 29)

The significance of this becomes clear when we consider the ways in which psychiatry has operated to ameliorate, and thereby to cover up for both the law and society's own responsibility for the mad criminal.

## (i)  Covering up for the law

The law's narrow individualistic test for responsibility threatens its own legitimacy when it is seen as unfairly convicting persons who acted under extreme social and psychological pressure, for example, when faced with dire poverty and a family to raise. Psychiatric testimony operates to stretch irresponsibility beyond the narrow bounds of the legal test. At the same time, it maintains the law's own project because it does not expose the link between social context and 'criminal' behaviour, portraying conduct as the result of *individual*, rather than social, pathology. In this way, psychiatry operates as a safety valve for the law, and this is seen in that psychiatric testimony will often overreach not just the legal criteria of insanity but its own criteria of what constitutes mental disorder or illness where a 'compassionate' response to crime is called for.

### (a)  Poverty and the insanity defence

In the nineteenth century, there were a number of cases in which mothers and sometimes fathers killed their children in conditions of abject poverty. The killing of small babies in particular was intimately tied up with 'the working class experience of poverty, illegitimacy, abortion, wet-nursing, and child-minding ("baby farms")' (Smith, 1981, 145). The case notes from Bethlem indicated that poverty was a major element in infanticide, that juries were reluctant to convict particularly women, and that some of those found to be insane were nothing of the kind (Smith, 1981, 149). These were not situations in which the M'Naghten test would exonerate the accused. Nonetheless, many of these parents were found insane by juries going beyond the letter of the Rules, often with the testimony of psychiatrists to support their verdict. Psychiatric discourse was a convenient aid to rescue the law from the embarrassing consequences of its harsh narrowness, while at the same time avoiding any focus upon the social conditions that gave rise to the crimes in question.

> The medical language of internal individual disorder emptied the violent act of external social meaning. The insanity verdict classified child-killing as a problem to be solved by custodial therapy and managed by society's delegated specialists. This was humanitarian (in Victorian terms), but it also detracted from examining women's position in relation to power and wealth. It is important to take seriously the words of women who killed their bastard children . . . Calling [the woman] insane emptied her act of meaning; she, and not society, had a problem. (Smith, 1981, 149–50)

The need to move beyond the juridical categories was seen in the two trials of Burton (or Barton) in 1848 (Smith, 1981, 104, 117). The accused, following financial ruin, had killed his wife and child because he was tormented with the thought of starvation and poverty. When he was tried for his wife's murder, the judge rejected the category of moral insanity, stating that 'it might be urged in justification of every crime known to the law' and instructing the jury to apply a M'Naghten-style right/wrong test. As a result, Burton was convicted, though his sentence of death was commuted after pressure was brought by local psychiatrists on the Home Secretary.

Nine months later, he was tried for the murder of his child, and this time acquitted on the ground of insanity. While the judiciary was extremely unhappy with a defence that effectively found dread of poverty to be an excusing condition, their limited range of dispositions did not fit a man like Burton, who was neither narrowly mad nor morally bad. Psychiatry provided the escape both from conviction *and* from the opening of a window on the social conditions of criminality. Psychiatry was the means of introducing a satisfactorily circumscribed compassion into the legal rules. A narrow *individualisation* of a social issue stood in place of the law's abstract *individualism* and in so doing helped to obscure the underlying social processes. This collusion between law and psychiatry has long been a feature of the legal processing of mad crime. In the 1920s, a psychiatrist could comment that the M'Naghten test was innocuous in its effect. It had 'not produced its logical consequences, because it has never been fully applied' (W C Sullivan, Medical Superintendent at Broadmoor, quoted in Smith, 1981, 89).

## (b)  Women and diminished responsibility

The compromise between law and psychiatry is apparent in the treatment of women in the criminal process. The psychiatric individualisation of problems melds with legal individualism to exclude women's experiences from the law (see generally Raitt and Zeedyk, 2000). This is seen in both the offence of infanticide and the diminished responsibility defence.

A conviction of murder can be reduced to the lesser offence of infanticide where a woman kills her child within twelve months of birth and if –

> . . . the balance of her mind was disturbed by reason of her not having fully recovered from the effect of giving birth to the child or by reason of the effect of lactation consequent on the birth of the child. (Infanticide Act 1938, s 1(1))

The medically individualised nature of this concession is highlighted by the connection it makes, now recognised as spurious, between mental imbalance and lactation (O'Donovan, 1984; see more generally Rose, 1986). The offence also fails to take into account the 'social and emotional pressures'[30] which are often the main root of the problem. There are clear limits to the law's ability to recognise such pressures without its denying its own rationale as a punitive mechanism relying upon individual responsibility. By hiving infanticide off into a category of crime with a less severe penalty than for murder or manslaughter, and by presenting the issue in medical terms, the law was able to maintain a general punitive stance to a social problem, laced with an unthreatening show of compassion in the individual(ised) case.

Paralleling infanticide, diminished responsibility has been particularly significant as the defence used where an abused woman kills her husband or partner. Three defences can in principle be relevant here, self defence, provocation and diminished responsibility. There is a tendency for the last of these to be the one used. Where a woman subjected to consistent abuse responds by killing her partner, it could be argued that this is a normal reaction to what has been done to her. She ought therefore to be able to use either self-defence or provocation as a defence. However, these two defences are hard to use in this situation for reasons that suggest that a 'male norm' of violent response is incorporated in the law (McColgan, 1993; Raitt and Zeedyk, 2000, 69–74). Accordingly, diminished responsibility is used to avoid the mandatory life sentence for murder, but in the process pathologises the battered woman's situation. Discussing *Ahluwalia* (1992), Raitt and Zeedyk comment:

Although Kiranjit Ahluwalia had suffered years of extreme abuse and was acting in fear of her life, the only explanation for her behaviour that the court would accept was that it was due to irrational, uncontrollable impulses brought on by psychological disorder. It was impossible for them to see it as 'reasonable', in the way that men's behaviour is seen as 'reasonable' when they act in self defence or are provoked . . . (2000, 75)

The classification of 'battered women syndrome' which is used in such cases was originally developed to explain why women who kill act normally in their circumstances. However, its inclusion in psychiatric-diagnostic frameworks has led to its becoming a way of diminishing the woman and her experience by viewing her as psychologically damaged. The category permits the law flexibility in sentence via the diminished responsibility defence, but in the process, it portrays the woman as 'unreasonable, abnormal, the result of mental malady' (Raitt and Zeedyk, 2000, 85). It therefore draws a veil over the problem of domestic violence in society.

*(c)   Limits to compassion and pragmatism*

Removing the need for outright fraud and collusion between lawyers and psychiatrists on M'Naghten, the mitigatory plea of diminished responsibility permits a general blurring of the line between psychiatric diagnosis and legal compassion.[31] Most of the time, the two professions get on extremely well. In around 85% of cases, the prosecution accepts a plea of diminished responsibility, and therefore the defence's psychiatric evidence (Mackay, 2000, 62) We have already noted the tendency of lawyers and psychiatrists to approach the test with 'compassionate pragmatism' so that the 'mercy killer' experiencing intense social and psychological pressures is included with the diagnosed psychopath in the same legal category.[32]

At the same time, the law retains the option of relying on its hard and fast legal tests when practical political circumstances, like those in the case of Peter Sutcliffe, dictate. Where the symbols of condign punishment, however inappropriate,[33] are required, the law is able to cast aside its alliance with psychiatry and wheel out the old retributive magic. Of Sutcliffe's murder conviction, *The Times* (23 May, 1981) commented that it produced a 'public catharsis' in seeing the wrongdoer convicted and punished. Within three years, Sutcliffe was transferred to a secure mental hospital where he remains to this day. The case dramatically illustrated the underlying conflicts in approach that are masked by the normal working of the defence.

## (ii)   Covering up for society: men killing women

One of the most horrific areas of crime with which the label of madness is frequently associated is brutal, sometimes 'serial', crime associated with a sexual element. There is a tendency for lawyers, politicians and media commentators to distance the perpetrators of such crime from what is normal in our society. The rapist is described as bestial, or as subject to a nature that society cannot tame; the sex killer is described as an inhuman, raging animal, evil or insane. Alternative medical terms are also readily available: if the criminal is not 'bad', he must be 'mad'. Recent socio-legal scholarship drawing upon feminist understanding of gender and sexual relations has challenged this construction of 'the other' by arguing that such crimes are in fact quite normal in our society. The perpetrator draws upon widely available and promoted cultural understandings about the nature of male and female sexuality, which he simply pushes beyond the normative boundary that society's laws establish. As Box says of non-insane rape, it 'is not the opposite to normal sex, but a grim, grinning caricature of it': the 'engine of rape is not to be found between a man's loins, but in his mind, and this in turn reflects cultural definitions of gender'.[34]

Such an account of rape and rapists who are adjudged sane can be extended into the area of insane sexual crime, and reveals once again the law's ability, abetted by the psychiatrist, to decontextualise social actions. In the trial of Peter Sutcliffe, the question for the jury was whether the accused was 'mad' or 'bad'. Through either mental illness or wickedness, Sutcliffe's conduct would be abstracted from what is 'normal'. Yet his actions were anchored in the popular cult created by 'Jack the Ripper' in the nineteenth century, and encouraged by countless films and books whose attitude is far from condemnatory. The actions of the 'Yorkshire Ripper' can be seen as participating in a cultural discourse that society has created, and which it encourages some to enact.[35] Sutcliffe's contempt for prostitutes was part of a much wider social attitude, present at many different levels of society, including that of legal practice.[36] In focusing on individual responsibility or mental illness, both law and psychiatry ignored the cultural context which gives rise to a Sutcliffe. Hollway makes the point in relation to psychiatry:

> The explanation that it was a delusion does not show *why* the voice told Sutcliffe to kill women. Whether it was God's voice, the devil's voice or the projected voice of Sutcliffe's own hatred makes no difference: the content derives from a generalised, taken for granted misogyny. (Quoted in Cameron and Frazer, 1987, 129)

Nor does the law's conception of an individual, responsible choice get us anywhere near the social *content* of the delusion. Why was it women and specifically prostitutes he was told to kill? This is not to say that a general culture of misogyny is *sufficient* to explain the existence of someone like Peter Sutcliffe, but it is necessary. It helps us to understand how the serial murder of women can be a possible focus for a Sutcliffe-like figure, and why serial killers should be predominantly male.[37] Mad sexual crime must be explained at two different levels, the individual and the social. While there is an irreducibly individual element, this is not artificially separated from the social context in which the individual is created.[38] Both the legal and the psychiatric categories obscure the social nature of sexual crime, and the extent that society itself bears responsibility for its commission by one of its members, whether or not he is insane.

## 6  CONCLUSION

### (i)  The nature of madness

This is a difficult chapter to conclude because its account of the conflict between law and psychiatry has evaded one fundamental question: what is the nature of madness in modern society? Few would sincerely claim that the narrow legal stance we have identified represents a valid account of the phenomenon of human madness, as opposed to one of its symptomatic components.[39] Reaching for the M'Naghten Rules is a way of denying rather than seeking to understand the nature of mental illness. At the level of the classification of syndrome, psychiatry's expanded conception of the different forms of madness seems clearly better.[40] Yet conventional psychiatry suffers the fatal flaw of a gulf between its identification of syndromes, which it describes in psychological terms, and of underlying causes, which it describes in physiological terms. The latter remain poorly understood, and the proof of this is seen in the failure of psychiatry to develop forms of medical intervention that actually produce sustained improvement in the mental health of patients, as opposed to controlling the effects of the illness (Hirst and Woolley, 1982, 99–105). It is because of this gulf that psychiatrists are so vulnerable in the witness box. They cannot ultimately back up diagnosis with a convincing account of the underlying physical mechanisms which instantiate the conditions described.[41]

It would be far beyond the bounds of this work to present an account of the nature of modern madness that can transcend the analyses of the lawyer or the psychiatrist, although it seems clear that such an account is needed. In particular, what is required is an analysis that can embrace the various manifestations of madness as they affect the will and emotions as well as cognition, and inform the personality of the mad person as a whole, even when they take the form of an apparently only 'partial' madness. Such an account would also need to explain the nature of madness as a social phenomenon. The disruptions to the personality that it occasions should not be seen as linked in the first instance to an underlying organic condition, except in clearly specified circumstances of organic failure (eg Alzheimer's disease). Psychiatry's failure to identify the causes of conditions such as schizophrenia, coupled with the clearly social nature of many of their manifestations, suggests the need for a qualitatively different understanding. Even if mental illness were shown one day to have an underlying physiological basis, this would still only partially explain the *social* content of mad behaviour such as misogyny. Nine-tenths of the explanation requires to be established not at the level of the individual but at those of culture and social psychology.

In terms of the latter, the approach of Harré and his colleagues (Harré, 1983; Harré, Clarke, De Carlo, 1985) perhaps provides a fruitful way into the issue. Harré argues that the mental furniture of the psyche, in terms of concepts of will, agency and selfhood, are all inherently social and historical phenomena. To be a human being in Western society is to possess a language or theory about the possibility of being a unitary mind and will, capable of acting on the world within a broader social and moral order. Put simply, it can be suggested that in cases of psychopathy and schizophrenia, what has happened is that the process of upbringing, or the life experience of the sufferer, has not permitted this process of normative and psychic coherence to occur in an individual life. What is important about this approach is not so much the detail of its application to a particular disorder. It is its ability to combine in one analysis an account of the individual within the social, and to avoid a reduction to the level of biology, where, as we have seen, there has been little success in establishing the claimed causal relations. Mind is an inherently social phenomenon that is at the same time emergent from matter. Orthodox psychiatry has spent all its time reducing mind to matter. The two are linked, but a more fruitful approach would be to begin with the social construction and instantiation of individual mind and meaning, as a means of then better isolating the interface between the mental and the organic. It is impossible to take this discussion forward here, but the above comments indicate, in a general way, how we might begin to integrate the analysis of social and individual conduct rather than to juxtapose them.[42]

## (ii)   Law and psychiatry: consensus and conflict

This, however, leads to a second question, the answer to which will allow us to conclude this chapter: why should it be that the dominant methods of understanding madness remain locked in a false dualism between a narrow, legal cognitivism (law) and an overbroad, reductionist physiologism (psychiatry)? The answer lies not at the level of ideas but at the level of power, where we started our discussion. The focus of this book has been the historical emergence of law as a form of social control in the first half of the nineteenth century, which presents itself as a sphere of individual liberties and responsibilities and which denies social conflicts by decontextualising action. Psychiatry developed as one of a broad range of human sciences, including criminology, psychology and psychoanalysis, which took the 'pathological subject' as their object of study in order to permit and legitimise intervention into individual lives. There was an enormous development of such disciplines from the late nineteenth century onwards, when it seemed that the combination of law and laisser faire economics would not, between themselves, ensure an efficient level of social order and control. The 'market' in human conduct, controlled by a legal framework, required various forms of state intervention to supplement it (Stedman Jones, 1971; Garland, 1985; Donzelot, 1980).[43]

   This then entailed an *individuation* of social problems, for to look too broadly at such problems would make individual interventions appear valueless, and might also have the effect of undermining the social edifice. Thus the individualising of human conduct by law and psychiatry, and the success of these two discourses, emerged out of, and was guaranteed by, the cumulative needs of two particular historical periods occurring at the beginning and end of the nineteenth century. Myopia was socially and politically determined, and this is the reason why, at the end of the day, law and psychiatry have more in common as co-workers at the coal face of social order than their ideological disagreements would lead us to believe.

   Support for this conclusion is provided by considering what happens to those who are disposed of by courts, either with or without a madness label legally attached to them (see Walker and Padfield, 1996, chs 21, 22). Those who are found insane may be inter alia confined to a 'special hospital' on order of the Secretary of State, and this is mandatory where the original charge was for murder.[44] Those who successfully plead diminished responsibility, along with all those convicted of an imprisonable offence, can be sent either to prison on a normal custodial sentence, or to a psychiatric or 'special' hospital on a 'hospital order'. This is either with or without a restriction on discharge, as individual circumstances require (Mental Health Act 1983, s 37). When in prison, it is possible to be transferred to a hospital, and when in a hospital, it is possible to be remitted back to prison (Mental Health Act 1983, ss 47–53). There is in other words a substantial flexibility of, and interchangeability between, the prison and the asylum.

   Further, Walker and Padfield note that the courts have a largely pragmatic attitude to the labels of guilt or illness when sentencing, and do not normally concern themselves to distinguish between them where the defendant appears mentally ill:

> If the offender's mental state seems to call for a psychiatric disposal rather than a sentence, it does not trouble courts or defending lawyers very much that the defendant is usually convicted before benefiting from psychiatry. (Walker and Padfield, 1996, 337)

The court, almost regardless of the juridical label, 'treats the appearance of the defendant in court as a proper occasion for ensuring that he receives the care or medication which his state seems to need', and the flexibility of the prison/hospital disposal system amply permits this. What really determines the disposal of the court is not the legal finding. Rather, it is the availability of places in hospital wards for the mentally ill offender, the inability of medical science to treat conditions such as personality disorder, or the refusal of medical staff to accept patients seen as disruptive or dangerous (Walker and Padfield, 1996, 337). At the end of the court process, when the symbolic games have been played, the practical effects of the different findings in law are largely irrelevant. Having struggled to understand the elaborate and confusing categories of insanity and diminished responsibility, law students are often bemused to find that, practically, at the end of the day, it does not make much odds one way or the other which legal category is applied. Only in cases of capital punishment, or when it is thought necessary to avoid a mandatory life sentence, or when it is deemed necessary to demonise an individual like Sutcliffe, is there any real bite in the law.

This is precisely the point to understand. It is the efficient *administrative* disposal of the defendant, under either a legal or a medical heading, that is ultimately significant. The rest is all more or less for show: a matter of cutting the ideological cloth of deterrence, retribution or compassion as circumstances dictate. It is at this level, of the trial and the law, that the conflicts emerge out of the historical and structural consensus that informs legal and psychiatric practice. In the meantime, people who are criminally mad may be contained for long periods either in prison or hospital, and the public is protected. But the underlying social conditions, which generate madness and reproduce mad crime, remain all the while untouched and untreated. Despite the evidence of the dramatic causes célèbres, the legal-psychiatric complex combines to process the individual symptoms of a desperate social problem without ever getting to its roots.

# Part V

# Concluding

# Chapter 10

# Sentencing

[D]ecisions at the sentencing stage affect the fundamental interests of the offender in just as coercive and intrusive a way as decisions at the conviction stage affect the defendant. Indeed, the possibility of the ultimate application of a sanction which deprives an offender of some of her most valued goods and freedoms is one of the most important reasons underpinning the need for certainty and procedural safeguards in the criminal law itself . . . Once we have conceived criminal justice as an integrated process with certain complex social functions, it almost amounts to bad faith to place so much emphasis on these doctrinal values at one stage of the process whilst virtually ignoring them at others. (Lacey, 1987, 222–3)

[T]his focus upon the individual was not just a convenient means of aligning two opposed positions at their point of intersection; it was also, *in itself*, a means of gaining entry into the common sense of British penal policy . . . And the major assumption of that policy was – and *is* – that the individual is always the proper locus of penal intervention and concern. (Garland, 1985, 176)

People are ultimately responsible for their actions, but if you look at the numbers of young people in prison and see that one in three of them were in care, it can't be a complete coincidence. (Tony Blair, *Sunday Times*, 3 June, 2001)

## I  INTRODUCTION

Throughout this book, I have probed a particular conception of the criminal law as a systematic attempt to govern human conduct by rules. That conception is central to the legitimacy of the modern state, and is most clearly presented in the work of doctrinal scholars operating within the liberal tradition where values of the rule of law and of individual justice are presented as central. I have sought to show that these values are essentially flawed. This is because the model of the abstract juridical individual at their heart constantly comes into conflict with the socio-political realities of crime on the one hand and the politics of the judiciary, as an arm of the state, on the other. Because of this double tension in the basic elements, the lines of legal doctrine are constantly disrupted as rules are tugged this way then that according to the tensions upon which they are founded. Nonetheless the substantive doctrine of the criminal law is rule-based, even if the nature of those rules cannot be adequately understood within a liberal, positivist framework. The general principles of the criminal law remain the very 'stuff' of legal analysis, even if the orthodox approach to them can never properly capture the law's working.

However, when we come to the sentencing stage of the criminal process, we find that once we get beyond the conviction of the accused, the rules and principles of the criminal law largely evaporate and the system becomes much more discretionary and less regulated by law. In terms of liberal theory, this is surprising. After all, it is the sentence of the court that deprives the individual of the liberty that the rule of law is supposed to protect and respect at the conviction stage. Indeed, as Lacey's comment at the head of the chapter indicates, without the sentence of the court, the hard edge of delivery of the criminal sanction, none of the paraphernalia of law at the earlier stage would make much sense. Yet now we come to 'the moment of penal truth', much of the legitimating symbolism of the rule of law is largely cast aside.

The situation might be compared to one of those competitions on the back of breakfast cereal packs. The questions posed are so easy that everyone knows that it is the tie-breaker ('Explain in no more than ten words why you like Krispy Korn Flakes') that determines who gets the prize, and this is decided according to the subjective preference of the judges. The questions become no more than a backdrop to the real process of determining the winner. Consequently, the competitor becomes cynical because it turns out that the competition is not the real basis for deciding who has won, and also because the actual decision is at the judges' discretion. The same might be said for the criminal law. Conviction does qualify the offender for sentencing but, without a proper set of rules to determine the latter, the most important matter is left in the hands, and at the discretion, of the judge.[1]

This overstates the issue, for it is not that discretion is complete. Sentencing maxima exist for many offences and minima are now established for some (Crime (Sentences) Act 1997, ss 2–4, consolidated in Powers of Criminal Courts (Sentencing) Act 2000, ss 109–111). Guideline judgments have also been issued by the Court of Appeal, which 'provide judges with a starting point or range of sentences, and indicate the considerations which ought to be taken into account'. However, such judgments 'do not assign weight to the various factors' (Ashworth, 2000, 34) to be considered and their authority is indicative rather than binding. They 'merely set the general tariff, but judges are free to tailor the sentence to the facts of the particular case' (Taylor, 1993, 130). This leads to 'considerable latitude, some variation and, inevitably, some inconsistency' (Ashworth, 2000, 31). Judges consider sentencing to consist in 'trying to reconcile a number of totally irreconcilable facts' (Lord Lane, quoted in ibid, 34), as art rather than science, and therefore as requiring substantial discretion.

Why should this be so? Why is sentencing only loosely regulated by law, prompting Lacey's suggestion that the system is in bad faith with its own premises as evinced at the stage of conviction? Her answer is to point to the disagreements of principle, the tensions between the underlying values, and the lack of consensus about the proper functions of the criminal law which underlie the sentencing stage. What needs to be added to this is the way in which these disagreements and tensions are generated by the limitations of the ideological forms that underlie the liberal conception of criminal law and criminal punishment.

Problems in the sentencing stage are not just the result of a plurality of competing values, but the product of the organic tensions within the liberal model of the punishable, juridical, individual. Enlightenment thought produced an abstract individual who furnished legal discourse with ideas of rationality, intentionality, voluntariness: in short, of responsibility. But this model was never just legal in a narrow sense. It was always at the core of a broader conception of social order and social control which was premised upon a moral, rational, individual response to the existence of criminal punishment. Homo juridicus lay at the heart of both legal doctrine and a philosophical plan for social order which involved a particular conception of punishment (Norrie, 1991). Just as our homuncular friend has proved an inherently unsound basis for the rational construction of legal doctrine at the level of the general principles of responsibility, so he has undermined any attempt to rationalise a system of punishment.

The criminal law has traditionally operated with four core ideologies of punishment which began to emerge from the time of the Enlightenment. It is these which provide the main rationales for sentencing decisions in the criminal justice system. They return us at the end of this book to our starting point in the philosophies of retributivism and utilitarianism. It is these theories of punishment which both provide the theoretical backdrop to the sentence of the court and generate the tensions which make the system so difficult to govern by law. These establish the primary ideological bases for sentencing, theories of retribution and deterrence. However, we will see that these theories of punishment also set up, by way of negation and opposition, the space for two other rationales of sentencing, reform (or rehabilitation) and incapacitation, to emerge in the late nineteenth century.

These further ideologies were constituted as a result of the *failure* of the classical ideologies to control the problem of crime, and they took as their basis a critique of the abstract individualism of the classical models. In its place, they substituted a model of human conduct as concretely determined by personal circumstance, and therefore treatable through state intervention. The resulting ideology substituted a model of concrete human individuality and individualised treatment for the classical model of abstract individualism. In so doing, it injected further competing and conflictual elements into the penal arena, alongside the conflicts already generated within the classical models. Substantial indeterminacy at the sentencing stage is the product of these multiple conflicts emerging from the historically generated, theoretically and practically unrealistic, ideological forms that govern the official understanding of crime, its control and punishment.

Is there any way around the problem of pluralism? One suggested solution is to declare 'a primary rationale, and to provide that in certain types of case one or another rationale might be given priority' (Ashworth, 2000, 63). This was, indeed, the approach embodied in the principal sentencing statute of recent years, the Criminal Justice Act 1991, where desert was the primary rationale but incapacitation took priority in certain types of case. When we have considered the four main ideologies of punishment, we will consider the suggestion that prioritising one rationale could rationalise and juridify a discretionary system.

## 2  DETERRENCE

We have seen that the two fundamental theories of crime and punishment underlying the Enlightenment movement to reform the criminal law were those advanced by the retributivists and the utilitarians (see above, Chapter 2). In the English context, the home grown and more pragmatic approach of the latter school was initially more influential. This is seen in the work of the Victorian Criminal Law Commissioners, for whom the central organising principle for the reconstruction of the criminal law was the concept of deterrence:

> The great object of penal law is to deter men from violating the law by holding out privation and suffering as the consequences of transgression. (Criminal Law Commissioners, 1843, 92)

As Thomas (1978, 19–27) has pointed out, the reform of the substantive law and the construction of an effective sentencing system were intertwined goals within the reform project. Without a clear and rationally established set of doctrines, punishments could not be rationally applied to malefactors. Of particular concern was the amount of discretion that the unreformed law gave to judges, and therefore the lack of advance knowledge of, or publicity that could be given to, punishments in individual cases. The result of this was a decline in deterrence:

> ... the legal definitions of offences are frequently of so large a description, and the criminal acts they include differ so widely in the mischief they occasion to society, that, without a definite scale, marking different degrees of criminality, appropriate punishments cannot be previously defined ... The consequence of which imperfection in the law is great uncertainty in the application of punishment, whereby the motive to abstain from the commission of offences is weakened. And this imperfection can only be diminished by defining the different degrees and aggravations of offences, and annexing to them punishments, which shall, after allowing a discretionary latitude to be exercised by the court within certain limits, be carried into execution. (Criminal Law Commissioners, 1834, 32)

Thus we can see the centrality of the ideology of deterrence to the substantive structure of the criminal law as well as to the aims of sentencing, and the interconnectedness of these goals. Those who laid the first stones in the modern edifice did so to make deterrence work, and it is therefore no surprise that the idea of deterrence should figure as one of the modern aims of the penal system.[2]

Yet we should also be alerted to the potential problems with such an ideology from our discussion in Chapter 2 of the abstraction and decontextualisation at the heart of the utilitarian project. In the work of Bentham and Beccaria, the 'economic man', capable of rational calculation of the consequences of his action, had very little connection with real men and women living in circumstances that encouraged little respect for the social order and its laws. Consequently, the abstract individualism at the heart of the deterrence ideology offered little hope of practical success in achieving the diminution of crime. Bentham himself, as we saw (above, pp 21–3), was alive to the need to cultivate the manners and develop the lifestyle of the poor alongside his penal code. His invention of the 'panopticon' as a principle for the widespread surveillance of the working classes in the prison, the workhouse, the factory and the school also offered a more pragmatic, but also 'non-juridical', solution to the problem of social order in Victorian England.[3]

Bentham was the English inventor of both the penal code and the principle of perpetual surveillance embodied in his design of a built environment that would control and render docile large groups of people who could not be relied upon to act 'rationally'. Whereas the former addressed a world of rational legal subjects, the latter was a 'mill to grind rogues honest' (Halevy, 1972, 82–4; Foucault, 1979). Yet if the world was really as the author of the penal code imagined it to be, it is hard to see why the 'panopticon' was required. If people really were the ideal rational calculators of costs and benefits according to the model of a code, then a system of legal deterrents could and should deliver social control by itself, without the need for an accompanying panoply of disciplines.

## (i)    Individual deterrence and its social context

Deterrence theory has spawned a massive modern literature, and it is not possible or necessary to delve deeply into it here. It will be sufficient to consider whether the main findings reflect the historical problem identified in the Benthamite project. Broadly, the current distilled wisdom of penologists is that there is no consistent deterrent effect from punishment in society, and that the use of the penal system and, in particular imprisonment as the most serious punishment available, is not an especially effective deterrent to crime.[4] Recidivism rates remain high among those who receive custodial sentences (in one year, approximately 50 per cent of adults and 66 per cent of juveniles were reconvicted within two years of a prior sentence),[5] and 'there is no evidence that longer custodial sentences produce better results than shorter sentences' (Brody, 1976, 39).

A vivid illustration of the problem with a deterrent strategy is seen in the case of exemplary sentencing. In the United Kingdom, one example is the 1957 sentencing of young men to exceptionally long periods of imprisonment following their involvement in racial attacks on black people in Notting Hill, as a result of which the attacks were said to have stopped. A second is the draconian sentences passed on youths in Birmingham in 1973 for a violent robbery at a time of 'moral panic' about the spread of 'mugging' in Britain (Hall, Critcher, Jefferson, Clarke and Roberts, 1978). With regard to the former, as Walker points out, attacks in the Notting Hill area did not completely stop after the punishments meted out in that case. To the extent that they died down, there was no evidence that this was because of the sentences passed, a variety of other reasons being available (Walker and Padfield, 1996, 101). In the 1973 case, a study carried out by Home Office researchers found that there was no evidence of a decline in comparable crimes following the widespread publication of the sentences handed down (Baxter and Nuttall, 1975).

Of more significance than the punishment itself appears to be the 'high subjective probability', the perception of the likelihood, of being caught. However, detection rates for many crimes remain low, and to increase them would entail substantial increases in police powers and numbers and the level of state surveillance in society. In effect, this would involve developing (more than has already occurred: Cohen, 1985; Mathiesen, 1983) a modern version of Benthamite 'panopticism', defending freedom by denying it. Such an increase in the powers of the state would not be without its own cost in terms of provoking other more serious kinds of crime such as riot.[6] On the other hand, some studies have revealed a deterrent effect in particular situations. There is also a general belief that, whatever the figures might show, the problem of crime would be worse were the deterrent threat of the criminal sanction completely removed. The state of current wisdom is that –

Naive claims that deterrent policies are highly effective – or totally ineffective – have been replaced by the less exciting realisation that *some* people can be deterred in *some* situations from *some* types of conduct by *some* degree of likelihood that they will be penalised in *some* ways; but that we do not yet know enough to enable us to be very specific about the people, the situations, the conduct, or the likelihood or nature of the penalties. (Walker and Padfield, 1996, 101; cf Beyleveld, 1980)

This gives rise to one central question: how does one explain the *relative* efficacy of deterrence, in that some people are deterred but not others? Penologists tend to explain such differentials in terms of differences within the social audience, which can be divided into three broad groups. These are, first, those who refrain from breaking the law because they believe it to be wrong; second, those who cannot be deterred because they have no 'conscience'; and, third, a significant group between these two extremes. The third group represents a growing number, who are no longer fully anchored in the value system of the society, but who still have sufficient to lose from being caught and punished. While the first group do not need to be deterred because they believe in law-abiding conduct anyway, and the second are beyond deterrence, the third are 'in the balance'. They may be deterred if punishments 'are substituted for those individual scruples which normally ensure "respectability"'. The broadest conclusion about relative efficacy from deterrence research is that –

> . . . amongst that section of the population *who are tempted to take risks but who have more to lose than to gain by being caught*, the most effective deterrent measures are those which make it obvious that success will be difficult. (Brody, 1979, 10) (emphasis added)

This dividing up of the population into groups is often expressed in individualistic psychological terms by penologists. Brody describes the 'undeterribles' as lacking a sense of the consequences of their action, as impulsive and neurotic, or as 'seriously unbalanced' in their attitudes to authority (Brody, 1979, 10). Yet there is a clear *social* distribution operating behind these individualistic labels. Those who are most likely to be deterred are those in society who 'have more to lose than to gain by being caught', those who still have a 'conscience'. Focusing on the relationship between economic conditions, crime and punishment, Box has synthesised a number of different criminological theories to explain why conventionally defined crime is likely to rise amongst the poorest and most deprived sections of society, particularly in a time of recession (Box, 1987, 36–52). What is significant amongst those who are likely to turn to crime is the coupling of 'thwarted ambition' with 'relative deprivation' in a situation of marginalisation from 'institutionalised organisations for social change', and alienation from the forces of law and order.

Box's argument is that those who see themselves as getting the least from society are those who are most likely to become alienated from it, to operate outwith both the law and conscience. Having an insufficient stake in society, they experience neither material nor moral disincentives to commit crimes. Such people, as a group, are the sociological, not psychological, undeterribles in our society, and they form the real counterpart to those whom Brody describes as still having 'more to lose than to gain by being caught'. Clearly, in any individual case, personal factors come into play,[7] but these exist within the confines of the broader social arena and structure where characters are formed and decisions made, where life chances are defined and personal conclusions drawn. In this regard, Garland's observation about the modern relevance of late Victorian 'penality' is correct:

> When we talk of the population of criminals dealt with by penality, we should not mistake this for a diverse amalgam of individuals randomly distributed throughout the general population. *Penality deals, and has always dealt, with a population overwhelmingly drawn from the working classes.* By the late nineteenth century, however, its major 'problem population' was no longer even the working classes in general. Instead, the penal institutions of the late Victorian era largely concerned themselves *with the lowest sections of the working classes* – the poor, the lumpenproletariat, the 'criminal classes'. Surveys of the prison population at the time of Du Cane suggest that the vast majority of offenders were illiterate, unskilled and often unemployed workers or their dependants – a population drawn from a very particular stratum of a very definite class. (Garland 1985, 37–8) (emphasis added)[8]

This social dividing up of the potential criminal population takes us to Foucault's (1979) account of the prison in modern society, and the dual role that it plays there. Those who are located at the 'bottom end' of the social structure, with least to gain from 'playing the game', are precisely those whom the prison system ends up containing. They cannot be deterred, but they can be removed from circulation for a period of time.[9] The prison thereby acts as a cordon sanitaire, between the relatively law-abiding and the rest. While containing the one group, it acts as a symbol to the other of the dangers of crossing the line between criminality and respectability. Those that it contains it has least chance of deterring, but their containment still serves to draw a line for the rest. It demonstrates the possibility and consequence of loss to those who have something to lose.

Once one realises that those who are being deterred and those who are being punished are primarily from two different but adjoining socio-economic groups, the apparent failure of the prison to deter (or indeed reform) its inmates becomes less important. The prison is still providing a deterrent function in relation to those who cleave to law-abidingness and their place in society. Thus the 'failure' or 'success' of deterrence, however one wishes to look at it, is tied to the social nature of crime and criminality, but only tangentially connected with the abstract rational calculating subject of deterrence theory. It is the subject's social location which is the primarily determinative context for calculation of conduct, not the sanction of the law.

### (ii)   Individual versus general deterrence

The Criminal Law Commissioners argued for a penal code that would allocate particular, graded punishments according to the severity of the crime. At their most ambitious, they established forty-five different classes of punishment, although the number fluctuated from one report to the next (Thomas, 1978, 25). Their aim of restricting judicial discretion was limited, however, by their recognition of the need to permit a measure of leeway within the bands that they had established. This was to permit a more precise tailoring of the punishment to the offence in individual cases, recognising that 'the degrees and shades of guilt are infinite' (Criminal Law Commissioners, 1843, 94). There had also to be some room to mitigate because of 'the condition and circumstances of offenders' (1836, 36), or to augment where there were aggravating circumstances (1843, 94). Committed to a rationalist legal enterprise, the Commissioners saw judicial discretion as an evil to be controlled as much as possible by legal rules. In particular, they opposed punishments which were the product of judges –

> . . . swayed by their own peculiar notions or even prejudices, *or by conceptions of policy formed on circumstances peculiar to the times*, on the necessity for a display of firmness and vigour to check the course of particular classes of delinquents, or according to numerous other collateral considerations widely varying in their nature and influence. (1843, 92) (emphasis added)

Their main argument was against the gross forms of discretion that existed under the old system, and its reliance on the death penalty. Such a system was ineffective because 'overstrained severity defeats its own end by rendering the conviction of offenders more difficult, and consequently diminishing the certainty of punishment'. Further, it was wrong, for the aim in producing the pain in punishment could only be to produce such suffering as was necessary to deter others from committing crime, a principle which tended 'to contract the limits of penal coercion' (1843, 93). Yet this liberal attempt to confine the extent of punishment and to avoid what we now refer to as exemplary punishments was undercut by the overall, utilitarian logic that the Commissioners themselves espoused.

Benthamism remained poised between not one but two standpoints: those of individual *and* general utility. From the point of view of individual utility (and therefore individual deterrence), the amount of punishment remained anchored to the extent of the wrong done, for the pain in the one had to match the pain in the other, and any excessive punishment would be needless. However, from the point of view of the general utility (and therefore calculations of general deterrence), the aim was to deter everyone from committing crime, and it might well be that the over-punishment of the one might deter the many. The balance of utility here would not assist the criminal, because now the evil visited upon him is measured not against the evil that he produced but against the sum total of such evils that might be produced in the whole society but for his punishment. In short, the amount of efficacious punishment that can be levied can vary radically, depending upon whether the calculation is from the point of view of what is necessary to deter the individual, or to provide a measure of general deterrence (cf Hart, 1968, 18–19). From the penal viewpoint, the individual's happiness is now weighed against 'the greatest happiness of the greatest number', in contrast to which it can only come off badly.

Benthamism was caught between egoistic individualism (the promotion of individual self-interest or utility), and general utilitarianism (Plamenatz, 1958; Halevy, 1972). In this, it mirrored the intellectual condition of a society in which the triumph of individual self-interest was stressed alongside the need for strong and efficient government to establish the conditions for successful capitalist industrialisation. The laisser faire individualist ideology of political economy was supplemented by the general utilitarian principle of 'the greatest happiness of the greatest number'. This accounts for the schizophrenic nature of Bentham's thought, and explains how the same man could espouse both the legal individualism of his penal code and the 'collectivism' of the panopticon.[10] But his general utilitarianism threatened to undercut the individualist premises of his penal code. For example, he suggested that a loss of deterrent value from a weak system of detection could be countered by an increase in punishment for those caught (Ashworth, 1983, 339) and he was sympathetic to the value of torture from a general utilitarian standpoint (Twining, 1973).

Drawn from the latter position, the principle of general deterrence is not logically able to withstand the over-punishment of one in order to deter the many.[11] In this theory, the state stands between two political logics. One logic constrains its sanctions in terms of the wrongs done by individuals, but the other uses punishment of the individual as a means to a general end. This second form cuts across the individualism of the first, and threatens to undermine it. It returns us to our discussion of the tension between legal individualism and social control (see Chapter 2, pp 26–8), for it is the corollary at the level of sentencing of all the examples in substantive doctrine of how 'policy' invades the logic of individual right and responsibility. This conflict in utilitarian sentencing theory reflects the position of the political state maintaining social control while attempting to do so through a mediating ideology of individual self-interest.

The theory of deterrence contains the two tensions that we have identified at the heart of the criminal law (above, pp 28–31; also pp 222–5). On the one hand, the theory of the rational, calculating individual stands in opposition to the contextualised nature of social action, and this conflict informs the failure of the system to deter lawbreakers, save in particular social contexts. On the other hand, the logic of punishment according to the dictates of individual action comes up against the logic of punishing for broader political ends. Within a deterrent strategy, as enunciated by the Criminal Law Commissioners, it is logically not possible to deny what they wished to deny. 'Conceptions of policy formed on circumstances peculiar to the times' or 'on the necessity for a display of firmness and vigour to check the course of particular classes of delinquents' have their place.

The 'proof of the pudding' is that English judges have frequently invoked the rationale of general deterrence or exemplary punishment.[12] Will *Cunningham* (1993) stop this practice? There, it was held that the Criminal Justice Act 1991, s 2 prohibits adding to a commensurate sentence 'simply to make a special example of the defendant'. However, *Cunningham* admits considerations of deterrence into the calculation of seriousness and accepts that prevalence of an offence is a relevant consideration. Thus the main ingredients for general deterrent or exemplary sentencing are present. *Cunningham* suggests that judges should be careful as to how they phrase an exemplary sentence, rather than that they should cease to give them.

## 3   RETRIBUTIVISM

While deterrence remains a central rationale of the criminal justice system, the other arm of Enlightenment thought, retributivism, also plays an important part. It is a philosophy that has not always been well understood in the Anglo-American world, being associated with a doctrine of giving punishment 'for its own sake', and without regard to any benefits it might achieve. As such, it was historically contrasted with what were regarded as more progressive approaches which stressed that the infliction of pain without gain was indefensible (Norrie, 1991, 116–25). One response to this is to argue that judicial, or state, retribution does have a valuable purpose in that it acts to declare the attitudes of the community, and to affirm its rejection of and revulsion at certain types of conduct. In so doing, it affirms the values of the community as a whole (Cross and Ashworth, 1981, 128–31; see also *Sargeant* (1974)). This, however, is a secondary meaning of the concept, when compared with the position of the classical retributivists,[13] and that position is both manifested within the sentencing process and plays an increasing role in debates about the nature of sentencing today.

### (i)    Introduction: 'just deserts' and sentencing

Retributivism's central meaning is that of 'doing justice' to the individual, regardless of any benefits to the society, or indeed the individual, that might accrue from punishment. A retributive justification of punishment looks back to the crime that has been committed and asks what the criminal merits in return for it, rather than forward to any benefits to the community or the criminal that might be derived from punishment. It stresses the criminal's 'just desert' for his actions, and therefore a principle of equality of treatment as between individuals, that they should be treated fairly in the way that punishments are allocated. It is concerned with punishing individuals justly and proportionately to their crime.

Such an approach operates implicitly in the English system, although not so as to gain the acceptance of modern 'just deserts' theorists. As Hart expressed it (1968, ch 1), the penal system operates with a utilitarian 'general justifying aim', the decrease of crime and protection of the public, but in applying punishments to individuals, it employs principles of distribution that are retributive. These principles cover both questions of individual responsibility and the allocation of punishment. Hart wrote as regards the latter that –

> The guiding principle is that of a proportion within a system of penalties between those imposed for different offences where these have a distinct place in a common-sense scale of gravity. (1968, 25)

The penal system recognises this principle both by possessing a rough-and-ready 'tariff system' by which an approximate 'going rate' can be known for particular crimes, and by recognising the role of factors which mitigate the guilt of the individual, or which aggravate the gravity of the offence. But the philosophical basis for establishing a scaling of the gravity of offences has never been properly articulated within the law of sentencing in the same way as the principles of fault have been elaborated within the substantive law. Nor have the judges sought to achieve a jurisprudence of sentencing on the basis of a retributive, or any other, systematic basis. The tariff is said to be calculated from 'a mixture of deterrent and desert principles' (Ashworth, 2000, 86; see also 130). Nonetheless, it can be argued that within the narrow limits of what the judges have been prepared to do in terms of developing a law of sentencing, retributive principles of justice and proportionality have played some part. Further, statutory reform (Criminal Justice Act 1991) asserts the importance of the 'seriousness' of an offence for the decision to impose a custodial sentence and in calculating its length (ss 1 and 2), and this was expressly based upon the retributive idea of 'just deserts'.[14] Its practical development has, however, been a source of disappointment to desert theorists (Ashworth, 2000, 84–89).

Retributivism has played an historical role in sentencing theory, but this has been diminished by the other sentencing rationales (general deterrence, rehabilitation and incapacitation) with which principles of individual justice have had to compete. It is out of dissatisfaction with the results of intermingling different rationales that a renewed movement in favour of sentencing reform on the basis of 'just deserts' has emerged since the 1970s. The movement started in the United States, where ideologies of reform and incapacitation (these are discussed below) led to substantial indeterminacy and discretion within the penal system. Strong arguments were made there for a return to a principle of 'just deserts' which would constrain discretion and limit the power of the state over the criminal (Von Hirsch, 1976; American Friends Service Committee, 1971). Those arguments have had some practical success in the creation, in some American states, of sentencing commissions and in a move to the use of sentencing guidelines which are meant to formalise and control the decisions of judges according to 'just deserts' criteria (Von Hirsch, Knapp, Tonry, 1987).[15]

In England, there has been a similar, though less strong, move to establish a more formal sentencing structure. This emerges from dissatisfaction with the current smorgasbord or 'cafeteria' approach to sentencing aims, which permits judges substantial discretion. In such an approach, there is always a reason to scale punishment up or down by shifting from one sentencing rationale to another. Were the 'just deserts' approach to become the primary sentencing rationale, it is claimed that uniformity of sentencing decisions would be more easily achieved (Ashworth, 2000), and the creation of guidelines, whether expressed numerically or verbally (Von Hirsch, 1987), would constrain the judges. At the same time, as its title suggests, the 'just deserts' approach sees itself as involved in the liberal project of delivering justice to individuals, thereby *legitimating* as well as *limiting* state violence as punishment. It is under these two heads that I consider the theory.

## (ii) Legitimating the allocation of punishment

In Chapter 2, we referred to the classical retributive justification of punishment propounded by Kant and Hegel. Although modern accounts do not follow their approach in toto, the following comment of Kant would still attract wide support from modern retributivists:

> Judicial punishment can never be used merely as a means to promote some other good for the criminal himself or for civil society, but instead it must in all cases be imposed on him only on the ground that he has committed a crime; for a human being can never be manipulated merely as a means to the purposes of someone else . . . He must first be found to be deserving of punishment before any consideration is given to the utility of this punishment for himself or for his fellow citizens. (Kant, 1965, 100)

The claim to legitimacy within retributive theory is stronger than that within utilitarianism, which uses the convicted person as a means to a social end. Punishment for the retributivist entails pain that is justly handed out, because it is what the criminal deserves. Individuals are treated as morally responsible agents according to a code of law founded upon moral principles:

> Condemning people for the *wrongful* acts they commit is part of having a morality that holds people *responsible* for their behaviour. When a misdeed has been committed, one

judges the actor adversely for having committed the wrongful deed . . . [T]he penal law embodies a considered judgment that the punished behaviour is wrong, and that people should take that judgment into account in forming their own standards of right and wrong. (Von Hirsch, 1986a, 50) (emphasis added)

Modern accounts of retributivism are committed to the idea of deserts, but less convinced than the classical theorists of the possibility of offering a theory that can provide a complete justification of punishment as a social institution. For Von Hirsch, the general justification for punishment is *consequentialist*, that is, justified in terms of utilitarian consequences such as crime prevention, but the allocation of punishment to individuals is based upon a theory of *censure*. Punishment operates by condemning certain forms of conduct, but it must do so in proportion to wrong-doing. Were it to over- or underpunish the wrongdoer, it would visit more or less censure on that person than his conduct justified (1986a, 34–7). Von Hirsch thus combines a utilitarian justification of the existence of punishment with a moral retributivist justification of punishment in individual cases. It is this latter element that vindicates the idea of 'just deserts' in punishment.

### (a)    The ideal and the actual in classical retributivism

In assessing this approach to doing individual justice, it is helpful to note a problem at the centre of Kant's classical retributive theory (cf Norrie, 1991, ch 3). Kant recognised that his justification of punishment was only achieved by making a distinction between ideal rational ('noumenal') individuals and the actual ('phaenomenal') individuals who were committing crimes.[16] In correspondence he drew the conclusion from this that his ideal, rational justification of punishment was hard to apply to the actual world of crime:

> In a world of moral principle governed by God, punishments would be categorically necessary (insofar as transgressions occur). But in a world governed by men, the necessity of punishments is only hypothetical, and that direct union of the concept of transgression with the idea of deserving punishment serves the ruler only as a prescription for what to do . . . (Zweig, 1967, 199)

There is, as one sympathetic to Kant put it, a substantial gap between the theory and the practice of punishment (Murphy, 1979, 86). On the one hand, an ideal rational (noumenal) person would agree to his punishment as a moral necessity, but such a person would, by definition, never need to be punished because he would never be so irrational as to commit a crime. On the other hand, the (phaenomenal) person, who is not subject to rational thinking, would break the law and need punishment but would not, by definition, be the kind of person who would grasp the rational necessity and justification for it. Punishment is justified to noumenal beings who do not commit crimes, but unjustified to phaenomenal beings who do commit them.

### (b)    'Just deserts in an unjust society'?

The modern denial of a systematic theory underlying the retributive element in the just deserts approach is linked to this uncomfortable problem of bridging the gap between the ideal and the actual (see Von Hirsch, 1986a, 57–60; Murphy, 1987;

Norrie, 1991, chs 3–5). In modern terms, this is translated into the problem of a gap between the abstract responsible individual and the social context in which the individual operates. More practically, it is the problem of how one can give just deserts when the decision to commit crime is the result of living in an unjust society.[17] We hold the individual responsible for what he has done to society when, in reality, his crime is the product of what society has done to him. The 'justice model', according to one writer, can make us 'forget that by the time many offenders get to this wonderful justice system the damage has already been done'. Five minutes in a court or prison would disabuse anyone of any preconceptions about the nature of the social problem of crime, or about the 'free moral choice' said to be exercised by the majority of criminals (Cohen, 1979, 35–41). Individual justice is inseparable from the broader question of social justice and injustice.

One solution to this latter-day Kantian problem is more strongly to detach the justification of individual punishment from any wider theory of social justice, in order to assert that the 'actor may be worthy of censure – even in an imperfect social system – if, for example, he victimises someone who is in no way responsible for those social inequities' (Von Hirsch, 1986a, 58). This begs the question, what if the victim *were* responsible for social inequities? Von Hirsch asserts that retributivism must involve condemning *wrongful* acts committed by *responsible* persons, but he does not explain why appalling social conditions do not affect the intrinsic wrongfulness of acts or the responsibility of persons. Decoupling the social from the legal theory does not avoid the broader questions, because to answer them in legal terms simply leaves the broader social questions begging, and this is a persisting problem in modern 'just deserts' theory.[18]

A second approach is to acknowledge the difficulty but to seek its resolution within the sentencing system. For Ashworth, racial discrimination exists in the social system and is therefore likely to appear in the criminal justice system. Race issues, however, cannot 'be isolated from more general social inequalities in matters of wealth, employment and housing' (Ashworth, 2000, 202). Structured, systemic social inequality underlies and therefore undermines the value of legal equality. Could it be acknowledged by systematic mitigation of sentence, or by a diminished responsibility-style defence? If there is evidence that 'a person's offending derives in some significant measure from upbringing or social background, that should be ground for reduced culpability' so that 'there are strong social grounds for recognising a diminished degree of responsibility among people with these characteristics' (Ashworth, 2000, 127). The problem here is to consider whether it is ultimately possible to reconcile such an approach with retributive values of proportionality and equality in sentencing. If legal equality is undermined by systemic social inequality, then importing considerations based on that inequality into sentencing will systematically undermine formal principles of equity (cf Hudson, 1998, 1999; Hutton, 1999; see also note 17). The desert theorist is ultimately thrown back on a separation of legal and social equality (and justice):

> The sentencing of convicted persons cannot wait until underlying social ills are remedied, nor can it be abandoned until they are addressed . . . Addressing fundamental social ills (desirable and, indeed, essential as this is) cannot constitute a substitute for trying to make sentencing policy more coherent and fair. (Von Hirsch, 1992, 98 quoted in Ashworth, 2000, 215)

As an observation on legal practice, this is truistic. In terms of questions of fairness, equity and moral legitimacy, however, sentencing *must* await the remedy of underlying social ills. This is, indeed, the central unresolved dilemma for a legal conception of equality. To say so is not to deny that 'Equality before the law is a fundamental value which cannot simply be cast aside' or that one ought to caricature it (Ashworth, 2000, 214). It is, however, to argue that one cannot judge legal equality properly in abstraction from the overall social context in which it operates.

The 'just deserts' approach to punishment has two main aims. The first is to legitimate the concept of punishment in modern society, the second is to affix determinate limits to the amount of punishment. The concept of *justice* implicit in the idea of 'just deserts' cannot be sustained, so that the legitimation function does not work (cf Norrie, 2000, ch 9). The problem lies with the abstract form of the individual at the heart of the retributive theory from the time of Kant onwards. For this reason, it would be more appropriate to describe the retributive approach as an 'equal misery' theory of sentencing to denote the commitment to proportionality but to be more honest about what its concept of justice offers. But even this description requires scrutiny, for we have yet to see what kind of equality this approach can achieve.

### (iii)   Limiting punishment through proportionality

#### (a)   The classical approach

It is questionable to what extent the 'just deserts' approach can achieve a determinate system of proportional punishments, given its foundation on conflicting theoretical positions. To understand the modern approach it is again necessary briefly to return to the classical. Both Kant and Hegel insisted on the need for equality between crime and punishment, but neither was able to establish a workable deduction of the one from the other (see Norrie, 1991, 59–61, 81–2). For Kant, the Lex Talionis ('an eye for an eye, a tooth for a tooth') was the appropriate measure, but the concrete pairing of crimes and punishments had clear limits. For example, Kant had some difficulty in considering the appropriate punishment for the rapist and the pederast, or how to fine the rich and the poor man justly for the same offence.

For this reason, Hegel rejected the idea of an actual matching of crime and punishment, preferring to remain at a metaphysical level of identifying the equal 'value' that lay within both as a result of their both being species of 'injury'. However, Hegel's problem was that from this metaphysical standpoint, he was left with no way of specifying the *actual* punishment for *specific* crimes. Matching crimes and punishments in the abstract was no easier than the concrete equations attempted by Kant. The problem, as the Criminal Law Commissioners recognised, was that –

> There is no real or ascertainable connexion or relation existing between crimes and punishments which can afford any correct test for fixing the nature or the extent of the latter, either as regards particular offences or their relative magnitudes. (1843, 92)

Their response was to establish the scale of punishment according to a utilitarian principle of deterrence, and the modern 'just deserts' theorist, having already moved to a utilitarian 'general justifying aim', does something similar.

## (b) Cardinal and ordinal proportionality

In setting the proportions of punishment to crime, Von Hirsch draws a crucial distinction between what he terms 'cardinal' and 'ordinal' proportionality. The ordinal magnitude of a punishment 'concerns how a crime should be punished compared to similar criminal acts, and compared to other crimes of a more or less serious nature' (Von Hirsch, 1986a, 40). Cardinal magnitude on the other hand involves the anchoring of the scale of penalties as a whole 'by fixing the absolute severity levels for at least some crimes' (1986a, 43). Ordinal proportionality involves the internal levels of punishment in the sentencing system, while cardinal proportionality fixes the outer limits, the minima and maxima, that will be permitted.

Whereas ordinal magnitude is fixed according to principles of desert, comparing crime against punishment within a range of punishments that has already been created by the determination of the cardinal limits, cardinal magnitude cannot be set in the same way. Because there are no 'natural' proportions between crime and punishment, the actual anchoring points of the system have to be set according to some criterion other than desert. Once the limits are given, proportionality within the system becomes possible. What then are the criteria for setting the cardinal limits? Von Hirsch considers the possibility of setting them according to the requirements of deterrence. Although he is sceptical about the value of such an approach (1986a, 94–5), he concludes that 'crime-prevention effects' (1986a, 170) together with other policy considerations, such as the availability of prison resources (1986a, 95–6) are relevant in anchoring the penal scale. Thus, whereas utilitarian criteria are used to fix the punitive scale as a whole,

> . . . once the scale has been so anchored, then desert requires that parity be observed among crimes of a given degree of seriousness – and that comparatively more or less serious crimes be ranked higher or lower on the scale. (1986a, 45)

The ordinal measure of seriousness is to be taken in terms of concepts of harm and culpability, but it is apparent that this ordinal ranking is already fundamentally compromised by its rooting within a cardinal system based upon criteria *other than* those of harm and culpability. No matter how offences are ordinally ranked internally, the scale of punishments will be set on a continuum based upon utilitarian criteria. Thus, if the cardinal limits of punishment in a state with scarce penal resources, or a sceptical and liberal orientation to imprisonment, are set at levels one to five, a medium severity punishment will be at level three. If the state is then won by a conservative administration dedicated to deterrence and prison-building, it then increases the upper cardinal limit by adding further levels of punishment up to a maximum of ten on the same scale. At that point, the ordinally judged medium severity punishment will be set at level five, two grades higher than it was previously, without any consideration of the harm and culpability criteria internal to the judgment of ordinal seriousness. This problem reveals that *both* ordinal and cardinal judgments are based upon utilitarian criteria. Its consequences are seen in practice. Although 'just deserts' was canvassed by liberal opponents of excessive sentencing, the outcome in certain conservative states of the United States of reform was an increase in the severity of sentences (Moerings, 1986).[19] More generally, the effect of just deserts sentencing has been fluctuating levels of punishment because 'so much depends on general political trends' (Ashworth, 2000, 73).

## (c)    The living standards analysis

Attempts have been made to develop the parameters of ordinal proportionality, and to relate these to the severity of punishment. Ashworth (2000, 96–103) draws upon von Hirsch and Jareborg's (1991) living standards analysis. This identifies different levels of harm and their impact on living standards. These are then mapped onto a seriousness scale, where they are married with concepts of culpability, judged with regard to the offender's relationship to the harm, assessed with regard to aggravation or mitigation, and finally matched with a commensurate sentence.

Ashworth anticipates the problems with such an approach. One criticism might be that 'the parameters are vague and indefinitely expressed' so that there will be 'inconsistencies in outcome between different people using the same scale'. Conceding this, he asserts that the criticism itself presupposes it is possible 'to devise a scale which has great numerical precision, and yet which is sufficiently sensitive to the different combinations of fact' (Ashworth, 2000, 98). This, however, is just what the conceded criticism does deny, and elaborating the living standards approach only confirms the intrinsic difficulties in the project. The seven stage approach ends up combining plural evaluations (harm to the victim, culpability of the offender), complexity (seven stages) and abstraction (levels of 'harm' and 'impact'), together with an acknowledgment of the role of contingency in the crucial matter of scaling punishments (2000, 102–3).

A second criticism is that 'the principles are far too complex to be of practical use'. Against this, Ashworth says that the living standards analysis is an attempt to 'formalise the intellectual processes which sometimes take place, albeit impressionistically and even inconsistently, in the minds of those who have to decide these questions' (Ashworth, 200, 99). Thus it renders explicit what is already implicit in practice. What, however, does practice reveal except that it is indeed 'far too complex' to ground a unified analysis? Rationalising the practical approach will as likely confirm the difficulties which the living standards approach hopes to cure as produce consistency in it.

## 4    REHABILITATION AND INCAPACITATION

We have now covered the two primary ideologies of sentencing which emerge from the Enlightenment and accompany the reform of the substantive law. These ideologies both instantiate and are vitiated by the contradictions of juridical individualism at the core of the criminal law. We turn now to the secondary late Victorian ideologies of rehabilitation and incapacitation which have been grafted on to the classical models. It is important to see that these ideologies are a response to the failure of the classical models to control crime and legitimate punishment.[20] Rehabilitation and incapacitation were born as the mirror image of the classical ideologies. To the classical form of abstract individualism they oppose a model of concrete individuality and individualisation of social control.

These ideologies have their roots in their own historical period, the late Victorian world of the birth of welfare state interventionism, which stands in opposition to the laisser faire individualism of the Enlightenment. By the end of the nineteenth century, profound changes had occurred in the economic system which were to affect the nature of the state and its relationship to the 'individual'. The economic system had developed in such a way that large industry and finance capital had come to dominate the national economy, and this dominance by monopolies was supplemented in the social and legal spheres by the policies of an increasingly interventionist state. In the context of international imperialist rivalry, there was widespread concern about the unhealthy state of the working classes, and the perceived danger that the 'lowest' elements, its 'residuum', would 'contaminate' and degrade the middling ranks. As a solution to this problem, there emerged the idea of the 'positive' state with developed welfare and control functions which would both ameliorate and control the position of the worst off (Stedman Jones, 1971; Garland 1985) through therapeutic intervention (Wiener, 1990).

To 'punishment', the late Victorians opposed a conception of welfare, or rather of a form of social control that took the form of welfare – a 'welfare sanction' (Garland, 1985). They thus added to the ideological brew of utilitarian deterrence and retributive justice new, *antithetical* views of the nature and role of punishment that have contributed to the elements of modern sentencing.

## (i)  Individualism versus individualisation

We saw in Chapter 9 that the law was prepared to enter into a pragmatic alliance with doctors around the question of the control of madness. The mad were an early group for whom the concept of medical or psychiatric treatment seemed appropriate. From the late nineteenth century, other groups of criminals were identified by other specialists as 'suitable cases for treatment.' The result of this development was the establishment of modes of supervision and segregation that went beyond those that existed for persons who could be classified as mentally ill. A broader range of psychologically or socially 'disturbed' criminals were identified, who could be treated or controlled by the penal system according to their 'needs' or the actual dangers they manifested. In this process, ideologies of *rehabilitation* and *treatment*, and of *incapacitation* and *dangerousness*, were born.

Central to these developments was the growth of the positivist school of criminology which developed in this period. The essence of this new 'science' was its claim to a knowledge of the nature, causes and treatment of criminality and delinquency, which held out the possibility of arresting its development in the social body. Like the doctors, the criminologists, in their programmatic statements,[21] rejected the classical ideas of the penal reformers concerning the responsibility and freedom of the individual. For the Italian leader of this group, Enrico Ferri, crime had its natural and social causes 'which lie outside of that mathematical point called the free will of the criminal' (Ferri, 1901, 81). The result was a fundamental shift from philosophical ideas of individual freedom to psychological, physiological and behavioural ideas of the causes of action. Criminality was to become the target of direct technologies of behaviour control, rather than the 'respectful' response to a pre-existing rational moral act.

One implication of these changes was a revision in the conception of imprisonment from a sanction essentially rooted in individual deterrence into a system for the rehabilitation of the offender on the basis of a scientific understanding of his character, and the application of penological techniques to his condition. A symbol of this is the injunction in Rule One of the 1964 Prison Rules that the purpose of imprisonment is to 'encourage and assist [prisoners] to live a good and useful life'. That idea goes back to the landmark report of the Gladstone Committee of 1895 which observed that –

> . . . prison discipline and treatment should be more effectually designed to maintain, stimulate or awaken the higher susceptibilities of prisoners, to develop their moral instincts, to train them in orderly and industrial habits, and whenever possible to turn them out of prison better men and women, both physically and morally, than when they came in. (Stern, 1987, 60)

This new approach shifted from an ideology of abstract individualism, in which imprisonment was seen purely as a harsh means of desert and deterrence, to one of 'concrete individuality'. In this approach, a deep interest in the personality of *this* criminal, rather than the general qualities of all criminals as rational and moral subjects, was cultivated. Individualism within the law was to give way to individualisation of the treatment of the offender. It was this move in political and social ideology which generated as its key elements an interest in our third and fourth rationales of sentencing. On the one hand, the state was now interested, if possible, in reforming the criminal, in his rehabilitation. On the other hand, if reform proved impossible, the state was prepared to establish more stringent forms of containment and prevention, extending beyond those available within the normal disposition of the court. It was prepared to consider modes of incapacitation for those who were especially dangerous or beyond reform. The interventionist state had a licence to move beyond the ideologies of deterrence and the individual tariff either to treat the criminal or, failing that, to defend society by incapacitating him through extended detention.

Rehabilitation and incapacitation represented the positive and the negative sides of a doctrine of extended state intervention and individuated treatment of criminality. They developed out of a dissatisfaction with existing retributive and deterrence oriented concerns, attacking their abstract individualism from their own ideological viewpoint of the concrete and determined individual subject. These new conflicting ideas then had to be incorporated into the penal system with the old ideas that, in principle, they sought to replace.

## (ii)    Individualisation and sentencing

### (a)    Rehabilitation

As regards the operation of the rehabilitation ideology within the penal system, there has been over the last twenty years a decline in belief in 'the rehabilitative ideal', such that in official pronouncements, less ambitious and more pragmatic goals are set. In 1979, the May Committee stated that the 'rhetoric of "treatment and training" has had its day and should be replaced'. They added, rather ambiguously, that 'the rhetoric alone should be changed and not all the admirable and constructive things that are done in its name' (May Report, 1979, para 4.27). Prisons should now provide custody 'which is both secure and yet positive' (May Report, 1979, para 4.26). It is not that there is a new attitude of cynicism about the ability of imprisonment to rehabilitate, rather that jaundiced views about the possibility of reform within the closed community of the prison, which have always existed,[22] are now in the ascendant. At a time when the interventionist project of the welfare state was under widespread attack, prisons were increasingly used to denote political toughness and as a means of containment, leading to a huge increase in prison numbers. The decline of rehabilitation ideology is accordingly linked to a deep sense of crisis and change within the penal system (Cavadino and Dignan, 1992). While there have been attempts to reaffirm and update rehabilitation (eg Rex, 1998), the 'rehabilitation of rehabilitation' must occur in a penal system where a climate of punitiveness prevails.

Yet the sentencing system itself remains imbued in many of its aspects with rehabilitative concerns. Many non-custodial sentences such as the probation order, the suspended sentence, and the community service order embody such concerns. The decision to impose a custodial sentence is also linked in the judicial mind, along with deterrent and retributive concerns, with the possibility of reform.[23] Similarly, the structure of the determinate and the life custodial sentence is affected by considerations of reform. Under the Criminal Justice Act 1991, ss 32–4, a system of parole and release on licence remains for prisoners serving any sentence over four years' imprisonment. Under this system, the basic considerations to be taken into account are 'the need to protect the public from serious harm from offenders'; and 'the desirability of preventing the commission by them of further offences and of securing their rehabilitation' (s 32 (6)).

## (b)  Incapacitation

While rehabilitation has declined in importance, the other individualised form of sanction, incapacitation, has enjoyed renewed interest. The crisis of the prison system of the 1980s, which was strongly linked with overcrowding, led to a growing interest in a bifurcatory approach to sentencing. Its aim was to ensure that the state imprisoned those who were the most 'dangerous' offenders.[24] Under the Criminal Justice Act 1991, ss 1 and 2, the judiciary is required to consider whether a custodial sentence is necessary on grounds of seriousness *or*, in violent or sexual offences, public protection. The length of the custodial sentence is to be governed by the seriousness of the offence *except* in the case of a violent or sexual offence when a longer sentence may be passed if this is 'necessary to protect the public from serious harm'. Thus public protection through incapacitation can be substituted for a tariff consideration of offence seriousness in relation to violent or sexual offences. This requirement of a longer sentence replaced the previous 'extended sentence', a specifically incapacitative measure, which was used infrequently.

The interest in incapacitation arose from a desire to imprison less, but more effectively. The 1991 Act was launched on the view that prisons were 'an expensive way of making bad people worse' (White Paper, 1990, para 2.7). However, a political volte face saw a different Home Secretary challenge 150 years' experience with a populist and punitive programme under the slogan 'prison works'. The upshot was that prison numbers increased dramatically and new legal measures were introduced which would contribute to the trend. Under the Crime (Sentences) Act 1997, ss 2–4 (Powers of Criminal Courts (Sentencing) Act 2000, ss 109–111), a number of American-style 'three strikes' rules were introduced. These mix deterrent and incapacitative objectives. Under s 2, a person convicted of a second 'serious offence' (including s 18 assaults, armed robbery, rape, manslaughter) must be given a life sentence unless there are 'exceptional circumstances' relating to offences or offender (on which, see *R v Offen* (2001)). Under s 3, a third time class A drug trafficker must receive at least seven years, and under s 4, a third time burglar must receive at least a three year sentence. Both provisions are subject to an exception where specific circumstances would make the sentence unjust.

Yet incapacitation remains inherently problematic as an ideology of sentencing because of the failure of its protagonists to show that it is possible to predict with a high degree of accuracy those who are specifically dangerous. Predictive studies generally achieve a success rate of less than 50 per cent, with the embarrassing and lingering problem of a high rate of 'false positives'.[25] The effect of this is that a strategy of incapacitation is as likely to detain a person wrongly as rightly in terms of the likelihood of reoffending.

Why should this be so? Proponents of incapacitation will insist that the problem is one of developing adequate predictive techniques. We should, however, remember that the predictions of individual dangerousness are made in relation to a *social* class of criminals, so that indicators which seek to separate out some individuals from within the class are likely to be unsuccessful. Alternatively, they will draw upon characteristics that are indeed common to the class as a whole, and thus end up with a surfeit of false positives.[26]

## 5   SENTENCING IDEOLOGIES: THE INTERNAL DYNAMIC OF CONFLICT

### (i)   The antinomies of sentencing

Having reviewed the internal problems of the four theories of punishment, I return to my introductory comments about the problem of discretion and its roots in conflicting and one-sided ideologies of sentencing (above, p 201). The underlying problem is that each judicial sentencing decision invokes questions of the right punishment, of deterrence, incapacitation and reform. Each of these ideologies reflects only one aspect of what punishment is supposed to achieve, so all are necessitated. No sentencing ideology is adequate by itself, but none can be reconciled with any other. Individualist rationales invoke the contradictory individualising counter-strategies and vice versa in a bid to do the 'best' justice. Further, the individualist rationales (deterrence and retributivism) are themselves in conflict, both with each other and within themselves. Deterrence generates both individual and general calculations as to the appropriate punishment. Retributivism asserts a just punishment before utilitarian calculations, but then invokes just such calculations to decide what the just punishment is. At bottom, the problem is conflicting theories of sentencing resting on partial ideological grounds of individualism and individualisation.

In light of this, it is not surprising that the sentencing decision is one that resists determinate legal statement. This is not, however, because the 'particularity of the individual' escapes any generally-stated rule. It is often said by judges that this is the problem, that there 'are too many variables for it ever to be possible to get consistency'.[27] The problem concerns rather the conflicting, one-sided, inadequate nature of the ideologies of sentencing deployed pluralistically to determine the sentence. The particular case will not easily fall under any one sentencing rationale, and therefore requires reference to others. In the theoretical context of a plurality of one-sided approaches to punishment, no one rationale can do all the work. To opt for one rationale by itself is simply to ignore the plural needs, and therefore conflicting characteristics, of the sentencing decision.

### (ii) A dominant rationale? The Criminal Justice Act 1991

In recent years, an influential academic approach has been to challenge the consequences of a pluralistic view. Rejecting the 'cafeteria' style of sentencing, it is argued that one sentencing rationale (retributivism) should be given priority, with the other rationales playing a role that is limited by just deserts (von Hirsch, 1993, Ashworth, 1992, 2000). One achievement of this approach was the reflecting of its ideas in the Criminal Justice Act 1991, which did indeed give priority to retributive ideas of offence seriousness and commensurate punishment. It is therefore interesting to review its impact on sentencing with regard to the control of competing sentencing aims.

At the time of its passing, it was hoped that the emphasis on just deserts would assist in structuring discretion by prioritising questions of offence seriousness and commensurateness over other considerations (Ashworth, 1992, 57–9, 69–72). There was, however, a contrary view, which was, first, that there was sufficient evidence of pluralism within the Act's framework to call into question the ultimate value of the prioritisation of 'seriousness'. Second, offence 'seriousness' was so vague a concept as to admit other apparently excluded sentencing aims into the calculation of the sentence. As regards the first issue, the criterion of offence seriousness was balanced against the dangerousness of the offence and the offender (Criminal Justice Act 1991, ss 1(2)(b), 2(2)(b)). Although rehabilitation was not a stated rationale, it was also possible for the court to take into account mitigating factors in awarding punishment (s 28), allowing reform-oriented thinking an entry by the back door. This looked pretty much like 'business as usual'. As Thomas put it, one could either see the Act as an innovative landmark in the history of sentencing or, taking account of its pluralism, as an exercise in teaching granny to suck eggs (Thomas, 1992, 232).

As regards the second criticism, the Court of Appeal in *Cunningham* (1993) made short work of the Act by finding that offence seriousness was to be calculated according to deterrent as well as retributive considerations. 'The purposes of a custodial sentence must primarily be to punish and to deter. Accordingly, the phrase "commensurate with the seriousness of the offence" must mean commensurate with the punishment and deterrence which the seriousness of the offence requires' (1993, 447). The just deserts emphasis had seemingly excluded specific reference to deterrence, but almost immediately, the court rejected this. Defending the Act, Ashworth has argued that, for all its faults, it represented a new start, and that it was torpedoed by an alliance of academic, judicial and political hostility (Ashworth, 2000, 85–7). Lord Taylor's judgment in *Cunningham* involved a 'flagrant misreading of the statute' (2000, 87) to permit matters of deterrence into the calculation of commensurate punishment. In terms of the formally declared aims of the Act, Ashworth has a point. However, it is questionable whether it was realistic to expect any sentencing statute, even one based on retributive goals, to exclude issues of deterrence.

It should be noted that the retributive approach has never, from Kant onwards, denied that deterrence is a material function of punishment. It has only said that deterrence must first be justified as deserved, so that deterrence is the unspoken purpose which retributivism legitimates. To exclude deterrence from the legal frame-work is therefore artificially to limit the range of sentencing ideologies available to the judge. It is not, therefore surprising that judges should at the first opportunity reinsert deterrence in the penal equation.

To this, Ashworth might respond that, even so, deterrence should be *limited* by retributive calculation of the seriousness of the offence. Is that a plausible argument given that retributive calculations are so abstract that they require 'fixing' by material calculations of a utilitarian character? Retributivism is itself the hostage to utilitarian calculation (above, p 213). To argue that retributive measures can limit deterrence considerations is like sticking one's finger in the dyke wall when one is already up to one's neck in water. At best, had *Cunningham* gone the other way, the 1991 Act would have required judges to act hypocritically, couching deterrence thinking in non-deterrence terms. This would not have been very hard for, as one writer predicted of the Act, 'factors which trigger defensive and strategic sentencing are also likely to aggravate perceptions of seriousness' (Cooper, 1992, 7). If a crime is in need of greater deterrence because, for example, it is more 'prevalent' (*Cunningham* (1993) at 448), does that not indeed make it more serious? Talk of offence seriousness would simply have become an undercover way of talking about what deterrence required.

One can see the history of the 1991 Act in this matter as the product of a botched process of law reform. The Act was insufficiently clearly formulated, and was sabotaged by judicial hostility. Alternatively, one can see what happened as the inevitable consequence of seeking to constrict artificially a necessarily pluralistic and conflicted practice. My argument has been that the latter view is more plausible because sentencing ideologies are one-sided and inadequate. None can therefore fulfil the role of a primary sentencing rationale.

## 6 CONCLUSION

In examining the principles and philosophies of sentencing, I have emphasised the plurality of rationales, and the inherent and dialectical character of the shifts from one ideology to another as politics have dictated. The problem is that these conflict-ing ideologies of sentencing both repudiate and invoke each other as first abstract individualism then concrete individualisation holds sway within a state and polity committed both to liberal ideology and the effective control of crime. But, as with our discussion of law and psychiatry, it is worth concluding not in terms of the conflict in sentencing rationales but in terms of what they have in common. The ultimate focus of the criminal justice system is the deviance of the lowest social strata of our society, those with the least to gain from law-abidance, for whom various inducements offered by the labour market or the state are insufficient to encourage commitment to the law. Of course, the criminal law is not applied in a way that directly targets those strata, so that it is quite possible for the middle class fraudster or killer to end up behind bars. Nonetheless, the example of white collar crime (see above, Chapter 5) reveals one of the ways in which statistically and structurally the system is socially directed at the lowliest and poorest sections of our society. Another way of seeing this directedness is by examining the social position of those who end up in prison.[28]

This social structuring of the criminal population is ignored or marginalised by all four ideologies of punishment, which focus upon the individual, either through their *individualism*, or their *individualisation* of the criminal. It is the 'social question' which undercuts every one of the ideologies of punishment. Whether it is deterrence with its cordon sanitaire around a criminal population that has no incentive to be deterred; or retributivism, with its abstract moral relationship between an ideal individual and the state; or rehabilitation and incapacitation, with their focus upon the reformability or segregation of particular individuals in isolation from the broader social factors that cause crime, the ideologies of punishment constantly fail to see the social wood for the individual trees.

At best the system is able to hold those who do least well out of it, containing the problem within institutions that address its effects rather than its causes. Criminal punishment can be seen as a lid stuck on a pot of boiling water, when no one turns off the hotplate. This, however, is a pot that has the singular demerit of never running dry, so that the steam continues to rise, and society must continue to find legitimations for keeping the lid shut. The key element in those legitimations in the Western system of criminal justice is the idea of the individual abstracted from his or her social relations *either* through the classical individualist ideology of the Enlightenment, *or* the late Victorian ideology of the individualisation of the problem of criminality. In both, the social context in which people live and character is formed is studiously pushed to the edge of the picture so that individuals can be blamed for, or 'cured' and controlled in relation to, the real problems of violence and poverty created by our society.

# Chapter 11

# Conclusion

And this universal language (law) comes just at the right time to lend a new strength to the psychology of the masters: it allows it always to take other men as objects, to describe and condemn at one stroke. It is an adjectival psychology, it knows only how to endow its victims with epithets, it is ignorant of everything about the actions themselves, save the guilty category into which they are forced to fit. (Barthes, 1973, 45)

When a science goes round in circles without managing to overcome its contradictions it is always because it is based on concepts, on a definition of its object, which have not been subjected to a sufficiently radical critique, one which is sufficiently well-informed philosophically. (Sève, 1975, 20)

## 1 THE POLITICAL NATURE OF JURIDICAL INDIVIDUALISM

In Chapter 1, I outlined the principles of individual justice and rational legalism which underlie the orthodox theory and practice of criminal law, and indicated at the same time the ambivalence within that theory to them. In Chapter 2, I suggested that the time had come to move beyond attempts to shore up or reconstruct the criminal law so as better to match principle to practice. I proposed an historical approach to the principles of the criminal law, and identified the link between the legal forms of social control that emerged in the early nineteenth century and the ideologies of the Enlightenment.

The link was provided by the two Enlightenment-inspired philosophies of retributivism and utilitarianism, and the key to understanding the nature of the law lay in the contradictions at the heart of these two philosophies of punishment. These contradictions were historically generated in the modern period by the interplay between an abstract individualist ideology of just punishment and the reality of crime as a social and political phenomenon. First, crime was the product of the conditions in which the lower social orders lived and against which they struggled, but in philosophical ideology it was the product of a free individual for which punishment was deserved. Secondly, this abstract ideology represented the social world as consensual, whereas in reality it was racked by social and political conflict.

These conflicts within ideology underlay the tensions and contradictions within the criminal law. Liberal theorists like Hart have elaborated the retributive and utilitarian principles which inform that law. If those philosophical principles are fundamentally flawed, we should expect to see the results of this in the law itself. The central ideological figure within Enlightenment thought is the abstract juridical individual. This book has explored the various ways in which this homuncular form operates within the criminal law, analysing the tensions and contradictions to which it gives rise.

## (i) Psychological individualism

There are two main elements within the ideological form of the juridical individual. One is a psychological individualism, which operates in two ways in the criminal law. First, it screens out a range of possible excuses that stem from the context within which individuals operate. Within the philosophy of punishment, it was the abstract freedom of the individual which justified punishment retributively (Norrie, 1991), and it was the contradiction between the ideal image of the free individual and the social reality of poverty and need that undermined that theory, leading to its historical downfall. Enlightenment-derived ideology legitimates punishment on the basis of individual responsibility. But in order to do so, it must ensure that the individual be 'sealed off' from the social relations which give rise to action. Within the criminal law, it is necessary for the practice of attributing fault to individuals that this abstract form of individualism be maintained through a variety of doctrinal mechanisms. The criminal law operates with a form of psychological individualism, and this central ideological form involves a constant work of political closure to keep the social context at bay.

The second, related operation performed by this psychological individualism is the apparent depoliticisation and de-moralisation of both the philosophy of punishment and the criminal law. Neumann wrote that:

> The philosophical system appropriate to the Rechtsstaat is that of Enlightenment . . . [B]ut only because man was seen as universal man, as infinitely perfect being without individual features . . . was . . . a pre-established harmony . . . between state and society . . . possible. (1987, 70)

Liberal theory wishes to portray the criminal law as existing within a consensual world in which all individuals qua individuals come together under the law. This is central to the theory and practice of the criminal law, as well as to the philosophical legitimation of the criminal justice system as a whole. But in a society based upon deep social and political conflicts, this representation can only be maintained if the conflicts can, so far as possible, be excluded from the court of law. Harmony between state and society in the context of the criminal process can only be maintained if social conflicts are filtered out in advance. The concept of the abstract psychological individual contributes to this political goal by removing such conflicts from the courtroom.

Thus the psychological individual at the heart of the criminal law is a political and ideological construction which operates to seal off the question of individual culpability from issues concerning the relationship between individual agency and social context. It seeks to exclude a broad view of social relations which would locate individual actions within their determinative context, and to exclude moral and political counter-discourses from the law. The concept of the abstract psychological subject or citizen which the law fashions stands as a denial of the social, moral and political context within which individuals operate. Presenting the question of responsibility in an apolitical, amoral and asocial form, it performs a negative and repressive political task of closure and exclusion.

In considering the nature of law, it is important to understand that the political element in this construction of the legal individual is an active though indirect one. Abstract psychological individualism is presented as an ideal and apolitical representation of human agency, but it stands in opposition to the realities of concrete social individuality, which threaten to undermine the conviction process. The work of excluding those 'external' realities is practical and ongoing, and determines the evolving shape of legal doctrine. The abstract form of the law is used to police the borders of the conviction process (that is, the law) against contextual raiding parties. There is a constant political task of maintaining the abstract psychological boundaries of doctrine against corruptive invasion from the socially, morally and politically constituted 'other'.

### (ii) Political individualism

The second main element within the law's abstract individualism, which is more immediately political, stems from the Janus-faced character of the legal form (Norrie, 1991, 199–203). The abstract psychological individual performs a negative and repressive role in establishing an ideal subject or citizen to 'stand before' the judge and to justify the state's punitive repression of actual individuals. However, the juridical subject also plays a positive and affirmative role in that it 'stands up for' the individual against the state even if it is presented in an abstract and repressive form. The citizen in law stands as an ideal representative of the real person against any overweening power claimed by the state. The liberal theory of citizenship denies actual subjectivity, but still establishes an abstract form of individual right. It is upon a conception of political individualism that the categories of responsibility within the criminal law are based, and they therefore stand as a potential defence against state power. The abstract juridical individual has a dualistic character: judged against the actualities of human life, it functions to repress individuals; measured against the strength of state power, it can act to defend them.

Thus the legal forms of subjectivity within the criminal law stand as potentially important controls upon what the state can do to individuals who come before its courts. This is true both in relation to the forms of responsibility which must be satisfied in order to convict, and in relation to potential controls on the disposal of convicted persons at the sentencing stage. But precisely because the ideology of juridical individualism establishes this positive protection of the subject, it becomes the site of a second tension within legal doctrine. Here the conflict is between the nature of the criminal process as a mechanism of social control in a divided society, and its ideological representation as the embodiment of free and equal citizenship.

The reality of crime control is primarily one of 'us and them', of the control of the lowest social classes by a social and political elite drawn from the middle and upper middle classes. The ideological representation is one of a world of free and equal subjects under the rule of law. Thus criminal doctrine is elaborated in terms of a logic of subjective individual right, but this logical and principled elaboration of the rules is constantly put under threat by a more direct set of political demands reflecting perceived social control needs. This socio-political conflict within the law is often referred to in orthodox thinking as a tension between 'principle' and 'policy', but there is a danger in this mode of representation that 'policy' becomes seen as an unthreatening technical addendum to an otherwise apolitical legal system. It is not that what goes on under the name of 'policy' represents the political conspiracy of an elite; rather, this conflict within the criminal law is inherent in a society in which ideological forms of free and equal individualism coexist with a socially structured world of crime and punishment. Viewed in this light, the demands of 'policy' are seen as a more systemic and structured set of socio-political imperatives than its polite quasi-technical appellation suggests. As with its psychological individualism, so with its political individualism, the law's essential form is crucially mediated by political concerns.

In reviewing the character of juridical individualism in the criminal law, I wish to indicate and underline the political nature of the liberal legal enterprise. This is not just at the 'obvious' level of the intersection between 'principle' and 'policy' around the concept of the legal subject. It is also at the deeper level of the structuring of the legal subject around a psychological individualism that excludes social, moral and political conflict from legal discourse. Politics does not overlay a set of pre-existing apolitical concepts: it contributes to the construction of their deep structure, and it polices the boundaries of legal doctrine in accordance with them. It has to do this, for the law's abstract individualism is the site of a tension between narrower (more individualistic) and broader (more contextual) conceptions of individual agency. The work of policing the boundaries is an essentially political task, a matter of choice that is not determined (although it is deeply influenced) by pre-existing legal materials. Judges choose to open up or close down the concepts because the contradictory form of the abstract individual forces them to go one way or the other. They normally tend towards the narrower, more individualistic, options that are available to them for the practical reason that this strengthens the conviction process.

## 2 JURIDICAL INDIVIDUALISM IN THE CRIMINAL LAW

My starting point is a theory of legal ideology that sees criminal doctrine as shaped by particular historical conditions and as founded on conflicts which express themselves as tensions and contradictions within the law. Criminal law is an expression of a social and political practice, and it bears the marks of the conflicts within that practice. Because it is founded upon the political ideology of the juridical individual, criminal law is constructed upon the conflicts inherent in that ideology. My aim has been to explain the problems of logic within the law as structural problems that can be contained or managed but not resolved. More than just the product of bad lawyering, they are at the very heart of the liberal legal project. They cannot be resolved by the further elaboration of a rational principled account of the law because such an account is impossible. The project is unachievable because it is inherently flawed.

In the first three substantive chapters, I examined the central elements in mens rea, intention and recklessness, and contrasted their development with the 'exceptional' situations of strict and corporate liability. In Chapter 3, I considered the law of intention and the division within the law between intention and motive. With the notable exception of Hall (1960), criminal lawyers have accepted the centrality of the division between intention and motive as a datum of the legal enterprise. While intention is central, motive occupies a peripheral role, scratching an existence at the edges of doctrine. Yet motive remains central to human agency and to broader moral and political claims about the nature of fault. The reason why this 'much more advanced level of ethical criticism' (Hall, 1960, 83) is ignored is that motive introduces the questions of social need and right that would directly challenge the allocation of fault. The focus on intention excludes the motives of those living at the margins of society and those whose political values the existing order wishes to marginalise.

Yet motive does not go away because the law's psychological individualism tells it to, and it persists as a problem within legal doctrine. While generally excluded from the conviction process, it is admitted at the politically more 'safe' stage of sentencing, where its effects are controlled by the application of judicial discretion. It is true that admission of individual particularity at this latter stage threatens to undermine equality of treatment under the ideology of the rule of law. But the administration of such equality through formal legal categories at the conviction stage is so morally inadequate that it can only survive on the basis that individuality is allowed in through the back door of mitigation.

Furthermore, motive remains as a constant challenge to doctrine in 'dramatic' situations such as those associated with duress and necessity, and in circumstances in which the formal categories have not been tightly enough drawn to exclude disruption of the law. In relation to the former situations, the strategy is to establish certain exceptional excuses which operate above and beyond the 'normal' requirements of mens rea. These permit a measure of 'special' justice, while legitimating its denial in the majority of cases which do not directly fall within the special category. In relation to the latter, the law can either use the distinction between motive and intention to fend off 'political' challenges to an 'apolitical' system (*Chandler* (1964)), or seek to find some abstract formulation to neutralise the direct moral-political challenge of the disruptive or troublesome citizen (*Ghosh* (1982)).

These cases reveal a central element of legal practice, although one that is normally presented as peripheral. It is the political use of a depoliticised or de-moralised individualism to exclude moral and political challenges to the order of things. From this starting point, the 'real' legal debate can take place, and it is here that the shifting terms of the law of direct and indirect intent become our focus. But even on doctrine's own terrain, there is no guarantee of a smooth development. Having drawn the line between abstract psychological individualism (intention) and social individuality (motive), legal debates find themselves impaled on the second conflict within juridical ideology between political individualism and socio-political power. This conflict emerges in the contradictions in the law of intention between narrower definitions reflecting subjectivist principle and broader accounts that rely on objective elements. The shifting positions on the mens rea of murder over the last thirty years can only be understood in terms of this conflict. Underlying this battle over intention are the moral issues that orthodox subjectivism reads in terms of psychological control and cognitive mental states. 'Moral substantivists' in legal theory seek to introduce these issues into the legal categories. However, they fail to understand that legal reasoning around the subjective categories is an *historical* as well as a philosophical task. They cannot see that matters of moral substance are necessarily limited in their purchase on formal legal categories. Such matters are there, but always in the background, never properly expressed within the law. The law's conflicts reflect their impact without directly embodying their substance.

The subjectivist/objectivist split within criminal liability is the central focus of Chapter 4, on the law of recklessness. The 'indefensible' character of the law in this area has been remarked upon by orthodox theorists (Smith and Hogan, 1999, 67). So, at the level of the conflict between individual right and socio-political power, the argument about contradiction within the criminal law is easily made. In this chapter, however, I have tried to show in a more fundamental way the interconnection between the two contradictions at the heart of the law. I argued that the subjectivist and objectivist dichotomy in the law of recklessness is itself the product of a prior historical depoliticisation and de-moralisation that occurred in the nineteenth century. The terms in which the conflict between subjective right and objective liability are fought out are *already* the product of a prior historical 'resolution' of a conflict in legal ideology. The inadequacies of the law of recklessness are the product of this layering of the contradictions within the legal form. As with intention, a *morally substantive* conception of recklessness is both invoked and excluded by the law's emphasis on abstract psychological categories.

It is because of this that philosophical attempts to reinstate a core of moral judgment within the law of recklessness founder. To succeed, they would have to confront the lack of consensus at the heart of the social order, and, as a consequence, to reverse almost two centuries of legal development. One important result of this historical-conceptual impasse is the unsatisfactory nature of *both* positions in the subjectivist/objectivist controversy. Neither side can capture the moral issues at the heart of fault because the necessary moral and political concepts have already been removed from the picture. The subjectivists' liberally minded insistence on a narrow definition of advertent recklessness both appears to be 'right' in terms of legal principle *and* to miss an important moral definition of fault. The problem for those taking an objectivist position is that they must conflate the deeper sense of individual moral fault that the subjectivist ignores with a form of liability that exceeds individual fault by virtue of a broad authoritarian standard of reasonableness in human conduct. The moral distinctions that would have to be made are impossible because of the fact-value split within criminal responsibility. But this is no 'mistake'. It is the product of a social and historical process that engineered the exclusion of moral and political issues from the field of individual responsibility in order to render criminal conviction more certain.

In Chapter 5, I compared and contrasted general mens rea in relation to individual crime with strict and corporate criminal liability. I argued that the problems associated with the social and legal control of corporations stem from the nexus between individualism and social class which lies at the heart of the general criminal law. The essential focus of the law is on harms associated with the lower social classes – 'street crime', committed by actual individuals. Corporate harm is accordingly doubly removed from the realm of 'normal' crime. As a matter of social and ideological construction, corporations are hard to perceive as criminals, and as a matter of legal practice, they are hard to capture within individualistic legal forms.

The effects of this double difference are seen in the areas of strict and corporate liability. With regard to the former, the ideological difficulty is to the fore, leading to a legal differentiation that cannot be substantiated. As Williams says, 'it is impossible to abstract any coherent principle on when this form of liability arises and when it does not' (1983, 934). The appeal to a formal distinction, which the law requires to make in order to legitimate itself as law, cannot obscure the real underlying socio-political differentiation. With regard to the latter, the use of an individualistic, anthropomorphic account of corporate responsibility serves only to obscure the socially organised nature of harm in a world where an increasingly naked profit motive drives the corporate organisation. The weakness of the 'head and hands' principle is in a political sense a strength because, in making conviction harder, it legitimates the view that corporate wrongdoing is indeed non-criminal. It also obscures the broader economic motives behind corporate harm by personalising and individualising blame in a way that reform proposals radically challenge. The problem for reformers is that in socialising fault, they threaten to indict the economic system as a whole and therefore to transcend and dissolve the realm of the criminal law as a distinct 'apolitical' entity.

In Chapters 6 and 7, I considered the role of abstract individualism in the construction of the central elements of actus reus. With regard to acts, my central focus was upon the requirement that an act be voluntary. The double play around the central antitheses of the juridical individual observed in intention is repeated. On the one hand, judges and orthodox scholars must police the boundaries of the concept of involuntariness so as to ensure that a broad, contextualised conception of 'moral involuntariness' is excluded or limited. The safety valve of necessity and duress operates to maintain the strict general principles of individual responsibility based on a narrow physical conception of involuntariness. On the other hand, the requirement of physical involuntariness is itself subject to attack through a kind of 'super-individualism' which traces voluntariness back to a prior, morally culpable voluntary act, albeit one that cannot be directly tied to the actual actus required by a formally and technically proper criminal law.

This 'super-individualism' stands in the same relation to subjectivist principle in the law of voluntary acts as do the objectivist positions in the law of intention and recklessness, although it involves a different modus operandi. It is a way of over-riding the established, principled stance in favour of a socio-political control objective, although this is couched paradoxically in the language of subjectivity. This is most clearly seen in the context of intoxication. That condition has the double demerit from the law's point of view of offering a potential excuse to the criminal actor through the denial of voluntariness (or intention) *and* of being a social phenomenon commonly linked with working-class crime.

The law of omissions performs a different function from the law of voluntary acts, but the crucial mediation is provided by the form of the juridical individual. Voluntariness locates responsibility in individual acts in isolation from their context, whereas the law of omissions is concerned with maintaining that isolation in relation to failures to act. The interconnectedness of social life raises the possibility of a broad conception of responsibility to prevent a wide range of structurally as well as individually induced harms: for example, the responsibility of the rich for the poor. The political aim of the criminal law of omissions is to establish a sphere of responsibility that does not encroach upon the 'normal' omissions of a society based upon economic laisser faire. The law of omissions draws on the key ideological form of the abstract individual who is only committed to the extent that he commits himself through his own prior act. A convenient nexus is established between individual economic and juridical activity, primarily through the ideology of contract or analogy with it. In the process, however, the law evolves so narrowly that even elementary duties of social help are excluded from the field of liability.

The political decision to formulate the law of involuntary acts and omissions narrowly through the use of an individualistic conception of duty can be contrasted with the different functional context provided by the law of supervening cause which I examined in Chapter 7. The theoretical problem for the law is the same, though the solution is different. In a socially interconnected world, individuals are both the producers of causes and themselves located within causal chains. At what point is the law to draw the line that delimits the effects of one person's agency from those of another? The use of broad and vague concepts of voluntariness and coincidence as the breaks on causal sequences contrasts with the narrow conceptions of involuntariness in the law of acts and of causal connection in the law of omissions. This can be understood in terms of the different socio-political goals in the three areas. In the law of acts, the idea of moral involuntariness is excluded, whereas it is accepted in the law of supervening cause. In the latter area we are concerned not with the acts of the criminal, but with those of the victim or a third party. The effect of a broad conception of involuntariness in relation to acts would be exculpatory, because it would broaden the range of claims available to the accused. The effect in relation to supervening cause, however, is the reverse because a broad conception of involuntariness works against the claim that a new cause has intervened.

In both areas of the law, the basic premise is that of individual agency and responsibility, but the actual construction of the legal concepts is dependent upon a political choice between more and less contextual conceptions of the juridical individual. The endorsement of a more contextual account of the individual in the law of supervening cause confirms both the tension within the basic legal form, and the role of political considerations in 'fixing' the law's form in particular areas. Similarly, we can compare the idea of a coincidental supervening cause in causation with the role of cause in the law of omissions. We note the broad and indeterminate character of the line drawn by the vague concept of coincidence in the law of causation (where indeterminacy increases inculpation). We can compare this with the narrow and determinate character of the line drawn in the latter by the precise concept of the duty to act (where precision increases exculpation). One can only understand these differences according to the functional context of increasing the likelihood of conviction in causation cases and decreasing it in situations of omission. The specific character of individual agency is shaped by the underlying socio-political agenda.

In the following two chapters, I considered two of the most important general defences within the law, and explored the nature of legal individualism within them. In Chapter 8, I examined necessity and duress and the role that these defences play within the overall logic of the law of criminal responsibility. The important links between the existence of these defences and the law of intention and agency have already been discussed. They operate as a safety-valve for the law: a box into which are pigeonholed those situations in which it is hardest to separate intention and agency from context. Yet because these defences operate against the logical grain of the law's abstract individualism, they sit uncomfortably with the standard legal categories. They occasion theoretical concern amongst criminal lawyers, some of whom would like to 'rationalise' the law by dissolving the defences into a capacious residual discretion at the sentencing stage. These defences challenge the law's psychological individualism, and the social control functions which underlie it, by opening up the legal sphere in which matters of social and political context can be contested. At worst, they threaten to be a contextual Pandora's Box, the opening of which generates a social and political counter-logic to that of the law. For these reasons, the very existence of necessity and duress as defences to some or all offences remains a permanent point of contention within judicial discourse. They play upon the fault line generated by the law's decontextualised individualism and this accounts for their continually 'provisional' character within legal discourse.

In Chapter 9, I considered the defences of insanity and diminished responsibility. Here the particular nature of the phenomenon of madness means that the law's abstract individualism appears in the shape of a narrow rationalist test of insanity. The position is complicated by the conflictual yet co-operative relationship between lawyers and doctors. The medical approach opposes an individuated and concretely determined model of the mad person to the law's test of rational individualism. Psychiatry thus plays on the other pole in the opposition between psychological individualism and contextualised individuality. However, the psychiatric point of view only opposes legal individualism to a limited extent, for what is lacking also within the psychiatric understanding is a recognition of the broader social context of mad behaviour. It is the limited nature of the psychiatric critique of the law that is both the cause and the effect of the political alliance between the two professions, at the same time as it is the source of occasional dramatic disagreements between them. They oppose each other in the ways in which they construct individual conduct and responsibility, but they agree in seeing the problem as being one of individual conduct. It is this situation of alliance without underlying ideological agreement that explains both the practical success and theoretical inadequacy of the partial defence of diminished responsibility.

Finally, in Chapter 10, I moved from the substantive law that governs the process of conviction to the sphere of broad discretion that exists at the post-conviction stage. For most orthodox criminal law texts, sentencing is not a topic that attracts detailed consideration. At one level, this is understandable, for sentencing has a different function to conviction, and therefore assumes different forms. Yet to recognise the differences is not to deny the fundamental ideological continuity between the two stages, and there is also a danger of not seeing that the differences at the sentencing stage are *determined by* what occurs at the conviction stage that has preceded it. In examining the law of intention and agency, we have seen how the problem of social context is either pigeonholed through the excuses, or postponed, finally to re-emerge as a relevant factor at the sentencing stage. The abstract individualism that governs the law is only possible on condition that a significant measure of discretion exists at the sentencing stage. Moral and political considerations have so far as possible been wrung out of the law, but they must find their place in the politically safe discretion of the judge once conviction is secured. A 'wise polity' must have the mechanisms strictly to control those forms of harm that endanger it, but must temper its legal 'justice' with individual 'mercy'. Individualism in the law and individuality in the sentence are organically linked elements in the criminal justice system.

Despite the differences, however, the same ideological forms which underlie conviction emerge once more at the sentencing stage, albeit in a less controlled form.

It is the law's psychological individualism that underlies retributive sentencing principles, but these are undermined by individualising and contextualising ideologies of rehabilitation and dangerousness. Ideas of just deserts also embody the values of political individualism within the legal form, but these are undermined by the politics of punishment associated with a general utilitarian theory. Seen in this light, the indeterminacy of the sentencing stage is not just the product of the determinacy required at the conviction stage. It is also the result of the setting loose of the contradictions inherent within the historical and ideological project that is the criminal law. With the strict legal requirements of the conviction stage slackened off, those contradictions are given freer rein. This is an embarrassment to the legal process, which prides itself on its formal determinacy of outcomes, but it cannot really be otherwise. Attempts to make things better through the prioritisation of 'just deserts' founder on the partial and one-sided character of retributivism's abstract individualism. The sentencing stage with its wide discretion can thus be seen as the culmination of a particular, historical form of social control. It can also be seen as confirmation of the central thesis of this book: that the criminal law is founded on ideological principles that are in their essence contradictory, so that rationalistic readings of the law are bound to fail.

## 3    CRIMINAL LAW AS PRAXIOLOGY

I have sought to portray both the practical and real quality of the law and its ideological character. I have also sought to show the law's illogicality and the historical logic that underlies it. The key to the critique presented here is the idea of law as a particular, historical form of social practice that is based upon an ideological representation of human life through the idea of the abstract legal individual. It is this responsible individual that the law respects through the 'rational' application of legal rules. That the matter of responsibility is much more complex than legal individualism can allow, or that the deduction and application of legal rules must be much less rational than orthodox legal theory is prepared to recognise, does not mean that the system is impractical. On the contrary, despite the deep flaws in its self-understanding and representation, criminal law remains a crucial and powerful social practice. As such, it is vital for political and ideological reasons that the law maintain its self-image as a system based upon individual responsibility and justice. It is for this reason that it is important to understand the limits of individual justice, and the political functions that it performs.

The concept of law as an ideological practice is also important in terms of the way that we understand the theory of criminal law. There is a tendency to see the law's concepts as reflecting the way individuals 'really are', or the way life 'really is'. To a point, this is true: individuals are agents, they do form intentions, they do take risks, and so on. But this is not the whole story; indeed it is a dangerous half-truth that obscures the significance of the social, moral and political context of agency which alone makes proper judgment of conduct possible. The concept of the abstract psychological individual suppresses the synthesis of individual form and social content necessary to such judgment, but this is what it is supposed to do. In Barthes's words, the language of the law lends 'a new strength to the psychology of the masters' precisely because it can 'describe and condemn at one stroke' while remaining 'ignorant of everything about the [criminal] actions themselves'.

Similarly there is a deep conviction reflected in legal practice and scholarship that law really is in principle a system of logically derived rules. Legal cases do indeed seek to present their conclusions in a formally rational way. The point, however, is that their rationality is undercut because of the social and political fault lines on which the doctrinal categories are built. Lawyers, nonetheless, continue to argue as if rational justification is possible. As part of an historical and practical control process, there is every reason why they should do so. Law can only operate on the basis that it has a formal existence above and beyond 'local' issues of morality and politics (cf Fish, 1993). But there is no need for a critical legal theory, seeking to get behind the legal forms and to relate them to their underlying historical and practical tasks, to take what is said at face value. Given the marked propensity of criminal law theory to 'go round in circles', there is every incentive to follow Sève's advice and to seek a deeper critique that can understand the underlying contradictions that operate as mental blocks in the way of theoretical progress. The problem with orthodox liberal, positivistic approaches to criminal law is that this is precisely what they fail to do.

Following Bhaskar (1979), I suggest that if we think of criminal law as a particular form of social and historical practice, we should consider its theory, which reflects and legitimates that practice, as a form of knowledge which can be described as a 'praxiology'. This term refers to any theoretical account of a form of social agency that, like law, is tied to, and limited in its level of understanding by, a set of possible practices and outcomes. The range of concepts available within a praxiology is governed by the set of social practices and outcomes that it represents, informs and legitimates. Because the practice of the criminal law operates with concepts of individualism and formal rationality, orthodox criminal law theory is also tied to these concepts, and cannot transcend them.[1]

The essence of a praxiology is that it takes the part represented by the practice to be the whole, and in so doing it both obscures the whole and, ultimately, misrepresents the practice. Criminal law theory, by ignoring the relationship between law, conviction and punishment on the one hand and the social context of crime on the other, is unable to see the broader picture. It cannot therefore get to the bottom of the conundrums of the criminal law itself. Praxiologies are condemned to repeat the problems that the practices to which they are attached give rise because they cannot get beyond them. Thus, for example, the old problems of individual versus social responsibility and of subjectivism versus objectivism remain unresolvable problems for criminal law theory because they stem from the historical practice of the criminal law. While a critique such as the present one cannot indicate how such problems would ultimately be resolved, it can indicate the basic historical foundations of the problem in the way that an 'internal' praxiological account cannot.

The praxiological explanation of juridical subjectivity sees the modern social fact of individualistically constituted legal responsibility as the basis for a descriptive and normative account of criminal liability, but as doing so in a onesided way. Individually instantiated social agency is translated into individualistically constituted, desocialised responsibility. Recognition of the social dimension of individual agency transforms our knowledge, understanding and judgment of the implications of such agency. Legal knowledge, tied to the criminal law practice of punishing *individuals*, is founded upon a misrecognition that is necessary to the legitimacy of the criminal law. Similarly, representation of the legal process as in principle rational is necessary for the law's legitimacy, but entails a misrecognition of the role of political judgment within the legal categories. It is these misrecognitions which both constitute the basis for the continuing practical 'success' of criminal law theory, and prevent it from transcending the idées fixes which govern the social practice of the criminal law. It is the social and historical practice of the criminal law that establishes both the practical necessity and the intellectual impossibility of the orthodox, liberal, positivist tradition in criminal law scholarship.

# Notes

## Chapter 1: Contradiction, critique and criminal law

1   See also MacCormick (1978, 41): 'since legal reasoning is a form of thought it must be logical, ie must conform to the laws of logic, on pain of being irrational and self-contradictory.' Philosophically, this position endorses a standard *analytical* account of legal thinking. In recent work, I have argued that such an account needs supplementing with a *dialectical* approach (Norrie, 2000, ch 3).

2   The political principle behind the rule is expressed in the following judicial observation from the nineteenth century. 'Mr Justice Blackstone well lays down the rule: "The freedom of our Constitution will not permit that in criminal cases a power should be lodged in any Judge to construe the law otherwise than according to the letter." Our institutions were never more safe, in my opinion, than at the present moment, but we must not lose any of the grounds of our security, no calamity would be greater than to introduce a lax or elastic interpretation of a criminal statute to serve a special but temporary purpose . . . [I]n a criminal statute you must be quite sure that the offence charged is within the letter of the law' (quoted in Radzinowicz, 1948, 105–6; cf A Smith, 1984, 48).

3   Williams, 1961, 589: 'In short, the rule is, or should be, merely this: that if an Act of Parliament is so drawn as to make it really difficult to say what was intended and what facts come within it, the benefit of that obscurity should be given to the accused person. For a recent discussion, see Ashworth (1999, 80–2). Ashworth counterposes the liberal principle of strict construction to a broader purposive approach. His analysis is noteworthy for its juxtaposition of conflicting interpretive techniques in the law. The historical roots of such conflicts are explored in the next chapter.

4   Compare the popular judicial refrain that the 'lifeblood of the law is not logic but common sense' (Lord Reid in *Haughton v Smith* (1975) at 500; cf Lord Edmund-Davies in *Majewski* (1976) at 157).

5   Thus it is relevant which judges sit on appeals (cf Sellers, 1978, 245), but only within the overall context of the judicial role and the framework of legal argumentation. Practical factors within these broader parameters, such as the procedural context, also play their part (Spencer, 1982).

6   Cf Moore (1984, 112): 'the very abstract view of persons in terms of autonomy and rationality is of course radically incomplete as a picture of any person we know.' For a brief critique of the internal contradictions of Moore's defence of this radical incompleteness, see Norrie (1986). See also Norrie, 2000, ch 5 for an extended discussion of Moore's work.

7   The discussion here and elsewhere in this book overlaps with important debates within the philosophy of punishment that cannot be adequately dealt with in the current work, but which are discussed in Norrie (1991) and (2000).

## Chapter 2: The historical context of criminal doctrine

1   The essentially retributive idea of individual criminal responsibility is the focus of Chapters 3–9 of this work. The operation of retributivism as a theory of punishment is considered in Chapter 10.

2 For a graphic illustration of the 'thief turned into the assassin' by indiscriminate punishment, see Winslow (1977).
3 Although the logic of the Benthamite position was flawed (Hart, 1968, 19). See Chapters 8 and 10 for discussion of the particular tension within utilitarian theory, and for consideration of deterrence as a utilitarian rationale for sentencing. See also Norrie (1991, chs 5, 6).
4 Under a fixed code of laws 'citizens acquire that sense of security for their own persons which is just, because it is the object of a human association, and useful, because it enables them to calculate accurately the inconvenience of a misdeed' (Beccaria, 1966, 17). See also Foucault (1979, 95, 98) and Kadish (1978, 1101).
5 'During the eighteenth century one legal decision after another signalled that the lawyers had become converted to the notions of absolute property ownership . . . The rights and claims of the poor, if inquired into at all, received . . . perfunctory compensation . . . Very often they were simply redefined as crimes: poaching, wood-theft, trespass' (Thompson, 1977, 240–1; cf Foucault, 1979, 84–5).
6 The middle class character of the interests embodied in the reform movement is seen in the petitions collated by Radzinowicz (1948, App 4). These include one from master calico printers whose 'property is much exposed . . . and great depredations are annually committed', and one from the bankers of 214 towns and cities 'deeply interested in the protection of property from forgery' and the London jurors' petition signed by 'upwards of 1100 merchants, traders, etc'.
7 'The more men become enlightened, the more they will contract a spirit of general benevolence, because the progress of enlightenment makes it evident that the interests of men are oftener harmonious than discordant . . . The work of Adam Smith is a treatise on universal benevolence, because it shows that commerce is equally advantageous to all parties' (Bentham, 1975, 265).
8 'By good laws almost all offences may be reduced to acts which can be repaired by a simple pecuniary compensation, and thus the evil of offences may be almost wholly done away' (Bentham, 1975, 289).
9 'We have' wrote one, 'before our eyes, the example of a great many people who freely lead a life harder than the hardest slavery' (quoted in Venturi, 1971, 106).
10 '[The logic of the will] seems often to be in opposition to that of the understanding' (Bentham, 1975, 229).
11 Compare this benign but hopeless reformism with the reality described by Fielding as regards the problems of drink: 'wretches are often brought before me charged with theft and robbery, whom I am forced to confine before they are in a condition to be examined; and when they have afterwards become sober, I have plainly perceived, from the state of the case, that the Gin alone was the cause of the transgression . . .' (quoted in Radzinowicz, 1948, 231–2).
12 In the early days at least. Later on, the utilitarians divided precisely on the issue of whether a society based upon individualism could solve the social questions of the day, or required measures of social reform (Halevy, 1972, 514). Note also the changing role of the state as social classes took over from individuals as the main perceived historical actors in later utilitarian thought. Where Malthusian economic pessimism concluded that there would inevitably be rich and poor, the role of the legislator would change: 'in the interests of all, the State should protect the property *of the rich against the poor*' (1972, 488) (emphasis added).
13 'Where liberty and property coincided, Coke was most eloquent and urgent' (1965, 257).
14 Approximately 95% of crime in England and Wales is against property. See further Lacey and Wells (1998, ch 3).
15 This is not to say that there is no room for political difference of opinion within the judiciary but that potential differences are circumscribed by their overall social position and outlook.
16 A term that is not neutral but constructed to reflect particular social interests and perceptions of the nature of social life, especially as it is lived by the 'lower' classes (Hall, Critcher, Jefferson, Clarke and Roberts, 1978). Cf Box, 1987, 135: 'there is a class "logic" not only in [the judiciary's] situation, but in the perception of their situation.'

## Chapter 3: Motive and intention

1 For example, a dishonest appropriation of property belonging to another with an intention permanently to deprive constitutes the mens rea of theft; an intent to kill or cause grievous bodily harm that of murder; an intention to have sexual intercourse in the knowledge of lack of consent that of rape.

2   The argument that the various particularisations of mens rea render a general discussion impossible (Sayre, 1931/32, 1026) is met by Hall (1960, 74–6). On the different usages of the term, see Smith, 1978.

3   Though motive may be relevant to sentence. The significance of this dichotomy is discussed below, and in Chapter 10.

4   'It is intolerable that . . . the law should permit "intention" to have some . . . undefined meaning. Legal concepts must be certain in advance if the principle of legality . . . is not to be infringed seriously' (Cross, Jones and Card, 1988, 175).

5   The language stems from the utilitarian psychology of James Mill, which was taken up by the legal philosopher John Austin. See Halevy (1972, 455–77).

6   On the social creation of individual emotions, see Harré (1983).

7   The threat of death was no idle one, and throws into the sharpest relief the real practical effects of the motive/intention distinction. Hall (1960, 100) recounts a forgery case of 1809 in which the defendants were described as 'all indigent and, many of them, very distressed persons, who were tempted to engage in this criminal practice, by the necessities of the moment . . .' Nonetheless, they were all hanged.

8   See further on the conflict between a theory of justice based upon the rule of law and one based upon human need, Hay (1977, 44). Hall (1960, 99) rationalises the denial of motive in terms of the need to maintain an abstract consensus around the law while excluding anarchic individuals' claims to challenge consensus. Yet his illustration of how 'consensus' operated (previous note) reveals its particular political content.

9   The last sentence quoted is from Hume. The practical context behind the legal principle is graphically illustrated in Hobsbawm and Rudé's account of rural riots in 1830. The rioters were 'not criminals' but believed in the 'natural right' to work and 'refused to accept that machines, which robbed them of this right, should receive the protection of law'. For the judges, it was a matter simply of *law*, not the grievances of the labourers (Hobsbawm and Rudé, 1969, 249, 259).

10  In the United States (Levitin, 1987; Bannister and Milovanovic, 1990), peace protesters have used the necessity defence to seek to achieve what *Chandler* failed to. Like duress, necessity occupies an uncomfortable position within the law because it can permit this kind of political argument into the court. See Chapter 8.

11  This problem parallels in theory the practical 'problem' of ensuring that juries will accept the moral values of the law in a society which Lord Denning (1982, 75–7) described as lacking 'homogeneity'. See Findlay and Duff (1988).

12  See the interesting discussion by Williams (1983, 726), and works cited there which reveal the ambivalence of many people towards respect for private property.

13  Cf Smith and Hogan (1988, 530): 'juries might legitimately differ on how they believe that ordinary people would regard the conduct in question.'

14  Cf Smith and Hogan (1988, 532): 'Not everyone has the sort of upbringing that acquaints him with community standards of what is honest and dishonest.'

15  See eg *Prince* (1874–80) and *Tolson* (1886–90). These cases are discussed in Chapter 5. More recently, see *Shaw v DPP* (1962) and *Knuller v DPP* (1973).

16  Cf Ashworth (1983, 450): 'the sentencing process is a disgrace to the common law tradition.' My argument is that the practical problems he describes are informed by the structural and ideological conflicts at the root of juridical individualism. I develop this argument in Chapter 10.

17  The necessity of the means or side-effect must be *known* to the accused.

18  In so far as one can tell in a judgment containing five different and conflicting opinions. The 'probable consequence' test was enshrined in Archbold's statement of the law and became the basis for the judge's direction to the jury in *Moloney* (1985).

19  Williams (1987) cites Lynn's illustration of the second meaning of 'natural': 'Conception is a natural consequence of sexual intercourse but it is not necessarily probable' or, of course, certain.

20  Since intention under the guidelines includes foresight of probable consequences, but this is denied under the law, it leads to an indefensible position: 'Where the jury are not satisfied that the achievement of the prohibited consequences was the accused's aim or purpose, the inference of intention from foresight postulated in *Moloney, Hancock and Shankland* and *Nedrick* is *nonsense*' (Cross, Jones and Card, 1988, 74).

21  In *Walker and Hayles* (1989), a case of attempted murder, the Court of Appeal sought to reconcile the conflict between the law and the guidelines by arguing that the gap between virtual certainty and very high probability is a matter of degree.

## Chapter 4: Recklessness

1 The precise words of the test are given below, p 63.
2 'It seems to me that, in redefining the limits of criminal liability in this way, his speech borders on the unconstitutional. Parliament, advised by the Law Commission, had chosen the point at which it thought that liability should attach' (A T H Smith, 1987).
3 '[T]he main reason why the subjective definition has met with resistance from the judges [is that t]hey are apprehensive that the jury will acquit too readily. The objective definition, in contrast, enables the jury to express its indignation at the defendant's conduct without bothering about what went on in his mind' (Williams, 1983, 99).
4 They wrote (1843, 25–6): 'The characteristic difference between the mens rea, as applicable to the two great classes which we have considered, consists in this, that in the latter the offender for want of exertion, does not foresee and avoid mischief when he might have done so; in the former he incurs . . . a far more serious degree of responsibility in knowingly and wilfully encountering the danger of causing the mischief which was, as he knew, likely to result.' In the 'former' category, the Commissioners include both direct intention and 'wanton', 'wilful' and 'reckless' exposure to danger (1843, 24). In the 'latter', they place the 'improvident rashness or negligence' of a party 'who is not reasonably vigilant in avoiding all risk of danger . . . which might by the exercise of due care have been avoided' (1843, 25). See also Austin (1869, Lecture XX). Austin distinguishes intention from 'rashness' in which 'The party runs a risk of which he is conscious . . .' and negligence and heedlessness which 'suppose *un*consciousness' (his emphasis, 1869, 441).
5 The discussion here is specifically of malice aforethought in murder, which includes intention and 'Knowledge that the act which causes death will probably cause the death of, or grievous bodily harm to some person' (1883, 119). That is, what we would now call recklessness, although the law of murder does not now incorporate this rule. This is compared with negligence, which involves 'not taking notice of matters relevant to the business in hand, of which notice might and ought to have been taken' (1883, 122).
6 Kenny distinguishes malicious assault, which can be committed intentionally or in knowledge of likelihood and with a feeling of recklessness (1902, 147), from an injury accompanied by 'mere negligence' (1902, 149). Similarly (1902, 40) he distinguishes, without giving names to the states, the minor liability which accompanies a failure to foresee a criminal consequence which could have been foreseen from the major liability which follows actual foresight.
7 But note that in this case, there was an added but unexplained gloss of 'indifference'. A man was reckless as to a woman's consent if he was aware of the risk she was not consenting or 'he *was indifferent and* gave no thought to the possibility that the woman might not be consenting in circumstances where if any thought had been given to the matter it would have been obvious that she was not' (Pigg, 1982, 772) (emphasis added). The addition may be significant in terms of the discussion of 'practical indifference' in Section 3.
8 In order not to care less, it must have crossed the accused's mind that there was something to care about (Smith and Hogan, 1988, 66). This interpretation is supported by the further phrase 'pressed on regardless' which has a subjective ring. The context for the decision was an explicit rejection of the *Caldwell* test, but the use of colloquialisms does permit other interpretations of the meaning of the words: Birch (1988), Gardner (1991).
9 Or in *Lawrence* ((1981) at 982) 'obvious and serious'.
10 See in particular the comment of the reporter of *Noakes* ((1866) 4 F & F at 920): 'the case . . . afford[s] a remarkable illustration of that which it has too often been said cannot be defined, and can only be described by means of illustrations, viz: culpable or criminal negligence. It is impossible to define it, and it is not possible to make the distinction between actionable negligence and criminal negligence intelligible, except by means of illustrations drawn from actual judicial opinions.'
11 Williams (1978, 227–8) illustrates the point with the facts in *Pike* (1961), who anaesthetised women to have sex with them when unconscious, using a dangerous chemical (carbon tetrachloride) to knock them out. As a result of so doing in one case, a woman died and Pike was convicted of manslaughter. On the objective *Bateman* test, it appears highly likely that Pike would have been convicted of gross negligence manslaughter. Using a dangerous chemical on another person in order to satisfy his own sexual needs revealed a high degree of disregard for the life and safety of his victim. But change the facts around, as Williams does, and see whether the conclusion looks so obvious:
'Carbon tetrachloride is a common household cleaner, and it has in the past been sold under a trade-name without warning of danger. Suppose that Pike, being unable to think of anything better

, do on a wet Sunday afternoon, had agreed with a [male] friend . . . to see if the vapour would ause the friend to lose consciousness. Suppose, further, that Pike had done this on several occasions with other friends without mishap; but on the present occasion the friend dies. With sex removed from the case it is unlikely that he would be prosecuted, and likely that, if he were prosecuted, the jury would have acquitted of manslaughter.'
The grossness of the negligence depends upon the way in which the conduct is socially or morally perceived rather than its inherent quality. Prosecution and conviction are therefore a matter of social perception and construction.

12 'If the prisoner had been a medical man I should have recommended you to take the most favourable view of his conduct, for it would be most fatal to the efficiency of the medical profession if no one could administer medicine without a halter round his neck . . .' (1 F & F at 520).

13 Under the Road Traffic Act 1991, s 1, a new offence of causing death by dangerous driving was substituted. Similarly, 'reckless driving' has been replaced by an offence of 'dangerous driving'. I use reckless driving as an example at p 75.

14 In *Seymour*, Lord Roskill added that the judge should tell the jury that the risk of death ensuing must be 'very high' (grossly so?). The capacity test proposed by Ashworth as a modification of the *Caldwell* rule in order to subjectivise inadvertent negligence does not help either, for it does not affect the question of the necessary extent of the negligence itself.

15 For a discussion of the gendered nature of the 'reasonable man', see Allen, 1988.

16 It is clear that prosecutors retain a discretion to prosecute, and magistrates and juries to construe the facts of a case as they see fit, sometimes perversely. But at least under a subjectivist approach, they have a 'factual' peg to hang their deliberations on. There is an important difference between the question 'did the *accused* foresee the risk of x?' and 'do I think there was an obvious and serious risk of x?' As Williams (1983, 99) (emphasis added) puts it, the latter 'enables the jury to express its indignation at the defendant's conduct without bothering what went on in his mind. But against this it may be said that to ask the jury whether the defendant departed grossly from the reasonable standard *leaves them to make a value-judgment with very little assistance*.'

17 Duff suggests (1990, 165) that the fact that the fire endangered Faulkner's own life is relevant as showing that he was not indifferent to the risk he created. But he could have been as indifferent to his own life as to the safety of the boat, as would be the case in the example of driving at 60 mph in a built-up area, an example Duff uses to support his concept of practical indifference (1990, 167).

18 Cf the comment on *Noakes*, quoted above at note 10.

19 'For if *we* ask how he could have failed to notice that risk . . .' (Duff, 1990, 162–30) (emphasis added).

20 '. . . the jury need not infer some hidden mental state . . .' (Duff, 1990, 166).

21 Note the shift from descriptive to normative mode in this passage.

22 Cf the illustrations given in Temkin (1983, 15).

23 For example, operators of aircraft, surgeons performing operations, and the promoter of a tightrope act in a circus: Smith and Hogan (1999, 60).

24 Cf Sanders, 1985. This is discussed further in relation to strict and corporate liability in Chapter 5.

25 On the modern communitarian theory of punishment, see Lacey (1988). For an ambivalent critique, see Norrie (1990a) and 2000, ch 6.

## Chapter 5: Strict and corporate liability

1 There are in fact a variety of possible ways of formulating liability so as to exclude standard mens rea requirements, but to include, for example, lesser fault elements such as a 'due diligence' defence. On the variety of formulations which can be said to be covered by the head of strict liability, see Ashworth (1999, 167–8).

In this chapter, my focus is upon strict liability in the context of those offences which regulate industry. Strict liability offences have of course also expanded into the regulation of individual conduct through, for example, the regulation of road traffic (see Lacey and Wells, 1998, 497). It seems to me, however, that the extension of the strict liability offence to penalise the 'respectable' individual citizen is not incompatible with the main argument presented in this Section.

2 Cf McBarnet (1981), who uses this term to explain the legitimation of another form of two tier justice: that provided by the magistrates' court.

3 Nor, pace Williams, is the argument of regulators that they do not have the resources to mount sophisticated legal cases without substance, as the statistics make clear. See Box, 1983, 44–7; and Brown 'Balance Sheets and Shrouds' *Guardian*, 16 November 1988.

4  The following account is drawn from the work of Carson (1974, 1979, 1980). Carson (1970) shows the continuities between the practices developed in the nineteenth century and those in place in modern Britain.

5  Then, as recently, the legitimacy of corporate activity was called into question by major accidents at work. In these early days of heightened social conflict, however, the legitimacy of the state had also to be secured through some appearance of concern and intervention. Carson (1980) quotes the following editorial from *The Times* of 1844: 'We warn legislators of the infallible result of their not carrying out the protective character of Government . . . Tell the British labourer that he must fight all his battles and make all his own conditions without help from the State, and what sort of feeling is he likely to have towards that State, towards its head and towards its aristocracy?'

6  In this chapter, as elsewhere, I use terms like 'moral', 'political' and 'socio-political' interchangeably, to indicate the operation of substantive value judgments operating within the law in opposition to concepts that are presented as formalistic, 'technical' or 'factual'.

7  One judge (Brett J) argued that there was no legal wrong done by the accused and that there was a general presumption of mens rea which ought to apply in this case.

8  The cases are only fourteen years apart and concern provisions of the same statute only one section apart. Although the arguments in *Tolson* proclaim consistency with those in *Prince*, there was a substantial gulf between the leading positions.

9  'The judgments are full of technical arguments purporting to justify the two decisions. But the real point was that the judges sympathised with Mrs Tolson but not with Prince' (Williams, 1983, 221).

10  The Offences Against the Person Act 1861, s 57 states that 'Whosoever, being married, shall marry any other person during the life of the former husband or wife . . . shall be guilty of [an offence].' This is subject to a proviso that the offence does not exist where the person waits seven years before remarrying.

11  Towards the end of his judgment, Stephen does also argue, redundantly given his main argument, that Mrs Tolson had not behaved immorally.

12  Compare *Prince* with *Instan* (see Chapter 6) and *Dudley and Stephens* (see Chapter 8).

13  The crucial difference is that in Stephen's argument the definition of morality rests in the hands of the judiciary, who will interpret the 'intention of parliament' as to which offences are strict, and without reference to the mind of the accused. In the latter situation, there is more scope for the introduction of political or moral argument into the courtroom by individual defendants.

14  See Williams (1983, 940–6) for a full discussion of *Warner* and the change in the law wrought by the subsequent Misuse of Drugs Act 1971.

15  The Misuse of Drugs Act 1971, s 8 confirmed the requirement of mens rea with regard to this offence.

16  See also *R v Lemon* (1979) which reads a strict liability element into the common law offence of blasphemous libel. In this case, the political concern was the control of homosexuality.

17  For the historical development, see Williams (1961, ch 22; Welsh, 1946; Wells, 2001).

18  The 192 deaths in the Zeebrugge disaster represented almost one third of the number of deaths classified as homicide in one year.

19  'The "brains" and "hands" dichotomy essentially represents vivid journalism. It is not a substitute for analysis' (Leigh, 1966, 570).

20  Donovan 'Safety Fears in Shadow of Zeebrugge' *Guardian*, 20 October, 1990.

21  Cf Clinard (1983, 18): 'In the case of large corporations . . . their primary goal is to maximise profits for the stockholders and, simultaneously and indirectly, for top management. Although large corporations may have other goals, such as the increase or maintenance of corporate power and prestige, along with corporate growth and stability, their paramount objectives are the maximisation of profits and the general financial success of the corporation . . .'

22  The argument is outlined in Section 2(iii), above. See Canfield (1914); Edgerton (1927).

23  Cf Coffee (1981, 397) who writes of the 'multi-divisional and often radically decentralised structure of the modern public corporation'.

24  This already happens in relation to the Health and Safety regulation of the building trade, where builders blame sub-contractors for breaches of regulations. The Health and Safety Executive's response is to prosecute middle managers and foremen, a solution that may lead to convictions of individuals but which lets companies off the hook: see Wells (1988, 798).

25  Similar arguments could be made in relation to a 'retribution trap' too: Fisse (1990, 214–19).

26  Cf Box's conclusion (1983, 79): 'If there is no way of implementing justice for the largest and worst offending corporations then it is surely unjust to pursue with such ruthless and cruel tenacity the majority of those eventually condemned to prison.'

## Chapter 6: Acts and omissions

1   Thus Sir Edward Coke, quoted in Williams (1983, 146): 'No man shall be examined upon secret thoughts of his heart, or of his secret opinion: but something ought to be objected against him that he hath spoken or done.'

2   For discussion of the historical centrality of the Hobbesian account of voluntariness to the liberal theory of punishment, see Norrie (1991, ch 2).

3   Hart (1968, 22–3) is more inclined to the narrower view. The broadest expression of what is meant by 'involuntary' comes out in Hart's work on causation: see pp 139–40. The reason for the different conceptions of involuntariness in the areas of act and supervening cause are considered at p 149.

4   Stephen (1883, II, 100) reports only one example of a case where a writer has bothered to state it.

5   I use the term 'moral voluntariness' to denote a broader normative conception of fault beyond the 'psychological' fault of physical voluntariness. I am not suggesting that the law categorises prior fault in this way, indeed the particular kind of fault recognised by the law is that of subjective recklessness (see pp 116–18). The term however indicates something of the nature of the moral argument that is being made when a prior act takes the place of the act required for the actus reus of the offence.

6   The case was apparently rather implausibly treated as one of non-insane, rather than insane, automatism, and is therefore of dubious significance, except that it so vividly indicates a judicial attitude to the requirement of unconsciousness. On the nature of insane automatism, a concept that also operates, in practice, to limit the use of involuntariness, see Chapter 9, p 180.

7   Cf Clarkson and Keating (1998, 106) for whom this is like saying it would be 'wrong to punish someone for having a common cold, but permissible to punish him for sneezing.'

8   Cf Fletcher (1978, 428) who supports the majority position in *Powell* that the proper distinction is acts versus non-acts (statuses, etc), rather than acts versus involuntary acts, but he does not test the strength of the conceptual distinction between a non-act and an involuntary act.

9   The tension within judicial thinking is most clearly seen in two comments by Stephen. In *Doherty* ((1887) at 308), he stated that 'It is almost trivial for me to observe that a man is not excused from crime by reason of his drunkenness. If it were so, you might as well at once shut up the criminal courts, because drink is the occasion of a large proportion of the crime which is committed.'

    Elsewhere (1883, II, 165), he wrote that 'The reason why ordinary drunkenness is no excuse for crime is that the offender did wrong in getting drunk.' It is necessary to establish a prior fault requirement because intoxication otherwise provides a genuine ground for saying that the accused was unconscious when he acted.

    A similar issue arises in relation to the law of mens rea where the parallel claim is that the intoxicated person failed to form the intention for the crime. The law's response (*Majewski* (1976)) is to permit intoxication to negate mens rea in relation to some offences but not others. A shadowy and unsatisfactory distinction is drawn between offences of basic and specific intent to rationalise a policy response, and an uncertain concept of prior fault is employed in place of mens rea to legitimate the denial of the defence in offences of basic intent. See Norrie (1991, 170–3, 181–3) for discussion of *Majewski*, and Lacey, Wells and Meure (1990, ch 3) for broader discussion of the interplay between politics, social policy and law in this area. For detailed reflection on a necessarily troubled area of the law, see Smith and Hogan (1999, 219–30).

10  Thus in relation to addiction, the addict can be blamed for 'letting himself go' in the first place. The argument is originally Aristotle's (1955, 90–1). For discussion, see Gordon (1978, 56–7).

11  Words can mean what one likes, but this is an unusual definition of a voluntary act! Compare Windeyer J's analysis with the more sober dissenting view of Barwick J.

12  Williams (1983, 148): 'If there is an act, someone acts; but if there is an omission, everyone (in a sense) omits. We omit to do everything in the world that is not done.' This goes too far, however, in that it fails to distinguish things that we could do from those things that it would be beyond our powers to do.

13  '... deviation from [humanly contrived normal conditions] will be regarded as exceptional and so rank as the cause of harm. It is obvious that in such cases what is selected as the cause from the total set of conditions will often be an omission which coincides with what is reprehensible by established standards of behaviour and may be inhibited by punishment' (Hart and Honoré, 1985, 38).

14  Hart and Honoré would not accept the terminology of proximate cause, but the analysis is in their spirit.

15  I focus on the need for a duty concept to provide a socio-political 'fix' for the potential results of a Hart-Honoré moral-common sense analysis. There are other reasons why a duty concept is valid. One

is that, as a matter of phenomenological description, it is sensible to talk of the person who is required to act in order to avoid omission liability as operating under an obligation, or duty to act. Another is that there is one category of omissions, so-called role omissions, where the holder of an office is duty bound to act in certain ways by virtue of tenure. It would be circumlocutory to describe such institutionally created duties in causation terms. On role omissions, see Honderich, 1980, 66–7.

16 See the discussion of Macauley at pp 124–5, 128–9, and also Stephen (1883, III, 10). For a defence, see Williams (1991, 88).

17 Like that endorsed by modern communitarian philosophy. See Ashworth (1989, 424; Lacey, 1988) and pp 128–31.

18 On the historical contribution of the British East India Company to starvation and the 'crime problem' in India, see Arnold (1985).

19 '. . . every legal duty is founded on a moral obligation . . . The prisoner was under a moral obligation to the deceased from which arose a legal duty towards her' (*Instan* (1893) at 453–4).

20 Hawkins J, who joined with Lord Coleridge's judgment, had suggested to defence counsel that the relationship amounted to an implied contract.

21 Glazebrook (1960, 407) suggests that the earlier Assize case of *Nicholls* (1874) is more important because there it was held that a destitute grandmother, who had taken in her grandchild and then neglected him, could owe a duty of care, yet there was no consideration in this case. This takes the contractual point too narrowly. There remained the fact that the grandmother had consciously taken the child in, and undertaken to care for him. Thus there was an analogy with the commitment required in a contract, if not the consideration.

22 Cf *R v Gibbins and Proctor* (1918), in which the female defendant was convicted of murdering her male partner's child by neglect on the basis of a duty of care impliedly undertaken by living with the man and taking money from him for food. It is noteworthy that in the explicit contract case of *Pittwood*, discussed below, both *Nicholls* and *Instan* are cited as authority for the duty principle arising out of a contract.

23 An effect of this Act was to provide a lesser offence of wilful neglect of a child which could be used in what would otherwise have to be a manslaughter case, although it is hard to see how the two levels of offence are distinguished, either on mens rea or actus reus terms. In *R v Lowe* (1973), the court distinguished a situation of wilful neglect resulting in death from manslaughter by omission by arguing that there was a clear distinction between acts of commission and omission for the purposes of liability. This argument does not hold: see Ashworth (1991, 263).

24 Lord Diplock expressly recommends the duty theory against the alternative 'continuing act' theory that had been espoused in the comparable case of *Fagan* (1969).

25 How far does the blood relationship go? Is the occupation of the room conjunctive or disjunctive with the blood relationship? If the two elements are conjunctive, does it mean that a blood relation living next door will not have a duty? Or that a close friend living under the same roof will not? See Ashworth (1989, 441–3).

26 Because the court uses evidence of practically undertaken chores as evidence of a commitment to carry them out, the defendant would have been best advised to do *nothing* to help the sister. This is the logical, though morally counterintuitive, result of deducing the latter illegitimately from the former.

27 Ashworth (1989), who also argues for a duty to take reasonable steps towards law enforcement. See Williams's (1991) response for the social and political issues raised by this.

28 But cf Weinrib (1980), and Feinberg (1984) who make the same argument through an extension of liberal individualist philosophy.

29 This is also Ashworth's (1989, 455) solution. It is hard to see why couching the matter in terms of 'no unreasonable risk' would make matters clearer than determining whether the risk was reasonable or not.

30 Cf Ashworth (1989, 442). The French *Code Penal*'s qualification to the duty of assistance cited by Ashworth (1989, 449) does not appear to meet this problem.

31 A parallel would be 'gross negligence' in manslaughter where precisely the concern is the 'at large' quality of the offence (see Chapter 4, pp 66–9), or, in relation to the law of theft, the definition of 'dishonesty' which is also left open (see Chapter 3, pp 41–3). The problem also has a parallel in the law relating to moral involuntariness (see the judgment of Dickson J in *Perka* (1984), above, p 114).

32 Similar forms of closure or 'fixing' of the forms of causation are explored in the following chapter.

33 The classical theoretical illustration of this process is the drift to authoritarianism in the Hegelian philosophy of punishment (Norrie, 1991, ch 5).

## Chapter 7: Causation

1   The other example, medical maltreatment, is discussed at p 146.
2   The Law Commission say (1989, 156): 'The refusal of the transfusion may be unforeseen by D and not reasonably foreseeable, but it is not sufficient in itself to cause death. *The death would not have occurred without the wound inflicted by D*' (emphasis added). In other words, this is a case of 'but for' causation.
3   One answer, though I shall argue an inadequate one, is given by Hart and Honoré (1985, 361), who claim that the relevant consideration is whether or not the victim's act was voluntary. The relevant case, *Blaue* (1975), is also discussed at p 143.
4   'Here is a capitalist among these antecedents; he shall be forced to pay' (quoted in Horwitz, 1982, 205).
5   Holmes, for example, recognised 'the inclination of a very large part of the community . . . to make certain classes of persons insure the safety of those with whom they deal' (quoted in Horwitz, 1982, 211).
6   See Chapter 2 and Chapter 10.
7   In criminal law, these questions are relegated to the philosophy of punishment, and in particular the never-ending philosophical debate about freewill and determinism: see eg Moore (1985); Fletcher (1978, 798–817), Norrie (2000, 105–7). They also crop up in different ways but are suppressed, through the legal attitude to motive (see Chapter 3); and they emerge through the excuses of necessity and duress, where they must be controlled (see Chapter 8).
8   For a helpful review of Hart and Honoré's work from a tort perspective, see Stapleton (1988).
9   At this point, a functionalist defence of legal practice may be offered which rests its case on the very fact that law is just one form of social control among many that happens to adopt an individualist approach (Fletcher, 1978, 800; Moore, 1985, 1144–8). The question, however, is not about what the law does, but whether it is justified in doing it.
10  Compare the approach here with the narrow conception of involuntariness in the law of acts (see pp 112–14). The reason for this different broader approach in the law of causation is discussed in the concluding section.
11  I use this term in the sense of indicating the interconnectedness of social relations, not in the Hart and Honoré sense of individuals providing opportunities for others to do wrong (1985, 51–9). Their sense of the term implies the legal model of a pair of isolated individuals interacting with each other, not of individuals located in particular social contexts, structures and relations independent of their own making.
12  Surely it would depend on our perspective in asking the question, as above, in considering what is normal and abnormal.
13  At one point, Hart and Honoré rely upon what they concede is a 'vague common-sense distinction' between accelerating and causing death (1985, 344–5).
14  Either directly in the case of physical self-preservation (1985, 330–3), or indirectly, as in 'inter-personal transactions' (1985, 51–7).
15  And likely to be used. Suppose an accused had planted a bomb leading to the death of a bomb disposal expert who had been warned of the danger of entering the building where the bomb was located. Given the attitude of the courts to this situation in the law of intention to murder (see Chapter 3, pp 52–5), it seems unlikely that the latter's acts would be interpreted as voluntary and breaking the causal chain.
16  Hart and Honoré also discuss a Rhodesian case, *McEnery* (1943), in which a white man entered a rail carriage reserved for blacks and began to assault them. One jumped from the train and was killed, the court holding that because he was surrounded by other blacks, his fear and need for self-preservation were ungrounded, and that therefore the causal nexus was broken. As with the example of molested women, the result of the causal inquiry depends not simply on causation, but upon an ability or desire, in this case lacking, to empathise with the position of the victim.
17  For murder on a felony-murder doctrine, for a lesser form of homicide in its absence.
18  This formulation was supported by the Court of Appeal in *Pagett* (1983). The subsequent finding in a civil action (*Guardian* 4, 5 December 1990) that the police had been negligent in their handling of the siege in which Gail Kinchen died reveals the two-sided character of the causation issue in this case. Looked at narrowly, Pagett did use Gail Kinchen as a hostage and fire a shot to which the police responded but, more broadly, the police actions can be interpreted as caused by their own negligent handling of the siege, removing the element of justifiability from their actions and negating the

imputation of causation to Pagett. Ultimately the causation issue can only be solved by a political judgment.

19 It is interesting to think how a court following Hart and Honoré might deal with a case in which the victim belonged to a religious sect so eccentric as to be on the furthest fringe of religious life. Would they accept the idea that such a person was 'bound' by principles that appeared quite bizarre? If not, why not? Another problem would be raised in a situation where a child of a member of a sect had been stabbed, but had only died through the refusal by an informed parent to allow medical treatment. On the law of homicide, such a refusal would be intentional and voluntary, so that the parent would be responsible for the child's death. Would the original assailant also be responsible through inter alia the causation rules? If the answer on *Blaue* is yes, then it would mean that the parents' actions were voluntary vis-à-vis their own liability, and involuntary vis-à-vis the assailants.

20 There is a tension in Hart and Honoré (1985, 356, 361) in their discussion of *Smith* and *Blaue*. They describe the court's method in the former, apparently supportively, as a 'common-sense causal approach', whereas in relation to *Blaue*, they write: 'The fact that the physical process started by accused (bleeding) continued up to the moment of death is not conclusive. What if . . . the doctor had refused to administer [treatment], saying that he preferred to play a round of golf, so that the victim died? In that case, . . . the bleeding would have continued until death but death would surely have been caused by the doctor's callousness, not the original wound' (1985, 361).

This example shows that *Smith*'s commonsense causal approach is not enough to conclude the imputation of causation where there is maltreatment. There can be further questions, discounted in *Smith*, concerning the nature of the medical negligence.

21 '. . . what is taken as normal for the purpose of the distinction between cause and mere conditions is very often an artefact of human habit, custom, or convention . . . [of] developed customary techniques, procedures, and routines to counteract . . . harm . . . When such man-made normal conditions are established, deviation from them will be regarded as exceptional and so rank as the cause of the harm' (1985, 37).

22 If a death from a wound had occurred during an ambulance strike because the troops used in substitution for the regular ambulance crews had got lost in the streets of London, would the assailant have been causally responsible? Presumably he would on *Smith*, but the case is eminently arguable on the Hart and Honoré principles.

23 The detaching of probability from foreseeability in the argument makes for a very broad rule of causation excluding many situations that would otherwise be seen as involving supervening cause. Cf Williams (1989, 402–4).

24 Cf Hart and Honoré (1985, 3–5), who argue that vague language like this obscures genuine principles which they uncover. The Law Commission remains content with the language the courts have provided.

25 One abiding memory of first year undergraduate criminal law for me was my feeling of the harshness of this rule. Cf Stapleton (1988, 130–1).

26 This is even more the case where in a New Zealand case, *Storey* ((1931); 1985, 347), the court was 'prepared to treat the victim's physical location as a coexisting circumstance which the wrongdoer took at his peril'. The authors cite this case without demur, despite its obvious conflict with their analysis (1985, 33–5).

# Chapter 8: Necessity and duress

1 For both sides of the argument, see Williams (1983, 588–92; cf Williams, 1982). Fletcher argues that 'So far as the defence exists in Anglo-American law, it is to be found in the interstices of particular offences . . .' (1978, 789). See also Glazebrook (1972).

2 He argues that where the actor is a third party who is not personally threatened, like a doctor aborting a foetus to save a mother's life or a policeman killing a lunatic shooting at a crowd, the question of *excuse* cannot arise: 'A finding of involuntary conduct is precluded because the actor's personal interests are not at stake.' This begs the question of how one defines 'personal interests'.

3 Discussions of Howe (J Smith, 1987; K Smith, 1989; Ashworth, 1999) suggest that the judges have moved more to a discourse of justification than excuse in this area, but this is only partly borne out by a reading of the case. It is true that Lord Hailsham talks of a 'lesser of two evils' approach. However, this is in the context of still talking of duress as a 'concession to human frailty' ((1987) at 782) and he speaks of necessity and duress situations as being ones where a 'person of ordinary

fortitude can be excused from' different types of pressure ((1987) at 777). On the other hand, it is true that he also conflates justification and excuse in his judgment ((1987) at 781). While there is confusion, the overall thrust of his argument relates to excusing, or not excusing, because of pressure to act.

4 Fletcher (1978, 826) modifies this view by seeing the decision as involving both justificatory and excusatory elements.

5 Dudley 'had, as they say in the Westerns, done what a man must do. Confronted by the dictates of necessity, he had risen to the occasion and steeled himself to the terrible act of killing the boy when his companions shrank from the deed. He had fulfilled a captain's role.' Dudley openly admitted what he had done and requested that he be allowed to keep his pen-knife (the weapon) as a memento of the act (Simpson, 1986, 89).

6 See the Home Secretary's deliberations on the matter in Simpson (1986, 246–7).

7 Baron Huddleston, who tried the case on Assize, was in fact the son of a sea captain who had risen in the world, marrying the daughter of a duke. Simpson (1986, 197) comments that such men 'sometimes fall into the tendency to reject the world out of which they have risen, and Huddleston was a snob'. A more direct connection between legal decision-making and survival cannibalism is seen in the decision ten years earlier not to prosecute a case where a wrecked boat was owned by a Conservative member of parliament notorious for the lack of safety of his ships, to avoid potential political embarrassment (Simpson, 1986, 192).

8 The same is also true in relation to necessity as justification. In Chapter 3 (see pp 36–9), I argued that the law of intention and motive excluded indigent social need and indignant claim of right. What is excluded there raises its head in relation to questions of justification (claim of right) and excuse (claim of need) in the law of necessity and duress. The two become merged in the moral defence that 'I could do no other' to a criminal charge.

9 Following Bannister and Milovanovic (1990), I draw here on the Weberian distinction between formal and substantive rationality. In several chapters (see especially Chapters 3–6) of this book, I have argued that the law's proclaimed formalism involves only an apparent exclusion of substantive moral and political arguments.

10 Lord Edmund-Davies spoke ((1971) at 180) of the 'deep depression' that anyone of 'even ordinary sympathy' would feel at the plight of the families.

11 In the contemporaneous case of *Buckoke v Greater London Council* (1971), he did suggest that in certain circumstances of necessity 'the police need not prosecute. Nor need the justices punish' ((1971) at 258). The case involved the question whether a fireman driving through a red light to a fire broke the law. Lord Denning's view was that he did (he had no defence of necessity) but that he should not be prosecuted: 'He should be congratulated'. See also above, pp44–6.

12 Dickson J follows the argument of Hart (see Chapters 1, 6, pp 11, 112).

13 See *R v Pottle and Randall* (1991) for a recent British illustration of how such a necessity defence might be used (see p 45).

14 In *Lynch*, the defendant had merely been the driver of a car, whereas in *Howe*, the accused had more actively participated in a series of horrific murders. In *Lynch* also, there was the possibility of a retrial (at which the defendant was again convicted) that did not exist in *Howe*.

15 For differing interpretations of the dicta in *Lynch* concerning the availability of the defence to an actual killer, see Lord Salmon's judgment in *Abbott v R* (1977) and Dennis (1980, 211–3).

16 An appeal to the House of Lords judiciary in their Privy Council capacity from the Court of Appeal in Trinidad and Tobago.

17 The majority never addressed the point that Smith and Hogan had made in the 1973 edition of their work (to which Lord Edmund-Davies had referred in *Lynch* ((1975) at 715)): 'The difficulty about adopting a distinction between the principal and secondary parties as a rule of law is that the contribution of the secondary party to the death may be no less significant than that of the principal.'

18 Lord Kilbrandon being the exception. See in addition to Lord Wilberforce, Lord Morris ((1975) at 670), Lord Edmund-Davies ((1975) at 709–10) and Lord Simon ((1975) at 690).

19 Wasik adds that the defence involves an 'appeal to moral notions of justice', apparently distinct from *legal* notions of justice.

20 But see at p 169 a discussion of *R v Graham* (1982).

21 For a similar argument conceptually, see Bayles (1987, 1212).

22 The passage is quoted by Lord Edmund-Davies in *Lynch* ((1975) at 709–10) without seeing its implication.

23 Williams's answer (1983, 625) is that 'Constraint is a defence only when it is of so immediate or pressing a character that it seems futile or unconscionably harsh to maintain the prohibition.' But the

examples given by Lord Simon are all of situations where the threats are of an immediate and pressing character for the individual concerned. Might not, to use Williams's own words, 'fear of economic ills' equally be immediate and pressing? Smith and Hogan implicitly acknowledge the problem by quoting Lord Simon's words without further comment, apparently thereby endorsing their logic (1988, 234).

24 On the power of the argument from terrorism to disrupt the categories of individual right, see Alldridge and Belsey (1989).

25 Cf Lord Lowry in *Gotts* ((1992) at 851): 'The defence is withheld on the ground that the crime is so odious that it must not be palliated; and yet, if circumstances are allowed to mitigate the punishment, the principle on which the defence of duress is withheld has been defeated.' What is true of a moral justification is as true of one based upon deterrence.

26 For a more detailed discussion of the decision in *Howe*, and the anomalies to which it gives rise, see Walters, 1988; Milgate, 1988; Smith and Hogan, 1999, 234–5.

27 Cf Smith (1989, 94–5).

28 'Lack of faith in the jury to detect the "bogus defence" probably lies at the root of the objective requirements. It is much the same as with mistake generally' (Smith and Hogan, 1988, 236).

29 It is an exclusion which arguably pulls most of the rug from under the 'terrorist's charter' argument which has proved so popular among the judiciary (Milgate, 1988, 72–3).

30 For further discussion of 'moral voluntariness' versus 'moral involuntariness', see Chapter 6, pp 112–15.

31 The authors point out the role of the state itself in producing this situation, making even more ambiguous the right of the state to punish. As Vandervort (1987, 219) puts it: 'Overtly political first order determinations – involving fundamental issues of social justice and affecting great numbers of persons [should] receive greater scrutiny. Judicial decisions about individual legal responsibility [should] more frequently be seen to be concerned not with individual choice alone, but *rather with the consequences of social policy mediated* by individual choice' (emphasis added).

32 Cf Naipaul (1981, 72) on Malik, the gangleader whose 'charter' was opposed by the courts in *Abbott*: 'The walls are still scrawled with the easy threats and easy promises of Black Power. The streets are still full of "hustlers" and "scrunters", words that glamourise and seem to give dispensation to those who beg and steal. Another Malik is possible.'

## Chapter 9: Insanity and diminished responsibility

1 In Britain, the trials of Dennis Nilsen and Peter Sutcliffe; in the United States, those of Mark Chapman, the killer of John Lennon, and John Hinckley, the would-be assassin of Ronald Reagan.

2 Sutcliffe knew both the nature and quality of his act, and that it was wrong according to law.

3 Compare with Lord Devlin's modern restatement (Smith and Hogan, 1999, 210): 'there is something logical – it may be astringently logical, but it is logical – in selecting as the test of responsibility to the law, reason and reason alone. It is reason which makes a man responsible to the law. It is reason which gives him sovereignty over animate and inanimate things. It is what distinguishes him from the animals, which emotional disorder does not; it is what makes him man; it is what makes him subject to the law. So it is fitting that nothing other than a defect of reason should give complete absolution.'

4 Pinel's account of insanity accompanied by lucidity was developed by Esquirol into the concept of 'monomania' – insanity that was all-consuming, but 'focused on one area of perception or action' (Smith, 1981, 36–7).

5 'The lunacy statutes gave medical men special rights and duties to certify insanity. Logically speaking, the same powers should have existed in the criminal law: if civil law accepted that alienists had valid empirical means of identifying insanity, then the same resources existed for the criminal law. However, this deduction was not often drawn, not even by alienists. Jurists certainly treated lunacy legislation and criminal law as having different existences without comparable internal logic and procedure' (Smith, 1981, 70).

6 'The law may be perfect but how is it that whenever a case for its application arises it proves to be of no avail? We have seen the trials of Oxford and MacNaughten conducted by the ablest lawyers of the day – and they *allow* and *advise* the Jury to pronounce the verdict of not guilty on account of insanity, whilst *everybody* is morally convinced that both malefactors were perfectly conscious and aware of what they did' (quoted in Walker (1968, 188)). The Queen's final comment captures the essence of the legal definition of insanity, expressed in the M'Naghten Rules.

7    'At any rate it is the sort of disease for which a person should be detained in hospital rather than be given an unqualified acquittal' (1961, 534).

8    'The purpose of the legislation relating to the defence of insanity, ever since its origin in 1800, has been to protect society against recurrence of the dangerous conduct' ((1983) at 677).

9    This distinction was drawn for the same reason that morally good motive is excluded from the law: that it might allow the insane person to claim a higher (albeit insane) morality as a justification for breaking the known law of the land (Walker, 1968, 115). The absurdity of the distinction is seen in this comment (Fitzgerald, 1982) on the conviction of Peter Sutcliffe: 'One might suppose that the [right/wrong] exception would extend to those who, like Sutcliffe, believe they are acting under God's commands. Not so! English law defines knowledge of what is wrong as knowledge that what one is doing is against the law of the land – on the quaint assumption that those who are so un-English as to put the edicts of God before the law of the land must be not mad but very wicked' (cf Stephen, 1883, II, 167).

10   ' "Mental responsibility" . . . is either a concept of law or a concept of morality; it is not a clinical fact relating to the defendant . . . It seems odd that psychiatrists should be asked and agree to testify as to legal and moral responsibility. It is even more surprising that courts are prepared to hear that testimony' (Committee on Mentally Abnormal Offenders, 1975, 242; see also Wootton, 1960).

11   'The step between "he did not resist his impulse" and "he could not resist his impulse" is . . . one . . . which the jury can only approach in a broad, common-sense way' (Lord Parker in *Byrne* (1960) at 5).

12   The conflict is explained by Smith (1981, 108): 'Alienists used "irresistible impulse" as a physiological term. In court it became a legal term and inevitably sounded like dangerous nonsense.'

13   As one Canadian judge put it, 'If you cannot resist an impulse in any other way, we will hang a rope in front of your eyes, and perhaps that will help' (quoted in Smith and Hogan, 1999, 205).

14   This formulation compounds the difficulties of interpretation because Lord Parker insists that he is referring to the 'popular' definition of insanity – whatever that might be. Perhaps the aim was, in the light of the confusion of legal and psychiatric concepts, to resolve the issue by means of gut reaction, in 'a broad common-sense way' (*Byrne* (1960) at 5).

15   'Inability to exercise will-power to control physical acts . . . is . . . sufficient to entitle the accused to the benefit of the section; difficulty in controlling his acts . . . may be' (*Byrne* (1960) at 5).

16   Smith and Hogan (1999, 214) note that the test is one of moral responsibility. 'A man whose impulse is irresistible bears *no* moral responsibility for his act, for he has no choice; a man whose impulse is much more difficult to resist than that of an ordinary man bears a diminished degree of moral responsibility for his act.' The odd fact is that *both* these conditions are treated as ones of *diminished* responsibility. See further Sparks, 1964, 16; Walker, 1968, 162; Moore, 1984, 355–6.

17   Compare the facts in the case of the sexual psychopath Byrne with those in the case of *Price* (*Times*, 22 Dec 1971). Price placed his severely handicapped son on a river and watched him float away. His 'sentence' was to 'undergo treatment as a doctor may prescribe for the next few weeks or so'. The child functioned only as a baby and had not long to live. See Dell (1984), and Williams (1983, 692–4) for further examples.

18   Cf Griew (1988, 78): 'The responses of the judges and the psychiatrists to section 2 have ranged from the very generous to the very strict – to an extent that might attract any of the epithets "flexible", "pragmatic" or "undisciplined", according to taste.'

19   For a helpful account of the historical development of psychiatry, see Miller (1986). As Unsworth has shown (1987), the late fifties represented the high water mark of psychiatric power and influence in mental health legislation. The recognition of the diminished responsibility defence in the criminal law is paralleled in the civil field by the Mental Health Act 1959.

20   The Model Penal Code of the American Law Institute, s 4.01 provides that: 'A person is not responsible for criminal conduct if at the time of such conduct as a result of mental disease or defect he lacks substantial capacity either to appreciate the criminality (wrongfulness) of his conduct *or to conform his conduct to the requirements of law*' (emphasis added).

21   For the libertarian critique of the 'authoritarian state', see Kittrie (1971); for an equally telling critique of the implications of the alternative juridical regime, see Rose (1986).

22   Thus a bad social background is as criminogenic a factor as mental disease, if not more so: Morris (1982, 61–4).

23   For philosophical discussion of the general issues raised for criminal responsibility by the free will/ determinism debate, see Hook (1961); Moore (1997, ch 12). I argue that the general debate involves a partial and one-sided understanding of human life which arises from the polarisation of concepts brought about by an abstract concept of freedom. To the idea of the ideally free 'man', there could only be opposed the idea of the concretely determined personality (Norrie, 2000, 105–7, 229).

24 There has been a somewhat similar conjunction of interests in relation to sentencing: see Chapter 10.

25 For discussion of these developments, and their relationship with the reform process in England, see Mackay (1987; 1988). 'Guilty But Mentally Ill' is interesting in that it offers a finding other than insanity where the accused is mentally ill but not legally insane. It has some of the characteristics of diminished responsibility, but because it provides an alternative to people 'getting off' through insanity pleas, it is actually used to maintain or increase, not mitigate, punishment: Mackay (1988, 92).

26 For an account of the trial, see Bland (1984, ch 8). For a critical psychiatrist's view, see Bennett-Levy, 1981.

27 Reflecting this conflict, Smith and Hogan (1988, 200) suggest that it is 'perhaps not obvious that D should have a defence to a charge of robbing a bank or reckless driving because he had a jealous delusional belief that his wife was committing adultery', although they also acknowledge that if the delusional belief reflects severe mental illness, the accused is set apart from the rest of humankind in terms of responsibility. They then wonder whether the main problem might not be what constitutes 'severe mental illness'. The more fundamental question, however, is whether conviction is to be decided on a psychiatric test of illness, or a legal test of responsibility. Butler is controversial because it opts for the former. See now Smith and Hogan, 1999, 209.

28 'Some people . . . take the view that it would be wrong in principle that a person should escape conviction if, although severely mentally ill, *he has committed a rational crime which was uninfluenced by his illness* and for which he ought to be liable to be punished' (Law Commission, 1989, 11.16) (emphasis added).

29 A second crucial issue that is not focused on here is that of how some groups such as women or black people are more prone to being labelled as mentally ill, and how psychiatric knowledge is constructed differently in relation to questions of class, race and gender. The same forces of power and inequality operate not only to structure life chances, but also the knowledges that seek to explain their effects (Edwards, 1981; Allen, 1986; Mercer, 1986).

30 Criminal Law Revision Committee (1980, para 102), but the Committee linked the question of social pressure to 'hormonal and other bodily changes' after birth. As O'Donovan (1984, 263) explains, this was necessary: '*to enable the court to take account of socio-economic factors*, the medical model was retained' (emphasis added).

31 A comparable use of the diminished responsibility plea is provided by the issue of pre-menstrual tension: *Sandie Smith* (1982), and see Edwards (1988). Luckhaus (1985) argues that while PMT, like infanticide, has been constructed by the medical profession and imposed upon women, it does reflect, in distorted fashion, real experience.

32 Some suggest, eg Dell (1984), that the only raison d'être of the diminished responsibility defence is to get around the mandatory sentence for murder; were that to be abolished, it would no longer be required because disposal would be left to the discretion of the judge. The removal of the issue to the sentencing stage would not resolve it, it would obscure it within a comforting blanket of discretion. The rigidity of the mandatory punishment for murder at least forces the law to articulate its conditions of responsibility (to a limited extent: cf Williams, 1983, 689–70).

33 For discussion of this case, see Burn (1984).

34 Box's position (1983, 150, 161) is summarised in his quotation from the work of Clark and Lewis (1977): 'The socialisation of both men and women takes coercive sexuality as the normal standard of sexual behaviour. Men are expected to apply a certain amount of pressure to have women submit ('agree') to sexual intercourse, and women are expected to resist such pressure, whatever their own desires might happen to be. Men are expected to be sexually dominant and to initiate sexual activity; women are expected to be somewhat passive and to agree to sex reluctantly. Understandably, those men who most strongly identify masculinity with sexual dominance and aggression are not likely to see any difference between what they call seduction and women call rape.' See also Lacey and Wells (1998, ch 4).

35 For a broader discussion of different kinds of sexual crime, see Cameron and Frazer (1987). Their thesis is that such crime is essentially gendered, something that men do to women, children and other men. There is no cultural code which provides the space within which such crime could be committed by a woman (although this could change: see 1987, 176). For discussion of the case of Myra Hindley, as a potential exception, see (1987, 144–8). See also Skrapec (1993).

36 This was made vivid by the response of a section of the football crowd at Leeds to the news that Sutcliffe had killed again (chants of 'Ripper 13, police 0' and 'There's Only One Yorkshire Ripper'). Consider also the statements of police and the Attorney-General, Sir Michael Havers, at the trial which implied that the death of prostitutes was less tragic than the death of his other victims: 'Some

were prostitutes, but perhaps the saddest part of the case is that some were not. The last six attacks were on totally respectable women' (see Bland, 1984).

37 See note 35 above. It is likely that the social-cultural pattern of abuse is directly linked to the individual's psychological problem. Cameron and Frazer interpret Burn (1984) to locate Sutcliffe's condition in the tension between the misogyny and machismo of the area in which he grew up, and personal anxieties about gender and masculinity from his childhood. See also Smith (1989, 147–50) for a similar argument. There is inevitably an element of speculation in such accounts, but they indicate a more plausible starting-point for enquiry than, for example, consideration of Sutcliffe's biogenetic make-up.

38 Cameron and Frazer's argument primarily addresses sexual crime at the social level, although they touch on the question of what social-psychological factors transform a person into a mad sex criminal. They relate Sutcliffe's problems to the gender conflicts inherent in his life and family. In relation to another case, however, they come close to following a rather 'juridical' model by suggesting that a man *decides* to become a sex-killer (while acknowledging that the choice is constrained by social structures: 1987, 116). This suggests too much that the decision to become a sex killer is as normal as the decision to steal a car. Because society provides scripts for sex killing to occur, we can say that sex killing is normal in our society. That does not mean to say that the individual sex killer is normal. Sutcliffe may have looked like anyone else, and not fitted the image of a beast, but that surely does not mean to say that he *was* like anyone else.

39 Even so resolute a defender of the legal approach as a realistic account of human conduct as Moore (1984, 47, 112) is forced to admit that it is 'radically incomplete'.

40 Although psychiatry must avoid the charge that some of its categorisations of behaviour involve a narrow, ethnocentric or sexist viewpoint (Allen, 1986; Mercer, 1986).

41 This is recognised to be the case in relation to psychopathy, but is also so in relation to other forms of madness such as schizophrenia, as the Sutcliffe case makes clear. See for general discussion Fulford, 1993.

42 Mention should be made here of one exemplary analysis of mad crime. In his account of Dennis Nilsen, convicted of murdering fifteen young men in London in the early 1980s, Brian Masters (1985) reflects on the failure of any of the available theories, medical or moral, to explain how a man like Nilsen became a mass murderer. His answer, the 'untutored intuition of a novelist', returns him to certain threads running through Nilsen's life. For Nilsen, the concepts of love and death were inextricably entangled. He sought love, but could only find it in the killing of young men and the care of their corpses. For Masters, the symbolic significance of this conjunction returns him, as it returned Nilsen, to the death of his grandfather, and the love, and the guilt about that love, that he felt:

'Andrew Whyte was the one love of Nilsen's infancy. The boy's last view of the loved object was as a body, which he only gradually perceived to be dead . . . Whyte was "parent" to Dennis Nilsen as no other member of the family had been. I believe that he never ceased wanting to be "like" him, as a demonstration of love, and that when Andrew Whyte was dead, the only way that Nilsen could still "feel" that love was in simulating his own death, and finally the death of others. The idea of death resurrected the idea of love as nothing else could. When simulation ceased, and reality took over, his behaviour towards the corpses of his victims (in the immediate aftermath) was that of an affectionate parent . . . Andrew Whyte had been a seafaring man, absent for long periods and frequently. Each departure must have seemed like a death to the child, and each return a renewal of love. Unable to accept that final departure meant the disappearance, for ever, of love, the boy morbidly clung to its last manifestation in the coffin, the last return' (Masters, 1985, 295).

The matter is inevitably more complex than this, and the analysis speculative, but Masters's sensitive analysis links Nilsen's emergent mentality to a context of paternal desertion and maternal distance in an isolated, lonely and fatalistic fishing community. He provides an account at the level of social psychology that links a set of preoccupations to a social world that shaped them and gave them their logic. His approach is far removed from the preoccupations of orthodox psychiatry or the judgments of law and conventional morality. It identifies Nilsen as neither mad nor bad, but as a person who is in many ways like the rest of us, and it explores the crucial intermediate link between individual mind and society, without reducing the analysis one way or the other.

43 Psychiatry has its beginning in the Enlightenment asylum, but develops its current medical form in the second half of the nineteenth century. This discussion of the (limited) 'socialisation' of individual problems is pursued in Chapter 10, pp 214–18.

44 Criminal Procedure (Insanity) Act 1964, s 5 as amended by the Criminal Procedure (Insanity and Unfitness to Plead) Act 1991, s 3. The recent reform of the law has introduced flexibility into dispositions after an insanity verdict except where there is a mandatory life sentence.

## Chapter 10: Sentencing

1 Discretion operates widely both before and after the criminal trial: 'the rules are no more than a thin spreading of jam between two thick slices of scarcely controlled discretion: the prosecutor's and the sentencer's' (Glazebrook, 1991, 33). The criminal law establishes a framework of maximum sentences for different crimes, but discretion within the maxima is broad.

2 Although it is apparently not an aim incorporated in the new Criminal Justice Act 1991. I discuss this at pp 207, 219–20.

3 On the panopticon and 'panopticism', see Foucault (1979). Foucault contrasts the disciplinary character of the closed institution, designed to regulate and individuate a recalcitrant population that is the object of control, with the concept of the free juridical subject. The Enlightenment gave birth both to a juridical ideology of the subject, and, as its 'dark' side, to the disciplinary techniques, of which the panopticon is representative. 'Panopticism' creates the space for forms of knowledge and control based upon appraisal of the character and condition of individuals though, as Garland (1985) points out, it took a change in the nature and function of the state at the end of the nineteenth century to develop the techniques that would fill it.

4 Nor, it should be noted, is there any special deterrent value in capital punishment: Walker and Padfield (1996, 96). In this chapter, I discuss punishment in the context of imprisonment as the most serious available punishment. For detailed consideration of custodial and non-custodial sentences, see Walker and Padfield (1996, Part III) and Ashworth (2000).

5 Ashworth (1992, 213–15). For general discussions, see Walker and Padfield (1996, ch 7); Brody (1976); Beyleveld (1980). A very useful brief summary is provided by Brody (1979).

6 Such crimes have accompanied attempts to deter by increased policing in inner city areas since the early 1980s: see Lord Scarman (1981). This was notoriously the case in the 1980s riots in Los Angeles (see Davies with Ruddick, 1988).

7 Nor is this to deny that there are individuals who commit crimes for individual 'pathological' reasons, although the connection between such reasons and the broader social context must itself be explored: see Chapter 9.

8 Garland describes the 'underclass' for whom penality operated in late Victorian times thus: 'Excluded by laws and property, marginalised by the labour market and political forces, this class stood outside respectable Victorian society, devoid of social attachment and the constraint it entails.' The modern link between crime, marginalisation and deprivation is sometimes made by senior police officers: see 'Imbert Links Crime Rise to Deprivation', *Guardian*, 30 July 1992.

9 A journalist in the United States quotes a conversation with a policeman following the capture of a young black man who has stolen his car: 'These people don't care if they're in jail or outside. It's all the same to them' (*Observer*, 30 July 1992).

10 Halevy (1972, 14–18) notes the existence of two standpoints in Bentham's work with regard to the question of social order. When discussing questions of political economy, he tended to the view that individual interests would naturally cohere ('the natural identity of interests'); but when discussing social questions, he tended to deny this in favour of the need for state regulation ('the artificial identity of interests').

11 Although a good part of the twentieth-century debate within the philosophy of punishment has been devoted to finding ways of avoiding this conclusion: see Norrie, 1991, ch 6; cf Lacey, 1988, ch 2.

12 On *Cunningham*, see further pp 219–20.

13 In this Section I focus on modern, policy-oriented positions informed by classical thinking, especially the work of Von Hirsch (1986a; 1986b). For a sympathetic but rigorous critique, see Ashworth (1989). Ashworth (1992, 2000) is constructed on a 'just deserts' foundation. For discussion of the development and decline of the classical retributive theory of punishment, and the historical roots of its trajectory, see Norrie (1991, chs 2–5). For a philosophical argument with and against Kant, see Norrie (2000, chs 1 and 9).

14 Criminal Justice Act 1991, ss 1, 2. The White Paper (1990) on which the Act is based enunciates a retributive philosophy. In the first edition of his work on sentencing, Ashworth (1983, 450) concluded that 'In short, the sentencing process is a disgrace to the common law tradition.' In his second edition (1992, 25–30), he notes some improvement in the judicial approach and expresses a measure of optimism that, with the Criminal Justice Act 1991, the system is moving in the right direction by prioritising one aim, proportionality, over a mix of aims. However, he still sees the judiciary as a potential obstacle to a more rational sentencing system (1992, ch 12). The latest edition is thematically similar, with the 1991 Act seen as a landmark, but let down by the absence of a transmission

mechanism to communicate to the judiciary. The new Sentencing Advisory Panel might assist this. The process is however strongly influenced by the impact of populist political strategies (2000, 357–62). I argue that the latter does not help, but is not the main problem (pp 218–21).

15  For discussion of similar moves in Canada, Australia and Scandinavia, see Ashworth (2000, 348–57).

16  'When . . . I enact a penal law against myself as a criminal it is the pure juridical legislative reason (homo noumenon) in me that submits myself to the penal law as a person capable of committing a crime, as another person (homo phaenomenon) along with all the others in the civil union who submit themselves to this law' (Kant, 1965, 105). For extended analysis and discussion of this issue, see Norrie, 1991, ch 3.

17  The attempt to establish 'a just system of criminal justice in an unjust society is a contradiction in terms' (American Friends Service Committee, 1971, 6). If, instead of following simply the legal categories of fault, one applies this insight by arguing that economic and social factors in offending should be taken into account in determining culpability (Ashworth, 1992, 117), the nature of the social distribution of processed criminality in Western societies would mean that one's theory of culpability would be swallowed up by one's theory of excuse.

18  Ashworth (1989, 354) makes the same argument more fully when he writes that 'one answer to those who complain that it is impossible to propound a "just deserts" approach to sentencing in the context of a fundamentally unjust society is that they misunderstand the function of sentencing. It should not be, and cannot be, a primary instrument of social reform. Sentencing is a public quantification of the individual offender's blameworthiness, determined according to acceptable standards of proportionality.' But precisely the same problem of how one *gauges* individual blameworthiness remains; to do so according to legal, not social, criteria, is to make a choice, not an argument.

19  Another effect of this approach to sentencing may well be that it simply relocates the operation of the discretionary power that used to accrue to sentencers to the plea and charge bargaining stages of the system (Tonry, 1987).

20  For analysis of the effect of this failure through the Victorian corruption of the classical retributive account of punishment, see Norrie (1991, ch 5).

21  As Garland (1985, part III) has shown, there was a substantial gap between the programme and the practice, in which compromise with existing legal approaches was normal. Compare with the discussion of the relationship between lawyers and doctors in Chapter 9.

22  Thus Foucault (1979, 264–8) lists a range of criticisms of prisons that appeared as early as 1820–45 and are still relevant today: prisons do not diminish crime rates; the quantity of crime remains the same or increases; detention causes recidivism; prisons actively produce disrespect for law; prisons encourage the organisation of delinquency; prisons stigmatise the criminal; prisons break up families.

23  This is sometimes called the 'beckoning candle philosophy', expressed by one judge thus: 'What I look for are signs of a present intention to avoid crime and a glimmer of a prospect that in the long, if not the short, run that intention will be fulfilled – not necessarily without lapses on the road.' ('The Beckoning Candle Philosophy', *Guardian*, 7 February 1990).

24  For discussion of the roots of this bifurcatory trajectory in criminological positivism on the one hand and 1970s penal policy on the other, see Bottoms (1977).

25  A rate of between 55% and 70% on one review of the literature (Bottoms, 1977, 80). According to Von Hirsch's analysis (1986a, ch 11) of one politically important American study in the 1980s, which reported a high degree of predictive success, the false positive rate was actually 56%. See also Ashworth, 2000, 68–70.

26  Thus in the study discussed by Von Hirsch (1986a), the factors used to predict dangerousness were prior conviction for same offence, incarceration for more than half of the preceding two years, conviction before the age of 16, time served in a state juvenile facility, previous drug use, and poor employment record. These factors do not individualise the delinquent, they describe a life pattern for a substantial proportion of the so-called 'underclass' in the United States.

27  An anonymous judge, quoted in 'The Beckoning Candle Philosophy', *Guardian*, 7 February 1990.

28  Actually, this is harder than might be thought because very little information is collected or published on these matters. One study in 1972 found that about a third were homeless, while the last jobs of three-quarters of the prisoners had been manual work. Only 35% were described as having stable work histories. Figures in 1986 showed that the proportion of black people in prison is about twice their proportion in society at large. There is also a high level of mental disorder: see Stern, 1987, 23–5). See also J Murphy, 1979, 113, who quotes the 1967 United States President's Commission on Law Enforcement and Administration of Justice: 'From the arrest records, probation reports and prison statistics a portrait of the offender emerges that progressively highlights the disadvantaged

character of his life. The offender at the end of the road in prison is likely to be a member of the lowest social and economic groups in the country, poorly educated and perhaps unemployed . . .' In the United States, after decades of cutting American welfare and urban aid programmes, this portrait is no different, though the amount of violent, and drug related, crime rises (Davies with Ruddock, 1988), as does the level of imprisonment. American society's, and, through the Supreme Court, the law's predominant response appears to be an increase in 'blaming the victim' for victimising others through the facilitation of 'assembly line' capital punishment that does not exclude the mentally subnormal, the mad, and children of 15 years of age at the time of their crime (*Panorama*, BBC Television, 3 August 1992).

## Chapter 11: Conclusion

1    Bhaskar (1979, 37) defines a praxiology as: 'a normative theory of efficient action, generating a set of techniques for achieving given ends, rather than as an explanatory theory capable of casting light on actual empirical episodes.'

His examples are forms of knowledge such as neo-classical economic theory, rational and public choice theories in the social sciences, utilitarian and liberal theory in the political sciences. Many of these theories share much in common with orthodox liberal legal theory. They all seek to explain and guide action individualistically while bracketing off historically given social relations, or denying their importance for the understanding of how economic, political and social relations actually operate.

# Bibliography

Alldridge, P and C Belsey (1989) 'Murder Under Duress: Terrorism and the Criminal Law' 2 *International Journal for the Semiotics of Law* 223

Allen, H (1986) 'Psychiatry and the Construction of the Feminine' in P Miller and N Rose *The Power of Psychiatry* Oxford, Blackwell

Allen, H (1988) 'One Law for All Reasonable Persons?' 16 *Internal Journal of the Sociology of Law* 419

American Friends Service Commission (1971) *Struggle for Justice* New York, Hill and Wang

Aristotle (1955) *Nichomachean Ethics* Harmondsworth, Penguin

Arlidge, A (2000) 'The Trial of Dr David Moor' *Criminal Law Review* 31

Arnold, D (1985) 'Crime and Crime Control in Madras, 1858–1947' in A Yang *Crime and Criminality in British India* Tucson, University of Arizona Press

Ashworth, A (1978) 'The Making of the English Criminal Law (4): Blackstone, Foster and East' *Criminal Law Review* 389

Ashworth, A (1983) *Sentencing and Penal Policy* London, Weidenfeld and Nicholson

Ashworth, A (1989) 'Criminal Justice and Deserved Sentences' *Criminal Law Review* 340

Ashworth, A (1989) 'The Scope of Criminal Liability for Omissions' 84 *Law Quarterly Review* 424

Ashworth, A (1991) *Principles of the Criminal Law* Oxford, Oxford University Press

Ashworth, A (1992) *Sentencing and Criminal Justice* London, Weidenfeld and Nicolson

Ashworth, A (1996) 'Criminal Liability in a Medical Context: the Treatment of Good Intentions' in A Simester and A T H Smith *Harm and Culpability* Oxford, Oxford University Press

Ashworth, A (1999) *Principles of the Criminal Law* (3rd edn) Oxford, Oxford University Press

Ashworth, A (2000) *Sentencing and Criminal Justice* (3rd edn) London, Butterworth.

Ashworth, A and E Steiner (1990) 'Criminal Omissions and Public Duties: the French Experience' 10 *Legal Studies* 153

Austin, J (1869) *Lectures on Jurisprudence* London, John Murray

Bannister, S and D Milovanovic (1990) 'The Necessity Defence, Substantive Justice and Oppositional Linguistic Praxis' 18 *International Journal of the Sociology of Law* 179

Barthes, R (1973) *Mythologies* St Albans, Paladin

Baxter, R and C Nuttall (1975) 'Severe Sentences: No Deterrent to Crime?' 31 *New Society* 11

Bayles, M (1987) 'Reconceptualising Necessity and Duress' 33 *Wayne Law Review* 1191

Beccaria, C (1966) *On Crimes and Punishments* Indianapolis, Bobbs-Merrill

Beldam, Mr Justice (1987) 'Prospects for Codification' in I Dennis *Criminal Law and Justice* London, Sweet & Maxwell

Bennett-Levy, J (1981) 'Psychiatric Diagnosis in the Witness Box: a Postscript on the "Yorkshire Ripper" Trial' 34 *Bulletin of the British Psychological Society* 305

Bentham, J (1962) *An Introduction to the Principles of Morals and Legislation* in J Bowring *Collected Works*, vol 1, New York, Russell

Bentham, J (1975) *Theory of Legislation* New York, Oceana

Berlin, I (1958) *Two Concepts of Liberty* Oxford, Oxford University Press

Berlins, M and C Dyer 'Perverting the Course of Justice?' *The Guardian* 22 January 2001

Beyleveld, D (1980) *A Bibliography on General Deterrence Research* Westmead, Saxon House

Bhaskar, R (1976) *A Realist Theory of Science* Leeds, Leeds Books

Bhaskar, R (1979) *The Possibility of Naturalism* Brighton, Harvester

Birch, D (1988) 'The Foresight Saga' *Criminal Law Review* 4

Blackstone, W (1769) *Commentaries* vol 4

Bland, L (1984) 'The Case of the Yorkshire Ripper: Mad, Bad, Beast or Male?' in P Scraton and P Gordon *Causes for Concern* Harmondsworth, Pelican

Bottoms, A (1977) 'Reflections on the Renaissance of Dangerousness' 16 *Howard Journal of Penology and Crime Prevention* 70

Box, S (1983) *Power, Crime and Mystification* London, Tavistock

Box, S (1987) *Recession, Crime and Punishment* Basingstoke, MacMillan

Braithwaite, J (1979) *Inequality, Crime and Public Policy* London, Routledge and Kegan Paul

Brody, S (1976) 'The Effectiveness of Sentencing – a Review of the Literature' *Home Office Research Study* 35

Brody, S (1979) 'Research into the Efficacy of Deterrents' *Home Office Research Bulletin* 7, 9

Buchanan, A and G Virgo (1999) 'Duress and Mental Abnormality' *Criminal Law Review* 517

Burn, G (1984) *Somebody's Husband, Somebody's Son* London, Heinemann/Pan

Buxton, R (1988) 'Some Simple Thoughts on Intention' *Criminal Law Review* 484

Cameron, D and E Frazer (1987) *The Lust to Kill* Oxford, Polity

Canfield, G (1914) 'Corporate Responsibility for Crime' 14 *Columbia Law Review* 469

Carson, W G (1970) 'Some Sociological Aspects of Strict Liability and the Enforcement of Factory Legislation' 33 *Modern Law Review* 396

Carson, W G (1974) 'Symbolic and Instrumental Dimensions of Early Factory Legislation' in R Hood *Crime, Criminology and Public Policy* London, Heinemann

Carson, W G (1979) 'The Conventionalisation of Early Factory Crime' 7 *International Journal of the Sociology of Law* 37

Carson, W G (1980) 'White Collar Crime and the Institutionalisation of Ambiguity: the Case of the Early British Factory Acts' in G Geis and E Stotland *White Collar Crime* Beverley Hills, Sage

Carson, W G (1981) *The Other Price of Britain's Oil* London, Martin Robertson

Cavadino, M and J Dignan (1992) *The Penal System* London, Sage

Chase, A (1985) 'Fear Eats the Soul' 94 *Yale Law Journal* 1253

Clark, L and D Lewis (1977) *Rape: the Price of Coercive Sexuality* Toronto, Women's Press

Clarkson, C (2000) 'Context and Culpability in Involuntary Manslaughter: Principle or Instinct?' in A Ashworth and B Mitchell *Rethinking English Homicide Law* Oxford, Oxford University Press

Clarkson, C and H M Keating (1998) *Criminal Law: Text and Materials* (4th edn) London, Sweet and Maxwell

Clinard, M (1983) *Corporate Ethics and Crime* Beverley Hills, Sage

Coffee, J (1981) 'No Soul to Damn: No Body to Kick': an Unscandalised Inquiry Into the Problem of Corporate Punishment' 79 *Michigan Law Review* 386

Cohen, J (1979) 'Guilt, Justice and Tolerance: Some Old Concepts for a New Criminology' in D Downes and P Rock *Deviant Interpretations* Oxford, Martin Robertson

Cohen, S (1985) *Visions of Social Control* Oxford, Polity

Collins, H (1990) 'Ascription of Legal Responsibility to Groups in Complex Patterns of Economic Integration' 53 *Modern Law Review* 731

Committee on Mentally Abnormal Offenders (1975) *Report* Command 6244

Cooper, P (1992) 'Commensurability After the Criminal Justice Act' Paper Given at Fulbright Colloquium on Criminal Justice in Theory and Practice, Stirling, September 1992

Corrigan, P and D Sayer (1985) *The Great Arch* Oxford, Blackwell

Criminal Law Commissioners (1834) *First Report* Parliamentary Papers XXVI

Criminal Law Commissioners (1836) *Second Report* Parliamentary Papers XXXVI

Criminal Law Commissioners (1839) *Fourth Report* Parliamentary Papers XIX

Criminal Law Commissioners (1843) *Seventh Report* Parliamentary Papers XIX

Criminal Law Revision Committee (1966) *Eighth Report* Command 2977

Criminal Law Revision Committee (1980) *Fourteenth Report* Command 7855

Cross, R (1978) Murder under Duress 28 *University of Toronto Law Journal* 377

Cross, R (1978) 'The Reports of the Criminal Law Commissioners (1833–1849) and the Abortive Bill of 1853' in P Glazebrook, *Reshaping the Criminal Law* London, Stevens

Cross, R and A Ashworth (1981) *The English Sentencing System* London, Butterworth

Cross, R, Jones and R Card (1988) *Introduction to Criminal Law* London, Butterworth

Cullen, F (1984) 'The Ford Pinto Case and Beyond: Corporate Crime, Moral Boundaries, and the Criminal Sanction' in E Hochstedler *Corporations as Criminals* Beverley Hills, Sage

Davies, M with S Ruddick (1988) 'Los Angeles: Civil Liberties Between the Hammer and the Rock' 170 *New Left Review*

Davis, D (1990) 'Capital Punishment and the Politics of the Doctrine of Common Purpose' in D Hansson and D Van Zyl Smit *Towards Justice? Crime and State Control in South Africa* Cape Town, Oxford University Press

Dell, S (1983) 'Wanted: an Insanity Defence that Can be Used' *Criminal Law Review* 431

Dell, S (1984) *Murder into Manslaughter* Oxford, Oxford University Press

Denning, Lord (1982) *What Next in the Law?* London, Butterworth

Dennis, I (1980) 'Duress, Murder and Criminal Responsibility' 96 *Law Quarterly Review* 208

Dennis, I (1997) 'The Critical Condition of Criminal Law' 50 *Current Legal Problems* 213

Devlin, P (1956) *Trial By Jury* London, Stevens

Devlin, P (1965) *The Enforcement of Morals* Oxford, Oxford University Press

Devlin, P (1979) *The Judge* Oxford, Oxford University Press

Donovan, P (1990) 'Safety Fears in Shadow of Zeebrugge' *The Guardian*, 20 October

Donzelot, J (1980) *The Policing of Families* London, Hutchinson

Dowie, M (1987) 'Pinto Madness' in S Hills *Corporate Violence* New Jersey, Rowman and Littlefield

Drummond, H (1980) 'Power, Madness and Poverty' *Mother Jones* 19

Duff, R A (1990) *Intention, Agency and Criminal Liability* Oxford, Blackwell

Duff, R A (1990a) 'The Politics of Intention: A Response to Norrie' *Criminal Law Review* 637

Edgerton, H (1927) 'Corporate Criminal Responsibility' 36 *Yale Law Review* 827

Edwards, S (1981) *Female Sexuality and the Law* London, Martin Robertson

Edwards, S (1988) 'Mad, Bad or Pre-Menstrual?' *New Law Journal* 456

Edwards, S (1990) 'Battered Women Who Kill' *New Law Journal* 1380

Elliot, D W (1989) 'Necessity, Duress and Self-Defence' *Criminal Law Review* 611

Feinberg, J (1984) *Harm to Others* Oxford, Oxford University Press

Ferri, E (1901) *The Positive School of Criminology* Chicago, Kerr

Field, S and N Jorg (1991) 'Corporate Liability and Manslaughter: Should We Be Going Dutch?' *Criminal Law Review* 156

Field, S and M Lynn (1993) 'Capacity, Recklessness and the House of Lords' *Criminal Law Review* 127

Findlay, M and P Duff (1988) *The Jury Under Attack* London, Butterworth

Fish, S (1993) 'The Law Wishes to Have a Formal Existence' in A Norrie *Closure or Critique: Current Directions in Legal Theory* Edinburgh, Edinburgh University Press

Fisse, B (1990) 'Sentencing Options against Corporations' 1 *Criminal Law Forum* 211

Fisse, B and J Braithwaite (1988) 'The Allocation of Responsibility for Corporate Crime: Individualism, Collectivism and Accountability' 11 *Sydney Law Review* 468

Fitzgerald, E (1982) 'Is the System Fair to the Likes of Peter Sutcliffe?' *Guardian* 25 March 1982

Fitzpatrick, P (1992) *The Mythology of Modern Law* London, Routledge

Fletcher, G (1974) 'The Individualisation of Excusing Conditions' 47 *Southern California Law Review* 1269

Fletcher, G (1978) *Rethinking Criminal Law* Boston, Little Brown & Co

Foucault, M (1965) *Madness and Civilisation* London, Tavistock

Foucault, M (1979) *Discipline and Punish* Harmondsworth, Peregrine

French, P (1984) *Collective and Corporate Responsibility* New York, Columbia University Press

Fulford, W (1993) 'Value, Action, Mental Illness and the Law' in S Shute, J Gardner and J Horder *Action and Value in the Criminal Law* Oxford, Oxford University Press

Gamble, A (1990) *Britain in Decline* London, MacMillan

Gardner, C and N Curtis-Raleigh (1949) 'The Judicial Attitude to Penal Reform' 65 *Law Quarterly Review* 196

Gardner, J 'On the General Part of the Criminal Law' in A Duff *Philosophy and the Criminal Law* Cambridge, Cambridge University Press

Gardner, S (1991) 'Reckless and Inconsiderate Rape' *Criminal Law Review* 172

Garland, D (1985) *Punishment and Welfare* Aldershot, Gower

Glazebrook, P (1960) 'Criminal Omissions: the Duty Requirement in Offences Against the Person' 55 *Law Quarterly Review* 386

Glazebrook, P (1972) 'The Necessity Plea in English Criminal Law' 30 *Cambridge Law Journal* 87

Glazebrook, P (1983) 'Criminal Law Reform: England' in S Kadish *Encyclopaedia of Crime and Justice*

Glazebrook, P (1991) 'Redesigning the Criminal Law Course' SPTL Newsletter

Gluckman, M (1963) 'The Reasonable Man in Barotse Law' in *Order and Rebellion in Tribal Africa* London, Cohen and West

Goff, R (1988) 'The Mental Element in Murder' 104 *Law Quarterly Review* 30

Gordon, G H (1978) *The Criminal Law of Scotland* (2nd edn) Edinburgh, W H Green & Co.

Gordon, R (1981) 'Historicism in Legal Scholarship' 90 *Yale Law Journal* 1017

Green, T A (1985) *Verdict According to Conscience* Chicago, University of Chicago Press

Greenawalt, K (1986) 'Distinguishing Justifications and Excuses' 49 *Law and Contemporary Problems* 89

Griew, E (1984) 'Let's Implement Butler' 37 *Current Legal Problems* 47

Griew, E (1988) 'The Future of Diminished Responsibility' *Criminal Law Review* 75

Griffith, J (1985) *The Politics of the Judiciary* (3rd edn) London, Fontana

Gur-Arye, M (1986) 'Should the Law Distinguish Between Necessity as a Justification and Necessity as an Excuse' 102 *Law Quarterly Review* 71

Hale, Sir M (1736) *Pleas of the Crown*

Halevy, E (1972) *The Growth of Philosophic Radicalism* London, Faber

Hall, J (1960) *General Principles of Criminal Law* (2nd edn) Indianapolis, Bobbs-Merrill

Hall, J (1976) 'Comment on Justification and Excuse' 24 *American Journal of Comparative Law* 638

Hall, S, C Critcher, T Jefferson, J Clarke, B Roberts (1978) *Policing the Crisis* London, Macmillan

Harré, R (1983) *Personal Being* Oxford, Blackwell

Harré, R, D Clarke, N De Carlo (1985) *Motives and Mechanisms* London, Methuen

Hart, H L A (1963) *Law, Liberty and Morality* Oxford, Oxford University Press

Hart, H L A (1968) *Punishment and Responsibility* Oxford, Clarendon

Hart, H L A and A M Honoré (1985) *Causation in the Law* (2nd edn) Oxford, Clarendon

Hay, D (1977) 'Property, Authority and the Criminal Law' in D Hay et al *Albion's Fatal Tree* Harmondsworth, Peregrine

Hill, C (1965) *Intellectual Origins of the English Revolution* Oxford, Oxford University Press

Hill, C (1967) *Reformation to Industrial Revolution* London, Weidenfeld and Nicolson

Hill, D (1983) *The Politics of Schizophrenia* London, University Press of America

Hills, S (1987) *Corporate Violence* New Jersey, Rowman and Littlefield

Hirst, P and P Woolley (1982) *Social Relations and Human Attributes* London, Tavistock

Hobsbawm, E and G Rudé (1969) *Captain Swing* London, Lawrence and Wishart

Honderich, T (1980) *Violence for Equality* Harmondsworth, Penguin

Hook, S (1961) *Determinism and Freedom in the Age of Modern Science* New York, Collier

Horder, J (1992) *Provocation and Responsibility* Oxford, Clarendon

Horder, J (2000) 'On the Irrelevance of Motive in Criminal Law' in J Horder *Oxford Essays in Jurisprudence* (4th series) Oxford, Oxford University Press

Horder, J (2001) 'How Culpability Can, and Cannot, be Denied in Under-age Sex Crimes' *Criminal Law Review* 15

Horwitz, M J (1981) 'The Historical Contingency of the Role of History' 90 *Yale Law Journal* 1057

Horwitz, M J (1982) 'The Doctrine of Objective Causation' in D Kairys *The Politics of Law* New York, Pantheon

Hudson, B (1987) *Justice Through Punishment* Basingstoke, MacMillan

Hudson, B (1998) 'Doing Justice to Difference' in A Ashworth and M Wasik *Fundamentals of Sentencing Theory* Oxford, Oxford University Press

Hudson, B (1999) 'Reply to Hutton' *Social & Legal Studies* 239

Hughes, G (1958) 'Criminal Omissions' 67 *Yale Law Journal* 590

Kadish, S (1978) 'Codification of the Criminal Law' 78 *Columbia Law Review* 1098

Kadish, S (1985) 'Complicity, Cause and Blame: a Study on the Interpretation of Doctrine' 73 *California Law Review* 324

Kant, I (1965) *The Metaphysical Elements of Justice* Indianapolis, Bobbs-Merrill

Kelman, M (1981) 'Interpretive Construction in the Substantive Criminal Law' 33 *Stanford Law Review* 591

Kenny, C S (1902) *Outlines of Criminal Law* Cambridge, Cambridge University Press

Kittrie, N (1971) *The Right to be Different* London, John Hopkins

Lacey, N (1985) 'The Territory of the Criminal Law' 5 *Oxford Journal of Legal Studies* 453

Lacey, N (1987) 'Discretion and Due Process at the Post-Conviction Stage' in I Dennis *Criminal Law and Justice*, London, Sweet and Maxwell

Lacey, N (1988) *State Punishment* London, Routledge and Kegan Paul

Lacey N, C Wells and D Meure (1990) *Reconstructing Criminal Law* London, Weidenfeld and Nicolson

Lacey, N and C Wells (1998) *Reconstructing Criminal Law* London, Butterworths

Lanham, D (1976) 'Larsonneur Revisited' *Criminal Law Review* 276

Law Commission (1989) *A Criminal Code for England and Wales* Law Commission No 177

Law Commission (1996) *Legislating the Criminal Code: Involuntary Manslaughter* Law Commission No 237

Leavens, A (1988) 'A Causation Approach to Criminal Omissions' 76 *California Law Review* 547

Lederman, E (1985) 'Criminal Law, Perpetrator and Corporation: Rethinking a Complex Triangle' 76 *Journal of Criminal Law and Criminology* 285

Leigh, L (1966) Note 29 *Modern Law Review* 570

Levi, M (1987) *Regulating Fraud: White Collar Crime and the Criminal Process* London, Tavistock

Levitin, J (1987) 'Putting the Government on Trial: the Necessity Defence and Social Change' 33 *Wayne Law Review* 1221

Little, D (1969) *Religion, Order and Law* New York, Harper and Tow

Lloyd-Bostock, S (1979) 'The Ordinary Man, and the Psychology of Attributing Causes and Responsibility' 42 *Modern Law Review* 143

Luckhaus, L (1985) 'A Plea for PMT in the Criminal Law' in S Edwards *Gender, Sex and the Law* Beckenham, Croom Helm

Macauley, Lord (1898) 'Introductory Report upon the Indian Penal Code, Note M' *The Works of Lord Macauley*, vol XI, London, Longmans Green & Co

McBarnet, D (1981) *Conviction* London, MacMillan

McColgan, A (1993) 'In Defence of Battered Women Who Kill' 13 *Oxford Journal of Legal Studies* 508

MacCormick, D N (1978) *Legal Reasoning and Legal Theory* Oxford, Clarendon

MacCormick, D N (1993) 'Reconstruction After Deconstruction: Closing in on Critique', in A Norrie *Closure or Critique* Edinburgh, Edinburgh University Press

Mackay, R D (1987) 'Craziness and Codification – Revising the Automatism and Insanity Defences' in I Dennis *Criminal Law and Justice* London, Sweet & Maxwell

Mackay, R D (1988) 'Post-Hinckley Insanity in the USA' *Criminal Law Review* 88

Mackay, R D (1990) 'Fact and Fiction About the Insanity Defence' *Criminal Law Review* 247

Mackay, R D (1995) *Mental Condition Defences in the Criminal Law* Oxford, Oxford University Press

Mackay, R D (2000) 'Diminished Responsibility and Mentally Disordered Killers' in A Ashworth and B Mitchell *Rethinking English Homicide Law* Oxford, Oxford University Press

MacPherson, C B (1962) *The Political Theory of Possessive Individualism* Oxford, Oxford University Press

Marcuse, H (1941) *Reason and Revolution* London, Routledge and Kegan Paul

Masters, B (1985) *Killing For Company* London, Coronet

Mathiesen, T (1983) 'The Future of Control Systems – the Case of Norway' in D Garland and P Young *The Power to Punish* London, Heinemann

Mercer, K (1986) 'Racism and Transcultural Psychiatry' in P Miller and N Rose *The Power of Psychiatry* Oxford, Blackwell

Milgate, H (1988) 'Duress and the Criminal Law: Another About Turn by the House of Lords' 47 *Cambridge Law Journal* 61

Miller, P (1986) 'Critique of Psychiatry and Critical Sociologies of Madness' in P Miller and N Rose *The Power of Psychiatry* Oxford, Blackwell

Moerings, M (1986) 'Prison Overcrowding in the United States' in B Ralston and M Tomlinson *The Expansion of European Prison Systems* Belfast, European Group for Study of Deviance and Social Control

Moore, M (1984) *Law and Psychiatry* Cambridge, Cambridge University Press

Moore, M (1985) 'Causation and the Excuses' 73 *California Law Review* 1091

Moore, M (1997) *Placing Blame* Oxford, Oxford University Press

Moran, L (1992) 'Corporate Criminal Capacity: Nostalgia for Representation' *Social and Legal Studies* 371

Morris, N (1982) *Madness and the Criminal Law* Chicago, University of Chicago Press

Murphy, J (1979) *Retribution, Justice and Therapy* Dordrecht, Reidel

Murphy, J (1987) 'Does Kant Have a Theory of Punishment?' 87 *Columbia Law Review* 509

Naipaul, V (1981) *The Killings in Trinidad* Harmondsworth, Penguin

Nelken, D (1987) 'Criminal Law and Criminal Justice: Some Notes on their Irrelation' in I Dennis *Criminal Law and Justice* London, Sweet and Maxwell

Neumann, F (1987) *Social Democracy and the Rule of Law* London, Allen and Unwin

Norrie, A (1986) 'Practical Reasoning and Criminal Responsibility: a Jurisprudential Approach' in D Cornish and R Clarke *The Reasoning Criminal: Rational Choice Perspectives on Offending* New York, Springer

Norrie, A (1989) 'Oblique Intention and Legal Politics' *Criminal Law Review* 793

Norrie, A (1990a) 'Review of Lacey, State Punishment' 18 *International Journal of the Sociology of Law* 112

Norrie, A (1990b) 'Intention: More Loose Talk' *Criminal Law Review* 642

Norrie, A (1991) *Law, Ideology and Punishment* Dordrecht, Kluwer

Norrie, A (1992) 'Subjectivism, Objectivism and the Limits of Criminal Recklessness' 12 *Oxford Journal of Legal Studies* 45

Norrie, A (1996) 'The Limits of Justice: Finding Fault in the Criminal Law' 59 *Modern Law Review* 540

Norrie, A (1999) 'After *Woollin*' *Criminal Law Review* 532

Norrie, A (2000) *Punishment, Responsibility and Justice* Oxford, Oxford University Press

Norrie, A (2001) 'The Structure of Provocation' *Current Legal Problems*

O'Donovan, K (1984) 'The Medicalisation of Infanticide' *Criminal Law Review* 259

Paulus, I (1975) *The Search for Pure Food* London, Martin Robertson

Plamenatz, J (1958) *The English Utilitarians* Oxford, Blackwell

Porter, R (1987) *Mind Forg'd Manacles*, London, Athlone

Quen, J (1968) 'An Historical View of the M'Naghten Trial' 42 *Bulletin of the History of Medicine* 43

Quinney, R (1980) *Class, State and Crime* New York, Longman

Radzinowicz, L (1948) *A History of English Criminal Law*, vol 1, London, Stevens

Raitt, F and S Zeedyk (2000) *The Implicit Relation of Psychology and Law* London, Routledge

Rex, S (1998) 'A New Form of Rehabilitation?' in A Von Hirsch and A Ashworth *Principled Sentencing* (2nd edn) Oxford, Hart Publishing

Rose, L (1986) *Massacre of the Innocents* London, Routledge Kegan Paul

Rose, N (1986) 'Law, Rights and Psychiatry' in P Miller and N Rose *The Power of Psychiatry* Oxford, Blackwell

Royal Commission on Capital Punishment (1949–1953) *Report* Command 8932

Sanders, A (1985) 'Class Bias in Prosecutions' 24 *Howard Journal* 26

Sanders, A and R Young (2000) *Criminal Justice* (2nd edn) London, Butterworths

Sayre, F (1931/32) 'Mens Rea' *Harvard Law Review* 974

Scarman, Lord (1981) *The Brixton Disorders 10–12 April 1981* Command 8427

Sellers, J (1978) '*Mens Rea* and the Judicial Approach to "Bad Excuses" in the Criminal Law' 41 *Modern Law Review* 245

Sève, L (1975) *Marxism and the Theory of Human Personality* London, Laurence and Wishart

Sheen, Mr Justice (1987) *MV Herald of Free Enterprise* Department of Transport, Report of Court, No 8074

Simon, R and D Aaronson (1988) *The Insanity Defense* New York, Praeger

Simpson, A W B (1986) *Cannibalism and the Common Law* Harmondsworth, Penguin

Skrapec, C (1993) 'The Female Serial Killer' in H Birch *Moving Targets* London, Virago

Smith, A T H (1978) 'On *Actus Reus* and *Mens Rea*' in P Glazebrook *Reshaping the Criminal Law* London, Stevens

Smith, A T H (1984) 'Judicial Law-Making in the Criminal Law' 46 *Law Quarterly Review* 48

Smith, A T H (1987) 'Law Reform Proposals and the Courts' in I Dennis *Criminal Law and Justice* London, Sweet & Maxwell

Smith, J (1989) *Misogynies* London, Faber

Smith, J C (1987) *Justification and Excuse in the Criminal Law* London, Stevens

Smith, J C (1991) 'Comment on *R v Reid*' *Criminal Law Review* 274

Smith, J C (2000a) 'Comment on *B v DPP*' *Criminal Law Review* 405

Smith, J C (2000b) 'Comment on *Attorney-General; Reference (No 2, 1999)*' *Criminal Law Review* 478

Smith, J C (2001) 'Comment on *Re A (Children)*' *Criminal Law Review* 400

Smith, J C and B Hogan (1983) *Criminal Law* (5th edn) London, Butterworths

Smith, J C and B Hogan (1988) *Criminal Law* (6th edn) London, Butterworths

Smith, J C and B Hogan (1992) *Criminal Law* (7th edn) London, Butterworths

Smith, J C and B Hogan (1999) *Criminal Law* (9th edn) London, Butterworths

Smith, K (1989) 'Must Heroes Behave Heroically?' *Criminal Law Review* 622

Smith, R (1981) *Trial by Medicine* Edinburgh, Edinburgh University Press

Smith, R (1985) 'Expertise and Causal Attribution in Deciding between Crime and Mental Disorder' 15 *Social Studies of Science* 67

Sparks, R (1964) '"Diminished Responsibility" in Theory and Practice' 27 *Modern Law Review* 9

Spencer, J (1982) 'Criminal Law and Criminal Appeals – the Tail that Wags the Dog' *Criminal Law Review* 260

Spencer, J (1984) Review of Simpson, Cannibalism and the Criminal Law 51 *University of Chicago Law Review* 1265

Spicer, R (1981) *Conspiracy* London, Lawrence and Wishart

Stapleton, J (1988) 'Law, Causation and Common Sense' 8 *Oxford Journal of Legal Studies* 111

Stedman Jones, G (1971) *Outcast London* Oxford, Oxford University Press

Stephen, J F (1883) *History of the Criminal Law of England* vol II, London, Macmillan

Stephen, J F (1887) *Digest of Criminal Law* London, MacMillan

Stern, V (1987) *Bricks of Shame* Harmondsworth, Penguin

Sutherland, E (1949) *White Collar Crime* New York, Holt, Luke and Rhinehart

Swigert, V and R Farrell (1980–81) 'Corporate Homicide: Definitional Processes in the Creation of Deviance' *Law and Society Review* 161

Syrota, G (1982) 'A Radical Change in the Law of Recklessness' *Criminal Law Review* 97

Taylor, Lord (1993) 'Judge and Sentencing' *Journal of Law Society of Scotland*, 129

Temkin, J (1983) 'The Limits of Reckless Rape' *Criminal Law Review* 5

Thomas, D (1978) *The Penal Equation* University of Cambridge, Institute of Criminology

Thomas, D A (1992) 'Criminal Justice Act 1991 (1) Custodial sentences' *Criminal Law Review* 232

Thompson, E P (1975) *Whigs and Hunters* Harmondsworth, Peregrine

Tonry, M (1987) 'Sentencing Guidelines and Their Effects' in A Von Hirsch, K Knapp and M Tonry *The Sentencing Commission and its Guidelines* Boston, Northeastern University Press

Tur, R (1985) 'Dishonesty and the Jury' in A Phillips Griffiths *Philosophy and Practice* Cambridge, Cambridge University Press

Turk, A (1969) *Criminality and Legal Order* Chicago, Rand McNally

Twining, W (1973) 'Bentham on Torture' in M R James *Bentham and Legal Theory* Belfast Northern Ireland Legal Quarterly

Unsworth, C (1987) *The Politics of Mental Health Legislation* Oxford, Clarendon

Vandervort, L (1987) 'Social Justice in the Modern Regulatory State: Duress, Necessity and the Consensual Model in Law' 6 *Law and Philosophy* 205

Venturi, F (1971) *Utopia and Reform in the Enlightenment* Cambridge, Cambridge University Press

Vining, J (1978) *Legal Identity* New Haven, Yale University Press

Von Hirsch, A (1976) *Doing Justice: the Choice of Punishment* New York, Hill and Wang

Von Hirsch, A (1986a) *Past or Future Crimes* Manchester, Manchester University Press

Von Hirsch, A (1986b) 'Deservedness and Dangerousness in Sentencing Policy' *Criminal Law Review* 79

Von Hirsch, A (1987) 'Guidance by Numbers or Words? Numerical Versus Narrative Guidelines for Sentencing' in M Wasik and K Pease *Sentencing Reform: Guidance or Guidelines?* Manchester, Manchester University Press

Von Hirsch, A (1993) *Censure and Sanctions* Oxford, Oxford University Press

Von Hirsch, A and N Jareborg (1991) 'Gauging Criminal Harm: a Living Standard Analysis' 11 *Oxford Journal Legal Studies* 1

Von Hirsch, A, K Knapp and M Tonry (1978) *The Sentencing Commission and its Guidelines* Boston, Northeastern University Press

Walker, N (1968) *Crime and Insanity in England and Wales, vol 1: the Historical Perspective* Edinburgh, Edinburgh University Press

Walker, N and N Padfield (1996) *Sentencing* London, Butterworths

Walters, L (1988) 'Murder Under Duress and Judicial Decision-Making in the House of Lords' 8 *Legal Studies* 61

Wasik, M (1977) 'Duress and Criminal Responsibility' *Criminal Law Review* 453

Wasik, M (1979) '*Mens Rea*, Motive and the Problem of "Dishonesty" in the Law of Theft' *Criminal Law Review* 543

Weinrib, E (1980) 'The Case for a Duty to Rescue' 90 *Yale Law Journal* 267

Wells, C (1985) 'Necessity and the Common Law' 5 *Oxford Journal of Legal Studies* 471

Wells, C (1988) 'The Decline and Rise of English Murder: Corporate Crime and Individual Responsibility' *Criminal Law Review* 788

Wells, C (2001) *Corporations and Criminal Responsibility* (2nd edn) Oxford, Oxford University Press

Welsh, R (1946) 'The Criminal Liability of Corporations' 62 *Law Quarterly Review* 3465

White Paper (1990) *Crime, Justice and Protecting the Public* Cmnd 965 London, HMSO

White, A (1991) *Misleading Cases* Oxford, Clarendon

Wiener, M (1990) *Reconstructing the Criminal* Cambridge, Cambridge University Press

Williams, B (1990) 'Voluntary Acts and Responsible Agents' 10 *Oxford Journal of Legal Studies* 1

Williams, G (1960) 'Constructive Malice Revived' 23 *Modern Law Review* 60955

Williams, G (1961) *Criminal Law: the General Part* (2nd edn) London, Stevens

Williams, G (1965) *The Mental Element in Crime* Oxford, Oxford University Press

Williams, G (1978) *Textbook of Criminal Law* (1st edn) London, Stevens

Williams, G (1981) 'Recklessness Redefined' 40 *Cambridge Law Journal* 252

Williams, G (1982) 'The Theory of Excuses' *Criminal Law Review* 732

Williams, G (1983) *Textbook of Criminal Law* (2nd edn) London, Stevens

Williams, G (1987) 'Oblique Intention' 46 *Cambridge Law Review* 417

Williams, G (1988) 'The Unresolved Problem of Recklessness' *Legal Studies* 74

Williams, G (1989) '*Finis* for *Novus Actus*?' 48 *Cambridge Law Journal* 391

Williams, G (1991) 'Criminal Omissions – the Conventional View' 86 *Law Quarterly Review* 88

Winslow, C (1977) 'Sussex Smugglers' in D Hay et al *Albion's Fatal Tree* Harmondsworth, Peregrine

Wootton, B (1960) 'Diminished Responsibility' 76 *Law Quarterly Review* 224

Young, J (1971) *The Drugtakers* London, Paladin

Zweig, A (1967) *Kant, Philosophical Correspondence 1759–99* Chicago, University of Chicago

# Index

# Index of names